*Death and the Prince*

# Death and the Prince

*Memorial Preaching
before 1350*

D. L. D'AVRAY

CLARENDON PRESS · OXFORD
1994

Oxford University Press, Walton Street, Oxford OX2 6DP

Oxford  New York
Athens  Auckland  Bangkok  Bombay
Calcutta  Cape Town  Dar es Salaam  Delhi
Florence  Hong Kong  Istanbul  Karachi
Kuala Lumpur  Madras  Madrid  Melbourne
Mexico City  Nairobi  Paris  Singapore
Taipei  Tokyo  Toronto
and associated companies in
Berlin  Ibadan

Oxford is a trade mark of Oxford University Press

Published in the United States
by Oxford University Press Inc., New York

British Library Cataloguing in Publication Data
Data available

Library of Congress Cataloging in Publication Data
D'Avray, D. L.
Death and the prince: memorial preaching before 1350 /
D. L. D'Avray.
p. cm.
Includes bibliographical references and index.
1. Death—Religious aspects—Christianity—History of doctrines—
Middle Ages, 600–1500.  2. Death—Religious aspects—Christianity—
Sermons—History and criticism.  3. Funeral sermons—History and
criticism.  4. Europe—Kings and rulers—Death and burial.
5. Sermons, Latin—History and criticism. I. Title.
BT825.D35  1994
236'.1'0902—dc20  94–8695
ISBN 0–19–820396–9

1 3 5 7 9 10 8 6 4 2

Typeset by Best-set Typesetter Ltd., Hong Kong
Printed in Great Britain
on acid-free paper by
Bookcraft Ltd., Midsomer Norton, Nr. Bath

*To Julia Walworth*

# Acknowledgements

Nicole Bériou and Louis-Jacques Bataillon, OP, dear *commilitones*, have put their learning and judgement at my disposal. I have also had cause to be grateful to David Anderson, Charles Burnett, Suzanne Cawsey, Michael Crawford, Martin Davies, Wendy Davies, Tony d'Avray, Carlotta Dionisotti, Manuel González Jiménez, Alan Griffiths, Jill Kraye, Rudolf Lenz, Peter Linehan, Timothy McFarland, John McManamon, SJ, Lauro Martínes, David Morgan, Charlotte Morse, Alexander Patschovsky, Darleen Pryds, Nazneen Razwi, Patricia Stirnemann, Michael Sylwanowicz, and Julia Walworth. The remarkable scholar whose name would come next in the sequence has made a professional principle out of anonymity. Finally, I should thank the many students at University College London who have delayed the book's progress, but increased the quota of intelligence in it.

D.L.d'A.

# Contents

*Abbreviations*                                                          xi

*Introduction*                                                            1

1.  Preliminaries                                                        12
2.  Individuals                                                          69
3.  The Prince                                                          117
4.  Death and the Afterlife                                             159
      *Excursus*: Some Recent Work on the History of
      Death                                                             177
5.  Representations and Reality                                         185

*Conclusion*                                                            222

*Appendix*: The Character and Contents of Key                          228
Manuscripts

*Transcriptions*                                                        232

*Endnotes*                                                              279

*Bibliography*                                                          287

*Index of Manuscripts*                                                  305

*General Index*                                                         307

# Abbreviations

| | |
|---|---|
| *AFP* | *Archivum Fratrum Praedicatorum* |
| BL | British Library, London |
| BN | Bibliothèque Nationale, Paris |
| CCSL | Corpus Christianorum, Series Latina |
| CCSM | Corpus Christianorum, Continuatio Mediaevalis |
| MGH | Monumenta Germaniae Historica |
| OESA | Ordinis Eremitarum Sancti Augustini |
| OP | Ordinis Praedicatorum |
| OSB | Ordinis Sancti Benedicti |
| PL | Patrologiae Cursus Completus, Series Latina, ed. J.-P. Migne |

# Introduction

MEMORIA, the liturgical commemoration of the dead, is one of the best-studied phenomena in medieval history, thanks to a brilliant galaxy of German scholars collaborating formally and informally.[1] From difficult sources such as 'Books of Life' and necrologies[2] (but also from other evidence, notably images and chronicles),[3] they have shown how the physically absent living and dead could in some sense be made present through the naming of their names in a liturgical setting, and how liturgy created real communities in which living and dead were drawn together.[4] Memorial sermons are one aspect of this liturgical 'memory' of the dead,[5] for they belonged to funerals and other

[1] K. Schmid and J. Wollasch (eds.), *Memoria: Der geschichtliche Zeugniswert des liturgischen Gedenkens im Mittelalter* (Münstersche Mittelalter-Schriften, 48; Munich, 1984), gives a good sense of the breadth and originality of this school's research. One must also make special mention of O. G. Oexle's 'Memoria und Memorialüberlieferung im früheren Mittelalter', *Frühmittelalterliche Studien*, 10 (1976), 70–95.

[2] On *Libri memoriales* and necrologies see K. Schmid and J. Wollasch, 'Die Gemeinschaft der Lebenden und Verstorbenen in Zeugnissen des Mittelalters', *Frühmittelalterliche Studien*, 1 (1967), 365–405.

[3] On images see O. G. Oexle, 'Memoria und Memorialbild', in Schmid and Wollasch (eds.), *Memoria*, 384–440 (wide-ranging and very original). G. Althoff, 'Beobachtungen zum liudolfingisch-ottonischen Gedenkwesen', ibid. 649–65, brings narrative and charter sources together with necrology evidence. See also his *Adels- und Königsfamilien im Spiegel ihrer Memorialüberlieferung: Studien zum Totengedenken der Billunger und Ottonen* (Münstersche Mittelalter-Schriften, 47; Munich, 1984).

[4] Oexle, 'Memoria und Memorialüberlieferung', 84.

[5] It is the liturgical setting of the sermons studied in this book which decisively marks them off from *Ehrenreden*, on which see below, ch 2, text at n. 243, and probably also from the secular commemorative addresses from Italy which are included in the *Oculus pastoralis*, on which see *Speeches from the Oculus pastoralis, Edited from Cleveland, Public Library, MS. Wq7890921M-C37*, ed. T. O. Tunberg (Toronto Medieval Latin Texts, 19; Toronto, 1990), 50–60. Phrases such as 'Vos autem qui uenistis ad obsequium sepulture, recedetis amodo . . .' (ibid. 54) suggest that they were in some way associated with the funeral (apart from the oration 'De mortuo in partibus remotis', pp. 58–60), but in view of the secular character of the collection as a whole it seems likely that the speeches were given by laymen and outside the liturgy proper. See also H. Kantorowicz, 'Über die dem Petrus de Vineis zugeschriebenen "Arenga"', *Mitteilungen des Instituts für österreichische Geschichtsforschung*, 30 (1909; repr. 1969), 651–4, at 653 ('Die Trauerrede . . .').

memorial services (above all after thirty days);[6] nevertheless, their evidence transcends the history of *Memoria* in that these sermons could broaden their scope to discuss a wide range of topics relating to this life and the next. Moreover, this class of source has not come within the scope of the German group's investigations. All the same, their many publications provide what is probably the best historiographical setting for the findings of this book.

The relevance of research on *Memoria* to this study became evident only when it was virtually complete, and its genesis must be explained by other influences. The course of this investigation has mirrored (albeit unwittingly) a wider move- ment of fashion in historical writing. Interest in past political events had ceased to be chic by the 1950s.[7] Undergraduates and perhaps most of their teachers continued to concentrate on traditional topics, but the social and economic historians felt themselves to be the professional avant-garde. In the 1970s, if not earlier[8], the search for 'new problems' led to a series of studies which went beyond social history, as it had earlier been

---

[6] On the origins of liturgical commemoration after thirty days (the 'month's mind') see M. Lauwers, 'La mémoire des ancêtres, le souci des morts: Fonction et usages du culte des morts dans l'Occident médiéval (diocèse de Liège, XIe–XIIIe siècles)' (École des Hautes Études en Sciences Sociales, thèse de doc- torat 'Nouveau Régime'; Paris, 1992), 115, 122. This important thesis could be regarded as an interesting hybrid of the German school of historians of *Memoria* and the French school of writing about the 'history of death'.

[7] Sir Lewis Namier's prosopographical method was focused on political structures rather than events.

[8] Georges Duby, in an article about modern French historical scholarship published in 1985, implied that the word belonged to the 1950s and was *passé*: 'die Mentalitäten, wie man in den fünfziger Jahren sagte. Die Historiker hüten sich jetzt, dieses Wort zu gebrauchen' ('Über einige Grundtendenzen der modernen französischen Geschichtswissenschaft', *Historische Zeitschrift*, 241 (1985), 543–54, at 550). One notes, however, that the article which immediately follows his in the journal is V. Sellin on 'Mentalität und Mentalitätsgeschichte' (pp. 555–98). As for French historians, the word by no means passed out of intellectually respectable use after the 1950s. Thus É. Le Roy Ladurie could write in evidently complimentary terms of 'une véritable histoire, sérielle et massive, des mentalités religieuses' ('Chaunu, Lebrun, Vovelle: La nouvelle histoire de la mort', in id., *Le Territoire de l'historien* (Paris, 1973), 393–403, at 403), and A. Vauchez could entitle a section of his classic *thèse d'état* 'Mentalité hagiographique et mentalité commune' (*La Sainteté en Occident aux derniers siècles du Moyen Âge d'après les procès de canonisation et les documents hagiographi- ques* (Bibliothèque des Écoles Françaises d'Athènes et de Rome, 241; Rome, 1981), 615).

conceived, and which were brought under the heading of 'history of mentalities'. The history of attitudes to death was prominent in this new wave.[9]

The high profile of the history of mentalities made it easier for scholars interested in medieval sermons to explain the value of their sources. This was a good time to be working on sermons for another reason also. The patient work of J. B. Schneyer, and above all his *Repertorium der lateinischen Sermones des Mittelalters*[10] had made the riches hidden in medieval sermon manuscripts relatively easy to locate. Among the treasures which the *Repertorium* disclosed were a large but not unmanageable number of sermons on the dead. When the history of death was the height of fashion, and sermons on the dead were there for the asking, a marriage of the concept and the data was on the cards, and in that sense this study is a predictable product of its historiographical time.

The conditioning by context did not stop here, for most of the research for this book was done while I was guiding bright young adults through an unwritten but inflexible History syllabus that their grandparents' generation would not have regarded as advanced. Although 'events history' and the study of kingship had played no part in my personal research, and looked *passé* to the historian à la mode, the old London History School, no more perturbed than Maigret by flashy modern theories, continued to investigate the doings of rulers.

That syllabus has now been pensioned off by my college to the Meung-sur-Loire of academic History schools, but one could not work with it for fifteen years and remain unaffected. Before the bloody civil war which ended the old regime, I had come to love this impersonal Big Brother. Though I read my way conscientiously through all kinds of sermons on the dead, I was drawn more and more to the ones which were about the lives of real rulers.

---

[9] On the 'history of death' see the excursus to Chapter 4.

[10] 11 vols. to date (Münster, 1969– ). Schneyer died after completing nine volumes, the body of the work; the indexes were undertaken under the auspices of the Raimundus-Lullus Institut in Freiburg im Breisgau. For plans to continue the *Repertorium* into the late medieval period see L. Hödl and R. Hetzler, 'Zum Stand der Erforschung der lateinischen Sermones des Mittelalters (für die Zeit von 1350–1500)', *Scriptorium*, 46 (1992), 121–30.

Though the sermons contained plenty of allusions to political action, they were not detailed enough to be used as a source for old-fashioned political history; besides which, it would have been artificial to separate the sermons about real rulers from model sermons 'on the death of a prince' or king. Still, there seemed no reason why the genre should not be studied in its historical right (rather as Helmut Beumann studied the image of kings in early medieval historians as a subject in its own right, and not just as a source for straight political history).[11]

Moreover, some obvious questions, bridging the gap between 'past politics' and 'mentalities', also presented themselves. In the last century Jakob Burckhardt argued that in the Middle Ages (by contrast with the Renaissance) people lacked the capacity to perceive individual personality. Though not many historians would now maintain this theory as a generalization, one may still usefully ask how far a given genre conveys the unique characteristics of particular people. Sermons in memory of real princes (though not the model sermons) lent themselves to this kind of enquiry, because enough is known about the men in whose honour they were preached to judge how good a likeness the preachers captured. It will be shown that in some cases a remarkably successful likeness is achieved, though the underlying idea of individuality seems different from the dominant modern one. These depictions of personality also look like a means of conveying messages about political ethics.[12]

---

[11] e.g. 'Betrachtet man etwa die Gesta Friderici Ottos von Freising einmal nicht als Nachrichtenarsenal für die Geschichte Friedrich Barbarossas und seiner Zeit, sondern als Denkmal für die Geschichte der Historiographie, so gewinnt der Text unter diesem Aspekt ohne Zweifel den Rang eines "Überrestes"; und dies gilt nicht minder, wenn man den gleichen Text nach der Stellung des Verfassers zu den politischen, staatsrechtlichen, sozialen, religiösen, kirchenpolitischen und geistigen Problemen und Verhältnissen seiner Zeit befragt' ('Die Historiographie des Mittelalters als Quelle für die Ideengeschichte des Königtums' (1955), repr. in id., *Ideengeschichtliche Studien zu Einhard und anderen Geschichtsschreibern des früheren Mittelalters* (Darmstadt, 1962), 40–79, at 42). Cf. also the comments of K. J. Leyser, *Rule and Conflict in an Early Medieval Society: Ottonian Saxony* (Oxford, 1989 edn.), 81.

[12] Another purpose in making the dead person seem real was doubtless to persuade people to help that person in purgatory, though this function does not seem to be particularly prominent in our sample. But see Penny Cole, D. L. d'Avray, and J. Riley-Smith, 'Application of Theology to Current Affairs:

The ideas of the preachers about political virtue were thus a natural topic for the next chapter (Chapter 2)—another theme, incidentally, which bridges the gap between political history and the study of mentalities. Though quite un-machiavellian (as one might expect), the preachers took a largely positive view of secular values and the things of this world, so that their political message is strikingly (and not so predictably) similar to that of humanist funeral orations.

That aspect of the sermons was balanced by emphasis on the 'last things'—death and the afterlife—themes which are the subject of a separate chapter (Chapter 4). These two chapters about the ideological message need to be taken together, however, because the equilibrium between this-worldly and other-worldly emphases is one of the genre's distinctive features.

In this way a contribution to the fashionable 'history of death' could be integrated, via questions about the ideology of government and the sense of the individual, with an old-fashioned interest in past politics. It must be said in retrospect, furthermore, that the attempt to combine some *histoire événementielle* with *histoire de mentalités* was itself a rather predictable move. Some such aim can be discerned behind, for instance, the recent study of William Marshall by Georges Duby.[13]

Perhaps most historical monographs could be similarly analysed as products of the historian's professional setting. The process selectively sketched above is not a negative sort of conditioning, for the approaches suggested by recent historical writing and even by traditional habits of teaching help scholars notice things in and about their sources which they could otherwise overlook.

The final chapter, on 'Representations', could be presented in similar terms. Literary theory was the badge of avant-garde historians in the 1980s, and the chapter does subject the sermons to a sort of literary criticism. The exposition then moves back and forth between representation and reality, in a way superficially reminiscent of the so-called 'New Historicism'.

Memorial Sermons on the Dead of Mansurah and on Innocent IV', *Historical Research*, 63 (1990), 227–47, at 231 and n. 27, 232–3, and 241.

[13] G. Duby, *Guillaume le Maréchal ou le meilleur chevalier du monde* (Paris, 1984).

These parallels would in fact be misleading. The first part of the chapter is uninfluenced by the Franco-American literary theory so recently in vogue (though it does owe something to German work on the aesthetics of reception,[14] which is more easily adapted to the needs of empirical history). As for the transition back from representation to reality, readers will find none of those interesting paradoxes which make new historicist writings seem like Borges short stories. The argument is crudely straightforward. It is that the sermons in memory of princes 'represent' political realities of their time by purifying and distilling attitudes that permeated the lives of princes in the century around 1300. The memorial sermons are a concentrated form of a balanced and stable compound of secular political and other-worldly preoccupations which was widely diffused in the atmosphere of that age.

The central argument of an academic book will be of little interest to a certain proportion of its readers, who, whether scholars or students, may nevertheless find one or other aspect of it useful. It would be arrogant to ignore this important constituency, and the following remarks are intended for it.

Many readers will be able to pass rapidly over Chapter 1, though it contributes to an aspect of the 'history of death' and supplies one of the larger pieces missing from the general picture of memorial preaching in the West, a subject on which non-medievalists have done and are doing important work. Chapter 2 may be read by students of early fourteenth-century political history and by anyone interested in the argument about the 'discovery of the individual', even if the rest of the volume lies outside their scope. Chapter 3 may have a subsidiary relevance for people studying the softer edges of political thought, the influence of Aristotle and Aquinas in the Middle Ages, the relation between Church and State, and Pope John XXII's conflict with Ludwig of Bavaria. Chapter 4 casts some light on attitudes to death and to the body–soul relationship, though it makes less sense in isolation than in the context of the book's overall argument. The final chapter will not be to

[14] See e.g. R. Warning, *Rezeptionsästhetik: Theorie und Praxis*, 2nd edn. (Munich, 1979).

everybody's taste because it brings together themes that may seem unrelated. The links are there, but readers are advised to be patient with it or omit it altogether, though for the author it is the cornerstone of the book.

## NOTE ON TRANSCRIPTIONS AND RELATED MATTERS

As a rule I have followed the scribe's spelling. However, this principle does not meet every case. *Dr̄ia* could be extended as *differentia* or *differencia*. One acceptable solution would be to follow the rule that the *c* should always be adopted rather than *t* if followed by *i* and then another vowel at the end of the word. Scribes do not invariably obey this rule, however, and I have preferred simply to normalize *c* and *t* to classical usage. There are also other cases where abbreviation commonly makes it impossible to follow the orthography of the manuscript, but where the classical spelling too is less standardized. Thus one can have *numquam* or *nunquam*, *sed* or *set*, etc. My general and perhaps rather pedantic solution is to italicize the letter or letters in doubt. I do not use *j* or *v*, which I normalize to *i* and *u* respectively (even for capitals). I try to adopt the scribe's abbreviation for books of the Bible, within the limits of typographical convenience, occasionally extending them a little when it might otherwise be hard to tell which book is intended. I supply scriptural verse-numbers after the chapter-number, in round brackets. Quotations from the Bible are italicized. If the wording departs substantially from that of the Vulgate in a way that seems important I return to roman type, but I have not attempted to fine-tune such typographical indications, since the textual background of the biblical lemmata in the sermons is not among the problems addressed in this book. For the same reason I have for the most part contented myself with the convenient (and inexpensive) Madrid edition of the *Vulgata Clementina*. Note, however, that for our purpose the Clementine Vulgate is not necessarily inferior to the standard critical edition of the Vulgate, which aims to reconstruct the pure original text, since the Clementine traces descent from one of the copies of the thirteenth-century Paris Bible, and thus comes close to a version readily available to preachers in our period.[15]

[15] Cf. R. Weber in *Biblia Sacra iuxta vulgatam versionem* (2 vols.; Stuttgart, 1969), vol. i, p. x: 'dieser Text hat die weitere Entwicklung bestimmt bis hin zur Pariser Bibel der Sorbonne im 13. Jahrhundert und ihren zahlreichen

When giving references *in propria persona* to the Bible I follow
Schneyer's conventions for the naming and numbering of books, apart
from some normalization to OUP style. Thus, for instance, I count
four Books of Kings (the first two corresponding to 1 Samuel and 2
Samuel), though I write 'Kgs.' where Schneyer would write 'Reg.'
When I give the scriptural *incipit* of a sermon as part of a reference to
Schneyer's *Repertorium*, I have not thought it necessary as a rule to
check the chapter- and verse-numbers he gives (though otherwise I
have tried to go back and check all references and transcriptions).

Since the unpublished texts on which the book is based are not only
sources for but part of the object of the investigation, and since
scholarly readers deserve the chance to assess the material for themselves, a good deal of this material is made available *in extenso*,
whether in footnotes or in the text, or in the transcriptions at the end
of the volume. Though I have tried to produce a 'reader-friendly'
book, this concern gets sacrificed when it obstructs the overriding
purpose of advancing understanding of a different world. At least
there are no untranslated passages of Latin in the text (the book is
intended for students as well as scholars); instead my policy has been
to give an English translation of the passage required for the argument, followed by the Latin, which anyone is free to pass over.[16] It is
not the most elegant of solutions, but probably the most practical one
in the circumstances, for the footnotes would otherwise have become
impossibly overblown: as it is, their capacity is stretched by those
passages to which reference is made without full quotation in the
text. One overblown footnote had to be removed, and appears as
Transcription D. The other transcriptions at the end of the volume are
designed to give scholars a small corpus of complete sermons against
which to test my general interpretations, and to which questions that
have not occurred to me may be posed.

Those transcriptions at the end of the book which are based on a
single manuscript, as also the transcribed extracts in the text and notes
in the body of the book, are in effect diplomatic editions, apart from
the limited normalization explained above, modern punctuation (in
the reader's interest), and correction of recognizable scribal errors.

---

Abschriften. Eine davon wurde die Vorlage der ersten gedruckten Bibel, von
der wiederum fast ohne Änderungen die folgenden Bibeldrucke abhängen,
sogar die offizielle Editio Sixto-Clementina.' (Weber's edition, incidentally, is
the standard critical text of the non-Clementine Vulgate.)

[16] The translations are moderately free, and sometimes silently settle the
interpretation of a word or phrase when another view could also be defended.
When anything important turns on the translation, scholars will want to con-
sult the Latin text as well.

When it is necessary to correct the manuscript's reading, the erroneous reading is always recorded in the notes. Note, however, that a different policy is followed with those transcriptions where more than one manuscript has been used. In these the apparatus of variants is streamlined according to principles explained below, and it seemed inappropriate to combine such principles with those of a diplomatic edition in which a scribe's every movement is recorded. With this subset of the Transcriptions, therefore, trivial errors, scribal corrections, etc. have not been recorded; see, however, the note on asterisks, at the end of this introduction.

The Transcriptions for which several manuscripts have been used are all of sermons by Bertrand de la Tour (most other sermons in memory of kings and princes seem to survive in only one manuscript). Though I have used all the manuscripts which I know to contain these texts, there are doubtless others I have missed. Still, I have tried to use a variety of witnesses to produce what could be called a 'critical transcription'.

A critical transcription is inferior in principle to an edition on the principles associated with Lachmann, but has advantages in practice, at least where late medieval texts are concerned. The Lachmannian approach possibly works best for classical texts where a few Carolingian copies of a lost late-antique exemplar have survived.[17] (I have also noted that editions of this sort are seldom attempted unless the text is already in print.) The problem that has especially weighed with me, however, is that 'no one ever checks anybody else's collations (or his own, for that matter) without finding mistakes in them'[18]—and it is not easy for editors in the Lachmann style to check their own initial observations. Either they must go over the collation of every manuscript twice or, if they delay checking until they have a provisionally completed text and apparatus, they must move their eyes continually between their version and this, that, or the other microfilm printout. The method I have adopted does not, needless to say, provide a guarantee against error, but it does make it easier to be accurate in detail and will commend itself to the obsessive checker.

In principle, a 'critical transcription' should produce a text identical to that of a 'Lachmannian' edition, though the critical apparatus will not record so many of the readings which the editor has discarded. The first stages are the same as with a full edition. One of the manuscripts is selected, because it promises to be good or, if one does

[17] J. Willis, *Latin Textual Criticism* (Illinois Studies in Language and Literature, 61; Urbana etc., 1972), 30–1.
[18] M. L. West, *Textual Criticism and Editorial Technique Applicable to Greek and Latin Texts* (Stuttgart, 1973), 63.

not know, for convenience, and transcribed. Next one makes a rapid working collation of the other manuscripts against this initial transcription. Then one works through transcription and collations, identifying significant scribal errors. Serviceable stemmatic relationships, if any, are worked out on the basis of these errors.[19] At this point one can also make an informed choice of manuscript for the final transcription: obviously, the one with fewest identifiable errors. If two or more are about equally 'clean', it does not matter greatly which one picks. Then one can embark on the final transcription. The chosen manuscript may be good, but it will not be perfect. When another manuscript has a better reading (or if one can guess a better reading), it goes into the text. If any stemmatic relationships have been uncovered, they may help one decide what is a better reading. At this point the apparatus will give the reading of the transcribed text as well as identifying the manuscript authority for the reading which has been preferred over that of the transcribed text. If several manuscripts have this preferred reading, only one will be noted unless one needs to show that this reading has a stemmatic argument behind it. In view of the way in which the final choice of the manuscript to be transcribed was made, the apparatus will be uncluttered. For the purpose of final checking one is dealing with a single manuscript most of the time, turning occasionally to photographs of the others, when they have a better reading, but not continually. Those who want to read a clean text without going over all the editor's judgements for themselves should get a product almost indistinguishable from a critical edition, but I have preferred the term 'critical transcription' to indicate that the apparatus is constructed on different principles and is more modest is scope.

To facilitate reference both in the apparatus and in the body of the book to specific sentences in the transcriptions, I have divided them into chapters and put a superscript 'verse'-number before each sentence. I do not remember seeing this system used except in editions of the Bible, where it seems not to irritate readers unduly. It soon ceases to be much more noticeable than punctuation.

I have not included among the transcriptions at the end any of the sermons in memory of kings or princes from the Angevin dynasty of Naples (though I have built large extracts into the main structure of the book). Taken together with sermons in memory of female members of that interesting royal family, these sermons constitute a corpus with a natural unity and deserve to be edited in a separate volume. Furthermore, they deserve to be studied together with the funeral

---

[19] Note that some serviceable stemmatic relationships can be discerned even in a contaminated tradition: see ibid., 38–9.

monuments which are another striking aspect of the dynasty's *memoria*.[20] In the present volume I have tried to avoid the temptation to follow the bias of the surviving evidence and concentrate on the Angevins, since the aim has been to bring out the relation of kingship to death in Europe as a whole, in a period when a genuinely secular political consciousness is found in an interesting relation to otherworldly priorities.

*Note on the use of asterisks.* An asterisk immediately before a word in a transcription indicates that an error too trivial to deserve a note has been corrected, or that the word follows a scribal deletion. In practice the asterisk is used only in the Transcriptions, where the sermon is attested by more than one known manuscript and space in the apparatus needs to be saved for variants.

---

[20] I plan to study the sermons together with funeral monuments and other memorial images in collaboration with Julia Walworth. The present volume has ignored tomb sculpture because I lack the necessary art-historical expertise, but there is an important literature on the subject. Note e.g. A. Erlande-Brandenburg, 'Le Roi est mort': Étude sur les funérailles, les sépultures et les tombeaux des rois de France jusqu'à la fin du XIIIᵉ siècle (Bibliothèque de la société française d'archéologie, 7; Geneva, 1975) (to give only one example).

# 1 *Preliminaries*

THE existence of a genre of sermons 'on the dead' (*de mortuis*) in the period before 1350 has become evident only recently.[1] The rubric 'de mortuis' in a manuscript is a rough-and-ready indication that a group of sermons should be included in the genre. Sometimes such sermons are for the feast of All Souls. Sometimes no occasion is specified. Some of the most interesting sermons in the genre, however, are unmistakably funeral or memorial sermons. Memorial sermons might be preached a year or perhaps every year after the person's death;[2] and it may also have been common to preach such a sermon a month after the death.[3] Sermons preached on the occasion of someone's death but not in the presence of the body (and perhaps in an entirely different town) are half-way between funeral sermons and memorial sermons in the narrow sense. In this study, as a convenient shorthand, 'memorial sermons' are taken to stand for both funeral and memorial sermons.

Since they commemorate and (as will be shown) also com-

---

[1] Largely thanks to J. B. Schneyer's *Repertorium der lateinischen Sermones des Mittelalters für die Zeit von 1150–1350* (Münster, 1969– ). Even before the *Repertorium* some good work had been done on limited sections of the material, notably R. Cruel, *Geschichte der deutschen Predigt im Mittelalter* (Detmold, 1879; repr. Hildesheim, 1966), 237–44; A. Linsenmayer, *Geschichte der Predigt in Deutschland von Karl dem Großen bis zum Ausgange des 14. Jahrhunderts* (Munich, 1886), 162–5, 213, 218, 277, 298; A. Dondaine, 'La vie et les œuvres de Jean de san Gimignano', *AFP* 9 (1939), 128–83, at 154–7; E. Winkler, 'Scholastische Leichenpredigten: Die Sermones funebres des Johannes von S. Geminiano', in *Kirche—Theologie—Frömmigkeit: Festgabe für Gottfried Holtz zum 65. Geburtstag* (Berlin, 1965), 177–86; T. Kaeppeli, 'Opere latine attribuite a Jacopo Passavanti, con un appendice sulle opere di Nicoluccio di Ascoli O.P.', *AFP* 32 (1962), 145–79, at 147–55 and 165–6; J. B. Schneyer, 'Der Beitrag des Johannes Regina von Neapel zur Entwicklung eigener Predigtreihen', *(Tübinger) theologische Quartalschrift*, 144 (1964), 216–27; Th. Woltersdorfer in Greifswald, 'Zur Geschichte der Leichenreden im Mittelalter', *Zeitschrift für praktische Theologie*, 6 (1984), 359–65; also (since Schneyer) E. Panella, 'Note di biografia domenicana tra xiii e xiv secolo', *AFP* 54 (1984), 231–80.
[2] See P. Cole, D. L. d'Avray, and J. Riley-Smith, 'Application of Theology to Current Affairs: Memorial Sermons on the Dead of Mansurah and on Innocent IV', *Historical Research*, 63 (1990), 227–47, at 239 n. 79, also 230 n. 20.
[3] Ibid. 230 n. 19.

mend a person on the other side of the grave, this genre has certain affinities with sermons in honour of saints. On the other hand, memorial sermons are not infrequently organized according to different states of life, which gives them a resemblance to *status* sermons (sermons to or about different sorts and conditions of people).[4] They are in fact a rich source for attitudes to social roles.

The present work deals with sermons on holders of a special social role, that of king or prince. Little of the evidence has been printed and less, if any, has been studied. It has much to tell us about attitudes to the individual, to his office, and to the afterlife. These compositions can also provoke reflection about the relation of representation in this genre to political realities.

The genre has continued in various forms from the period covered here to the present. A subsidiary purpose of this book is to supply the missing first chapter of what should be a continuous story and, in the more immediate term, to supply materials for comparative study. Though much scholarly effort and indeed huge quantities of research money have been lavished on the history of memorial preaching in later centuries, the grip of scholars on the formative medieval period has been shaky and insecure.

Though a full review of the scholarly literature on other periods would be out of place here,[5] one must at least mention important work done on the Byzantine period,[6] on later medieval England,[7] on humanist Italy,[8] on sixteenth-century

---

[4] It was Nicole Bériou who pointed out to me the double affinity with *de sanctis* sermons on the one hand and *status* sermons on the other.

[5] For a most useful bibliography see R. Lenz (ed.), *Leichenpredigten: Eine Bestandsaufnahme. Bibliographie und Ergebnisse einer Umfrage* (Marburger Personalschriften-Forschungen, 3; Marburg, 1980).

[6] A. Sideras, 'Die byzantinischen Grabreden: Prosopographie, Datierung, Überlieferung, mit 24 Erstausgaben' (unpublished Habilitationsschrift; Göttingen, 1982 [not seen]), cited and summarized in id., 'Byzantinische Leichenreden: Bestand, Prosopographie, zeitliche und räumliche Distribution, literarische Form und Quellenwert', in R. Lenz (ed.), *Leichenpredigten als Quelle historischer Wissenschaften* (3 vols.; Vienna and Marburg, 1975–84), iii. 17–49.

[7] S. Powell and A. J. Fletcher, '"In die sepulture seu trigintali": The Late Medieval Funeral and Memorial Sermon', *Leeds Studies in English*, NS 12 (1981), 195–228 (excellent); P. J. Horner, 'John Paunteley's Sermon at the Funeral of Walter Froucester, Abbot of Gloucester (1412)', *American Benedictine Review*, 28 (1977), 147–66.

[8] J. M. McManamon, 'The Ideal Renaissance Pope: Funeral Oratory from the

France,[9] and above all on early modern Germany, where there is a whole institute devoted to the study of German *Leichenpredigten* from Luther to the eighteenth century.[10] Under the aegis of its director, furthermore, three volumes of conference proceedings[11] have been produced in which studies of different countries and periods are brought together, so that the genre's potential as a field of comparative history has already become evident. Though I shall not draw explicit comparisons with later periods in the present study, as I have tried to do elsewhere,[12] the present work should not be regarded as an isolated project but as a contribution to an informal collaboration.

Some preliminary questions about the origins, transmission, and functions of the genre in the Middle Ages must be answered before the real work of interpretation can begin. The first is simple: how and when did the tradition of memorial preaching develop in the West? Some supplementary questions follow naturally. Were sermons in memory of princes as rare as might be supposed? At what sort of audience were the sermons directed and in what language were they preached? How different are they from poetic speeches commemorating great men (*Ehrenreden* etc.)? Do memorial sermons have the same functions as other liturgical ways of honouring the dead? For what reasons were the sermons written down and preserved? How did the preachers themselves conceive the function of a memorial sermon? The answer to this last question will take us on to a principal argument of the book, about this world and the next.

Origins first. The funeral orations of Ambrose of Milan make

Papal Court', *Archivum Historiae Pontificiae*, 14 (1976), 9–70; 'Innovation in Early Humanist Rhetoric: The Oratory of Pier Paolo Vergerio the Elder', *Rinascimento*, 2nd ser., 22 (1982), 3–32; and above all his admirable *Funeral Oratory and the Cultural Ideals of Italian Humanism* (Chapel Hill and London, 1989).

[9] V. L. Saulnier, 'L'oraison funèbre au XVIᵉ siècle', *Bibliothèque d'humanisme et renaissance*, 10 (1948), 124–57. In connection with early modern France one should also mention J. Hennequin, *Henri IV dans ses oraisons funèbres, ou la naissance d'une légende* (Bibliothèque française et romane, ser. C, Études Littéraires, 62; Paris, 1977).

[10] The Forschungsstelle für Personalschriften at the University of Marburg, directed by Dr Rudolf Lenz.

[11] Lenz (ed.), *Leichenpredigten als Quelle historischer Wissenschaften*.

[12] D'Avray, 'The Comparative Study of Memorial Preaching', *Transactions of the Royal Historical Society*, 5th ser., 40 (1990), 25–42.

as good a beginning as any, in that they are a point of overlap between the end of the history of the classical *laudatio funebris* and the beginning of Christian memorial preaching in the West.[13]

Like a traditional Roman *oratio funebris*, these orations of Ambrose combine praise of the deceased with lamentation.[14] However, they are designed to console, which appears to be a departure from the Roman tradition.[15] Though the change was consonant with the new, Christian message, it was apparently influenced by the third-century Greek rhetorician Menander, either directly or through speeches written under the influence of Menander's doctrines.[16]

Christians and pagans alike participated in the rhetorical culture of late antiquity, and Ambrose's funeral orations fit into this background. For example, his description of the body of the dead emperor Valentinian II may have been directly or indirectly prompted by a suggestion of Menander.[17] The message about virtue conveyed by the rhetoric has a good deal in common with that of the pagan Roman funeral oration, but seems to have undergone a subtle Christianization.[18] A more obvious change, perhaps the salient one (together with the

---

[13] An alternative beginning, perhaps rather too distant from the main business of this book, would have been the Christian funeral oratory in the Greek East in the 4th cent. For a brief account see S. Rusterholz, *Rostra, Sarg, und Predigtstuhl: Studien zu Form und Funktion der Totenrede bei Andreas Gryphius* (Studien zur Germanistik, Anglistik und Komparatistik, 16; Bonn, 1974), 20–6. For a recent assessment of St Ambrose's place in the history of the classical *oratio funebris* see W. Kierdorf, *Laudatio Funebris: Interpretationen und Untersuchungen zur Entwicklung der römischen Leichenrede* (Beiträge zur klassischen Philologie, 106; Meisenheim am Glan, 1980), 126–30; also the studies cited by O. Faller in *Sancti Ambrosii Opera, pars septima* (Corpus Scriptorum Ecclesiasticorum Latinorum, 73; Vienna, 1955), 80* n. 123. I have not been able to see F. Rozynski, *Die Leichenreden des hl. Ambrosius, insbesondere auf ihr Verhältnis zur antiken Rhetorik und der antiken Trostschrift untersucht* (Breslau, 1910).

[14] On these features in the pagan Roman *oratio funebris* see Kierdorf, *Laudatio Funebris*, 135: 'Dieser Tenor von Lob und Klage, wobei das Lob dazu dient, die Trauer um den Toten zu rechtfertigen und anzuregen, ist, soweit wir es beurteilen können, für die pagane Leichenrede insgesamt kennzeichnend.'

[15] '. . . nicht mehr das Lob des Toten und die daraus entspringende Klage, sondern das konsolatorische Räsonnement bestimmen letzlich das Ziel der christlichen Leichenrede' (ibid. 129; Kierdorf believes this to be the 'erste wirklich grundsätzliche Wandel der Leichenrede', ibid.).

[16] Ibid. 86, 128, 129, 134. On Menander, ibid. 54, 56–8.

[17] Ibid. 130, where Ambrose is succinctly situated in his rhetorical context.

[18] Ibid. 127–8.

new emphasis on consolation), is that Ambrose shows little
interest in *bona externa*—the family, education, offices, and
honours of the deceased.[19] Praise of such *bona externa* had been
an important element in the pagan *oratio funebris*.

Four memorial sermons by Ambrose are extant. Two were
on his brother Satyras, one of them preached at the funeral
itself, the other on the seventh day after it.[20] Another oration
was preached at the (much-delayed) funeral of the emperor
Valentinian II,[21] and one forty days (inclusive) after the death
of the emperor Theodosius.[22] Each of these speeches would
appear to have undergone some modification for 'publication':
indeed, in the case of the sermon on Theodosius, a long excursus on Constantine, his mother Helena, and the finding of
the true cross would seem to have been added after delivery to
the version put into written circulation.[23] Since sermons in
memory of rulers are the theme of the present book, it is worth
looking more closely at the two orations on emperors, the *De
obitu Ualentiniani* and the *De obitu Theodosii*.

Both orations successfully convey some sense of the dead
man's individual personality. Ambrose said that guilty people
hoped to find in Theodosius the anger that they would have
feared in anyone else, since the angrier he became, the nearer
he was to forgiveness.[24] If this was a topos, which I doubt, it
captured what seems to have been a distinctive feature of his
character.[25] Valentinian II is represented quite vividly as a
very high-minded young man, who firmly suppressed his little
weaknesses. It had been said that he was too eager for lunch,

[19] 'nicht mehr . . . christlichen Leichenrede', 127.
[20] F. Homes Dudden, *The Life and Times of St Ambrose* (2 vols.; Oxford, 1935),
i. 181–4; Ambrose, *Opera*, ed. Faller, pp. 81*–88*.
[21] Dudden, *Life and Times*, ii. 419–21; cf. Ambrose, *Opera*, ed. Faller, pp.
101*–106*.
[22] Dudden, *Life and Times*, ii. 439–40; cf. Ambrose, *Opera*, ed. Faller, pp.
114*–117*. Kierdorf, *Laudatio Funebris*, 126, implicitly discounts this as an *oratio
funebris* (he does not mention it with the other three), presumably because it
was not preached at a funeral. This seems an unduly narrow definition of the
genre.
[23] Ambrose, *Opera*, ed. Faller, pp. 88*–89*, 106*, 117* (note that on this page
'§ 41' must be a misprint for '§ 51').
[24] '. . . tunc propior erat ueniae, cum fuisset conmotio maior iracundiae.
Praerogatiua ignoscendi erat indignatum fuisse et optabatur in eo, quod in aliis
timebatur, ut irasceretur' (sect. 13, pp. 377–8 Faller).
[25] Dudden, *Life and Times*, i. 173–4.

for instance, so he started to give big banquets for his companions through which he would sit hungry.[26] Valentinian's special affection for his sisters is also ably portrayed.[27]

Ambrose neatly uses his picture of Valentinian's feelings for his sisters to make a point about his public virtue as a ruler. When a legal case about land came before him in which his sisters were involved, he would not take it himself, but referred it to a judge, and even persuaded his sisters—girls worthy of such a brother (Ambrose says)—into a willingness to give up rather than cause embarrassment (*uerecundiam*) to him.[28] Ambrose also praises Valentinian's good judgement and freedom from paranoia when a great man was accused of treasonable ambition,[29] his willingness to defend the empire,[30] his firm refusal to impose more taxes,[31] and his steadfastness when faced with powerful pressure at a high level to restore alleged pagan rights.[32]

Theodosius too is praised for his policy towards paganism (against which he had legislated).[33] Other virtues praised are his mercy (as we have seen),[34] his humility, as evidenced by his willingness to do penance[35] (Theodosius' public penance for a massacre at Thessalonike was indeed an astonishing submission), his love of God and even of his enemies,[36] his willingness to accept the burden of empire in troubled times,[37] and his faith.[38]

---

[26] 'Iactabant inuidi, quod praemature prandium peteret: coepit ita frequentare ieiunium, ut plerumque ipse inpransus conuiuium solemne suis comitibus exhiberet, quo et religioni sacrae satisfaceret et principis humanitati' (sect. 16, p. 338 Faller); see also Dudden, *Life and Times*, ii. 412.

[27] 'Manus, capita sororibus osculabatur, inmemor imperii, memor germanitatis. Et quanto magis aliis potestatis iure praestaret, hoc se magis humilem sororibus exhibebat' (sect. 36, p. 347 Faller).

[28] *De ob. Ual.* 37, pp. 347–8 Faller.

[29] Ibid. 18, p. 339 Faller.

[30] Ibid. 2, p. 330 Faller.

[31] Ibid. 21, pp. 340–1 Faller.

[32] Ibid. 19–20, pp. 339–40 Faller.

[33] *De ob. Th.* 38, p. 391 Faller.

[34] Ibid. 12–14, pp. 377–8 Faller; cf. above, n. 24.

[35] Ibid. 27–8, pp. 384–5 Faller; 34, p. 388 Faller.

[36] Notably ibid. 17–18, pp. 380–1 Faller.

[37] '"Portauit iugum graue", quando subiit pietatis exilium, quando infusis Romano imperio barbaris suscepit imperium. "Portavit iugum graue", ut tyrannos Romano imperio dimoueret' (ibid. 53, p. 399 Faller).

[38] Ibid. 7, p. 375 Faller.

Because he laboured here, says Ambrose, Theodosius now enjoys rest.[39] Ambrose is entirely optimistic about the fate of Theodosius and Valentinian II in the next world, which gets a fair amount of attention in the sermons. In order to gain a coherent picture of Ambrose's doctrine of the afterlife these sermons need to be studied together with his other works,[40] but it is worth listing some themes that stand out in one or both of these texts. At least some of what he says is, of course, the kind of thing that might be said in many periods.

As we have seen, he thinks that death can mean rest.[41] The separation of soul from body is presented as a liberation, in passages that could bear a mildly dualist reading.[42] Even though he had not received baptism, Valentinian is saved, for he ardently desired it.[43] He can turn again and show his glory to his sisters and to the rest before hastening on to the Holy Jerusalem.[44] Theodosius, Ambrose hopes, will be 'the helper and protector of his children with Christ'.[45]

Death and reunion are associated. In both sermons reunion with the emperor Gratian, elder brother of Valentinian II and co-emperor of Theodosius, is described in powerful language.[46] Conversely, Maximus (who had overthrown Gratian) and Eugenius (the tame emperor of the man who had humiliated

[39] 'Sed quia hic in labore, ibi in requie' (ibid. 53, p. 399 Faller).

[40] This has been done by Dudden, *Life and Times*, ii. 650–72, esp. 650–8.

[41] See also *De ob. Th.* 29–30, pp. 386–8 Faller, and 36, pp. 389–90 Faller. Cf. also sect. 37, p. 390 Faller, where Ambrose describes the holy mountain of the Lord as the place 'ubi perennis uita, ubi corruptelae nulla contagio, nullus gemitus, nullus dolor, nulla consortia mortuorum'.

[42] 'Ideoque regio illa uiuorum est, ubi anima est, quae "ad imaginem et similitudinem" dei facta est, non caro figurata "de limo". Ideo caro in terram reuertitur, anima ad requiem festinat supernam' (ibid. 30, p. 387 Faller); 'speciosos enim processus habuisti in corpore, tamquam calciamento eo usa, non ut inuolucro, ut quasi superior et eminentior, quo uelles, tuum circumferres sine ulla offensione uestigio, uel certe sicut calciamentum illud exsolueres, sicut Moyses fecit, cui dictum est: *Solue calciamentum pedum tuorum*' (*De ob. Ual.* 67, p. 361 Faller).

[43] See Dudden, *Life and Times*, ii. 420–1.

[44] 'Conuertere ad nos "pacifica", ut gloriam tuam sororibus tuis monstres et incipiant se tuae quietis et gratiae securitate solari. Semel tantum ad nos conuertere, ut te uideamus, et rursus conuertere atque ad Hierusalem illam ciuitatem sanctorum tota intentione festina' (*De ob. Ual.* 65, p. 360 Faller).

[45] I borrow the translation in Dudden, *Life and Times*, ii. 440.

[46] *De ob. Ual.*, esp. sects. 71–9, pp. 362–6 Faller; *De ob. Th.* 39, pp. 391–2 Faller.

and perhaps ordered the death of Valentinian II) are represented in the *De obitu Theodosii* as being in hell.[47] They and
their fate are described in terms of night.[48] The happiness of
the just, on the other hand, is represented in terms of light.[49]
Again, Ambrose pictures Valentinian II ascending towards God
like an eagle.[50]

It is hard to separate images from religious content in
Ambrose's representation of the afterlife; the same may be said
with respect to his use of Old Testament images,[51] and also,
more generally, of the scriptural quotations that are woven into
his rhetoric. Furthermore Ambrose's moving references to his
own personal and religious relationship with each of the two
emperors,[52] which contribute to the impact these speeches
make even on a modern reader, also illustrate the difficulty
of separating the ideas from the aesthetic, emotional, and
rhetorical efficacy of the medium.

These two memorial orations have deserved a relatively extended treatment[53] not only because they are the beginning of
this particular story, but also because they lend themselves
readily to comparison with the medieval sermons on dead
rulers. It is true that the late fourth century was a different
world from that of the thirteenth and fourteenth centuries.

---

[47] 'Contra autem Maximus et Eugenius in inferno quasi *nox nocti indicat
scientiam* docentes exemplo miserabili, quam durum sit arma suis principibus
inrogare' (*De ob. Th.* 39, p. 392 Faller).

[48] Ibid.: 'nox nocti . . .' (Ps. 18: 3).

[49] 'Transiuit enim pius de caligine seculari ad lumen aeternum' (ibid.);
'Prospicis igitur nos, sancta anima, de loco superiore tamquam inferiora re-
spiciens. Existi de tenebris istius saeculi, et "ut luna" resplendes, "ut sol"
refulges. Et bene "ut luna", quia et ante, in umbra licet istius corporis, re-
fulgebas et terrarum tenebras inluminabas et nunc lumen a sole iustitiae
mutuata clarum diem ducis' (*De ob. Ual.* 64, p. 359 Faller).

[50] 'Uidere igitur uideor te tamquam de corpore recedentem et repulsa noctis
caligine surgentem diluculo sicut solem, adpropinquantem deo et rapido uolatu
sicut aquilam, quae terrena sunt, relinquentem' (ibid. 64, pp. 359–60 Faller).

[51] e.g. 'Quis splendidius celebrauit quam qui sacrilegos remouit errores,
clusit templa, simulacra destruxit? In hoc Iosias rex superioribus antelatus est'
(*De ob. Th.* 38, p. 391 Faller).

[52] Cf. *De ob. Ual.* 79b, p. 367 Faller; and *De ob. Th.* 33–5, pp. 388–9 Faller,
e.g. '"Dilexi" uirum, qui me in supremis suis ultimo spiritu requirebat' (sect.
35, p. 389).

[53] Nevertheless a brief one in proportion to their length. It may have been
possible to capture the ideas in the foregoing summary, but not the emotional
impact.

Moreover, the oration on Theodosius, at least, is very much
the product of a particular historical moment, when Ambrose
was anxious to ensure that the dead man's style of government
should be continued under his sons.[54] However, the desire to
use the dead ruler as a model, if we abstract it from the
particular circumstances, is, as we shall see, a common factor
shared with medieval memorial sermons.

It has in fact been possible to put to these orations of Ambrose
much the same questions that will be asked of medieval
memorial sermons. The salient findings, for comparative purposes, are as follows. Ambrose successfully communicates the
individuality of the dead man, though (in the case of the
oration for Theodosius at least) this is probably not his primary
purpose. He praises qualities of justice, mercy, humility, love
of God, willingness to defend the empire, commitment to its
Christianity. He is confident that the men he praises are
already enjoying their eternal reward, one aspect of which is
reunion with loved ones. It is hard to separate the aesthetic
qualities of the orations from the content of the religious
message.

In the balance held between attention to this life and the next
these orations resemble their medieval counterparts. Indeed, it
is not easy to put concepts to the contrast which anyone who
compares the medieval texts with Ambrose must obscurely
feel. One difference is that some medieval sermons (like pagan
Roman and like fifteenth-century humanist *orationes funebres*)
show a definite interest in *bona externa*. Again, I know of nothing
in the medieval texts quite like the descriptions in Ambrose's
orations of reunion with Gratian and other loved ones.

After Ambrose, the sources seem to say nothing pertinent to
our theme for centuries. The sermon by Hilarius of Arles on his
predecessor St Honoratus (d. 429) should perhaps be classified
as a saint's-day sermon rather than as a memorial sermon
proper,[55] though the line between the genres may not be very
firm here. Ludwig Ruland was quite probably right to think

---

[54] *Opera*, ed. Faller, p. 116*.
[55] 'Die Rede des Hilarius von Arles auf seinen Vorgänger Honoratus gehört
nicht in unseren Rahmen. Sie ist eine Festpredigt am Jahrestag dieses Heiligen'
(L. Ruland, *Die Geschichte der kirchlichen Leichenfeier* (Regensburg, 1901), 162).

that from the patristic period to his own time there had never been a century which had not known the funeral oration;[56] but this was probably a guess, as the evidence which has so far been brought to light is scanty.[57] It is quite possible that references would be uncovered by anyone who worked systematically through the Scriptores volumes of the Monumenta Germaniae Historica, looking for accounts of how bishops and abbots (and perhaps also rulers) were buried. As things now stand, however, one must move forward to the tenth century for clear evidence of memorial preaching. It is a reference in Gerhard's Life of Bishop Ulrich of Augsburg, who died in 973. The sermon was delivered between the funeral mass and the burial.[58] Gerhard says that the preacher (another bishop) told those present to pray for Ulrich's soul, so that, freed from the bond of sins, it might by the gift of God be worthy to enjoy eternal happiness with the saints and the elect of God. The report is brief,[59] so we cannot be sure whether or not other themes were also broached.

We have a fuller report of the content of a memorial sermon delivered about a century later, in 1075. The preacher was Archbishop Anno II of Cologne; the dead man, a certain Herimannus, prior of a monastery where Anno spent much of his time near the end of his life.[60] The author of the *Uita Annonis* makes it clear by a charming story that Anno and Herimannus had been close enough friends to tease each

[56] 'Daß es aber in der Zwischenzeit von den Vätern bis auf uns kein Jahrhundert gegeben hat, das nicht auch die Leichenrede gekannt hätte, scheinen viele nicht zu wissen' (ibid. 211).

[57] Cf. the brief (and useful) remarks in Cruel, *Geschichte der deutschen Predigt im Mittelalter*, 75, 237; F. Jürgensmeier, 'Die Leichenpredigt in der katholischen Begräbnisfeier', in Lenz (ed.), *Leichenpredigten*, i. 122–41, at 128–9; Kierdorf, *Laudatio Funebris*, 131–2.

[58] See next note.

[59] It is as follows: 'Insuper etiam, publica missa expleta, omnes in commune sobrio et cauto sermone [admonuit], ut pro illa sancta anima intima intentione cordis deuote exorarent, ut ab omni uinculo delictorum absoluta, Deo donante, perenni gaudio in aeuum cum sanctis et electis Dei perfrui mereretur. Oratione autem secundum uerbum eius ab omnibus peracta, episcopus corpus sepeliuit, et animam omnipotenti Deo deuotissime cum lacrimis commendauit' (*Gerhardi Uita Sancti Oudalrici Episcopi*, p. 415 ed. MGH (Scriptores, 4; Hanover, 1841)).

[60] 'Igitur dilectissimus Deo praesul ultimum agens annum, dilectum sibi montem plus solito frequentabat' (*Vita Annonis Archiepiscopi Coloniensis*, 3. 1, p. 498 ed. MGH (Scriptores, 11; Hanover, 1854)). (Kierdorf, *Laudatio Funebris*, 131–2, steered me to this interesting report.)

other.[61] Anno's sermon, like the sermon on Ulrich, seems to have been given between the funeral mass and the burial.[62] The author of the *Uita Annonis* purports to give the sermon verbatim, and if his version is at all close to the live original it was an address that conveyed great unhappiness of spirit. It begins by using the presence of the dead man's body to make concrete the idea that death is inevitable for all, that doom comes just when men feel secure.[63] The author then turns to his personal grief. He has recently lost his beloved nephew, and now he is officiating at the funeral of a man especially dear to him, the more so since 'this place'—presumably he means the monastery—has cause to lament the deceased's death with perpetual grief, since his efforts had done so much for its monastic *disciplina*.[64] The author can imagine nothing worse than these trials, through which 'his place' is made vulnerable to the Devil.[65] His own death is all that remains, and he warns those present that it will not be long delayed.[66]

We may disentangle at least three themes here: a vivid

---

[61] 3. 2, pp. 498–9 ed. MGH.

[62] '. . . post consummationem sacramentorum retro feretrum stans, hanc orationem nimis luctuose prosecutus est' (ibid. 3. 2, p. 499 ed. MGH). Then, after the sermon: 'Ad hanc uocem multorum lacrimis excitatis, corpus ex more terrae traditum est' (3. 3, p. 499).

[63] 'Nostrarum miseriarum negocium prae manibus habemus, et quem conditionis nostrae finem habituri simus singuli, ipsis oculis considerare datur. Hae uos monent exequiae, quia dies Domini, sicut fur in nocte, ita ueniet. Cum enim dixerint pax et securitas, tunc repentinus eis superueniet interitus, sicut dolor in utero habentis, et non effugiet. Quicquid hinc excogitare potest homo, quicquid eloqui ualet lingua, totum hoc expositum nobis oculorum nostrorum acie fas est penetrare' (ibid. 3. 3, p. 499 ed. MGH).

[64] 'Unde generalem compendiose percurrens sermonem, ad meorum casuum specialem conuerto miseriam. Proh dolor! Anno puer, quo nullus umquam mihi dilectior in hac mortalitate, praecedentibus non minus decem diebus hinc abiit. Dolor quem inde contraxi nec ad momentum quidem conquievit; et ecce, sepulturae illius hodie deseruio, qui mihi non sicut quilibet carorum meorum lugendus est. Amplius multo uir lacrimarum mearum quaerit effusionem, quoniam hic est, quem et locus iste sempiterno planctu non immerito flere habet. Heu! quae spes ultra poterit esse de statu loci, cum iaceat exanimis, cuius industria processit hactenus hic disciplina religionis?' (ibid.).

[65] 'Erat quoquomodo tolerabile, quicquid huc usque diuino permissu me appetiit; intima sunt ualde quae nunc me coartant, nec potest exquisitioribus manus Domini me tangere plagis, quam his quibus in periculum loci mei grassandi copia offertur aduersario' (ibid.).

[66] 'Restat ut et me cunctis debita finiat mors, habetque testimonium ex me hodie, quisquis adest, antistem uestrum non plures ex hoc superuiuere dies' (ibid.).

message about death, lament at the speaker's loss, and praise for the virtue of the deceased. The sermon actually delivered may of course have been much longer than the report in the *uita*.

A few years later, in 1089, Gilbert bishop of Évreux preached at the funeral of William the Conqueror,

telling how he had valiantly extended the frontiers where the Norman law prevailed; how, more than all his ancestors, he had brought greatness to his people; how he had maintained justice and kept the peace in all his dominions, had effectively chastened thieves and robbers with the rod of law, and bravely protected clerks and monks and the defenceless populace with his strong sword. When he had ended his oration he made a request to the people, saying to the multitude, who wept out of respect and listened attentively, 'Since no mortal man can live all his life without sin, I beg you all for the love of God to intercede with almighty God for the dead duke, and if he has ever done you any wrong to forgive him freely.'[67]

If this account by Ordericus Vitalis is at all close to the original sermon, it shows that even in the eleventh century a memorial preacher could give great emphasis to tough, this-worldly royal virtues. Was it common at this time, and perhaps even earlier, to preach about dead rulers and to adopt this robust tone? It does not seem unlikely but it has not been proved.

Another brief chronicle reference, by Hugh of Flavigny, to a sermon at the funeral of an abbot in 1099,[68] need not detain us, for by this time evidence for memorial preaching is beginning to increase. The relatively plentiful twelfth-century evidence has, furthermore, been reasonably well studied.[69] Perhaps the

---

[67] *The Ecclesiastical History of Ordericus Vitalis*, 7. 16, ed. and trans. Marjorie Chibnall (6 vols.; Oxford, 1969–80), iv (1973), 104–7.

[68] '. . . in crastinum congregata est omnis ciuitas ad sepeliendum eum; et missa dicta, sermone dato, terrae redditus est, resurgendus in gloria et nobiscum semper spiritualiter conuersaturus' (*Chronicon Hugonis monachi Virdunensis et Divionensis Abbatis Flaviniacensis*, 1, p. 500 ed. MGH (Scriptores, 8; Hanover, 1848)). The dead man was Rodulphus, abbot of St Vitonus.

[69] Accordingly, I do not try to discuss every record of memorial preaching: what follows is a sketch of the main lines of development, with special reference to unexploited manuscript evidence. For a useful bibliography see Peter von Moos, *Consolatio: Studien zur mittellateinischen Trostliteratur über den Tod und zum Problem der christlichen Trauer* (4 vols.; Münstersche Mittelalter-Schriften, 3 (1–4); Munich, 1971–2), i. *Darstellungsband* (1971), and ii. *Anmer-*

best known is a memorial sermon which St Bernard integrated
into his series on the Song of Songs, after the death in 1138
of his brother Gerard; its context in this series—a different
'setting in life' from a funeral or memorial service—puts it
near the borderline of our genre.[70] Peter von Moos, who has
studied this sermon exhaustively,[71] characterizes it in terms of
Bernard's double relationship to Gerard, who was his fellow
monk as well as his brother; thus personal emotion was connected with instruction of his community.[72]

St Bernard's sermon is moving, but a full précis would take
us far from our theme. It may be noted in passing that there
are certain parallels with Ambrose's sermon in memory of his
brother.[73] Our next sermon seems closer (perhaps because of
the way it has been transmitted) to the tenth- and eleventh-
century cases just discussed. Like the sermon on Ulrich of
Augsburg, it is by a bishop on a bishop (Imbrico of Würzburg
on Otto of Bamburg).[74] As with Prior Herimannus, a chronicler
gives what purports to be a verbatim report of the sermon.[75]

*kungsband* (1971), paras. 56–7 (the bibliographical notes are arranged according
to these marginal paragraph-numbers in vol. i). Note that the sermon on Louis
IX by Jean de Samois to which von Moos refers is not a memorial sermon of the
sort studied in this book, for it was preached after he had been declared a
saint.

[70] '... Deshalb wählt er nicht die selbständige Redeform der Leichenrede
oder Totenklage, sondern spricht die Mönchsgemeinde als Seelsorger im
Rahmen einer Predigt an, die zum Zyklus der im Kapitelsaal gehaltenen,
später zum fortlaufenden Kommentar vereinigten Vorträge über das Hohelied
gehört' (von Moos, *Consolatio*, i. *Darstellungsband*, 279). (Charlotte Morse, *nisi
fallor*, first drew my attention to Bernard's sermon.)
[71] Von Moos, ibid. 278–331.
[72] 'Das doppelt nahe (verwandtschaftliche und monastische) Verhältnis
zwischen ihm und Bernhard bestimmt die eigne Gestalt einer Rede, die das
"Private" auf eine höhere gemeinschaftliche Ebene erhebt und das "Klöster-
liche" mit dem persönlichen, affektiven Impuls verbindet. Bernhard stellt den
Verlust nicht als ein für sich stehendes Thema dar, sondern geht davon aus,
um seine ihm geistlich gleichverbundenen Brüder zu lehren' (ibid. 279).
[73] Ibid. 329–30.
[74] On this sermon see Cruel, *Geschichte*, 75, 237. On neither page does Cruel
give references, but I suspect he may have unconsciously conflated two chronicle sources. See next note.
[75] Two chronicle accounts complement each other in an interesting way.
One might be understood to imply that Imbrico gave two sermons, one to
the people (presumably in the vernacular), the other to the clergy: 'Deinde
missarum celebritate a uenerabili Imbricone Wirtzeburgensi episcopo celebrata,
idem praesul sermone suauissimo ad populum habito—erat enim magnum

This time the report is relatively long, and it is easily accessible and so need not be retailed in detail here. Otto is compared to Martha receiving Christ, and a little later to a mother. The preacher, who refrains from talking about all his many virtues, singles out his mercy (*misericordia*). Imbrico talks of his personal loss, then of the loss to the episcopal order, for Otto was a model bishop, the loss to the pope and the emperor (the preacher dwells a little on his service to the empire), and to monks. He describes how Otto used holy guile to steer secular wealth, and sometimes also the owners of it, into monasteries. Because he was merciful and humble he will receive mercy, with the intercession of Mary, St Michael, etc., even if some trace of concern for human praise should have blemished his good and merciful deeds—for nothing is completely pure in the presence of the supreme judge. Imbrico therefore asks his audience to pray that any such blemish be removed by Christ.[76]

The German sermon which Imbrico apparently preached to 'the people' before this one[77] has not survived, but we do have at least two Middle High German memorial sermons from the first half of the twelfth century.[78] A recent commentary on them is rather blunt:

uerbi tonitruum—testimonium Jheremiae prophetae pii Ottonis personae adaptauit: *Oliuam uberem, pulchram, fructiferam, et speciosam uocauit Dominus nomen tuum*, tantaque mellifluae praedicationis suauitate se cunctis mirabilem fecit, ut uere Spiritus sanctus per os eius credatur esse locutus' (*Ebbonis Vita Ottonis Episcopi Babenbergensis*, 3, p. 881 ed. MGH (Scriptores, 12; Hanover, 1856)). The other source gives what would presumably be, from its content, a report of the second sermon (though he does not include any initial scriptural text): *Herbordi Dialogus de Vita Ottonis Episcopi Babenbergensis*, 1. 42, ed. R. Köpke (MGH Scriptores, 20; Hanover, 1868), 721–3. (This is the original version of Herbord's work: J. Petersohn, 'Überlieferung und ursprüngliche Gestalt der Kurzfassung von Herbords Otto-Vita', *Deutsches Archiv*, 23 (1967), 93–115, argues that 'die Kurzfassung von Herbords Otto-Vita nicht als Vorstufe des Dialogs zu betrachten ist, sondern daß sie als Bearbeitung dieses Werks entstand' (p. 111). In fact there seems virtually no difference between the text of Imbrico's sermon in the 'Dialogue' and the short version.)

[76] This is a free summary of MGH Scriptores 20, pp. 721–3.
[77] See above, n. 75.
[78] There is a critical edition of the sermons in *Speculum Ecclesiae: Eine frühmittelhochdeutsche Predigtsammlung (Cgm. 39)*, ed. G. Mellbourn (Lund and Copenhagen, 1944), Nos. 68–9, pp. 154–5; they are also reprinted in A. M. Haas, *Todesbilder im Mittelalter: Fakten und Hinweise in der deutschen Literatur* (Darmstadt, 1989), 47 (note that the words 'unde spil' are omitted from the last line of No. 68). Anton Schönbach described both sermons as 'Leichenreden': 'Studien zur

One is struck by a certain poverty of thought in both these model sermons (*Predigtmustern*): the surrender of earthly goods in death, the certainty of death and at the same time the uncertainty about the moment of it, and the consequent call to make oneself ready for the grace of God—these are the themes, which are presented briefly and without adornment.[79]

Though these sermons from the Middle High German *Speculum Ecclesiae*[80] (not to be confused with the more properly named *Speculum Ecclesiae* discussed below) may well be the earliest evidence of a practice of writing down memorial sermons in Middle High German, they are not the only such traces to survive from the central Middle Ages.[81] This may be an interesting peculiarity of the German-speaking area, for I know of nothing like them from Italy, France, or England.

The *Speculum Ecclesiae* proper, that is to say the remarkable collection of model sermons written in Latin by a shadowy figure known as Honorius Augustodunensis,[82] is more directly relevant to our specific theme, because it includes a model of how to preach to the people at the exequies of a *potens*, a man who had possessed power.[83] It is the earliest known medieval Latin model sermon for memorial preaching.[84]

This sermon has more than once been summarized in secondary works by German scholars,[85] so it is possible to be

Geschichte der altdeutschen Predigt; 1. Über Kelle's "Speculum Ecclesiae"', *Sitzungsberichte der philosophisch-historischen Classe der kaiserlichen Akademie der Wissenschaften*, 135, III. Abhandlung (Vienna, 1896), 138. This is clear at least in the case of No. 68, which includes the words 'Allez, dez dirre göte man in dirre werlt besezzen hete, dez hât er allez hie lazzen' (p. 154 Mellbourn).

[79] Haas, *Todesbilder*, 47.
[80] The name seems to have been imposed on the work by the first editor. See the comments by Schönbach, 'Studien . . . 1', 2.
[81] See Endnote 1, below, p. 279.
[82] To attempt to reconstruct his identity is to enter a quicksand. For a recent attempt to reach some conclusions about him see M.-O. Garrigues, 'L'Anonymat d'Honorius Augustodunensis', *Studia Monastica*, 25 (1983), 31–71.
[83] 'Si potens defunctus est sepeliendus, taliter populus est admonendus' (in *Speculum Ecclesiae*, ed. PL 172 (Paris, 1895), 807–1108, at 1081–6).
[84] Valerie Flint suggests a date in the very early years of the 12th cent., if not earlier: 'The Chronology of the Works of Honorius Augustodunensis', *Revue bénédictine*, 82 (1972), 215–42, at 221 (and cf. 225).
[85] Cruel, *Geschichte*, 238–9; Linsenmayer, *Geschichte*, 163; Haas, *Todesbilder* (following Cruel), 45–6.

brief. Honorius talks about Adam's sin (the long-term cause of death), about transitoriness, about readiness for death, about the afterlife, including purgation, and about helping the dead. Near the end he gives exempla to bring home the possibility of doing this. Since his sermon is a model, it is not surprising that there is nothing about the dead man's individuality, but there is not much about his role in the world either: only a reminder of how the glory of this world passes:

he was a flower of the world, the glory of his land (*patriae*), the honour of the kingdom; all the distinction of his family's nobility was apparent in him; he was honoured by princes, he was venerated by his equals, he was feared by those subject to him, he was[86] honoured by all the people. Now, if you take away the pall with which he is covered, all of you who were his dearest friends shrink from looking at him or approaching him, and you judge any man, however poor, so long as he is alive, to be better than him. Moreover, if you were to see him in his tomb after a few days, you would certainly flee the smell of his corruption as fast as you could. For the more well-fed (*pinguior*) a person has been, the more unbearable the stench will be. Today, dearest brethren, pray for his soul . . .[87]

This passage is of course not only the preamble to a request for prayers for the dead man, but also a *memento mori*, as Honorius had made clear just above.[88] This simple and powerful line of argument, or assault on the imagination, is a recurrent theme in medieval funeral preaching.

A sermon in memory of William II of Sicily (d. 1189) by Thomas, archbishop of Reggio, is quite different (at least as printed) both from Honorius' sermon on a powerful man and from the later sermons in memory of kings discussed in this book.[89] The style is classicizing, in a highly rhetorical manner

---

[86] Edition has 'honorificatur (*sic*)'.

[87] PL 172, 1083–4.

[88] 'Dicit Scriptura: *Melius est ire ad domum luctus quam ad domum conuiuii* (Eccle. vii). In conuiuio quippe homines mortis et aeternae vitae obliuiscuntur; in luctu mortui hominis futurae mortis recordabuntur. Si homines nobis mori referrentur, forsitan non crederemus; ecce cottidie ante oculos mortuos cernimus, et nos aeternos putamus. En cujus corpus inpraesentiarum conspicitis' (PL 172, 1083).

[89] I. La Lumia, *Storia della Sicilia sotto Guglielmo il Buono* (Florence, 1867), 339 n. 2, and app. II (which seems to be an edition of the sermon). See too N. Kamp, *Kirche und Monarchie im Staufischen Königreich Sizilien*, i. *Prosopographische Grundlegung: Bistümer und Bischöfe des Königreichs 1194–1266*, pt. 2. *Apulien und*

which derives, it has been suggested, from the school of
Orleans.[90] This florid language is the vehicle of a long lament
at the loss of the king—giver of peace, etc., etc.[91] The ex-
clamatory and iterated expressions of grief are more or less
unrelieved by any other theme until the end, when there is
a brief allusion to William's happy afterlife.[92] In the other
sermons on kings and princes which will be examined in this
book the theme of lament is much less dominant, the range of
religious ideas rather wider, and the style far more straightforward. The contrast is in fact so striking that one must hesitate
to describe this sermon as a forerunner of that tradition of
preaching in memory of kings and princes which was so firmly
established in southern Italy in the fourteenth century, as we
shall see.

After this sermon on William II there is no evidence known
to me of preaching in memory of a king or prince until the
death of the Emperor Frederick II's son Henry (d. 1242). We do
have a description of a sermon on a man who had been regent
of England, as well as (by common consent) the finest knight
of Christendom. This is the report given by the verse Life of
William the Marshall of Archbishop Stephen Langton's[93]
sermon at the Marshall's funeral in 1219—an occasion that
Honorius' rubric, 'if a *potens* who has died is to be buried',
would have covered quite nicely. As reported, the content was
more like Honorius' sermon than that of the archbishop of
Reggio. According to the verse Life, Langton said that his
audience could see what William, the best knight in the world,
had come down to; they have before them a mirror of their
own death; they should pray that God receive William into his
glory.[94]

---

*Kalabrien* (Münstersche Mittelalter-Schriften, 10/I. 2; Munich, 1975), 917–19
(notice on Thomas) and esp. p. 918 and n. 15, on the sermon, giving further
references.

[90] Kamp, *Kirche und Monarchie*, i/2. 918.

[91] La Lumia, *Storia*, app. II, pp. 395–7 *passim*.

[92] Ibid. 398.

[93] *L'Histoire de Guillaume le Maréchal*, ed. P. Meyer (3 vols.; Paris, 1891–1901),
iii. 266 n. 7.

[94] 'Quant li cors dut estre enterrez | Li archevesques dist: "Veez, | Seignor,
comme li secles vèt: | Quant chascuns est a sa fin trait, | Ne puet l'en en lui nul
sens querre, | N'est puis fors atretant de terre. | Veez ici a la roonde | Le meillor

Who knows how close this is to the sermon Langton actually preached? One can, however, at least say that the sentiments are just what most earlier traces of the genre's history would lead us to expect. We find much the same topos in a sermon 'to those who are mourning the death of people near to them' (*ad dolentes de morte propinquorum*), one of two with this rubric which Jacques de Vitry (d. 1240) included in his collection of sermons to different sorts and conditions of men and women.[95]

For today the Lord shows you two teachers and a twofold teaching. For you have one to preach to you by word, and one to preach to you by example. But the teaching of example is more effective than the teaching of the word. For the dead preach to you by example that you should despise the transitory glory of this world and the emptiness of the present time ... Therefore a dead man is a good teacher, and the burial of the dead is a good book ... In this book we read the general law of death ... Therefore when the dead man lies on the coffin or a board, we can read from him, as boys read from an alphabet attached to a board.[96]

Nam hodie duos doctores et duplicem doctrinam Dominus exhibet uobis. Habetis enim qui predicet uobis uerbo, et qui uobis predicet exemplo. Efficacior est autem doctrina exempli quam doctrina uerbi. Mortui quidem uobis exemplo predicant ut mundi huius transitoriam gloriam et presentem uanitatem contempnatis ... Bonus igitur doctor est homo mortuus, bonus liber mortuorum sepultura ... In hoc libro

chevalier del monde | Qui a nostre tens i fust unques | & por Deu! que direz vos donques? | A cest point covient toz venir; | Ne puet autrement avenir | Que chascuns muire a son jor, | Vez ici nostre mireor, | Autresi nostre comme vostre. | Die chascuns sa paternostre, | Que Deus icestui chrestïen | En son reigne celestïen | Receive en sa glorie [o] le[s] suens, | Si cum nos creons qu'il fu buens' (ll. 19065–84, ii. 325–6 Meyer). Meyer gives what seems to be a slightly abridged modern French translation in vol. iii, p. 267, and Sidney Painter an English version, apparently done from Meyer's modern French: Painter, *William Marshall, Knight-errant, Baron and Regent of England* (Baltimore, 1933), 289.

[95] For a good recent introduction and further bibliography see Nicole Bériou in N. Bériou and F.-O. Touati, *Voluntate dei leprosus: Les Lépreux entre conversion et exclusion aux XII$^{eme}$ et XIII$^{eme}$ siècles* (Centro Italiano di Studi sull'Alto Medievo; Spoleto, 1991), 38–40, 83–4, with further references, especially to work by J. Longère, in the notes. It appears that MS BN lat. 3284, though 16th-cent., gives a good text (Bériou, ibid. 83–4); however, for convenience, and because it is adequate for my limited purpose, I have used MS Troyes 228.

[96] The last clause has some interest for the history of literacy, on which see now the thoroughly updated new edition of Michael Clanchy's seminal *From Memory to Written Record: England 1066–1307* (rev. edn., 1993).

legimus regulam mortis generalem ... Quando igitur mortuus iacet super sarcophagum uel tabulam, possumus legere in eo sicut pueri legunt in alphabeto tabule affixo.[97]

A fuller analysis than is appropriate here would be necessary to do justice to these two sermons of Jacques de Vitry. They are relatively rich in ideas and make a strong appeal to the imagination, especially through fleeting images (notably scriptural ones) and through exempla. The theme of transience is prominent, and could be illustrated at considerable length, but the passage just quoted must stand for the rest. Jacques touches on other themes as well: preparation for death (a theme closely connected with the transience motif);[98] the metaphorical 'death of grace' (illustrated by exempla, including a memorable one about a monk who was ordered to bless then curse the bones of the dead);[99] the distinction between different kinds of 'death';[100] grief and mourning for someone who has died (Jacques believes it should be kept within bounds);[101] and

---

[97] MS Troyes 228, fo. 146[va]; from a sermon on the text *Nolumus uos ignorare* (1 Thess. 4: 12); Schneyer, *Repertorium*, iii. 218, No. 412.

[98] 'Acceleranda est penitentia, et toto tempore uite agenda. Si enim Noe centum annis arcam fabricauit in qua se ad horam a morte temporali saluaret, quanto magis arcam, id est animam tuam, toto tempore uite tue debes preparare, ut mortem eternam possis euitare' (MS Troyes 228, fo. 145[vb], from a sermon on text 1 Thess. 4: 12; Schneyer, *Repertorium*, iii. 217, No. 411).

[99] 'Est mors gratie, de qua Apostolus (Coloss. 3: 3): *Mortui estis, et uita uestra abscondita est cum Christo*, quando scilicet homo moritur mundo uel peccato ... Et de quodam abbate legitur quod nouitium quendam misit ad benedicendum (*corr. from* benedicenda?) ossa mortuorum, postmodum ad maledicendum, et querenti quid respondissent ossa, dixit nouitius: "Nichil, sed tacuerunt." Cui abbas: "Ita te oportet esse mortuum, si uis in hoc seculo permanere ut nec benedictione nec maledictione mouearis."' (MS Troyes 228, fo. 146[vb], from a sermon on the text *Ego sum resurrectio et uita* (John 11: 25); Schneyer, *Repertorium*, iii. 218, No. 412).

[100] 'Similiter est multiplex mors et multiplex uita. Est enim mors nature a qua nullus excipitur ... [*fo. 146[vb]*] ... Est enim mors culpe ... Est mors gratie ... Est mors gehenne': (MS Troyes 228, fo. 146[va–b], same sermon). The *distinctio* on *mors* is followed by one on *uita*. On this technique see R. H. and M. A. Rouse, *Preachers, Florilegia and Sermons: Studies on the* Manipulus florum *of Thomas of Ireland* (Studies and Texts, 47; Toronto, 1979), 7–9, and their 'Biblical Distinctions in the Thirteenth Century', *Archives d'histoire doctrinale et littéraire du Moyen Âge*, 41 (1974), 27–37, which gives further bibliography.

[101] To give some extracts: 'Uel interius gemere moderate conceditur, huius affectus naturalis compassionis non reprobatur, dummodo mensuram non excedat nec inconsolabiliter doleat' (MS Troyes 228, fo. 145[ra]). But a few lines above: 'quasi dicat: plangendus est impius, qui ita ab hac uita egreditur, quod

ways in which one can help someone who has died—charitable works, masses, prayers, other good deeds, and speedy execution of the terms of the dead man's will that are aimed at helping his soul.[102]

The sermons also contain specimen 'commendations' of imaginary dead individuals. The preacher was evidently expected to praise the life of the deceased as well as expatiating on death. The commendations in the second sermon deal with different states of life, but the one in the first is more generic. It concentrates on the imaginary dead man's long-term preparation for death, his reception of the sacraments, his alms, reconciliation to all with whom he has had a dispute, his will, and his good death.[103]

The second sermon to mourners (Schneyer No. 412) includes no fewer than five specimen commendations: for a 'prelate or priest', for a member of a religious order, for a knight, for a townsman (*burgensis*), and for a matron. The address in memory of a knight will serve as an example:

This noble knight, who has recently passed happily away, was not high and mighty because of his family's nobility, nor proud of his riches and dignities, nor brutalized by his strength and power. In the midst of pleasures he avoided dissolution, and he refrained from extravagance when surrounded by a varied abundance of possessions. In the midst of plenty he was self-restrained, and he was chaste when surrounded by women. With a wide choice of dishes, he was sparing, among proud men he was humble, and among the envious and

nec ad regionem spirituum nec ad illum qui fecit ipsum reuertatur. In legenda autem beate Agnetis dicitur quod, ipsa mortua, parentes eius nullam penitus tristitiam habentes cum omni gaudio corpus eius sepelierunt' (ibid.). Note also the following passage: 'Cum igitur amici nostri bene moriuntur, licet aliquantulum doleamus ex compassione uel naturali affectione, nichilominus gaudere debemus ex caritate. Teste enim Ecclesiaste (7: 2): *Melior est dies mortis quam natiuitatis*. Talis enim mors transitoria (trasitoria *ms*) et corporalis finis est miserie' (ibid., fo. 145[rb]). All three extracts are from the first of the two sermons, Schneyer, *Repertorium*, No. 411.

[102] 'Unde et amici eius accelerare debent eius liberationem operibus misericordie et missarum celebratione, orationibus et aliis bonis operibus, et fideliter atque festinanter ea que in testamento suo pro anima sua reliquit persoluendo absque ulla diminutione, ne proditionis argui possent coram iudice uiuorum et mortuorum' (MS Troyes 228, fo. 146[ra], first sermon; Schneyer, *Repertorium*, No. 411).

[103] See Endnote 2, below, pp. 279–80.

malicious he was kind. He was patient and gentle among the evil-tempered, fervent in spirit and devout among the slothful and idle, generous among the avaricious, restrained among the greedy, continent and decent among the lustful; a lamb among lions, a dove among hawks; he conducted himself in a praiseworthy manner among men *of a corrupt and perverse generation* [cf. Phil. 2: 15]; he showed himself to be a refuge of the oppressed,[104] a protector of the poor, the hope of the wretched, a guardian of orphans, a judge for widows, an eye for the blind, a tongue for the dumb, a staff for the old to lean on, an avenger of crimes, a terror of the evil, the glory of the good, a hammer of tyrants. He knew well how 'to spare the submissive and to war down the proud', sparing the humble and administering retribution to the proud, snatching the helpless man from the hands of those stronger than he, and the needy and poor man from those who despoiled him; bringing low the head of the powerful, giving humble obedience to those set over him,[105] giving assent to ecclesiastical teachers, honouring members of religious orders, powerfully defending ecclesiastical rights, strongly opposing himself to tyrants, heretics, pagans, schismatics, and other enemies of the faith of Christ, banishing from his land thieves, plunderers, killers, traitors, usurers, adulterers, public prostitutes, dicers, actors, and other pestiferous men, *so that he might cut off all the workers of iniquity from the city of the Lord, and in the morning putting to death all the sinners of the earth* [cf. Ps. 100: 8]; showing himself courteous to the poor, gentle to the gentle and humble, merciful to the afflicted and needy; to the cruel, hard and cruel, rising up against rebels: as is written (2 Kgs. 22: 27; Ps. 17: 27): *with the holy, you will be holy, and with the perverse, you will turn perverse;* fitting in prudently with religious and with secular men in accordance with the words of the wise man: 'I do not want you to be a monk with secular men, nor a secular man with monks.' To those who sought pardon he showed himself merciful, knowing that to forgive is a glorious kind of revenge. Noble is the magnanimity which, when it has an enemy in its power, judges that to have had the power to take revenge constitutes the revenge. Mercy gives birth to love, justice to fear. Just as love is preferred to fear, so is mercy to justice. A prince is slow to punish, swift to reward, and he is a man who grieves whenever he is forced to be fierce.

Iste uero miles nobilis, qui nuper diem ultimum feliciter clausit, de generis nobilitate non elatus, diuitiis et dignitatibus non superbus, de

---

[104] *oppressorum* here is probably from the participle *oppressus* rather than the substantive *oppressor*, to judge from context, though they are indistinguishable in the genitive plural.

[105] This is probably a reference to specifically ecclesiastical authorities.

fortitudine et potentia non efferatus; inter delicias non dissolutus, inter uarias rerum copias non superfluus; in ubertate modestus, inter mulieres castus; inter uaria fercula parcus; inter superbos, humilis; inter inuidos et malitiosos, benignus; inter iracundos, patiens et mansuetus; inter accidiosos et pigros, spiritu feruens et deuotus; inter auaros, largus; inter gulosos, sobrius; inter luxuriosos continens et honestus; inter leones agnus; inter acipitres columbinus; inter homines *praue et peruerse nationis* (Phil. 2: 15) laudabiliter est conuersatus; refugium oppressorum; aduocatum pauperum; spem miserorum; tutorem pupillorum; iudicem uiduarum; oculum cecorum; linguam mutorum; baculum senum; ultorem scelerum; malorum metum; bonorum gloriam; et malleum se exibuit tyranorum. Nouit utique 'parcere subiectis et debellare superbos', humilibus parcens et reddens retributionem superbis; eripiens inopem de manu fortiorum eius, egenum et pauperem a diripientibus eum; magnatis caput humilians; prelatis suis humiliter obediens; doctoribus ecclesiasticis acquiescens;[106] uiros religiosos honorans; iura ecclesiastica potenter deffendens;[107] tyrannis, hereticis, paganis, scismaticis et aliis fidei Christi inimicis fortiter se opponens; fures, predones, homicidas, proditores, feneratores, adulteros, publicas meretrices, deciorum lusores, hystriones, et alios pesti|feros [*fo. 147ʳᵇ*] homines de terra sua exterminans, *ut disperderet de ciuitate Domini omnes operantes iniquitatem et in matutino interficiens omnes peccatores terre*[108] (Ps. 100: 8); pauperibus affabilem se exhibens,[109] mitibus et humilibus mitem, afflictis et egenis misericordem, crudelibus durum et crudelem, rebellibus rebellem: sicut scriptum est (2 Reg. 22: 27; Ps. 17: 27): *cum sancto, sanctus eris, et cum peruerso, peruerteris*; religiosis et secularibus prudenter se coaptans, iuxta illud sapientis: Nolo te esse cum secularibus monachum, nec cum monachis secularem; ueniam petentibus misericordem se exhibuit, sciens quod gloriosum genus uindicte est ignoscere: generosa magnanimitas, que cum inimicum habet in potestate,[110] uindictam iudicat uindicare potuisse. Misericordia parit amorem, iustitia timorem. Sicut amor prefertur timori, ita misericordia iustitie. Est piger ad penas princeps, ad premia uelox, quique dolet, quotiens cogitur esse ferox.[111]

This commendation was worth giving in full because most of it might be used as well for a prince as for a knight. Much the

---

[106] acquiescens] acquescens *ms*
[107] deffendens] *corr. to* defendens *in ms?*
[108] terre] *scribal correction?*
[109] exhibens] *corr. from* exibens
[110] potestate] potestatem *ms*
[111] MS Troyes 228, fo. 147ʳᵃ⁻ᵇ.

same speech turns up, later in the century, in one of the sermons to mourners of the Franciscan Guibert de Tournai, whose enormous debt to Jacques de Vitry is well known in other contexts.[112] His sermons to mourners—and not just the specimen commendations—are strongly reminiscent of those of Jacques de Vitry, as we would expect. The big difference (which is typical of their relation in general, so far as I have studied it) is that Guibert tries to impose an explicit overall plan.

Guibert's material is arranged in explicitly partitioned sets and subsets, in accordance with the new sermon form which became current in the middle decades of the thirteenth century and which is variously described by scholars as 'the modern method' or as 'scholastic preaching', but which might perhaps more usefully be described as the 'artistic' method,[113] because it is the method described in *Arts of Preaching* and since its divisions and distinctions have a pronounced aesthetic character.[114]

The division at the start of the first of Guibert's sermons to people in mourning derives three headings from the biblical text, to each of which a whole sermon is devoted. The headings are: 'the diffinitive sentence of dying', the 'presence of death', and the 'differentiation of the dead'.[115] The first sermon could be described as an attempt to make religious sense of death; the second is about readiness for death; and the third is mainly

---

[112] MS BN lat. 15,943, fo. 174[va–b] (I have used this manuscript for convenience, and because it is quite adequate for the present purpose); from the sermon—really a set of commendations—numbered 265 under Guibertus de Tornaco in Schneyer, *Repertorium*, ii. 304. Nos. 261–4 are listed as 'Ad eos qui dolent . . .', and will be analysed below. For one study of Guibert's borrowings from Jacques (and his original contribution) see D. L. d'Avray and M. Tausche, 'Marriage Sermons in *Ad status* Collections of the Central Middle Ages', *Archives d'histoire doctrinale et littéraire du Moyen Âge*, 47 (1980), 71–119, at 85–118.

[113] Prof. Siegfried Wenzel suggested the term to me, though he himself has preferred 'scholastic' (which I avoid because these sermons do not usually include 'quaestiones' or explicit logical argument).

[114] Cf. S. Wenzel, *Preachers, Poets and the Early English Lyric* (Princeton, 1986), ch. 3.

[115] '*Omnes morimur et quasi aque dilabimur in terram que non reuertuntur*, ii R(eg). xiiii (14): In uerbis propositis notatur diffinitiua moriendi sententia, cum dicitur *omnes*; mortis presentia, cum dicitur *morimur*; mortuorum differentia, cum dicitur *et quasi aque*, etc.' (MS BN lat. 15,943, fo. 167[va–b]; Schneyer, *Repertorium* ii. 304, No. 261).

about this world and the next (purgatory, hell, and heaven). These three sermons are thus constituent parts of an integral whole. A preacher could have adapted them to make a single sermon, perhaps moving the model commendation at the end of the first sermon to the end of the block of three.[116] Each of these three sermons is further divided into neatly ticketed parts. The first of the three, for instance, is structured by a 'distinction': death is a sentence which is 'general', 'penal', 'rational', and 'curative' or 'medicinal'.

Death is 'general' in the sense that everyone has to die.[117] In the section which shows how death is 'penal' Guibert makes a slightly more complex point. In death, elements come into conflict; the harmony of body and soul is destroyed, and decomposition follows.[118] Death is bitter, and sometimes the elect have a harder death, like Lazarus (the suffering beggar at the rich man's gate).[119] When good people are dying there is no cause for grief, because they are purified here through their death and, once purified, enter the Kingdom.[120] As for the 'rationality' of death, what Guibert means by this is that it is a logical consequence of original sin. He tries to bring his point home with images, including a comparison with the crime of *lèse-majesté*, which brings punishment down on all the descendants of the criminal.[121]

[116] This commendation is for a man 'who died today or whose anniversary we are celebrating': 'Se*d* uir sanctus qui hodie defunctus aut cuius anniuersarium celebramus' (MS BN lat. 15,943, fo. 168ᵛᵃ), which is a good indication of the sort of occasion for which the model sermons (as well as the commendations) were intended. The commendation closely resembles the one in the first sermon for mourners by Jacques de Vitry.

[117] 'Quantum ad primum dicit diffinitiuam sententiam moriendi. Ipsa enim mors sententia est generalis. Quis est enim homo qui uiuet et non uidebit mortem?' (MS BN lat. 15,943, fo. 167ᵛᵇ).

[118] 'Est etiam ista sententia penalis, quia in morte confligunt elementa, soluitur corporis et anime armonia, caro resoluitur in putredinem, putredo in uermem, uermis in cinerem' (ibid.).

[119] 'Unde mors ab amaritudine nomen accepit, et electi aliquando durius moriuntur, quia in eorum morte dolor intenditur per quem uenialia resecantur. Sic purgatus in uia Lazarus moritur et ab angelis in sinum Abrahe deportatur. Et licet dolor sit in carne, tamen consolatio interius est in anima' (electi aliquando] alti quando *ms*) (ibid.).

[120] '... et ideo iusti morientes plangendi non sunt, quia hic in morte purgantur, et purgati regnum ingrediuntur' (ibid., fo. 168ʳᵃ).

[121] 'Est etiam ista sententia rationabilis, quia *per unum hominem peccatum intrauit in mundum, et per peccatum mors*, Ro. v (12), *ita in omnes homines mors*

The final part of the distinction that gives structure to the first sermon is that the sentence of death is *medicinalis*. Guibert seems to have more than one idea in mind here. He starts by saying that we are freed from original sin by Christ's death.[122] Then he moves on to the salutary effect which the fear of death and the subsequent punishment has on our conduct.[123] The section concludes with a graphic description of the state of mind of a dying sinner.[124]

The specimen commendation[125] to which reference has been made (to be distinguished from the commendations by *status* which come at the end of the sermons proper) makes a sharp contrast: the tone is up-beat. This in its turn ends with a reminder to carry out the dead man's will, advice which is the cue for the story (borrowed from Jacques de Vitry) of the knight fighting in Spain with Charlemagne, whose bequest of a horse was not executed by his fellow knight and relative.[126]

The next two sermons, as noted above, concentrate on readi-

---

*transiuit in quo omnes peccauerunt.* Ergo per illum omnes supplicia susceperunt. Tota enim natura humana in primis parentibus fuit, et in eis creatori suo contumeliam facit. Si enim in semine tota arbor, ergo in uitio seminis dicetur uitium arboris. Fluuius uitiatur in fonte, fructus in semine, posteritas in origine. Et sicut pro crimine lese maiestatis tota progenies punitur, ita in proposito pro peccato parentum omnes morimur' (ibid.).

[122] 'Est etiam ista sententia medicinalis, quia per mortem Christi liberati sumus a reatu originalis, ut sicut *unius delicto regnauit mors, multo magis uita regnet per unum Iesum Christum*, prout dicit Apostolus (Rom. 5: 17)' (originalis] *read* originali *or add* peccati) (ibid.).

[123] 'Mortis etiam sententia primo (*read* post?) cohibet a mortali culpa. Quia enim mortem timemus et ea que secuntur post mortem, abstinemus ne perpetremus multotiens iniquitatem. Unde anime sancte semper cogitant de morte eterna' (ibid.). A little later there is a striking remark: 'Infirmitates enim et tribulationes quas patimur sunt quasi citatio dilatoria, mors autem citatio peremptoria' (ibid., fo. 168rb).

[124] 'Et, si placet, statum anime morientis uideamus, ut ad medicinam quam inducit mortis timor, hoc est ad penitentiam nos preparemus. Anima enim peccatrix, cum a uinculis carnis incipit solui, timore concutitur, remordente conscientia stimulatur' (ibid.)—the description ending thus: 'Tunc oculi contabescunt, pectus palpitat, guttur raucum hanelat, dentes nigrescunt, ora pallescunt, membra rigescunt, et exutam animam legiones demonum secum ferunt' (ibid., fo. 168va). The style of this description suggests to me that Guibert may have borrowed it from an earlier writer.

[125] Begins ibid., fo. 168va, and ends fo. 168vb.

[126] Ibid., fo. 168vb. Cf. F. C. Tubach, *Index Exemplorum: A Handbook of Medieval Religious Tales* (FF Communications, 204; Helsinki, 1969), p. 156, No. 1931.

ness for death and on purgatory, hell, and heaven. We may pass over them to the fourth sermon, which has a fresh text (Eccli. 7: 37). It sets out how one should react to bereavement. This sermon too has a clearly marked framework. There are two main sections, each divided into four subsections. The first main section deals with the four things we owe to the dead,[127] while in the second main section we are presented with a symmetrically opposite set of evil attitudes.[128] Some of the main points made are: that grief is good but must be kept in perspective and within limits;[129] that we should wear a brave face to console others;[130] and that we should help the dead.[131] The end of this sermon leads directly into the models for panegyrics for prelates, members of the secular clergy, members of religious orders, knights, citizens, and matrons.[132]

[127] 'Quatuor autem debemus mortuis: naturalem affectio|nem, [*fo. 171$^{va}$*] in affectione moderationem, in moderatione consolationem, in consolatione orationem et subuentionem' (MS BN lat. 15,943, fo. 171$^{rb-va}$; from sermon on the text *Mortuo non prohibeas gratiam* (Eccli. 7: 37); Schneyer, *Repertorium*, ii. 304, No. 264).

[128] 'Sed proch dolor! Compassionem tollit duritia, moderationem stultitia, consolationem tristitia, subuentionem nequitia' (MS BN lat. 15,943, fo. 172$^{vb}$).

[129] For example: 'Conceditur flere super mortuum naturali compassione, sed longe plus plorare debemus super illos qui peccando incurrunt mortem anime' (ibid., fo. 171$^{va}$). Or again: 'Dolemus quia mundum reliquerunt; ipsi uero condolent sorti nostre, quos adhuc seculi carcer includit, quos cotidie in acie preliantes, nunc ira, nunc auaritia, nunc uariorum incentiua uitiorum protrahunt ad ruinam; et hoc solatio erigamur quia in breui uisuri sumus eos quos dolemus absentes' (ibid., fo. 173$^{va}$).

[130] 'Sicut enim magni duces militum in aduersis hylaritatem de industria simulant et aduersitates eorum adumbrata letitia abscundunt, ne militum animi frangantur, si ducis sui mentem uiderint esse fractam, sic in proposito faciendum est ut induamus uultum animo nostro dissimilem, et si non possumus omnem dolorem prorsus abicere, saltem introrsus abscondatur ne appareat, quia non poterimus [*fo. 172$^{ra}$*] esse aliorum consolatores, si dolori nostro nimis indulserimus' (ibid., fos. 171$^{vb}$–172$^{ra}$).

[131] In the first section, the subsection beginning 'De quarto: ii Mach. Iudas' (ibid., fo. 172$^{va}$), and in the second, the subsection beginning 'Nequitia tollit subuentionem' (fo. 173$^{vb}$).

[132] '. . . de quo frustra post mortem uenia postulatur. Non tales sunt mortui de quibus memoriam agimus uel officium celebramus, ut pie credimus. Et tunc potest fieri commendatio mortuorum secundum differentias meritorum et statuum. Aliter enim commendandi sunt prelati et seculares clerici, aliter reli|giosi, [*fo. 174$^{ra}$*] aliter milites, aliter ciues, aliter matrone, et sic de aliis. Rogemus ergo etc.' (*ibid.*, fos. 173$^{vb}$–174$^{ra}$). Then follow the commendations, which are marked off by an initial, as if they together made up a separate sermon, in this manuscript at least, and which Schneyer has numbered as one sermon: *Repertorium*, ii. 304, No. 265.

However derivative—to speak of plagiarism would be ana-chronistic—these commendations and much of the material in the sermons are, Guibert made his contribution by impressing his own form (or rather, the preaching form of his day) upon the sermons that precede the commendations.

During his time at Paris, Guibert[133] would probably have met Eudes de Chateauroux, author of some of the most fascinating memorial sermons to survive from the Middle Ages. (Eudes also has a kind of connection with Jacques de Vitry, since they both reached the position of cardinal bishop of Tusculum—leaving aside some looser parallels between their careers.) Eudes was one of the great men of his day. The scholar who has the courage to write the full study we lack will have traced the histories of Paris University at a formative moment, of the orthodox reaction against prophetic heresy, of papal canon-ization, of the condemnation of the Talmud, and of Louis IX of France's earlier crusade, where Eudes was the papal legate who worked alongside the king.[134] A large number of sermons by Eudes have survived, and rubrics such as 'At the council for the Mongol business', 'At a procession held on account of the flood of waters', 'On the conversion of the Jews', 'On account of the fear of an earthquake'[135] suggest that there are many treasures to be found in them. Eudes de Chateauroux's future historian will have to be equally at home with the history of religious sentiment and high politics. Some of his sermons on the dead, too, relate to the big news stories of thirteenth-century history. There is, for instance, a sermon 'In obitu domini Iohannis episcopi' (?)Gunthoniensis'.[136] Reading through it, one gradually realizes that it must be about John Gervais of Winchester (*Wintoniensis*), who was one of the bishops in the party of Simon de Montfort during the period of the Barons'

---

[133] For Guibert's Paris career see d'Avray, *Preaching of the Friars*, 145 (where further references are given).

[134] References in Cole, d'Avray, and Riley-Smith, 'Application', 227 nn. 1–5 and 229–39. (I have felt free to plagiarize from my own remarks in this article.)

[135] Ibid. 228 ('the flood of waters' could also be translated with the indefinite article).

[136] MS Arras, Bibliothèque Municipale 137 (876), fo. 163$^{va}$ (ends fo. 165$^{ra}$), from a sermon on the text *Est uia, quae uidetur homini justa* (Prov. 14: 12); Schneyer, *Repertorium*, iv. 466, No. 890.

wars and the Legate's peace in England.[137] Eudes describes how the bishop had got into trouble with the pope.[138] The bishop may have thought that he was defending the rights of the Church and guarding other people's rights, says Eudes, but really he was subverting the Church in England and indeed subverting the whole kingdom.[139]

Though I do not know of any sermon by Eudes in memory of a secular ruler in the normal sense,[140] we do have a sermon in memory of Pope Innocent IV that in a sense comes within the scope of this study, since Eudes includes remarks on the pope as ruler of the Papal States. He says that Innocent had already acquired part of the land of the Church when he died, but that the final victory was reserved for another.[141] Eudes speculates that he might have been denied full triumph because he had sinned in the enterprise (*facto*) by oppressing the churches for its sake, or that perhaps his heart had been raised up, and the Lord did not want his efforts to do harm to himself.[142] Eudes evidently feels that the conflict itself was

---

[137] F. M. Powicke and C. R. Cheney, *Councils and Synods with other Documents Relating to the English Church*, ii. *A.D. 1205–1313*, pt. II. *1265–1313* (Oxford, 1964), 726. See also s.v. 'Gervais, John, bishop of Winchester, . . .' in the index to F. M. Powicke, *King Henry III and the Lord Edward: The Community of the Realm in the Thirteenth Century* (2 vols.; Oxford, 1947), ii. 816.

[138] 'Sic uenerabilis episcopus cui exequias exsoluimus hiis de causis uel aliqua earum uel aliis deceptus fuit ut credimus, et fecit aliqua que facere non debebat. Et ideo dominus noster summus pontifex, uolens eum ab inuio reuocare, citauit eum ut personaliter ad suam presentiam accederet' (MS Arras, Bibliothèque Municipale 137 (876), fo. 164^va). The bishop obtained absolution: 'Tandem Dominus qui non uult mortem peccatoris se*d* magis ut conuertatur et uiuat uirga infirmitatis eum percussit, qua deiectus humiliauit se Domino et dixit (Act. 9: 6): *Domine, quid uis me facere?* Hoc dixit uicario eius, petens ab eo beneficium absolutionis; qui misit eum ad alterum Ananiam, id est ad dominum [*fo. 164^vb*] Ostien(sem), ut eum absolueret iuxta formam ecclesie, quod et fecit' (ibid., fo. 164^va–b).

[139] '. . . sic et iste misericordiam consecutus sit eo quod ignorans fecerat quod fecit, credens se in hoc libertatem ecclesie defensare quo ad aliqua et iura aliquorum tueri. Se*d* non bene considerauit quod resistendo mandatis apostolicis et non obediendo illi qui ob hoc uenerat ut ecclesia et etiam totum regnum ad bonum statum reducerentur, non tantummodo libertatem ecclesiasticam non deffendebat, se*d* omnino destruebat in illis partibus, et ecclesiam anglicanam, i*m*mo totum regnum, subuertebat' (ibid., fo. 164^vb).

[140] I do not exclude the possibility that I have missed one.

[141] Cole, d'Avray, and Riley-Smith, 'Application', 239.

[142] The passages are discussed in Chapter 2, in connection with the representation of individuality.

just, as he compares the recovery of the Papal States with the
occupation of the promised land (by the Jews).[143] He also
alludes with approval to Innocent's hard line against the Holy
Roman emperor Frederick II, saying that 'the obstinate, and
those who knew they were usurping the rights of others or
holding on to what they had usurped, he used to strike down
with his judgements, and with the rod of his mouth he killed
that man of great impiety, Frederick [II]'.[144] The last clause is
probably an allusion to the excommunication and deposition of
the emperor.

Eudes has a high opinion of Innocent IV's capacities as a
judge, praising his efficiency in expediting legal business.[145]
Here Eudes probably does not primarily have in mind Innocent's role as secular ruler of the Papal States, but as the
Church's supreme judge. By and large, general presentations
of the medieval papacy do not adequately convey how much
this ecclesiastical justice differed from that of secular kings in
content, but in form the analogies are close, which is a further
reason for dwelling on this sermon of Eudes. Other aspects of
it, such as his list of three things which are found only in
the supreme pontiff and which are very useful to the whole
Christian people,[146] must not detain us further, though it should
be said that the sermon casts a fascinating light on relations
between pope and cardinals in the mid-thirteenth century.[147]

As a cardinal, Eudes must have spent a good deal of time in
Italy, so he should perhaps be regarded as part of the Italian
tradition of funeral preaching. For there is some reason to
think that sermons on the dead were something of an Italian
speciality.[148] The always informative Salimbene gives a hint
that the tradition had especially deep roots in southern Italy.
He tells us that at the funeral of Emperor Frederick II's un-
fortunate son Henry VII 'Princes and barons, knights and
judges gathered together to bury him, in the absence of the

---

[143] Cole, d'Avray, and Riley-Smith, 'Application', 239–40.
[144] Ibid. 240.
[145] Ibid. 241.
[146] Ibid. 242.
[147] Ibid. 242–6.
[148] It was L.-J. Bataillon who first drew my attention to the importance of
Italian Dominicans in the history of the genre.

emperor. Brother Luca da Bitonto, the Apulian who is re-membered for his sermons,[149] was also present with them, so that he might preach at the funeral, according to the custom of Apulia.'[150] (This remark, incidentally, may help to explain why a disproportionately large number of the sermons coming within the scope of this study are in memory of kings and princes from the successor dynasty in southern Italy, the Angevins of Naples.)

The earliest surviving Italian memorial sermon known to me[151] is one of the sermons which appear to have been preached in the year 1233 by the bishop of Pistoia, Graziado Berlinghieri.[152] The dead man is not a ruler but a priest,[153] so not directly within this study's scope. A large part of the address is taken up with *distinctiones* on the words 'death' (*mors*)[154] and 'passing over' (*transitus*).[155]

Soon, however, *de mortuis* sermons, in one or another of the senses discussed at the start of this chapter, become more plentiful. The dogged reader of Schneyer's *Repertorium* will come across more than a few *de mortuis* sermons from the century or so before 1350, though the majority of these are probably from the last half-century covered. As the volume of material increases, coverage must be more selective, and from here on only collections whose influence was particularly great, or which include sermons in memory of princes, will be noted

---

[149] See d'Avray, *Preaching of the Friars*, 108–9, 156.

[150] Salimbene, *Cronica Fratris Salimbene de Adam*, ed. O. Holder-Egger (MGH Scriptores, 32; Hanover, 1905–13), 87–8. The funeral took place in Cosenza, so also in the south.

[151] It is known to me thanks to the generosity of Prof. S. Zamponi, who discovered it and the set of sermons to which it belongs and communicated them to me, as also to Nicole Bériou, who has in mind an edition.

[152] L.-J. Bataillon, 'Prédication des séculiers aux laïcs au XIIIᵉ siècle de Thomas de Chobham à Ranulphe de la Houblonnière', *Revue des sciences philosophiques et théologiques*, 74 (1990), 457–65, at 459 n. 14. Bataillon is speaking of the same sermons, in MS Pistoia Arch. Capitolare C 112. (For a brief description of the relevant part of the manuscript see Nicole Bériou in Bériou and Touati, *Voluntate dei leprosus*, 81.) The sermon in question is on fos. 45ᵛ–46ʳ. The rubric, fo. 45ᵛ, is 'Sermo domini episcopi quando obiit frater (frt̄) Nibaldus', and the text is '*Transibo ad locum tabernaculi amirabilis . . .* (Ps. 41: 5)'.

[153] 'Hodie honorastis illum bonum, uirum scilicet (.s.) et sacerdotem, *im*mo Christum in ipso' (MS Pistoia Arch. Capitolare C 112, fo. 45ᵛ).

[154] 'Est enim mors mortis, mors ad mortem, mors contra mortem, mors momentanea, et mors (?) eterna' (ibid., fo. 46ʳ).

[155] 'Est transitus bonus et malus, et est multiplex' (ibid.).

in any detail. Guibert de Tournai qualified because his sermons
to mourners are part of a widely diffused collection, Eudes de
Chateauroux because he talked about Innocent IV's political
and legal activity.

Other collections from the half-century or so before 1300
must get shorter shrift. Sermons in memory of particular individuals are included in the collection of sermons by Federico
Visconti, the archbishop of Pisa from 1254 to 1277, which
are transmitted in MS Florence Laurenziana, Plut. 33. sin. 1
(but nowhere else so far as is known).[156] Though Visconti's
memorial sermons are interesting and important in themselves,
none is in memory of kings or princes; in any case the collection
as a whole is in the best of scholarly hands and should soon
become readily accessible in a model edition.[157] One must,
however, at least note in passing a rubric which helps to explain
how some *de mortuis* sermons in memory of real people have
been preserved: 'On the death of the prior of the Dominicans;
and it can be adapted for any cleric.'[158] Before leaving the
thirteenth century one must also at least mention the rich
hoard of material in the Franciscan library at Assisi,[159] the
austere little series by 'Johannes de Opreno',[160] and the Dom-

---

[156] Incipits in Schneyer, *Repertorium*, ii, s.v. 'Fredericus Pisanus', esp. pp.
89–90. There is a remarkable study of the collection by A. Murray, 'Archbishop
and Mendicants in Thirteenth-century Pisa', in K. Elm (ed.), *Stellung und
Wirksamkeit der Bettelorden in der städtischen Gesellschaft* (Berliner historische
Studien, 3, Ordensstudien, 2; Berlin, 1981), 19–75. See also next note.

[157] A team directed by A. Vauchez and E. Cristiani, and including notably
Isabelle le Masne de Chermont and Nicole Bériou, is preparing a complete
edition, in which Bériou will provide analyses of the individual sermons.

[158] 'In obitu prioris Ord. Praed. et potest adaptari pro quolibet clerico'
(Schneyer, *Repertorium*, ii. 89, No. 69).

[159] The extremely important manuscript collection now housed at the Sacro
Convento in Assisi (I believe it is also still deemed to be part of the Biblioteca
Comunale, where it used to be physically housed) contains a large number of
*de mortuis* sermons, which are easy to find through index entries in C. Cenci's
admirable *Bibliotheca Manuscripta ad Sacrum Conventum Assisiensem* (2 vols.; Il
Miracolo di Assisi, 4; Assisi, 1981). Cenci dates some of the many anonymous
sermons to the 13th cent.

[160] MS Troyes 1729, fo. 248$^{va}$: 'Incipiunt quosdam (*sic*) sermones pro defunctis
(defuctis *ms?*)'. I have looked only cursorily at the short series that follows. The
first two or three at least (Nos. 402–4 in Schneyer's list, *Repertorium*, iii. 645;
fos. 248$^{va}$–249$^{rb}$ in MS Troyes 1729) might be sermons for All Souls' Day or
general sermons on the dead, rather than memorial sermons. On the other
hand, No. 409 in Schneyer's list (*Repertorium*, loc. cit.), on the text *Mortuus est
Abraham in senectute bona* (Gen. 25: 8), begins 'Hic circa prelatum defunctum
(defuctum *ms?*) nota tria' (MS Troyes 1729, fo. 250$^{rb}$).

inican Aldobrandino da Toscanella's fascinating collection, rich in the science and philosophy of his day.[161] At least a selection of these and no doubt other thirteenth-century *de mortuis* sermons deserve to be edited, though some make tough reading.[162]

Another Dominican, Remigio de' Girolami (a name well known to the numerous historians of Florence), whose career began in the thirteenth century but takes us into the fourteenth, left a marvellously rich set of sermons in memory of identifiable individuals,[163] including two on French kings; for which reason he cannot be passed over so briefly. The following remarks will be superseded when the critical edition now under way is completed,[164] but they may be useful as context for analyses of

[161] For Aldobrandino da Toscanella's use of philosophy and science in his *de mortuis* sermons see d'Avray, 'Sermons on the Dead before 1350', *Studi medievali*, 3rd ser., 31/1 (1990), 207–23, at 214. Though I have made a working transcription of the majority of Aldobrandino da Toscanella's *de mortuis* sermons in MS Vatican Ottobuono latino 557, fos. 180[ra] ff. (see Schneyer, *Repertorium*, i. 246–7), and found them most interesting, I have no current plans to work further on them. One cannot assume that they are all for funerals or memorial services (and the last of them, on the text *Miseremini mei* (Job 19: 21), MS Vatican Ottobuono latino 557, fo. 203[ra–vb], Schneyer, *Repertorium*, i. 247, No. 320, is for All Souls' Day), but at least one of them almost certainly is, since it has the words 'et quia mortuum habemus pre manibus, ideo de morte aliquid dicamus': see d'Avray, 'Sermons on the Dead before 1350', 214 n. 35.

[162] When the preacher's identity is unknown one must rely on palaeographical dating to get a rough *terminus ante quem*, which makes it hard to assign a set of sermons with any certainty to the 13th cent. (The dating of Assisi manuscripts by Cenci, to which reference was made above, is an atypical case: a relatively homogeneous set of manuscripts kept together in one place where a good specialist had plenty of opportunity to get his manuscript-dating eye in.) One set whose author has been identified and who may have entered the Dominican Order well before the middle of the century is 'Albertinus Dertonensis', on whom see *Scriptores Ordinis Praedicatorum Medii Aevi*, ed. T. Kaeppeli (Rome, 1970– ), i. 26. I have not seen the 'Sermones pro defunctis' in MS Paris, St.-Geneviève 2775, to which Kaeppeli alludes in his 'B. Jordani de Saxonia Litterae Encyclicae (1233)', *AFP* 22 (1952), 177–85, at 178, and do not know whether these are the same as the sermons on the dead in MS BL Arundel 395, fos. 102[vb]–106[rb], which are attributed to 'Adelbertino de ordine predicatorum'.

[163] MS Florence, Nazionale, Conv. soppr. G.4.936, includes a substantial batch of memorial sermons, some of which are printed, thought not always *in extenso*, by G. Salvadori in G. Salvadori and V. Federici, 'I Sermoni d'occasione, le sequenze e i ritmi di Remigio Girolami Fiorentino', in *Scritti vari di filologia: A Ernesto Monaci gli scolari, 1876–1901* (Rome, 1901), 455–508, at 487–500. See also E. Panella, 'Un sermone in morte della moglie di Guido Novello o di Beatrice d'Angiò?', *Memorie domenicane*, NS 12 (1981), 294–301.

[164] E. Panella and a collaborator have in hand an edition which will include these memorial sermons.

Remigio's sermons on Philip the Fair and Louis X of France in the next two chapters.[165] Some or all of his memorial sermons are surely records (in some cases exceedingly brief) of 'live' preaching; perhaps Remigio wrote them up from the notes he made before preaching or from 'reportations' taken down during his sermons. However, the occasional remark addressed to the user[166] suggests that the sermons were intended to serve as models. A fair number of them deal with the qualities of the deceased from a positive point of view (sermons on Dominican confrères and on female religious tend to take this form). Usually, in these cases, one is presented with an abstract pattern of virtues. In one or two cases, notably the sermon on Philip the Fair, one is given some impression of the dead person's individuality. Though Remigio states in a passage to which we must return that one of the purposes of a *de mortuis* sermon might be to get people to help the dead, exhortation to pray for the dead is less prominent in his memorial sermons (at least as transmitted) than his general statement might lead one to expect. However, purgatory does have quite a high profile in remarks about the likely fate of the deceased after death. In several places he gives a picture of the good death: confession, making good those wrongdoings that could be made good, communion, extreme unction. A substantial proportion of the sermons deal with the subject of death, in a fairly general sort of way, without too much reference to the deceased—except that Remigio likes to take the deceased individual's name as a starting-point, sometimes giving both Latin and vernacular forms, and to build symbolism upon it. Remigio's principal technique, perhaps, is one very common in the preaching of the period: hopping from scriptural text to scriptural text, using images and symbolism from these texts as a vehicle for his ideas. Exempla are not particularly plentiful. He likes quoting Aristotle, notably but by no means exclusively from the *Ethics*.

A penchant for quoting Aristotle is also a feature of what

---

[165] My remarks are based on a reading of most of this batch of memorial sermons, escept that I did not work systematically on the sermons squeezed into the margins of the manuscript.

[166] '. . . expone sicut expositum est supra de papa Clemente' (*Scritti vari . . . Monaci*, 492) (this instruction is in the sermon in memory of Philip IV of France, which will be analysed in the next chapter).

amounts to a *Summa* of model sermons on the dead by a Dominican active in the early fourteenth century, Giovanni da San Gimignano.[167] This has been analysed both by Antoine Dondaine and by Eberhard Winkler,[168] and is relatively accessible in early modern editions (which do not, however, dispense one from manuscript work).[169] The collection includes model sermons in memory of temporal rulers, as well as prelates and a wide assortment of conditions of men and women. This part of the work has obvious affinities with *ad status* sermons.[170] The memorial sermons for different sorts of people are themselves a subset of this remarkably comprehensive set of models, among which a preacher could find packaged material on the contempt for the world, the dreadfulness of death, the explanation of why everyone has to die, the separation of soul and body in death, the need to keep one's future death in mind, what happens to body and soul after death, how to help the dead, and how much mourning is appropriate (he says that moderate grief is permitted, but he concentrates on reasons for being consoled).[171] Thomas Aquinas is an important influence,[172] and Giovanni seems interested in natural science. Exempla are not at all common, but the work is full of fragmentary images, above all scriptural ones.

Since Giovanni da San Gimignano's collection got into printed editions, it presumably reached more readers and users at the end of the Middle Ages and in the early modern period

[167] See Dondaine's valuable 'La vie et les œuvres de Jean de San Gimignano', 154–7, for the *de mortuis* sermons. Giovanni was still alive in the early 1330s: ibid. 134.

[168] See previous note and Winkler, 'Scholastische Leichenpredigten'. I have Rudolf Lenz to thank for procuring a photocopy of this for me.

[169] See Dondaine, 'La vie ... Gimignano', 155. In general, early modern editions should be checked against at least one 'respectable' manuscript. I have used MS Siena F. X. 24 when quoting from Giovanni in later chapters, though I initially read through the whole work in editions. According to Dondaine, loc. cit., 'le texte des éditions n'est pas toujours fidèle à celui des manuscrits'. (He finds interpolations where doctrine has been 'précisée'.)

[170] On *ad status* sermons proper see e.g. d'Avray, *Preaching of the Friars*, index, s.v. '*ad status* sermons'. For an example of how *ad status* sermons can be exploited see C. Casagrande, *Prediche alle donne del secolo XIII: Testi di Umberto da Romans, Gilberto da Tournai, Stefano di Borbone* (Milan, 1978).

[171] For an efficient summary see Winkler, 'Scholastische Leichenpredigten', 178–9.

[172] Dondaine, 'La vie ... Gimignano', 178–80.

than did any other collection produced before 1350. Before Giovanni's *de mortuis* sermons were printed, however, the collection by another Dominican, Nicoluccio di Ascoli, was by far the most popular in this genre, if known surviving manuscripts are any indication. For this reason it deserves more than a cursory mention, even though it does not contain sermons in memory of princes.

Nicoluccio's collection seems to have been a sort of abridgement of a collection (not widely diffused) by the famous Dominican Jacopo Passavanti. It appears that Passavanti had originally intended to write a *de mortuis* series but had found himself incorporating much other preaching material as well.[173] So Passavanti's collection would seem to be on the margins of the genre.

Nicoluccio di Ascoli, however, sticks firmly within the *de mortuis* genre. Once again, Aristotelian philosophy is prominent. Once again, the preacher shows an interest in natural science. More abstract ideas are combined with concrete and biblical modes of thought. Teleology (understanding things in terms of the end or aim to which they tend) and the *viator* mentality (by which life is perceived as a journey) are synthesized. Merit in this life is associated with reward in the next, but this is combined with a Thomist form of predestinarian teaching. On the whole, the preacher assumes optimistically that the deceased is already in heaven. In some cases, there is an implication that it was confession that made this possible. There is some mention of extreme unction (the sacrament especially associated with the dying) and in some places a strong emphasis on the importance of the Eucharist. Purgatory does not bulk large, but is mentioned more than once. There are a large number of biblical *figurae*—stories taken to stand for a non-literal message. (He likes to take them from Genesis and

---

[173] For an admirable introduction to Nicoluccio and his source for the series see T. Kaeppeli, 'Opere latine attribuite a Jacopo Passavanti': pp. 147–55 on Passavanti's 'Sermones de Tempore (de mortuis) adaptabiles ad omnem materiam' (pp. 147–9 on the manuscripts); pp. 165–6 on the relation between this collection and Nicoluccio's 'Sermones (collationes) de mortuis sec. evangelia dominicalia'. I have only dipped into Passavanti's collection, but have read through Nicoluccio di Ascoli's *de mortuis* collection with some care, using MS Munich, Staatsbibliothek Clm. 2981.

seems to have a particular fondness for stories about Joseph.) Bestiary-type exempla are common, but narrative exempla (apart from biblical stories) are not a salient feature. Augustine and Gregory the Great are frequently cited; so, from time to time, is Seneca. Fasting, prayers, and alms-giving are often mentioned. The collection, rather curiously, is arranged as if it were a set of Sunday sermons.[174] In at least one manuscript (Munich, Staatsbibliothek Clm. 3555, fos. $108^{ra}$–$109^{rb}$) we find lists linking individual sermons to the death of a particular sort of person, or to a particular kind of death, but this probably does not go back to the author since there is sometimes internal evidence in a sermon that the deceased was not in the category listed in Clm. 3555.

We may now turn to five preachers—Jacopo da Viterbo (an Augustinian Hermit), Federico Franconi da Napoli, OP, Giovanni da Napoli, OP, Bertrand de la Tour, OM, and Juan de Aragón—who may be grouped together because of the curious fact that they all preached memorial sermons on members of the Angevin royal family of Naples. (In fact Eudes of Chateauroux and Remigio de' Girolami did so too, but not to my knowledge on princes who had the chance to exercise real political authority, as opposed to queens and princes who died young.[175]) Quite why so many surviving memorial sermons are on members of that family is unclear. The passage from Salimbene about the tradition of funeral preaching in Apulia may be a clue—such sermons could simply have been more frequent—or the explanation might have more to do with the way the sermons have been transmitted. Whatever the explanation, these sermons are a gift to the historian, and incidentally also a reminder to historians not to neglect this fascinating dynasty.

---

[174] Cf. Schneyer, *Repertorium*, iv. 215–19.

[175] Eudes de Chateauroux: Schneyer, *Repertorium*, iv. 466, No. 889: 'De obitu Beatricis illustr. reginae Siciliae'. Remigio de' Girolami: ibid. v. 94, No. 463: 'Nobilis grandis intuitu (Ez. 22: 5)—Dominus Karolus filius domini principis . . .' This is in memory of Carlo d'Acaia (son of Prince Philip of Taranto), who died at the battle of Montecatini in 1315. See E. Panella, 'Un Sermone in morte . . . Beatrice d'Angiò?', 299. The main subject of this article is a sermon in memory of another Angevin, Beatrice, daughter of Charles II and sister of King Robert, whose first marriage to Azzone d'Este attracted Dante's hostile attention (see ibid. 298). I have doubtless missed some sermons in honour of Angevins, if not by these then by other preachers.

Jacopo da Viterbo (d. 1308) is perhaps best known as a political thinker but is also important as a preacher. A major collection of his sermons survives in MS Archiv. Capit. S. Petri D 213 in the Vatican Library.[176] Among them are several that nearly come within our range, but not quite. There is a sermon in memory of a queen of Hungary, who was probably the Angevin princess Isabelle who married Ladislaus IV, king of Hungary.[177] This has virtually nothing on rulership in the literal sense, though some interesting remarks on the threefold kingdom in man.[178] There are sermons on St Louis of France (who was of course brother of the first Angevin king of Naples-Sicily), but these are saint's sermons so do not fall within our genre.[179] As for Louis of Toulouse, the manuscript has an interesting story to tell about a corrected slip which anticipated his canonization.[180] But in any case Louis was never a prince. Though his chances of becoming king must have seemed high, his heart was set on the Franciscan life.[181]

[176] My attention was drawn to the manuscript by L.-J. Bataillon. I am also grateful to David Anderson for sending me a copy of his unpublished paper on the sermons in honour of Louis of Toulouse. See also 'P.D.G.', 'De Vita et Scriptis Beati Jacobi de Viterbio, II. De Scriptis', *Analecta Augustiniana*, 16 (1937–8), 282–305, at 297–8. Though I expect that the confidence about Jacopo's authorship is justified, the words 'beati patris Francisci' and 'de glorioso patre Francisco' in the sermon on the text *Noe uir iustus atque* (adque *ms*) *perfectus*...(Gen. 6: 9), in col. 264, should be noted. Perhaps not only Franciscans thought of Francis as their father. On Jacopo as a political thinker see e.g. J. B. Morrall, *Political Thought in Medieval Times* (repr. Toronto etc., 1980), 88–9.
[177] Sermon beginning '*Regina autem domum conuiuii ingressa est*, Dan. v (10). Hic commendatur hec nobilis domina...' (col. 27). The medieval table of contents at the front of the manuscript gives this text and column-number for a sermon 'In m. Regine Ung.' Near the beginning of the sermon, col. 27, we find the words 'Fuit secundum statum seculi regina quia regis sponsa et regis filia.' All this fits Isabelle, daughter of king Charles I. See Detlev Schwennicke (ed.), *Europäische Stammtafeln: Stammtafeln zur Geschichte der europäischen Staaten*, NS 2. *Die außerdeutschen Staaten: Die regierenden Häuser der übrigen Staaten Europas* (Marburg, 1984), table 15.
[178] 'Est autem triplex regnum in homine, scilicet corporale, quo anima regit corpus, sensuale, quo ratio regit sensualitatem, rationale, quo ratio superior regit rationem inferiorem, quia temporalia sunt disponenda in ordine ad eterna. Ideo ratio inferior a superiori regenda; sic sensualitas rationi; sic corpus anime' (MS Bibliotheca Apostolica Vaticana, Archiv. Capit. S. Petri D 213, col. 27).
[179] See Endnote 3, below, pp. 280–81.
[180] It is for David Anderson to tell the story, in a paper to appear in a Festschrift. L.-J. Bataillon made the same observation independently.
[181] On Louis of Toulouse see M. Toynbee, *S. Louis of Toulouse and the Process of Canonisation in the Fourteenth Century* (Manchester, 1929).

One sermon by Jacop*liminaries*
scope of this study. The ... brought within the immediate
Raymond, son of the king'.[18]... 'On the death of the lord
who came well down the list of ...1st be Raymond Berengar,
but who had already acquired the ... II's many sons in age,
the kingdom and count of Piedmont, a..f grand seneschal of
the time of his death at the age of 23 ... as various fiefs, at
from the rubric, there is a reference in the s... [183] Even apart
as grand seneschal.[184] ...n to his office

As seneschal Raymond Berengar exercised real ...thority,[185]
and in fact the sermon does allude to his value to ...e State
more than once. He was 'very necessary and useful ...the
State'.[186] He gave justice to all,[187] and devoted his mind to
looking after the State.[188] 'Among the Romans, those who
devoted their attention to the State and fostered its development were called "Fathers of the Kingdom"; so too, in the
kingdom of France, those who direct the kingdom and keep it
going are called "Fathers". He was one of the Fathers of this
kingdom.'[189]

---

[182] 'In morte domini Raymundi filii Regis' (MS Bibliotheca Apostolica
Vaticana, Archiv. Capit. S. Petri D 213, col. 261; the sermon continues into col.
264).
[183] On Raymond Berengar's career see G. M. Monti, *La dominazione angioina
in Piemonte* (Biblioteca della Società Storica Subalpina, 116; Turin, 1930), 73–9.
Note the following remark in the sermon: 'Licet enim iste non esset unigenitus,
quia plures fratres habuit, nec primogenitus, quia plures ante eum prius geniti,
tamen ita carus erat parentibus et populo quod quasi unigenitus et primogenitus
putabatur' (MS Bibliotheca Apostolica Vaticana, Archiv. Capit. S. Petri D
213, col. 261).
[184] 'Secundo, dignitate regiminis, quia Senescallus regni magnus' (ibid., col.
264). Earlier, Jacopo had said that 'specialiter quo ad hunc est consolatorium
quod deus, qui hunc dedit et nunc abstulit, alios fratres eius uiros probos nobis
reseruauit'. (ibid., col. 262). (I tentatively assign 'adhuc', which follows 'reseruauit', to the next sentence.) The *preux* brothers would be Robert, the future
king; Philip of Taranto; and perhaps also John of Durazzo and Peter of Eboli
(1292–1315), if they were not too young at the time of the sermon to be
included among the *uiros probos*. (For their dates see Schwennicke, *Europäische
Stammtafeln*, vol. ii, table 15.)
[185] Cf. Monti, *La dominazione angioina in Piemonte*, 74, 78; but, on the other
hand, p. 79.
[186] '... rei publice multum necessarius et proficuus' (MS Bibliotheca
Apostolica Vaticana, Archiv. Capit. S. Petri D 213, col. 261).
[187] '... propter iustitiam (*suppl. in marg.*) quam omnibus reddebat' (ibid.,
col. 263).
[188] 'Tertio propter prouidentiam qua rei publice consulebat' (ibid.).
[189] '... apud romanos hii qui rei publice consulebant et (*after deletion*) eam

50

Ch... ct of the sermon's first part,
The emotion of grief is full and differentiated analysis
and Jacopo gives a relating the words that label different
of it. He begins by eye states the principle that lamentation
varieties of grief.[190] So far as it is kept within the bounds of
for the dead is generalizes this, in passing, to a principle
reason.[191] (Jaco emotion.[192]) The first thing required if
applicable to to be rational is an appropriate motive, and
lamentation a breakdown of such motives. One would be a
Jacopo gi with the dead person—an emotional attachment,
connect whether 'natural' (arising out of family relationship?), civil (a
social/political relationship?), or 'from grace' (i.e. derived from
charity, presumably of the supernatural sort).[193] Other motives
for grief would be that the deceased was valuable to the State,
or that still better things might have been expected of the
person if he or she had lived.[194] These generalizations are then
applied to Raymond Berengar's case.[195]
If grief is to be rational it should also take into account the

alebant patres uocabantur; sic et in regno Francie dicuntur patres regni (repeated
and deleted in ms) qui regnum dirigunt et manutenent. Hic erat unus de patribus
huius regni' (ibid.). Earlier, Jacopo had said that 'Fuit enim pater huius totius
regni et huius ciuitatis specialiter' (ibid.). The city is presumably Naples.
   [190] 'Primo notatur affectus tristitie quem debemus ostendere, cum dicitur
Plangite. Nam plangere signum est tristitie. Ostenditur quidem tristitia interior
quandoque per fletum. Flere autem est ubertim lacrimas fundere, quasi fluere.
Quandoque ostenditur per ploratum. Est autem plorare cum uoce flere.
Quandoque ostenditur per planctum. Est autem plangere cum lacrimis pectus
aut faciem tundere' etc. (ibid., col. 261).
   [191] '. . . considerandum est quod planctus pro mortuis laudatur et approbatur
in scripturis in quantum ordinate et rationabiliter fit' (ibid.).
   [192] 'Affectio enim quelibet in tantum laudabilis est in quantum regulata et
ordinata ratione' (ibid.).
   [193] 'Planctus autem est rationabilis et ordinatus tripliciter. Primo si habeat
motiuum et causam. Causa autem que rationabiliter mouere potest ad
plangendum mortuum est coniunctio nostri ad ipsum et ipsius ad nos, uel
secundum affectum naturalem, uel ciuilem, uel gratuitum, scilicet caritatis' (et
ipsius ad nos] supplied in marg.; I conjecture et, which is concealed) (ibid.).
   [194] 'Alia etiam causa est si persona mortui est utilis rei publice. Et etiam si
speratur de profectu ipsius in melius. De morte (mote ms?) namque illorum qui
(deleted word follows) uiuebant in periculum et dampnum reipublice, uel de
quibus presumitur (suppl. in marg.) quod in deterius procedant, magis
gaudendum est quam dolendum' (ibid.).
   [195] 'In morte autem huius bene subest motiuum et causa doloris et planctus,
quia nobis (deleted word follows) dilectione coniunctus, nos diligens, et a nobis
dilectus' etc. (ibid.).

state of life of the deceased. Thus one should grieve more for a prince than a knight.[196] (This is, incidentally, a reminder that, then as now, the death of public figures—some of them, anyway—was supposed to occasion collective grief. Funeral or memorial sermons could thus serve to orchestrate public emotion.)

Finally, grief should not be vehement beyond measure, should not go on too long, and should be mixed with consolation. When grieving, we should think upon things that console us, such as: the fact that death is unavoidable (!); the good way in which the deceased met his end (in the unity of the Church and the true faith, with the sacraments, after self-examination, and after making the right dispositions for his soul and his property); and the hope of resurrection, immortality, and eternal reward.[197]

Now Jacopo turns to the specific case of Raymond Berengar, pointing out, among other things, that good could come of his death since, 'when we are punished by losing him, the terror of divine judgement is brought home to us and a change of our life for the better follows'.[198] This is a commonplace of memorial preaching, less individual than some of Jacopo's other observations seem to be. The section ends with a doctrine which also has a familiar ring: better to be dead in flesh than in spirit.[199] Then he turns to the subject of the honour which

---

[196] 'Secundo si habeat gradum et differentiam, quia non equaliter de omnibus plangendum est et dolendum, se*d* consideratis causis predictis uel aliis: de aliquibus plus de aliquibus minus. Plus enim dolendum de principe quam de milite' (ibid., col. 262).

[197] 'Tertio si habeat te*m*pus et mensuram. Dolor quippe de mortuis debet habere mensuram et te*m*pus, et quantum ad affectionem, ne sit extra modum uehemens, et quantum ad diuturnitatem, ne sit diu permanens. Ut autem habeat mensuram et modum, debet misceri consolatio dolori, ut dolendo cogitemus que consolari nos possunt, quorum unum est moriendi necessitas, aliud est modus mortis, ut si mortuus sit in unitate ecclesie, in recta fide et sacramentis, in recognitione sui, in bona dispositione anime sue et rerum suarum. Tertium est spes resurrectionis, i*m*mortalitatis et remunerationis eterne' (ibid.).

[198] 'Adhuc, quia iudicia dei occulta sunt, se*d* iusta et bona, fortassis ex huius morte alica bona eliciet, quia dum per eius subtractionem punimur, diuini iudicii terror nobis incutitur et (*deletion follows*) emendatio nostre uite subsequitur' (ibid.). ('Adhuc' might conceivably go with the preceding sentence: see above, n. 184.)

[199] 'Multo enim a*m*plius plangere debemus uiuentes in carne se*d* mortuos in spiritu quam mortuos in carne et uiuentes in spiritu. Unde Iere. 22 (10): *Nolite*

should be paid to the dead. On this other aspect of the relation of the living to the dead his ideas are not banal. More of them below.

Jacopo da Viterbo was a great man in his day—a Master of Theology at Paris, then successively archbishop of Benevento and Naples.[200] In comparison with him Federico Franconi da Napoli is a minor figure, but from our limited perspective he is rather central, since he was the author of a substantial batch of sermons on Angevin kings and princes, some of which are exceptionally interesting. Frequent reference will be made to them in subsequent chapters, so here the bare biographical details of the preacher will suffice.

Federico Franconi, OP,[201] was prior of S. Pietro a Castello at Naples in the years 1337–9, inquisitor in 1334–5 and 1340–1, vicar general and prior provincial of the Dominican province of the *Regno*.[202] So far as his career is known, therefore, it was set in Angevin south Italy. Sermons by Federico, including the ones that concern us, are preserved in a Munich manuscript.[203]

Federico had probably met Giovanni Regina di Napoli, also a Dominican associated with Angevin Italy, but better known.[204] Giovanni seems to have had a special relationship with the Angevin royal family. In 1298 King Charles II arranged for him to be given a sum of money by two fellow Dominicans

---

*flere mortuum, neque lugeatis super eum in fletu. Plangite eum qui egreditur, quia non reuertetur ultra, nec uidebit terram natiuitatis sue.* Hic autem est ille qui a deo recedit peccando, qui per se non reuertitur, nisi ei gratia diuina succurrat. Et sic patet primum principale' (ibid.).

[200] M. Grabmann, 'Die Lehre des Jakob von Viterbo (†1308) von der Wirklichkeit des göttlichen Seins: Beitrag zum Streit über das Sein Gottes zur Zeit Meister Eckharts', in id., *Mittelalterliches Geistesleben: Abhandlungen zur Geschichte der Scholastik und Mystik,* ii (Munich, 1936), 490–511, at 492–3.

[201] Otherwise Fridericus Franconus (de Franconibus) de Neapoli.

[202] T. Kaeppeli, 'Dalle pergamene di S. Domenico di Napoli: Rilievo dei domenicani ivi menzionati con due appendici sui priori conventuali e provinciali fino al 1500', *AFP* 32 (1962), 285–326, at 321 n. 11; also *Scriptores Ordinis Praedicatorum,* ed. Kaeppeli, i (Rome, 1970), 402–3.

[203] Staatsbibliothek Clm. 2981. Schneyer lists Federico's sermons under Nicolaus de Asculo (whose sermons on the dead are also in this manuscript). The sermons that especially concern us are Schneyer, *Repertorium,* iv. 223, Nos. 216–22; see also No. 223: 'In exequiis dominae Blancae filiae principis.'

[204] Schneyer, 'Beitrag' (this article was of immense value when I was collecting the materials on which this book is based). See also T. Kaeppeli, 'Note sugli scrittori domenicani di nome Giovanni di Napoli', *AFP* 10 (1940), 48–76.

when he was a student at Bologna.[205] In 1307 the same king intervened again, asking the Master General of the order to send Giovanni, then lector at the convent in Naples, to lecture on the Sentences at Paris.[206] (Only a few theologians got so far: it was the preliminary to becoming a Master of Theology and should not be confused with selection to study theology at Paris at a lower level.[207]) Giovanni was sent, perhaps after a delay, and duly achieved the Mastership, probably in 1315, and occupied one of the Dominican chairs of Theology at Paris until 1317, when he was sent back to Naples as a lector.[208] We know that he was used as a theological consultant on a marriage question by Pope John XXII.[209] At Naples his special relationship with the Court continued,[210] which may explain why he preached so many sermons in memory of Angevins (there are surviving sermons in memory of King Charles II and of two of his sons, John Prince of Durazzo (d. 1335), and Philip Prince of Taranto (d. 1331/2)).[211]

Another sermon in memory of Philip of Taranto was preached by Juan de Aragón,[212] a youthful Spanish prelate who ended up as patriarch of Alexandria, his rapid rise being connected no doubt with the fact that he was a son of King James II of Aragon.[213] James II had married a daughter of Charles II of Anjou—a marriage alliance which helped put an end to the conflict between Aragon and Naples—so Juan was the nephew

[205] Kaeppeli, 'Note sugli scrittori domenicani', 48. I do not fully understand the form taken by the transaction, as related by Kaeppeli (it was done via inquisitors), but assume that it was just a convenient way to transfer money to a Dominican.

[206] Ibid. 49.

[207] See d'Avray, *Preaching of the Friars*, 134–5, with further references.

[208] Kaeppeli, 'Note sugli scrittori domenicani', 50–1.

[209] Ibid. 51.

[210] Ibid. 52–3.

[211] Kaeppeli noticed these sermons long ago: see ibid. 61 and 67–8. (Giovanni's sermons on Angevins will turn up frequently in the course of this book.) There seem to be two views on the date of Philip of Taranto's death. Kaeppeli (ibid.) gives December 1332, whereas É. Léonard, *Les Angevins de Naples* (Paris, 1954), 297, gives 1331.

[212] MS Valencia Cat. 182, fos. 127$^{vb}$–128$^{rb}$, sermon on the text *Princeps et maximus cecidit hodie* (2 Kgs. 3: 38); Schneyer, *Repertorium*, iii. 314, No. 255.

[213] Juan was a pious and rather touching figure. For a sensitive sketch see J. Ernesto Martínez Ferrando, *Jaime II de Aragón: Su vida familiar*, i. *Testo* (Consejo Superior de Investigaciones Científicas, Escuela de Estudios Medievales, Estudios, 9; Barcelona, 1948), 141–51.

of Philip of Taranto. Juan also preached other sermons relevant
to this study—notably one 'For his deceased father the king
and for his brother, succeeding to the throne'—and we shall
return to him in the next chapter.

Juan de Aragón's sermons are heavily abridged. The sermon
in memory of Charles of Calabria (Juan's cousin, incidentally)
by Bertrand de la Tour makes a striking contrast. As transmitted, it is by far the longest sermon in memory of an Angevin
king or prince. Bertrand de la Tour was a Franciscan who
reached the rank of cardinal under Pope John XXII. Charles of
Calabria was heir to the kingdom of Naples, son of Robert the
Wise.[214]

This sermon on Charles is hidden in the midst of a collection
of model sermons on the dead. Bertrand de la Tour (like
Giovanni da San Gimignano though not on such a grand scale)
wrote model memorial sermons for men or women of a particular state of life, including a number in memory of kings or
princes. These are an important source, and frequent reference
will be made to them.[215] Another of Bertrand's sermons, which
is a sort of miniature synthesis on the topic of death, but
which he indicated could be used when preparing a sermon in
memory of a king or prince, will be analysed in Chapter 4.

Two sermons in memory of a prince, the attribution of which
to Bertrand may eventually be established although it is not yet
beyond question, should also be mentioned here.[216] One is
very brief. The principal theme or themes are the universality,
power, and destructiveness of death (and of course the need to
prepare for it); the death of a prince brings it home that escape
is impossible.[217]

---

[214] Thus Charles of Calabria, like Juan de Aragón, was a nephew of Philip
of Taranto.

[215] They are Transcriptions B:a–B:d at the end of this book.

[216] Schneyer gives incipits of what looks to me like the same sermon in four
different places. The first is under 'Bertrandus de Turre': *Repertorium*, i. 574,
No. 1006. He lists MS Naples, Nazionale, VIII. A. 36 (which I have not seen) in
black type (when Schneyer does this he can usually be relied on) and some
other manuscripts in ordinary roman. Then there are two appearances under
'Sermones Fratrum Min.': ibid. vii. 148, No. 84 (MS Barcelona, Archivo de la
Corona de Aragón, Ripoll 187), and ibid. 454, No. 30 (MS Troyes 2001). Finally,
see ibid. ix. 824, No. 80 (MS Bibliotheca Apostolica Vaticana, Archiv. Capit. di
San Pietro G 48). The other sermon which may or may not be by Bertrand is
discussed below.

[217] See Transcription D at the end of the book.

The other[218] has a quite different balance of emphasis. It too evokes the fragility of life. For all the prince's greatness, he was brought low by death—though he died with the sacraments and will rise to enjoy eternal glory.[219] However, such other-worldly reflections are offset by teaching which relates mainly to the present life (though naturally the angle is religious). An early section of the sermon praises the prince's nobility: royal ancestry on both sides, and a soul decorated with virtues—the most evident sign of nobility.[220] Then, after speaking about death and heaven, the preacher returns to the subject of the prince's qualities as a ruler, in a lengthy and subdivided passage which takes up more than half the sermon and brings it to its conclusion.[221]

We are already on the edge of the 'anonymous' category, the transit-camp for sermons whose authors may or may not one day be identified. At present the number of inmates is small, though it could contract or expand as preachers are identified or as new anonymous sermons with rubrics like 'for the death of a prince' turn up in manuscripts. In the absence of an identified preacher, the inclusion of a sermon in a study of the period before 1350 depends on palaeographical dating (not an exact science) unless the sermon is on a real person, in which case it was probably preached not too long after the death.

On that assumption the set of anonymous sermons in memory of Edward I of England which survive in MS Rome Angelica 158 were preached in 1307 (just conceivably in 1308, on his anniversary, but I would not expect so many sermons except shortly after his death). These sermons are of great interest, and it will be necessary to return to them repeatedly in the following chapters. A lot lower down the scale of historical significance is a sermon 'On the death of some prince' in a Troyes manuscript.[222] It is mainly about the fragility of life and the misery of the human condition.[223] Taken by itself, it would give a misleading idea of memorial sermons for princes, for it lacks the emphasis on this-worldly values that is

[218] See Endnote 4, below, p. 281.
[219] See Endnote 5, below, p. 281.
[220] See Endnote 6, below, p. 281.
[221] See Endnote 7, below, pp. 281–2.
[222] See Endnote 8, below, p. 282.
[223] See Endnote 9, below, p. 282.

quite commonly combined with teaching about death and
the afterlife. An intriguing anonymous sermon in MS Berlin
Staatsbibliothek Theol. lat. Q. 298 also talks about the transitoriness of life and worldly greatness, in the second and final
part of the sermon; but, on the other hand, the first part is a
particularly well-defined case of the tendency of sermons in
memory of kings to take a positive view of the things of this
world—an aspect of the sermon which will be discussed in
Chapter 3.[224]

It will have been noticed that the surviving evidence for
memorial preaching is more plentiful with each succeeding
century (after the long gap from late antiquity to the central
Middle Ages). This pattern is as one would expect by analogy
with other categories of medieval source. How far there was an
actual increase in memorial preaching, as well as an increasing
amount of evidence for it, is as usual difficult to determine. It is
possible that a papal decree which was put into wide circulation
from 1317, and which included among many other things a
declaration that Franciscan and Dominican friars were free to
preach at funerals, may have given some stimulus to what was
no doubt already a common practice.[225] However that may be,
it seems fairly clear that more ready-made models for this kind
of preaching were available in the fourteenth century than ever
before, and that there was a demand for them.[226]

---

[224] For the whole sermon see below, Transcription A.

[225] '... ad funera ... mortuorum ... possunt iidem fratres et liceat eis libere
praedicare, nisi forte illa hora, qua solet ad clerum in praedictis locis Dei
uerbum proponi, episcopus uel praelatus superior clerum ad se generaliter
conuocaret, aut ex aliqua ratione uel causa urgente clerum ipsum duceret
congregandum' (*Clementinarum Lib. III. Tit.* VII, cap. 2, ed. Aemilius Friedberg,
*Corpus iuris canonici* (2 vols.; 1879, repr. Graz, 1955), vol. i, col. 1162). On the
diffusion of the Clementine Constitutions see J. F. von Schulte, *Die Geschichte
der Quellen und Literatur des canonischen Rechts*, ii. *Von Papst Gregor IX. bis zum
Concil von Trient* (1877 edn.; repr. Graz, 1956), 45–50. M. Rubin, in her important *Corpus Christi: The Eucharist in Late Medieval Culture* (Cambridge, 1991),
181–5, has shown what a difference the promulgation of this collection made
to the diffusion of the feast of Corpus Christi. On the early history of the burial
of lay people in Franciscan and Dominican churches and cemeteries see J.
Moorman, *A History of the Franciscan Order from its Origins to the Year 1517*
(Oxford, 1968), 122, 177–8.

[226] E. Winkler has already drawn attention to Giovanni da S. Gimignano's
remark that 'in locis et ciuitatibus *plurimis* consueuerunt in defunctorum
funeribus praedicationes ad populum fieri' ('Scholastische Leichenpredigten',
177).

The frequency of preaching in memory of princes and kings is a further problem. Would this not by its nature be a rare type of preaching, since the number of kings was limited? In fact, however, sermons in memory of kings and princes could have been much commoner than might at first appear. To begin with, the death of one ruler could give rise to a number of sermons. Sermons could have been preached at the commemoration services held, say, a month or a year after the death[227] (and perhaps even on subsequent anniversaries). Furthermore, the same preacher might preach several sermons on the death of a given prince. No fewer than four sermons in memory of Charles II of Anjou by Giovanni da Napoli are preserved.[228] They presumably go back to sermons actually preached—on different occasions, obviously. Moreover, memorial sermons could be preached far away from the body and the funeral. This is clearly the case with Bertrand de la Tour's sermon in memory of Charles of Calabria, for Bertrand speaks about the news or rumours of the death.[229] Again, it seems likely, even though one cannot be categorical, that Remigio de' Girolami was in Italy when he preached in memory of Philip IV of France and his successor Louis X.[230]

Even apart from the possibility that the death of an important person might give rise to a multiplicity of sermons, there is reason to think that a good deal of preaching must have fallen into the category of sermons envisaged by this study. The category may be defined as sermons in memory of men whom we would describe as 'secular rulers' and whom their contemporaries would have described as kings or princes. One may also add the appellation 'duke' (*dux*: 'leader' might be a better translation), since it seems to merge into 'prince'. The

---

[227] Cf. Decreti secunda pars, Causa XIII, Quest. II., c. 24, ed. Friedberg, *Corpus*, vol. i, col. 729. I am assuming that these periods were reckoned from the day of death.

[228] Schneyer, *Repertorium*, iii. 607, Johannes de Neapel, Nos. 35, 37, 38, 39. See below, ch. 2 n. 145, where I argue that No. 36, which would appear from the rubric to be another sermon about Charles II, is in fact probably about someone else.

[229] 'Rumores flebiles et lugubres audiuimus ... de subtractione ... ducis Calabrie' (MS Kremsmünster 44, fos. 121[vb]–122[ra], from a sermon on the text *Propter sapientiam* (Prov. 28: 2); Schneyer, *Repertorium*, i. 583, No. 1123).

[230] For details of Remigio's movements around these points in his career see E. Panella, 'Per lo studio di Fra Remigio dei Girolami (†1319): *Contra falsos ecclesie professores* cc. 5–37', *Memorie domenicane*, NS 10 (1979), 230–2.

rubric of the sermon by Bertrand de la Tour in memory of
Charles of Calabria indicates that it can be used for the exequies
'of some great leader or prince'.[231] Charles, who would have
become king of Naples had he not predeceased his father
Robert, was not only duke of Calabria but lord of Florence,
at the Florentines' request, and leader of their forces.[232] The
content of the same sermon reinforces the idea that the word
*dux* had a flexible meaning. On the one hand he describes
Charlemagne and St Louis as 'leaders' (*duces*) from the house of
France.[233] On the other hand the word is also used of Joshua,[234]
who was the successor of Moses as the leader of the Israelites
in the period before they were given a king, and Jonathan the
Maccabee, who was a resistance leader of his people. Bertrand
quotes 1 Macc. 9: 30: 'We have chosen thee to be our resistance
leader and prince, to fight our war'[235]—another case of the
versatility of the words *dux* and *princeps*.

The biblical use of the word *princeps*, in the Vulgate version
that the preachers used, is probably a safe enough guide to the
sense of the word in the thirteenth and fourteenth centuries. A
text used more than once for preaching in memory of a prince—
at least twice in memory of Philip of Taranto, the uncle of
Charles of Calabria and brother of King Robert, for instance—
is 2 Kings 3: 38, 'a prince and a great man is slain this day in
Israel'.[236] The original prince in question was Abner, the power
behind the throne of Saul until he went over to King David's
side. Presumably the word *princeps* here means a man who

---

[231] '. . . in exequiis alicuius magni ducis uel principis et cetera' (MS
Kremsmünster 44, fo. 121[vb]).

[232] Léonard, *Les Angevins de Naples*, 246–7.

[233] 'De domo autem Francie fuerunt multi duces contra istos commutatos et
filios doloris, sicud . . . Karolus magnificus, sanctus Ludowicus' (MS
Kremsmünster 44, fo. 124[ra]).

[234] 'Est autem sciendum quod iste nobilissimus uir fuit figuratus in scriptura
per quattuor nobilissimos duces, scilicet, per Iosue ratione fidelitatis . . . Dico
primo quod figuratus fuit per Iosue ratione fidelitatis . . . De Iosue enim legitur
in libro suo quod fuit fidelissimus Moysi cuius erat minister fidelissimus et
populo cuius erat rector fidelissimus' (ibid., fo. 123[vb]).

[235] Ibid., fo. 124[vb].

[236] In memory of Philip of Taranto: Juan de Aragón, Schneyer, *Repertorium*,
iii. 314, No. 255; Giovanni da Napoli, ibid. 606, No. 26. See also Giovanni da
San Gimignano, ibid. 762, No. 505; Bertrand de la Tour, ibid. i. 581, No. 1100;
and the sermon which may or may not be by Bertrand discussed above, n. 216.

exercised great political and military power, without enjoying formal supremacy. The loose sense of *princeps* (or of *dux*) fits the situation not only of a Philip of Taranto,[237] but also that of despots or *Signori* of Italian cities, as well as 'princes' in Germany (where the term had a more technical sense)[238] and rulers like the dukes of Brittanny or Burgundy.

There are few certainties about the audience for which the sermons studied here were designed. Whoever had these sermons written down presumably had two sorts of recipient in mind: listeners, to whom the sermons would be preached (and had perhaps already been preached) and, proximately, readers or users of the manuscript, for whom the sermon could serve as a model. This applies to the bulk of medieval preaching and is probably the general rule with our corpus of material also.

As for the listeners, we know that they were not necessarily lay even for sermons in memory of a king, for three of the rubrics for sermons in memory of Edward I of England specify a clerical audience.[239] (This fits the hypothesis holding the field, which is that the sermons were given before the papal court at Poitiers.[240]) Only the 'engineer's inference',[241] however, would lead us from this to the conclusion that the listeners

---

[237] Cf. Léonard, *Les Angevins de Naples*, 201–2 and 297–8 for Philip's territories. (I leave out of account Philip's claim to be emperor of Constantinople as a little unrealistic.)

[238] E. E. Stengel, 'Land- u. lehnrechtliche Grundlagen d. Reichsfürstenstandes', *Zeitschrift d. Savigny-Stiftung für Rechtsgeschichte, germanistische Abteilung*, 66 (1948), 294–342, and H. Koller, 'Die Bedeutung d. Titels "princeps" in der Reichskanzlei unter den Saliern u. Staufern', *Mitteilungen des Instituts für österreichische Geschichtsforschung*, 68 (1960), 63–80. Before getting down to his main argument, Koller remarks 'Daß daneben in anderen Quellen als "principes" nicht nur Kaiser und Könige, sondern auch andere mächtige Persönlichkeiten bezeichnet werden, ist nicht auffallend, wenn man bedenkt, daß die Bibel, deren Sprachgebrauch im Mittelalter häufig vorbildlich war, bedeutende Personen einfach "principes" nennt. Auch Isidor von Sevilla bezeichnet als "princeps" offenbar jede höhere Persönlichkeit und führt den Rang eines "dux" als entsprechend an' (p. 65).

[239] Transcriptions C:a, C:c, C:e (see rubrics at the head of the sermons).

[240] D. L. d'Avray, 'Sermons on the Dead before 1350', *Studi medievali*, 3rd ser., 31/1 (1990), 207–23, at 211 n. 19.

[241] An engineer, a historian, and a pure mathematician on a Scottish walking-tour saw a black cow. The engineer inferred that all cows in Scotland were black, the historian that some were black, and the mathematician that one was black on one side.

were always clerical. The easiest assumption would be that
sermons in memory of princes were normally preached to
courtly congregations (this could include papal and episcopal
courts). Yet there is no reason to suppose that this was exclusively the case, especially once one admits the possibility
that memorial sermons were not given only at funerals and
that a number might be delivered at different places about the
same man.

One thing which differentiates the audience, or rather the
whole 'setting in life', of this genre from, say, vernacular
memorial poems is that as a rule the sermons would presumably
have been preached at liturgical services—if not at funerals,
then at anniversary or other memorial services.[242] In the case of
a genre like the *Ehrenrede* (a member or relation of the rather
miscellaneous category of the poetic lament), in particular,
the practical difference would be considerable: the probable
context of this genre was the (one suspects) rather jolly one of
the eating and drinking that came after the solemn liturgical
rituals.[243]

Indeed, the functions of memorial preaching cannot be clearly
marked off from those of other liturgical acts relating to the
dead. Jacopo da Viterbo's analysis of the rationale of the
liturgical honour paid to the dead could be read as a functional
analysis of memorial preaching also. He lists three functions.
The first is to console the living and relieve sadness at the
person's death. The next reason for the honour paid to the
dead is 'testimony or sign'—testimony to their past virtuous
life or to their future life in glory. Finally, the *cultus* of the dead
is to help them, since it induces us to pray for them etc.[244]
There is a family resemblance between this list of functions
and the analyses by preachers of the functions of memorial
preaching itself which are discussed later in this chapter.[245]

---

[242] See Endnote 10, below, pp. 282–3.
[243] 'Für die zum Vortrag bestimmten Ehrenreden trifft wohl die Annahme
Primissers zu, daß sie ''nach der Tafel'' vorgetragen wurden. . . . Die Ehrenreden
wären dann im Rahmen des Gedächtnismahls zum Vortrag gekommen' (Nolte,
*Lauda post mortem*, 42). Nolte also raises the possibility, without committing himself, that 'einzelne Texte, etwa die umfangreichen epischen Ehrenreden, . . .
nur schriftlich überreicht wurden' (ibid.).
[244] See Endnote 11, below, p. 283.
[245] See below, text at nn. 255–69.

Thus Giovanni da San Gimignano includes consolation of the listeners and commendation of the deceased among the aims of memorial preaching, and Remigio de' Girolami includes both the presentation of the dead person's life as a good example and inducement of people to help the dead.

Liturgical services for a dead individual, and concomitant preaching, would presumably stand somewhat outside the routine of day-to-day liturgical observance, and all the more so if a king or prince was being commemorated. The average listener would be a little less likely to daydream through a sermon on an occasion of this kind than during a routine Sunday service. It is not so much their liturgical context alone, or the importance of the occasion alone, as the combination of the two, which we need to bear in mind when assessing the genre's impact.

The impact would of course be minimal if the sermons were preached in a language that the congregation did not understand, but there is no known evidence that this was the case. The sermons are transmitted in Latin, but that does not in itself tell us anything about the language in which they were preached before they were written down as models or when the models were used. Here the principles that hold for the preaching of the friars in general must be applicable in the main.[246] Before the higher clergy, on any kind of formal occasion, a sermon would almost certainly have been delivered in Latin. If the congregation consisted overwhelmingly of uneducated lay people, the vernacular would have been used. However, these principles may not account for every situation one could envisage, including two which could well have arisen with this particular genre. The genre, or at least surviving evidence for it, is especially associated with Italy, where the level of lay Latin culture was exceptionally high.[247] If a memorial sermon were preached before an audience composed of high-ranking laymen together with important clerics—as must often have been the case with sermons in memory of kings—it would be rash to exclude the possibility of delivery in

---

[246] D'Avray, *Preaching of the Friars*, 90–5.

[247] Albertano da Brescia is a fascinating example of the precocity of high lay culture in Italy. See now J. M. Powell, *Albertanus of Brescia: The Pursuit of Happiness in the Early Thirteenth Century* (Philadelphia, 1992).

Latin. Again, if the congregation consisted of both educated and uneducated elements, but the sermon was directed primarily at the literati, then the rest might have had to sit through a sermon they did not understand. This is all speculation. One may be confident, however, that memorial sermons would have been preached in a language comprehensible to at least a significant proportion of the listeners.

We shall never know the exact words the listeners heard because—as with any other form of oral communication in the Middle Ages—we have to work from written sources; so it is important to ask why the sermons were written down at all. It was suggested above in passing that they were written down as models. This is not so evident as with sermons for Sundays and feast-days transmitted in large numbers of manuscripts,[248] for nearly all the sermons in memory of kings and princes that have come to light survive in one manuscript only. Nevertheless, to make a model available was probably the ostensible[249] reason for recording them. Memorial sermons by Federico Visconti provide interesting evidence for this. The rubric of one of them—'On the death of the prior of the Dominicans; and it can be adapted for any cleric'—has already been noted.[250] Another sermon by Visconti, for the anniversary of an archbishop (whom he identifies), provides further evidence to the same effect.[251] After discussing death and the afterlife, and speaking of the dead archbishop's life, he continues: 'But if you wish to end the sermon about another dead cleric or layman, you may proceed as follows.'[252] By this Federico probably means that the section which followed could take the place of the section on the archbishop's life that had gone before (though it is perhaps conceivable that he was envisaging some kind of double anniversary sermon). In any

---

[248] Cf. d'Avray, *Preaching of the Friars*, II.iii and iv.

[249] Preachers may also have been motivated, perhaps only half-consciously, by a feeling that their sermon or sermons had value and should not be lost.

[250] See above, n. 158.

[251] 'Sermo quem dominus fecit in anniuersario domini Ugonis archiepiscopi Nicosien. presente clero Pisan. apud sanctum Petrum ad uincula' (MS Florence, Laur. Plut. 33 Sin. 1, fo. 96[vb], from a sermon on the text *Homo cum mortuus fuerit* (Job 14: 10); Schneyer, *Repertorium*, ii. 89, No. 66). (Incidentally, this sermon is very interesting on the topography of the afterlife etc.)

[252] 'Si autem uis de alio mortuo clerico uel laico terminare sermonem, sic procedas' (ibid., fo. 98[va]).

case it is clear both that the written sermon had been preached in the past and that it was intended as a model for future preaching.

Another confirmation that live sermons could be turned into models is Bertrand de la Tour's in memory of Charles of Calabria (d. 1328). The written text retains the heat of Bertrand's feelings about Ludwig of Bavaria and the antipope he had set up. It is hard to believe that this sermon was not delivered: at the very least, Bertrand must have planned to preach it live. Yet the rubric is 'Sermon 67. This can be preached at the exequies of some great leader or prince, etc.'[253] This leaves little doubt that it was intended to serve as a model, like the other sermons in memory of kings and princes with which it travels, which seem to be quite free of contemporary allusions.[254] These and other models which make no reference to actual historical persons or events are good evidence for attitudes to political power and the afterlife, because they tell us what ideas were thought applicable to the death of any prince. Nevertheless, the sermon on Charles of Calabria and the others we have on historical personages are valuable because they give us a more vivid sense than the others can normally do of what 'live' memorial preaching was like.

We may now turn to the distinct question of the function of memorial preaching itself (as opposed to the reason for writing the sermons down). Some of the preachers gave their own account of the function of *de mortuis* preaching, and should now be allowed to speak.

Juan de Aragón says in one place that sermons on the dead (*pro mortuis*) have a double purpose: to get the living to help the dead, and to bring home to the living their present state of misery.[255] In another place he mentions only the second

---

[253] 'Sermo lxviii.$^{us}$ Qui potest fieri in exequiis alicuius magni ducis uel principis, etc.' (MS Kremsmünster 44, fo. 121$^{vb}$; Schneyer, *Repertorium*, i. 583, No. 1123).

[254] See Transcription B, *passim*.

[255] 'Sermones pro mortuis sunt ex duplici causa, scilicet pro auxilio defunctorum cum uiuis procurando, et pro statu presentis miserie ipsis uiuentibus demonstrando. Predicant enim nobis ipsi defuncti in hoc plurimum, sicut iste presens defunctus' (MS Valencia, Cat. 182, fo. 129$^{ra}$, from a sermon on the text *Memor esto iudicii mei* (Eccli. 38: 23); Schneyer, *Repertorium*, iii. 314, No. 258).

of these two functions, namely, to convey a message about transitoriness:

Holy mother Church, founded on and ordered and regulated by the Holy Spirit, considering and procuring, like a merciful mother, what is useful for her children, began the practice of commemorating the dead, not so much to be useful to the dead themselves, for whom she employs the helps of prayer and alms and other works of mercy, as to be useful to the living, whose fragile and transitory condition she is anxious to recall to their minds, to stimulate and induce them to live good lives and do good works . . . So if this holds true of the death of any person, much more so of the deaths of nobles and magnates, who, though they seem high up, powerful, and very illustrious according to the fallacious judgement of the world . . .

Santa mater ecclesia, spiritu sancto fundata et ordinata et regulata, ta*n*quam pia mater utilitatem filiorum suorum considerans et pro-curans, co*m*memorationem fieri instituit pro defunctis, non tam pro utilitate ipsorum mortuorum, pro quibus suffragia orationis et elemosinarum et aliorum misericordie operum i*m*pendit, quam ipsorum uiuorum, quorum fragilem et caducam conditionem ad memoriam reducere intendit, ut ad bene uiuendum et operandum eos prouocet et inducat . . . Si hoc ergo in morte cuiuslibet ueritatem habet, multo fortius [*col. b*] in morte nobilium et magnatum, qui licet iuxta mundi fallaciam alti, potentes, et clarissimi uideantur . . .[256]

Remigio de' Girolami has a less exclusively other-worldly formula for the functions of *de mortuis* preaching. His com-pressed statement implies that it is about virtue in this life as well as about death and the duty of helping the dead:

Therefore note that someone preaching about the dead ought to preach about three things or about one of them: that is, either for example—and this is the life of the dead person; or for teaching—and this is the nature of death; or for assistance—and this is the help and remedy of the prayers of the people.

Unde nota quod predicans de mortuis de tribus uel uno horum debet predicare, scilicet aut propter exemplum, et hoc est uita defuncti; aut propter documentum, et hoc est natura mortis; aut propter adiutorium, et hoc est suffragium et remedium orationum populi.[257]

---

[256] MS Valencia Cat. 182, fo. 129[va–b], from a sermon on the text *Regina corruit et in pallorem* (Esther 15: 10); Schneyer, *Repertorium*, iii. 314, No. 260.

[257] MS Florence, Nazionale, Conv. Soppr. G. 4. 936, fo. 396[rb], from a sermon on the text *Cum dederit dilectis suis* (Ps. 126: 2); Schneyer, *Repertorium*, v. 95, No. 481.

The first of these three topics would seem to be the presentation of the dead person's life as a moral example—
presumably a good example, which would imply praise. The
practice of the period corresponds to Remigio's theory: medieval memorial sermons, as well as humanist ones, 'sought to
depict an inspirational image of the deceased'.[258] The second
topic is probably meant to include a wide range of doctrines
bearing on death, from its origins in human nature and/or
original sin to the fate of body and soul in the afterlife.[259]
The meaning of the third topic—'the help and remedy of the
prayers of the people'—is self-evident. Eudes de Chateauroux's
sermon in memory of Pope Innocent IV is a not unsubtle
instance of how a preacher might persuade listeners that the
deceased was in purgatory and in need of help, while at the
same time presenting the pope as a moral exemplar.[260] However, in our particular corpus, sermons in memory of secular
rulers, it seems a relatively subordinate theme, at least in terms
of the amount of space devoted to it. On the other hand, one
must take into account what a discourse does, as well as what
it says. It may be that people would be reminded to pray for
the dead by the very fact of listening to a memorial sermon,
even if it did not dwell explicitly on Remigio's third topic for
long. (Nevertheless, the present study will conform roughly to
the balance of explicit emphasis in the sermons themselves,
and concentrate on the lives of dead princes as presented in
the sermons, on the idea of political virtue, and on conceptions
of death and the afterlife.)

Giovanni da San Gimignano is less succinct than Remigio,
but he too orientates his remarks to this world as well as to the
next. He suggests that though funeral sermons are occasioned
by death, they are primarily for the consolation of the living
and the instruction of listeners.[261] The preacher should therefore

---

[258] Cf. McManamon, *Funeral Oratory and the Cultural Ideals of Italian Humanism*,
33. Excellent on the humanists, this fine book overdraws the contrast with their
medieval predecessors. See Chapters 2 and 3 below.
[259] See Chapter 4 below for an analysis of this kind of instruction on death.
[260] See Cole, d'Avray, and Riley-Smith, 'Application', 239–41.
[261] 'Quia in locis et ciuitatibus plurimis consueuerunt in defunctorum
funeribus predicationes ad populum fieri, que etsi pro mortuis occasionaliter
fiant, id est occasione ipsorum, magis tamen pro consolatione uiuentium et
doctrina audientium eas fieri est credendum' (MS Siena Comunale F. X. 24, fo.
1$^{ra}$, from the prologue).

aim at three things in his sermon: instruction of the people, the honouring of God, and, if possible, some kind of commendation of the deceased.[262] Giovanni goes on to suggest what might usefully be preached. Some of what he says is on the theme of the contempt of the world (as with Juan de Aragón). Those who seek worldly things have laborious effort while they live and pain when they have to part from them at death. He also recommends themes which will lead sinners to repent, such as the sterility of sin and the retribution which follows it. Again, it incites sinners to repent if one arouses fear of death and judgement.[263] After a passage about the duties of the preacher, Giovanni becomes more specific about the functions of this kind of sermon. He makes it clear that so long as the life of the deceased was not deserving of detestation (and even then, if it ended with edifying repentance), the functions of the genre include praise:

A third thing, however, is required in a preacher, which is that at funerals he should preach on behalf of those who have died—that is, to commend them, so that (viz. if they have lived good lives) their works, being praised, should serve as an example to others. And indeed, it is safer to praise good men when they are dead than when they are alive . . . If, however, the dead person should not be a man of distinguished life or reputation, one should concentrate more on the instruction of the living than on the praises of a dead man of this sort. Indeed, if he should be a man of detestable life, one should cease from praise altogether, lest scandal rather than edification be the outcome among those who know his life; unless perhaps clear and known testimony be available concerning his reconciliation and final penitence,

[262] '. . . oportet in predicationibus talibus, que scilicet ad funera fiunt, predicatorem ad tria precipue intentionem habere, . . . Et primo quidem ad eruditionem populi. Secundo ad honorem dei. Tertio quoque (*ms adds and deletes* supponit) si possit ad aliqualem commendationem defuncti' (ibid.).
[263] '. . . que ipsius auditores ad mundi contemptum inducunt, predicando uidelicet eis et labores et dolores mundana diligentium, . . . laborem uiuentium et mundana querentium, et dolorem morientium et ea deserentium. Item talia esse uidentur que debet etiam considerare ut predicet que peccatores ad compunctionem reducunt: siue exaggerando peccatorum iniquitatem . . . siue ostendendo peccati uilitatem . . . siue etiam declarando peccati sterilitatem, propter quam peccatores inutiles nec mittunt semina operum nec recolligunt premia fructuum. . . . siue etiam predicando (predicendo *ms*) retributionis calamitatem (calamitates *ms*) . . . Sunt etiam in predicationibus talibus non modicum utilia populo que mortis uel diuini iudicii peccatoribus timorem incutiunt, quia scilicet ex tali timore ad contritionem et penitentiam magis sollicitantur' (ibid.).

which it will certainly be no bad thing to recount to the people, to console those near to him, and as an example of penitence to others.

Tertium[264] autem in predicatore requiritur, ut scilicet in funeribus predicet pro hiis qui mortui sunt, scilicet commendandis: ut uidelicet, si bene uixerunt, eorum laudata opera sint aliis in exemplum. Et tutius quidem est laudare bonos uiros mortuos quam uiuentes . . . [*fo. 1ᵛᵃ*] . . . Si uero qui[265] mortuus fuerit homo non extiterit clare uite uel fame, magis est doctrine uiuentium quam talis defuncti laudibus insixtendum. Inmo, si uite detestabilis[266] fuerit, omnino est cessandum a laude, ne apud eos qui eius uitam nouerunt scandalum potius quam hedificatio generetur, nisi forte de reconciliatione eius et penitentia finali clarum et notum testimonium habeatur, quod certe ad consolationem suorum et ad penitentie aliorum exemplum non reprehensibile[267] erit populo recitare.[268]

In short, while Giovanni does not believe in praising non-existent virtues, he seems entirely in favour of praise in funeral sermons if the dead man's life was praiseworthy.

Federico Franconi da Napoli also believes in praising the dead person. In a memorial sermon for King Charles II of Naples he says that there are three reasons for commemorating the dead to the living (he may have memorial sermons especially in mind here, and can hardly be excluding them), and of these three the first, at least, would seem to involve praise:

The dead are brought back to the memory of the living for three reasons: firstly, by reason of the virtue they had, as is read in the histories of the philosophers and Romans; sometimes by reason of prayer which should be offered up, just as a commemoration is made for all the faithful departed; sometimes by reason of great sanctity, just as there is a memorial [day] for all saints.

Mortui reducuntur ad memoriam uiuorum triplici de causa. Primo ratione uirtutis habite, sicut legitur in Ystoriis philosophorum et Romanorum. Aliquando ratione orationis fiende, sicut fit conmemoratio omnium fidelium defuntorum. Aliquando ratione sanctitatis magne, sicut fit memoria omnium sanctorum.[269]

---

[264] Tertium] Tertio *ms*
[265] qui] *followed by line-filler?*
[266] detestabilis] *ms adds and deletes* erit omnino
[267] reprehensibile] prehensibile *ms*
[268] MS Siena Comunale F. X. 24, fo. 1ʳᵇ⁻ᵛᵃ.
[269] MS Munich, Staatsbibliothek Clm. 2981, fo. 130ᵛᵃ, from a sermon on the text *Memoriam abundantiae suavitatis tuae* (Ps. 144: 7), Schneyer, *Repertorium*, iv. 223, 'Nicolaus de Asculo', No. 217.

The preponderant testimony of the foregoing passages is that memorial preaching in the period is about life as well as death. Examination of the content of the sermons will bear this out. The next two chapters, accordingly, are about attitudes to this world: ideas about kingship in general but also, first, about the way in which the personalities of particular kings were perceived and represented.

# 2   Individuals

IN the Middle Ages, according to a nineteenth-century classic, 'Man was conscious of himself only as a member of a race, people, party, family, or corporation—only through some general category.'[1] Though the idea has been resilient and is still alive in a modern classic,[2] it was pointed out long ago that a Salimbene or a Dante had no difficulty in painting vivid verbal portraits of individual personality.[3] A schematic contrast between 'Middle Ages' and 'Renaissance' or 'Modern Times' is unhelpful here. Nevertheless, the question of how individuality was perceived remains a useful one to put to certain genres, and seems especially appropriate for memorial sermons, above all when they are about historical individuals well known from other sources. To texts of this kind we may in fact put the same kind of questions that can be asked about historical portraits.

A fundamental study of memorial images by G. O. Oexle has argued that liturgical commemoration was by its nature orientated towards individuality—the naming of the dead person's name was crucial to it; accordingly, *Memoria* can be regarded as a condition for the appearance of the individual and finally of the portrait-like representation of persons in works of art.[4] Memorial sermons too were intrinsically linked

---

[1] J. Burckhardt, *The Civilization of the Renaissance in Italy* (New York, 1960 edn.), 121.

[2] A. Gurevich, *Categories of Medieval Culture* (London etc., 1985), 302: 'the individual is known only through what is common to a whole category of persons, not through the organisational centre of his own individual inner life.'

[3] W. Goetz, 'Zur Geschichte des literarischen Porträts', *Historische Zeitschrift*, 92 (1904), 61–72, esp. 69; also his 'Die Quellen zur Geschichte des hl. Franz von Assisi', *Zeitschrift für Kirchengeschichte*, 24 (1903), 165–97, at 195.

[4] Oexle, 'Memoria und Memorialbild', in K. Schmid and J. Wollasch (eds.), *Memoria: Der geschichtliche Zeugniswert des liturgischen Gedenkens im Mittelalter* (Münstersche Mittelalter-Schriften, 48; Munich, 1984), 384–440: 'Im Zentrum der mittelalterlichen . . . Memoria steht die Person des einzelnen Toten, der in der Nennung seines Namens evoziert wird und damit einen sozialen Status erhält. . . . Wenn aber die Namensnennung das konstitutive Moment der Memoria war, so ergibt sich daraus, daß diese ihrem Prinzip nach auf Individualität ausgerichtet gewesen ist' (p. 437); 'Die These, daß es in der Geschichte der europäischen Personendarstellung einen "Übergang" gebe

to liturgical *Memoria*, and it could be argued by analogy that to this extent they also are orientated towards individuality. The sermons would encourage listeners to pray for the dead person, who would presumably matter as an individual to at least some of those present. Again, if the liturgical commemoration was a way of making the dead person in some sense present, the discourse would tend to further this end even if the person was presented only through rather general categories. These inferences seem attractive and plausible, but even if they are granted it need not follow that representing individuality was the only or even the primary function of memorial sermons. That matter must now be investigated on the basis of surviving sermons about real individuals.

It is easier to take in a reproduction of a portrait than the translation of an entire sermon,[5] but an initial effort to make direct contact with the genre must now be asked of the reader. The following sermon in memory of King Edward I of England is one of a set which lay undiscovered until a few years ago in a manuscript of the Bibliotheca Angelica in Rome.[6] It is possible that they were preached in the course of the exequies performed for Edward I at Poitiers in the presence of Pope Clement V in the week ending 28 July 1307.[7] At any rate, we know that the following sermon was addressed to a clerical audience.

---

"vom Typus (!) zum Individuum" im Sinne eines Übergangs vom Typus zum Porträt, dessen Anfänge ins 14. Jahrhundert zu datieren seien, diese These wird man unter sozialgeschichtlichen Aspekten in Frage stellen müssen. Sozialgeschichtliche Sachverhalte mahnen nämlich zur Zurückhaltung gegenüber der These, daß Individualität in der bildlichen Darstellung Lebender und Toter etwas sei, das erst in dem Moment und nur in dem Maß in Erscheinung trat, wie die Memoria verblaßte und an Bedeutung verlor. Sozialgeschichtliche Sachverhalte legen vielmehr die entgegengesetzte Annahme nahe: daß nämlich die Memoria — weil sie ihrem Prinzip nach auf Individualität ausgerichtet war — geradezu als eine Bedingung für das Erscheinen individueller und schließlich porträtähnlicher Personendarstellungen in der Kunst aufgefaßt werden muß' (pp. 438–9).

[5] Entire, that is, as transmitted.

[6] MS Rome, Angelica 158, fos. 156^vb–157^rb, 157^rb–vb, 158^ra–b, 158^rb–va, 158^va–b. The preacher/author is unknown, but it is tempting to suggest that he was Thomas Jorz, OP, who had been Edward I's confessor before being made cardinal in 1305. See *Dictionary of National Biography* (Oxford, 1917–ʻ ), x. 1091 (the entry is by Charles Lethbridge Kingsford).

[7] See W. Ullmann, 'The Curial Exequies for Edward I and Edward III', *Journal of Ecclesiastical History*, 6 (1955), 26–36, at 30.

### Address to the Clergy on the Death of a King

*Alexander reigned for twelve years and died.* Although this text, which is from the first book of Maccabees chapter 1 (8), was said in connection with (*in persona*)[8] Alexander the Great, the king of the Greeks, we may nevertheless conveniently take it for our purpose as being said about our most illustrious lord Edward king of the English, because truly, if his deeds and works were set down in writing (*scriptis*) as the deeds and works of Alexander were recorded in books, Edward's works would appear no less, indeed perhaps more, worthy of praise and splendid than the works and deeds of Alexander.

And we can say that the condition of this most illustrious king is made known and manifest to us in the text in two ways: firstly with respect to the singular excellence of his rule, when it is said in his person: *Alexander ruled for twelve years*; secondly, with respect to the final sentence (*terminatiuam sententiam*) of his end, when *and died* is added.

Firstly, therefore, the condition of that most illustrious king is made known and manifest to us with respect to the singular excellence of his rule, when it is said in connection with him: *Alexander ruled for twelve years.* For if Alexander the Great, king of the Greeks, ruled in the equity of justice, in the power of warring down his enemies, and in energy and wisdom of mind, as the books written about him make clear, we may say with justice that this most illustrious and holy king ruled as Alexander did with respect to these three things. For, firstly, he ruled not with a tyrant's evil character, but with unmixed equity and justice, doing justice to all his subjects, great and small, and administering hard-hitting punishment to those who wished to play the tyrant and act unjustly. Therefore we are justified in expounding with reference to him that text of the Psalm (44: 8): *You have loved justice and hated iniquity, therefore God, your God, has anointed you with the oil of joy beyond your fellows.* For since he loved not just any justice, but legal justice, which is all virtue and all justice, and hated not just any iniquity, but hated that iniquity which is all vice and all injustice, since *all sin is iniquity*, as John says in his canonical epistle (1 John 3: 4; cf. 5: 17), therefore God anointed him as king of that people *with the oil of joy*, that is, with the grace of the Holy Spirit, *beyond* all his *fellows*, that is, beyond all other kings; since, truly, in my [*or* our] times no king's kingdom was made firm and strong with so much justice and so much mercy as was that kingdom through the good rule of this most holy king. Therefore the text of Proverbs 20 (28): *Mercy and justice guard the*

---

[8] I have varied the translation of the recurrent phrase *in persona*.

*king, and his throne will be made strong by mercy,* can be clearly applied to
him.

Secondly, he ruled with the power of warring down his enemies.
For he warred down and overcame the enemies of Christ and holy
mother Church, even exposing himself and his people to peril of
death in order to overcome them. Therefore if it was written of
Alexander, Maccabees book 1 (1: 2–3), that *he killed the kings* of the
peoples, *and crossed to the boundaries of the earth and took the spoils of a
multitude of peoples, and the earth was quiet before him,* much more can it
be said of that most illustrious king that he crossed the boundaries of
the earth, since he traversed *Outremer* and the east to war down the
enemies of Christ and holy mother Church. He also tried to war down
and subdue all who wished to throw his people and commonwealth
into confusion. Therefore we may truly apply to him the text from the
first book of Maccabees chapter 3 (4–5): *He was made like unto a lion in
his works, and like a lion's cub roaring in his hunting. He went after evil
men, and he burnt with flames those who were disturbing his people.*

Thirdly, he ruled with energy and wisdom of mind. For he did not
rule in a frivolous state of mind, nor under the influence of flatterers
and evil counsellors, as many kings do today, but with his mind full
of energy and wisdom and with the prudent counsel of good and wise
men. Therefore we can in truth understand those words to have been
said to him which were said to Solomon in the third book of Kings
chapter 3 (12): *Behold, I have given you a wise and understanding heart* to
rule your people, *insomuch that there has been no one like you before you,
nor will follow after you.* Therefore that most illustrious and holy king
ruled as Alexander did with equity and justice, with the power of
warring down his enemies, and with energy and wisdom of mind. For
this reason his condition is clearly manifested to us with respect to the
outstanding excellence of his rule, when it is said and applied to him
that, firstly, *Alexander ruled twelve years.*

Secondly, his condition is made known to us with respect to the
final sentence of his end, when it is added: *and died.* And we can say
that this most holy and illustrious king died and did not die. For he
died because of the condition of human nature. For since he derived
originally from procreation by the first parents, to whom it was said,
Genesis 3 (3–4):[9] *In what* hour *soever you shall eat of the tree of good and
evil, you shall die the death,* it is necessary that he and every other man
should incur the sentence imposed on them, so that just as everyone
is a sharer in their guilt and transgression, so too everyone should be

---

[9] Genesis 3 (3–4)] closer to Gen. 2: 17.

a sharer in the punishment. Therefore it is written in Ecclesiasticus 8 (8): *we all die, and* want *to attain to* eternal *joy.*[10]

We can say, however, that he is not dead, in that he leaves a good inheritance, because he has left us good heirs from his seed and a good first-born son who should rule in his place over that kingdom; may the lord Jesus Christ deign to anoint him with the oil of his grace, so that he may be able to follow in the footsteps of his father in equity and justice, in the power of warring down his enemies, and in energy and wisdom of mind, that we might be able to say of him the words that are written in Ecclesiasticus 30 (4): *His father is dead, and it is as if he is not dead, for he has left one like to himself on earth.*

Similarly, we can say that he is not dead, in that he participates in eternal life, since, though he is dead with respect to this animal and bodily life, yet we should firmly believe that he may live (*uiuat*) with Christ with respect to spiritual and eternal life. May this be granted to him and to us by Christ, who with the Father, etc.[11]

The extent to which this represents Edward I's individuality can be best judged by bringing into play what historians have learnt about his personality and also by drawing comparisons with representations of him in other genres. We think of Edward as a legislator, the most important since Henry II.[12] The preacher may have had Edward's legislation in mind when he says that he 'loved not just any justice, but legal justice'. The reference to his 'energy and wisdom of mind', and to his reliance on 'the prudent counsel of good and wise men' is also a defensible interpretation of Edward's political character. Edward did indeed choose able advisers, and he valued their opinion.[13] Sir Maurice Powicke wrote eloquently about this:

In the years before the Hundred Years War, clerical advisers and agents whose memories went back to the time of Edward I looked back to it 'as the one understandable period in their official careers',

---

[10] 'omnes morimur et in gaudium eternum uolumus peruenire'. Contrast the Vulgate reading 'omnes morimur et in gaudium nolumus uenire' ('we all die, and are not willing that others should rejoice at our death').

[11] See Transcription C:a.

[12] On his legislation see M. Prestwich, *Edward I* (London, 1988), ch. 10. This is now the standard biography of Edward, based as it is on a thorough exploration of the manuscript sources. F. M. Powicke's *King Henry III and the Lord Edward* (2 vols.; Oxford, 1947) remains valuable for its insights.

[13] On Edward's council see Prestwich, *Edward I*, 436–40.

when plans could be made effective and things could be done. They doubtless had too rosy a view, but in the main they were right. King Edward was well served, and especially happy in his relations with his servants during the sixteen years after his coronation when Burnell was chancellor, and the class of 'king's clerks', to which Burnell belonged, was busy in all sorts of ways and even conscious of itself as the *élite* element in the personnel of royal administration.[14]

Effective co-operation with Robert Burnell and others would appear to lie behind Edward's achievements in the legal sphere.[15] The claim of the preacher that Edward did justice to all his subjects, great and small, would not be easy to defend today. It has been plausibly argued that he went beyond what was permitted by the standards of the time in his acquisitive policy towards the earls.[16] The view of the leading specialist on Edward is that he 'was fully prepared to bend the law to suit his own interests, but . . . felt strongly about corruption and miscarriages of justice', as when he 'wrote a severe letter to the Earl of Cornwall, his lieutenant in England, on behalf of a laundress who had followed him abroad to complain that she had not received justice in a rape plea'.[17] If we make allowance for the rosy tint almost inescapable in the genre of memorial sermons, the preacher's remarks about justice and good counsellors look more realistic and less of a stereotype than they might seem to be if we knew nothing about the deceased. Because we know a lot about a king like Edward, the modern reader of a text such as this is a little nearer to the position of a contemporary listener—personally acquainted with the deceased—than can often be the case with surviving memorial sermons.

In selecting Edward's martial qualities for emphasis the preacher is giving an equally or perhaps still more realistic picture. Edward was on crusade when he inherited the throne— hence the reference to 'Outremer'—and though he did not achieve much, his international reputation was enhanced.[18]

[14] F. M. Powicke, *The Thirteenth Century, 1216–1307* (London, 1964), 340.

[15] Ibid. 339–40; Prestwich, *Edward I*, 269–70; id., *The Three Edwards: War and State in England 1272–1377* (London, 1980), 21–2.

[16] K. B. McFarlane, 'Had Edward I a Policy towards the Earls?', *History*, 50 (1965), 145–59.

[17] Prestwich, *The Three Edwards*, 22.

[18] Id., *Edward I*, 81; Powicke, *King Henry III*, ii. 688.

Giovanni Villani, recording Edward's death in his *Cronica*, calls him 'bene avventuroso' in his enterprise against the Saracens in Outremer, as also against the Scots and in Gascony against the French.[19] Our preacher may be referring to these, among other wars, when he says that Edward 'tried to war down and subdue all who wished to throw his people and commonwealth into confusion'. As for the comparison with Alexander the Great, it was apt enough, once we remember that the Alexander of medieval romance, rather than 'our' classical Alexander, is in question.[20]

Thus the sermon *Regnauit Alexander* gives a definite 'likeness' of Edward I. The virtues singled out are conventional enough, but then, as Powicke said, 'he was a consistent and also a very conventional Christian in his outlook on life',[21] 'a conventional man in an age of change'.[22] All the same, one could say of this sermon that 'the individual is known only through what is common to a whole category of persons, not through the organisational centre of his own individual inner life'.[23] The 'likeness' is achieved by emphasizing virtues which kings in general were expected to aspire to but which Edward possessed to a higher degree than usual.

Another sermon in memory of Edward I, in the same manuscript and possibly by the same author, comes a little closer to the 'individual inner life'.[24] The preacher takes a long time to get on to the subject of Edward himself, but when he does so he shows what many scholars may feel to be real insight:

Among all the kings and princes there have been in our times who would have wished to know much about the changes and variations

[19] 'Nel detto anno MCCCVII, del mese di giugno, morì il buono e valente Adoardo re d'Inghilterra, il quale fue uno de' valorosi signori e savio de' Cristiani al suo tempo, e bene aventuroso in ogni sua impresa di là da mare contra i Saraceni, e in suo paese contra gli Scotti, e in Guascogna contro a' Franceschi' (Giovanni Villani, *Nuova cronica*, 9. 90, ed. G. Porta (3 vols.; Parma, 1990–1), ii. 177).

[20] G. Cary, *The Medieval Alexander* (Cambridge, 1956); D. J. A. Ross, *Alexander Historiatus: A Guide to Medieval Illustrated Alexander Literature* (London, 1963); F. Avril and P. Stirnemann, *Manuscrits enluminés d'origine insulaire, viiᵉ–xxᵉ siècle* (Paris, 1987), notice 171, p. 137.

[21] Powicke, *The Thirteenth Century*, 228.

[22] Ibid. 230.

[23] See above, ch. 2 n. 2.

[24] MS Rome, Angelica 158, fo. 157^{rb–vb}: Transcription C:b.

of the world, he stood out,[25] in that he never knew how to be at rest, and carried out that which is written in Ecclesiastes 9 (10): *Whatsoever your hand is able to do, do it instantly. For he leaned down from this to that,* crossing from England to Spain, being knighted there with honour, travelling, indeed, at one time right through *Outremer,* subduing enemies of Christ there with his power; at one time or other also to Wales, to Flanders, to Scotland, and to Gascony, setting out himself with his people, enlarging and augmenting his kingdom. Similarly he *leaned down from this to that,* that is, from a magnificent condition to a small one, for in his deeds he wished to seem at one moment a king, at another a knight, at another an esquire, at another a rich man, at another a poor man; at one moment a judge casting down the powerful, at another an advocate freeing the poor.[26]

The historian's own mental picture of Edward will affect their estimate of this likeness,[27] but it does not look ready-made; indeed, it seems a genuine attempt to penetrate below the surface of the dead king's personality. In one way it is more effective than a visual portrait could easily be, for it conveys a strong sense of the movement in Edward's life.

Yet if we juxtapose either of these sermons with the literary portrait by Nicholas Trevet, in his *Annales,* they look pale and abstract.[28] Trevet not only describes Edward's appearance, but also how it changed over time: his hair was light and silvery when he was a boy, turned very dark in manhood, and eventually became as white as a swan. He knows how to pick out detail: the lisp, the droop of the left eyelid. Edward's character and spirit are illustrated by a vivid anecdote.

Once, when he was engaged in catching birds with falcons by a river, he gave a dressing down to one of his companions on the other side of the river who was not attending properly to a falcon which had caught a duck in some willows. When the man didn't seem to take

---

[25] A free translation of 'ipse fuit unus'.

[26] Transcription C:b, **3**: 3–5.

[27] '. . . he never knew how to be at rest': again it is worth quoting Powicke: 'His quick response to every occasion, whether this were a casual difficulty or a public scandal or emergency, was informed by a sense of obligation' (*The Thirteenth Century*, 228). On the other hand: 'Yet in spite of his energy there was a dreamy, slothful strain in him' (ibid.).

[28] Powicke saw the value of Trevet's portrait and incorporated a close paraphrase of it into his own: *King Henry III*, ii. 686–7, after Trevet's *Annales*, ed. T. Hog (London, 1845), 281–3.

enough notice, he added threats. But the man realized that there was no bridge or ford nearby, and replied somewhat flippantly that it was enough for him that they had a river between them. Provoked by this, the king's son [*Edward had not yet succeeded to the throne*] crossed the river on his horse, which had to swim—Edward had plunged into the water without knowing its depth. With difficulty, he climbed the channel's bank, which had been hollowed out by the rushing of the river, and, pulling out his sword, he pursued the other, who had already mounted his horse[29] and fled. In the end, despairing of escape by flight, the man pulled his horse round, bared his head, put his neck forward, and surrendered himself to Edward to do with as he wished. At this, the anger of the king's son subsided[30] and he put his sword back in his scabbard; and the two returned from there peacefully and dealt with the falcon they had left.[31]

We note how Trevet helps the imagination by filling in concrete details—the overhanging bank, the horse pulled round, etc.—and the story perfectly makes his points about Edward's impatience of injuries, oblivion to danger, and willingness to abandon his resentment.[32] This story and the rest of Trevet's portrait make the sermons examined above look rather abstract.

We find much the same if we compare the sermons with a quite different sort of text, the *Commendatio lamentabilis* on Edward attributed to one 'John of London'.[33] Its eminent editor remarked that it 'has no particular merit of its own' and that 'its illustrations are hackneyed and threadbare', but he could also justly point out that 'there is scarcely a characteristic feature of the king and his reign that is not in one way or another touched upon for praise'.[34] John of London invents a series of laments by different individuals and classes of people: the pope, other kings, Edward's widow, bishops, earls, barons, knights, clergy, and laity.[35] This is actually an effective tech-

[29] Assuming that 'jam equo conscenso' does not refer to Edward.
[30] '... ab impetu suo fractus'. One might also interpret the phrase, as Powicke does (*Henry III*, 687), to mean that Edward checked his horse.
[31] Trevet, *Annales*, pp. 282–3 Hog; cf. Powicke, *Henry III*, 687.
[32] 'Inerat ei animus magnificus, injuriarum impatiens, periculorum obliuisci cogens dum uindicari cuperet, qui tamen facile humilitate exhibita potuit emolliri' (Trevet, *Annales*, p. 282 Hog).
[33] In *Chronicles of the Reigns of Edward I and Edward II*, ed. W. Stubbs, ii (Rolls Series; London, 1883), 3–21.
[34] Ibid., pp. xiii and xviii.
[35] For a good summary both of the laments and of the description of Edward which precedes them, see Stubbs's introduction, ibid., pp. xiv–xviii.

nique, structurally similar to that used by Orson Welles in the film *Citizen Kane*. We see Edward reflected, as it were, in the eyes of many different people. Stubbs called the *Commendatio* 'a sort of mortuary Éloge or funeral sermon on the death of Edward I',[36] but in its manner of representation (as opposed to the values it emphasizes) it does not have much in common with the sermons on Edward's death in MS Angelica 158, and on the whole it would give anyone not already informed a more concrete picture of the man than these two sermons do.

There are three further sermons on the death of Edward in the same manuscript,[37] but on the whole these give less rather than more of a sense of Edward's personality than the ones we have considered. A sermon on the text *Rex in eternum uiue* (Dan. 3: 9) says that

after he was made king of that people he did not live by unspiritual and fleshly and animal desires, but by the workings of his intellect. . . . Secondly, he lived with his subjects through the observation of justice and merciful compassion. . . . The poor, too, could always look to him for protection and relief . . . he not only protected and defended the faith of Christ in his people and in his realm, but, like Christ's champion and warrior, he travelled through *Outremer* to war down the Saracens and rebels against the Church and unbelievers, exposing his body and the bodies of his subjects to danger.[38]

It is on the mark as far as it goes—we have Edward's crusading, good justice, and unscandalous private life[39]—but it is less personalized than, at any rate, the second of the two sermons analysed above.

A sermon on the text *Quoniam rex sperauit* (Ps. 20: 8) says that Edward understood and delighted in the words of God, detested sins and vices, and did good works, observing the commandments of God and providing relief when it was needed by his neighbours.[40] The sermon on the text *In uirtute tua domine* (Ps. 20: 2) claims that he 'rejoiced in the strength of God, which in this life never deserted him in adverse circum-

[36] Ibid., p. vii.
[37] Transcriptions C:c, C:d, and C:e.
[38] Transcription C:e, **5:** 1–7: 1.
[39] 'Edward appears to have been remarkably faithful to his queens': Prestwich, *Edward I*, 131.
[40] Transcription C:d, **3:** 6–9.

stances, because although he was surrounded by many dangers, at sea and on land and among Saracens and Christians, he was none the less never abandoned by the strength of God, but was saved from them all'.[41] Still, 'he had not been raised up to pride in the midst of the successes and victories of this world, but, rather, humbled',[42] and he had purified his conscience through contrition and by receiving the sacraments.[43] All this makes interesting reading, but if his representation has the same aim as Trevet's, then it is less successful by a long way.

By this point readers may feel that they are receiving conflicting signals. At first attention was drawn to sermons or parts of sermons which realistically portray aspects of Edward's personality, but then it was argued that even these passages do not give nearly such a full picture of his individuality as do Nicholas Trevet or 'John of London', while the other sermons on Edward in MS Angelica 158 fall even further short of this standard. However, there is not necessarily a contradiction here. It may be proposed as a working hypothesis that preachers of memorial sermons in this period were capable of representing individual character traits successfully, but that they did not try to do this systematically or all the time, for reasons which we must try to elucidate after reviewing some more evidence.

So we may turn to a sermon on the death of Edward I's relative and rival, King Philip IV, preached by the Florentine Dominican Remigio de' Girolami.[44] The likelihood must be that it was preached at Florence, but at some point before 1303 Remigio had been sent to Paris to lecture on the *Sentences* of Peter Lombard,[45] so there must be a high probability that he had lived there when Philip was already king.

---

[41] Transcription C:c, **3**: 1.

[42] Transcription C:c, **4**: 1.

[43] Transcription C:c, **5**: 1–2. I am not sure whether the preacher had in mind Edward's habitual practice, or the way he met his end.

[44] There is a large literature on Remigio. See especially E. Panella, 'Per lo studio di Fra Remigio dei Girolami (†1319): *Contra falsos ecclesie professores* cc. 5–37', *Memorie domenicane*, NS 10 (1979), *passim*, and the preface by C. T. Davis to Remigio's *Contra falsos ecclesie professores*, ed. F. Tamburini ('Utrumque Ius', Collectio Pontificiae Universitatis Lateranensis, 6; Rome, 1981).

[45] Cf. Davis's preface (n. 44), p. iii: 'Fra Remigio . . . taught at S. Maria Novella in Florence for most of the period from about 1273 until a few years before his death there in 1319', and p. iv: 'We know of only two long absences from the city that can be confidently attributed to Remigio after he took up his

As with the texts already examined, one cannot answer the question 'Does it portray the king's individuality?' with a straight 'yes' or 'no'. Philip is described as 'fair (*pulcher*) in body and soul, since he was abstinent, generous to the poor, (*elemosinarius*), a hearer of the [liturgical] Office and of sermons, and always had a special confessor, etc. Again, he was truthful and taciturn in speech, mild in his behaviour: example about the lady of Provence [provincial lady?] who called him dumb; and just in his expeditions or deeds.'[46] This is compressed, and one could comment upon it at length.

As with Edward, one's feelings about the portrait depend on one's feelings about the original. Scholars notoriously disagree about Philip. The basic facts of his reign are not in dispute, and one could hardly improve on a summary of them written in 1329:

Philip was a handsome man. During almost all his reign he waged war with the Flemings and the king of England, leading his people to complain because of the many different exactions which he imposed on his subjects and because of the manifold mutations of the coinage, to which he excessively attended. He expelled the Jews from the kingdom; he brought the Templars to nothing. He also had his grandfather Louis canonized by Pope Boniface, with whom later all was not well.[47]

lectorate in the early 1270's. One was at Paris at an undetermined date, but before Boniface VIII's death in 1303, where Remigio went to read the *Sentences* and thereby qualify for the *magisterium*. The second was at the papal court in Perugia, probably from early 1304 at least to late 1305.' Panella, 'Per lo studio . . .', 230, does not commit himself to a location for the sermon (and on the same page, apropos of another sermon, he raises the possibility that Remigio was in France at some point between 5 June 1305, and 14 April 1314).

[46] '. . . pulcher in corpore et in anima, quia abstinens, quia elemosinarius, quia auditor officii et predicationum, quia habebat semper confessorem specialem &c. item fuit uerus et taciturnus in sermonibus, mansuetus in moribus: exemplum de domina provinciali que uocauit eum mutum; et iustus in expeditionibus seu operibus' (G. Salvadori and V. Federici, 'I sermoni d'occasione, le sequenze e i ritmi di Remigio Girolami fiorentino', in *Scritti vari di filologia: A Ernesto Monaci gli scolari (1876–1901)* (Rome, 1901), 455–508, at 492; a substantial sample of Remigio's *de mortuis* sermons are printed in this article).

[47] Pierre Jacob of Montpellier, trans. E. A. R. Brown in 'Persona et Gesta: The Image and Deeds of the Thirteenth-century Capetians, 3. The Case of Philip the Fair', *Viator*, 19 (1988), 219–38, at 221.

The great debate is about Philip's relation to his counsellors: did they control the king, or vice versa?[48] However, if one leaves aside this particular issue, which Remigio's sermon (unsurprisingly) does not touch upon, there is a good deal of consensus in modern work on Philip, and it tends to confirm that Remigio's portrait is accurate so far as it goes. That he was 'taciturn in speech' is agreed, whether it was because he was 'incapable de s'extérioriser'[49] or because he had learnt from the *Secretum secretorum* to abstain from speaking much.[50] Historians who disagree about his influence on policy converge to emphasize his piety. According to Elizabeth Brown, 'Philip's inordinate fear of sinning and of being chastised by the church led him to secure a host of unusual papal dispensations for deeds he had committed or thought he might commit and to take extraordinary measures to justify actions (including wars) whose legitimacy he judged might be questioned.'[51] Whether or not he was objectively 'just in his expeditions or deeds', this sort of justice entered largely into his thinking. Bautier has documented his religious foundations and his other charities.[52] Philip could indeed be called *elemosinarius*. Moreover, there is a

---

[48] For a recent restatement of the former view, systematically supported by diplomatic evidence, see R.-H. Bautier, 'Diplomatique et histoire politique: Ce que la critique diplomatique nous apprend sur la personnalité de Philippe le Bel', *Revue historique*, 259 (1978), 3–27: 'Jusqu'à la défaite de Courtrai, le roi semble peu appliqué aux affaires' (p. 15); after the defeat Philip was 'galvanisé pour venger l'humiliation' (p. 16); however, 'le roi s'est laissé jeter le grappin par un personnage inquiétant et qui va avoir sur lui une influence déterminante, Nogaret' (p. 17). I prefer this interpretation, but for a fascinating restatement of the idea that Philip was his own master see Brown, 'The Case of Philip the Fair', which is full of other insights into the reign. For general surveys of the reign see J. Strayer, *The Reign of Philip the Fair* (Princeton, 1980), and J. Favier, *Philippe le Bel* (Paris, 1978).
[49] Bautier, 'Diplomatique', 27.
[50] Brown, 'The Case of Philip the Fair', 233, draws attention to this teaching and points out that one of Philip's most trusted notaries owned a copy of the work.
[51] Ibid. 235.
[52] Bautier, 'Diplomatique', 20–2 (on other gifts to the church, ibid. 19, 21). For Bautier, the years 1308–10, 'marquées par toutes ces fondations royales, sont significatives de la montée de la religiosité du roi: le souci de son âme et de celle de sa défunte épouse devient sa préoccupation essentielle' (ibid. 20–1). On his lavish testamentary bequests see Brown, 'The Case of Philip the Fair', 235.

striking similarity between Remigio's characterization of Philip's
piety and the description of it by a monk of Saint-Denis, who
also speaks of his devotion to worship and to abstinence (and
tells us that his confessor used to administer the discipline to
him with a little chain).[53]

The oddest part of Remigio's miniature is the phrase 'mild in
behaviour' (*mansuetus in moribus*), illustrated by the enigmatic
allusion to the lady who called him dumb. This was the reign
in which the Templars, perhaps the hardest body of knights in
the history of the West, broke down in France *en masse* under
torture, when Pope Boniface VIII was remorselessly pursued
even after death, and when the alleged lovers of Philip's
daughters-in-law were flayed alive, castrated, quartered, and
hanged in front of the whole Court.[54] As for the woman who
called him dumb, one is immediately reminded of Bishop
Bernard Saisset's comparison between Philip and the owl,
which does not respond but simply passes air;[55] but in the case
of Saisset the outcome was his arrest (with the final struggle
between Philip and Boniface VIII as sequel). Remigio's exemplum presumably told a different kind of story. Is Remigio
then wildly off the mark? Not necessarily. The monk of Saint-
Denis also describes Philip as *mansuetus*, and explains the
tension between his mildness and his political actions (admittedly, here, his financial exactions) by his excessive trustful-
ness towards his counsellors, whom he believed to be more
like himself than perhaps they were.[56]

---

[53] '. . . humilitate ac mansuetudine praecipuus, a turpibus auditum auertens
sermonibus, ad Dei seruitium audiendum ordinateque fiendum sedulus et
deuotus; abstinentiae deditus, utpote feria secunda et quarta a carnibus
abstinens; feria sexta, abjectis piscibus et lacticiniis, solis pulmentis contentus.
Cilicio carnem frangens, eamque pluribus disciplinis per manum confessoris
cum quadam cathenula deuote susceptis edomans, a multis annis pro camisia
ueste linea utebatur. Et quia cum bonis operibus in aduersisque regni sui
euentibus cordis et labiorum seruauit munditiam, ipsum habuisse amicum
credimus Christum regem' (in *Recueil des historiens des Gaules et de la France*, ed.
M. Bouquet *et al.*, xxi (Paris, 1855), 205; according to Bautier, 'Diplomatique',
22, the name of the monk is not Guillelmus Scotus but 'Yves').

[54] Cf. Bautier, 'Diplomatique', 23.

[55] Brown, 'The Case of Philip the Fair', 228 (her English wording).

[56] 'Humilium namque ac mansuetorum, nulli male consulere uolentium, esse
uidetur ut aliis faciliter adsentiant, credentes alios non sibi uelle male consulere, sicut nec aliis male consulere ipsi uellent. Mansuetus itaque et humilis
rex Philippus, ex suae conscientiae fidelitate consiliariorum suorum, in praefatis

This makes Remigio's judgement look more plausible. Even if wrong, a writer in a better position to know (presumably) could make the same mistake. (In fact it may not be a mistake. The interpretation of the Saint-Denis monk, transferred to the sinister *causes célèbres* of the reign, seems at least to be the most charitable explanation of Philip's part in them.[57])

All things considered, therefore, Remigio's miniature is a reasonable likeness of the public image of Philip's personality,[58] if one may so put it. Accurate or not, however, it can hardly be said to dominate the sermon. The passage which surrounds the portrait is about the (impersonal) power of the king of France. According to Remigio, the French king is most powerful (*potentissimus*) in five ways: with respect to the breadth (*latitudinem*) of his kingdom; the great size of the population; the valour of its knights (*militie strenuitatem*); overflowing wealth (*opulentie ubertatem*); and his, the king's, position at the top of

---

suum forte commodum plus quam regis quaerentium, fidelitatem mensurans et judicans, eisdem ad talia facienda plus quam oporteret credidit et consentit' (*Recueil des historiens . . .* , xxi. 205). See also Ch.-V. Langlois, *Saint Louis. — Philippe le Bel: Les Derniers Capétiens directs, 1226–1328* (Histoire de la France depuis les origines jusqu'à la Révolution, ed. E. Lavisse, 3/2; Paris, 1901), 121, 123. Cf. The story quoted by Elizabeth Brown (who does not commit herself to its truth) that 'Uidi regem Francorum salutantem in Piccardia tres uilissimos ribaldos qui inclinabant se illi, et uolentes illi loqui equitare ad latus ejus et ipsum singulos patienter audire' ('The Case of Philip the Fair', 229 and n. 45).

[57] I am glossing over some crucial but perhaps unanswerable questions, especially: Did Philip knowingly 'frame' the Templars as sodomites, sorcerers, blasphemers, and idolators? This involves not only the question 'How much did Philip's aides tell him?', but also the question 'How much truth was there in the accusations?' There are good historians who feel that there was some fire behind the smoke, but I am swayed by the argument which Heinrich Finke formulated long ago: 'Wer jetzt noch für die Wahrheit der Anklagepunkte eintritt, der muß auch den Mut haben, seinen Glauben an die Erscheinung des Teufels in Gestalt eines Katers bei den Templerfesten zu bekunden; denn dessen Erscheinen, und zuweilen auch seine Buhlschaft mit ihnen in Gestalt einer schönen Frau, haben, wie wir jetzt wissen . . . , zahlreiche, wahrscheinlich Dutzende von Templern ebenso bejaht und beschworen wie die andern Anklagepunkte' (*Papsttum und Untergang des Templerordens* (2 vols.; Vorreformationsgeschichtliche Forschungen, 4; Münster am Wien, 1907), vol. i, p. x). See also M. Barber, *The Trial of the Templars* (Cambridge, 1978).

[58] Cf. Brown's account of descriptions of Philip which his ministers presented to Clement V, in 'The Case of Philip the Fair', 234–5, especially the phrase 'persona . . . mansueta' (ibid. 235 n. 75), and her remark that 'Their delineation is a verbal icon, an abbreviated Mirror of Princes, intended, like the statues of Philip the Fair, for public view' (ibid. 234).

# 84 Chapter 2

# 84 Chapter 2

the hierarchy (*praesidentie sublimitatem*), since he has the kings of England, Navarre, and Apulia beneath him—because they hold land from him—and no kings above him.[59] The miniature of Philip is somehow introduced into the section on the kingdom's wealth.[60] Moreover, this celebration of the French monarchy's greatness is balanced, and its significance transformed, by the second part of the sermon, which is about mutability and transitoriness.[61] So even if Remigio does convey a good deal about Philip's personality, the likeness would seem to be quite subsidiary to his main argument.

In Remigio's sermon on the death of Philip's successor Louis X (d. 1316) the king's individuality does not even make the subordinate but intense appearance that Philip's does in the sermon just examined—perhaps because Louis X was a less intense personality.[62] The sermon is fascinating for its analysis of the differences between kingship and tyranny, and we shall return to it in the next chapter, but it seems to have little to say about Louis's personality except that he was young and that he made efforts to ensure that the Church got a pope.[63] This must

[59] p. 492 Salvadori and Federici.
[60] A quotation from Psalms seems to be the link in the train of thought: 'quarto, quantum ad opulentie ubertatem, iuxta illud psalmi: "Potentissime, specie tua et pulchritudine tua intende, prospere procede et regna; propter ueritatem et mansuetudinem et iustitiam; et deducet te mirabiliter dextera tua". ubi nota quod bis nominat pulcritudinem' (ibid.). Read by someone without knowledge of Philip IV's image in the early 14th cent., Remigio's analysis (which follows at that point) of Philip might seem to be derived solely from the biblical text. In reality, Remigio probably selected a text which encapsulated things he felt he could say about Philip.
[61] For an analysis of the highly compressed and interesting train of ideas see D. L. d'Avray, 'The Comparative Study of Memorial Preaching', *Transactions of the Royal Historical Society*, 5th ser., 40 (1990), 25–42, at 31–2.
[62] '. . . he seems to have been a weak and ineffectual figure . . .' (Elizabeth M. Hallam, *Capetian France 987–1328* (London and New York, 1980), 283.)
[63] '. . . circa secundum nota quod ipse uidet Dominum per sincerissimam fidem, unde sollicitissime procurabat quod fideles haberent caput, idest papam' (p. 493 Salvadori and Federici). The passage continues: 'Dicitur prima Co(r). 13 (12): *Uidemus nunc per spe(culum) in e(nigmate).* Et in hoc habuit animi fortitudinem, iuxta illud prima Pe(tri) 5 (9): *cui,* scilicet diabolo, *resistite fortes in fide'* (MS Florence, Nazionale Conv. soppr. G. 4. 936, fo. 389ʳ, upper margin). It should be said here that Salvadori and Federici print only a little of this sermon, which begins in the right-hand margin of fo. 388ʳ, continues in the lower margin of this page, then leaps to the upper margin of fo. 389ʳ, continuing in margins until it finally ends on fo. 390ᵛ. This arrangement and the reasons for it are elegantly set out in E. Panella, 'Un Sermone in morte della moglie di

be an allusion to the election of Pope John XXII. The account in the textbooks is that it was Louis's brother Philip 'le long' who chivvied the cardinals into finally electing a pope.[64] Perhaps Remigio knew better, but it seems more probable that he was giving Louis credit for his brother's activity. Either way, we do not get much in the way of verbal portraiture.

The same may be said of the surviving summaries of sermons on royal personages by that youthful prelate, Don Juan, the son of King James II of Aragon.[65] (Before his death in 1334 at the age of (probably) 33, Juan had been archbishop of Toledo, archbishop of Tarragona, and patriarch of Alexandria.[66]) Although he was preaching about relatives, one would pick up almost nothing about their characters from these sermons.

Among these relatives—the sermon rubric makes the point explicitly[67]—was Philip V of France, the same who pressurized the cardinals into choosing a pope. There is nothing at all

Guido Novello o di Beatrice d'Angio?', *Memorie domenicane*, NS 12 (1981), 294–301, at 299–300. Panella and another will edit the series to which this sermon belongs, but in the meantime I have read it on microfilm. The only other passage which seems to come at all close to Louis X's personality is an omission supplied in the left-hand margin of fo. 389[r] (apparently attached to the section on *mors luctuosa*): 'Et sic est mors istius regis propter multa: tum quia iuuenis et quia sine prole mascula; tum quia sollicitissimus pro papa fiendo, tum etiam propter uxorem iuuenculam de cetero innubilem.' (The last three words have come out badly on microfilm, so I have made my best guess. It is not clear what they mean, though it is true that Louis X's widow, Clemence of Hungary, did not remarry: see the notice by M. Prevost in *Dictionnaire de biographie française* (1933– ), viii (1959), 1419–20.)

[64] H.-G. Beck, K. A. Fink, *et al.*, *From the High Middle Ages to the Eve of the Reformation* (Handbook of Church History, ed. H. Jedin and J. Dolan, 4; New York and London, 1970), 308; G. Mollat, *Les Papes d'Avignon, 1305–1378* (Paris, 1930), 42.

[65] See above, ch. 1, at nn. 212–13. I have read the sermons discussed below in a microfilm of MS Valencia, Cat. 182. Though I have not been able to obtain Ignacio de Janer, *El patriarca Don Juan de Aragón, su vida y sus obras (1301–1334)* (Tarragona, 1904), which, to judge by entry NJ 0042366 in the US National Union Catalogue, was printed in only 100 copies, my friend Dr Dillwyn Knox has examined a copy in the New York Public Library, and tells me that Janer does not edit the sermons in question.

[66] J. Ernesto Martínez Ferrando, *Jaime II de Aragón: Su vida familiar* (2 vols.; Consejo Superior de Investigaciones Científicas, Escuela de Estudios Medievales, Estudios 9–10; Barcelona, 1948), i. 151.

[67] 'Item de mortuis: pro Rege Franc. Philippo consanguineo suo' (MS Valencia, Cat. 182, fo. 128[vb], sermon on the text *Spiritus domini rapuit Philippum* . . . (Acts 8: 39); Schneyer, *Repertorium*, iii. 314, No. 257).

about this, nor anything else specific to Philip, in the sermon, which, as transmitted to us, contains nothing but two theological schemata and scriptural texts to back them up.[68] The sermon in memory of another Philip, Juan's maternal uncle the prince of Taranto (son of Charles II of Anjou and Naples, who was Juan's grandfather), gives only a little more detail. Juan calls him the 'most distinguished prince of Taranto, who was a very great prince among the people of Christendom, with respect both to the renown of his line and to the power of his lordship, and to the abundance of his possessions'.[69] He tells us that Philip is buried at the convent of the Dominicans.[70] Philip I, prince of Taranto, is indeed buried in S. Domenico Maggiore at Naples, which shows us that Juan was well informed.[71] Not a lot is made of any inside knowledge he may have had. We are informed that 'Although he was a great and powerful prince, still death did not spare him, for death, as Boethius says in the second book of the *Consolation*, spurns high glory, envelopes equally the humble and the high head, and makes the greatest heights equal to the lowest depths.'[72] Philip is being used as a vehicle for a message about the universality of death. Juan continues to present him in this way—more as an exemplum

---

[68] The theological schemata (if the phrase is not too grandiose) are as follows: (1) 'Tria describuntur: diuine uoluntatis adimpletio . . . ; mundane calamitatis euasio . . . ; superne felicitatis adeptio . . .' (MS Valencia, Cat. 182, fo. 128$^{vb}$); (2) 'Rapuit eum Christus de:—luto criminalis corruptionis per gratiam iustificantem;—bello hostilis temptationis per gratiam adiuuantem;—puteo penalis afflictionis per gratiam glorificantem' (ibid.).

[69] 'Item pro mortuis: pro domino Philippo principe Tarentino auunculo suo. *Princeps et maximus cecidit hodie in Israel* ii R(eg.) iii° (38). Uerba proposita dicta a Dauid rege de morte principis Abner congrue [*fo. 128$^{ra}$*] applicari possunt ad loquendum de morte precelsi principis Tarentini, qui princeps maximus tam generis claritate quam dominii potestate et possessionum facultate extitit in populo christiano' (MS Valencia, Cat. 182, fos. 127$^{vb}$–128$^{ra}$; Schneyer, *Repertorium*, iii. 314, No. 255).

[70] 'Potuerunt etiam dicere predicatores apud quos sepultus est' (MS Valencia, Cat. 182, fo. 128$^{ra}$).

[71] See T. Kaeppeli, 'Note sugli scrittori domenicani di nome Giovanni di Napoli', *AFP* 10 (1940), 48–76, at 61.

[72] 'Quamuis magnus princeps et potens, tamen non pepercit ei mors, que, ut dicit Boetius, ii° *De Consol.*, spernit altam gloriam, inuoluit humile pariter et celsum capud, equatque summa infimis' (MS Valencia, Cat. 182, fo. 128$^{ra}$). The Boethius reference is to *Philosophiae consolatio*, 2, M. 7, ll. 12–14, ed. L. Bieler (CCSL 94; Turnhout, Brepols, 1957), 34 (for 'summa infimis' in Juan, the edition has 'summis infima').

than as an individual. The sermon as we have it is, in a sense, not about him at all. Thus, in the first subsection of the second principal section, the idea that each man falls from grace into guilt is developed as follows:

On the first fall, Matthew 17 (14): the father of the lunatic boy said to the Lord: *Lord, have pity on my son, because he is a lunatic and suffers much, for he often falls into the fire and frequently into water.* We are lunatics, since we put our faith in the earthly things which fail us, and thus we frequently fall into the fire of avarice and the water of lust. But that lord, even if he fell—because there is no man who is without sin—yet through penance he rose again. This is what we should do.[73]

Though quite a close relative, Philip lived a long way away (as did his more distant relative Philip V of France), so the impersonal tone is not particularly surprising. It is a little odder in sermons about his immediate family. The historian's pulse quickens in anticipation of human interest at the sight of the rubrics 'For his deceased father the king and for the king, his brother, succeeding to the throne',[74] and 'on the anniversary of his parents',[75] but the individuality is tuned out here as well. The sermon on his father and his brother (Alfonso IV) would seem to have been delivered where the former was buried or perhaps in the presence of the body before burial. Juan does say a little about his father, but the level is abstract, as the following passage shows:

On the second point: the judgement of God is twofold, that is, the one of rigorous justice, and the one of loving mercy. We do not ask for the first for our lord king; indeed, we say with him (Ps. 142: 2): *enter not into judgement with your servant,* etc. For we know it to be written

---

[73] 'De primo casu, Mathei xvii° (14) dixit pater pueri lunatici Domino: *Domine, miserere filio meo, quia lunaticus est et male patitur: nam sepe cadit in ignem et crebro in aquam.* Lunatici sumus, quia in defectu terrenorum confidimus, et sic in ignem auaritie et aquam luxurie frequenter cadimus. Set iste dominus, etsi cecidit—quia non est homo qui non peccet—tamen per penitentiam resurrexit. Ita debemus facere' (MS Valencia, Cat. 182, fo. 128^{ra}).

[74] 'Item de mortuis: pro rege (Re *ms?*) patre suo defuncto et rege fratre suo succedente' (MS Valencia, Cat. 182, fo. 128^{rb}, sermon on the text *Deus iudicium tuum regi da* . . . (Ps. 71: 1); Schneyer, *Repertorium*, iii. 314, No. 256).

[75] 'Item de mortuis: in anniuersario parentum suorum, prima Oct. Epiphanie, in monasterio Sanctarum Crucum' (MS Valencia, Cat. 182, fo. 127^{va}, sermon on the text *Honora patrem tuum* . . . (Exod. 20: 12); Schneyer, *Repertorium*, iii. 313, No. 254).

(Wisd. 6: 6); that *a most severe judgement shall be done to them that bear rule*. But we ask that he be given the judgement of mercy by God, which is fittingly said to be God's for the time of grace, and this Isaiah says, chapter 16c (5): his *throne shall be prepared in mercy*—Christ's throne, that is—*and he will sit upon it in truth in the tabernacle of David, judging and seeking judgement.*

We can indeed presume and hold, with all likelihood, that this judgement has been given to our lord king. For when he lived, he judged himself through diligent examination of conscience and confession of sins. But St Paul says, 1 Corinthians 11 (31): *if we would judge ourselves, we should not be judged.*

He also prepared himself by doing a multiplicity of good and charitable [*or* pious] works, and through the devout reception of all the sacraments. For he knew that it was written: *Happy is the man that shows mercy and lends; he orders his words with judgement* (Ps. 111: 5).

There is a third reason why we can hold this, for he was most merciful, and therefore he has I hope found a merciful judge.

De secundo: Est duplex dei iudicium, scilicet districte iustitie et pie misericordie. Primum non petimus pro domino nostro rege, immo cum ipso dicimus; *non intres in iudicium cum seruo tuo* etc. Scimus enim scriptum (Sap. 6: 6) quod *iudicium durissimum hiis qui presunt fiet*. Sed postulamus sibi a deo dari iudicium misericordie, quod dicitur proprie suum pro tempore gratie, et hoc[76] est quod dicit Ys. xvi.c. (5): *preparabitur in misericordia solium* eius, scilicet Christi, *et sede(bit) super illud in ueri(tate) in taber(naculo) Da(uid), iudi(cans) et quer(ens) iudi(cium).*

Possumus autem uerisimiliter presumere et tenere quod istud iudicium datum fuerit domino nostro regi. Nam ipse dum uiueret iudicauit se per diligentem conscientie discussionem et peccatorum confessionem. Dicit autem Apostolus, Prima ad Cor. xi° (31): *si nosmetipsos iudicaremus, non utique iudicaremur.*

Preparauit etiam se per bonorum operum et piorum multiplicationem, et sacramentorum omnium deuotam receptionem. Sciebat enim scriptum (Ps. 111: 5): *Iocundus homo qui miseretur et comodat. Disponit[77] sermones suos in iudicio.*

Tertium est quare hoc tenere possumus, quia clementissimus fuit, et ideo clementem iudicem spero inuenit.[78]

It is the same with the sermon in memory of his parents: it says little or nothing about their personalities.[79]

[76] hoc] hos *ms?*
[77] *Disponit*] Disponet *in Vulgate*
[78] MS Valencia, Cat. 182, fo. 128^va.
[79] The sermon is on fos. 127^va–127^vb of MS Valencia, Cat. 182. Readers may be spared another lengthy quotation.

One must bear in mind, however, the possibility that
personal details and anecdotes had been included when the
sermons were actually preached. In his sermon 'on the anniversary of the queen of Castille'[80] he says at one point 'Speak
here about her wisdom, and how she ruled the kingdom, and
how she behaved in difficult matters and great dangers.'[81] Our
conclusion on the basis of these sermons by Juan must therefore
be negative in the neutral sense. They do not support the
hypothesis that memorial sermons paid attention to the dead
person's individuality, but are not absolutely incompatible with
it. What one can say is that in Juan's case the representation of
personality can hardly have been the primary point.

Juan was related through his mother to the Angevin dynasty
of Naples (we have seen that Philip, prince of Taranto, son of
King Charles II and brother of Robert 'the Wise', was his
maternal uncle). The family is one of those great dynasties
around which the political history of later medieval Europe
could be (though by and large it is not) written. As was noted
in the previous chapter, moreover, these Angevins are important in the history of *de mortuis* sermons because for some
reason, perhaps the tradition of funeral oratory in Apulia,[82] a
disproportionately large number of sermons on members of the
family have survived—a veritable portrait gallery. In analysing
these sermons it has seemed desirable to fill in more of the
biographical background than seemed necessary with Edward I
of England and Philip IV 'le Bel', who are familiar to the
scholarly and student public. Such details are also more
necessary than with Juan's father James II of Aragon, whose

[80] '... in anniuersario regine Castelle' (MS Valencia, Cat. 182, fo. 129[va],
supplied in margin (the sermon ends fo. 130[rb])); the text is *Regina corruit*
(Esther 15: 10); Schneyer, *Repertorium*, iii. 314, No. 260).
[81] 'Dic de eius sapientia, et qualiter rexit regnum, et qualiter se habuit in
arduis et magnis periculis' (MS Valencia, Cat. 182, fos. 129[vb]–130[ra]). I assume
that the queen in question is Maria de Molina, to whom C. W. Previté-Orton
went so far as to attribute 'political genius' (*The Shorter Cambridge Medieval
History* (2 vols.; Cambridge, 1966), ii. 904–6). Juan gives a similar indication
that much has been omitted in the written version a little further on: 'Dic hic de
eius elemosinis. Texe hystoriam breuiter, ut sequitur exponendo. Ecce ergo
karissimi de nobilitate huius domine corporali, que nichil ei profuit, et de
spirituali, quam ex bonis operibus eam arbitror habuisse, quam modo sentit.
Intendamus ergo karissimi ad istam. Dilata' (MS Valencia, Cat. 182, fo. 130[ra]).
[82] See above, ch. 1, text at nn. 150 and 175–214.

personality is hardly relevant to the memorial sermons on him since there are virtually no allusions to it to be explained. Against the background of Italian and dynastic history, by contrast, the sermons on the Angevins at times convey a vivid if compressed sense of individuality.

A striking case is a sermon on Charles II which brings his father Charles I and his son Robert the Wise into the picture, bringing out the contrast between their achievements and personalities. The author is Federico Franconi.[83] Some commentary will be needed, and the rhetoric of scriptural citations is an obstacle to the modern reader, but it is remarkable how succinctly and successfully he represents three generations of the dynasty's history.

The sermon is on the text *The lord our king shall sit for ever* (Ps. 28: 10),[84] and the image of sitting is the basis of the contrast: 'it should be known that sitting belongs to the person who triumphs, to the person who shows pity, to the wise man, and to the person who is at rest.'[85] The last kind of 'sitting' need not concern us here, since it is about Charles II's rest in the afterlife. The first three kinds, however, refer to Charles I, Charles II, and Robert the Wise respectively.

Firstly, I say, it belongs to the person who triumphs. For after a prince has had a triumph, he sits. Therefore after the triumph of Christ it is concluded, in the last chapter of Mark (16: 19), [Jesus] *sits at the right hand of God.* And in that way King Charles I sits; after many victories he sits on the throne of the Kingdom (*or Regno*), so that one may apply to him the text of Revelation 3 (21): *To him that will overcome, I will give to sit on my throne.* There are three things here.—Firstly, the glory of the one who triumphs: *to him that will overcome.* Secondly, the rights of the one who holds possession: *I will give to him.* Thirdly, the excellence of the one who sits in authority: *to sit on the throne.* On the first, Apocalypse 6 (2): *He went out,* that is, from France, *conquering that he might conquer.* On the second: that is, because the kingdom was given to him by the Church, and thus he has the rights

---

[83] See above, ch. 1, text at nn. 201–3.

[84] 'In annuali eiusdem regis. *Sedebit dominus rex noster in eternum,* Ps. Seruitoribus et amicis dei promictitur sedere et quiescere in eternum' (MS Munich, Staatsbibliothek Clm. 2981, fo. 131$^{ra}$ (sermon ends fo. 131$^{vb}$); Schneyer, *Repertorium,* iv. 223, 'Nicolaus de Asculo', No. 218).

[85] 'Circa primum sciendum quod sedere est *triumphantis, condolentis, sapientis et quiescentis*' (MS Munich, Staatsbibliothek Clm. 2981, fo. 131$^{rb}$).

of a possessor. And thus the words of Genesis 13 (15) can be said to him: *All the land which you see I will give to you and to your seed for ever.* And afterwards (Gen. 17: 6): *Kings shall come out of you*—because not only over one kingdom, but two, that is, the kingdom of Sicily and that of Hungary. On the third point, Hebrews 1 (8): his *throne is for ever and ever.*

Secondly, I say that to sit is the act of one who shows pity. Therefore Job, grieving, lay on the ground; similarly his friends, Job 2 (12). And in that way King Charles II sits, sitting with those in grief and affliction and poverty, through his sense of compassion; this the alms and benefits which he bestowed freely on poor religious and churches demonstrate, so that one might apply to him the words of Job 29 (25): *When I sat like a king with the army standing about* me, *yet I was a comforter of them that mourned.* Behold that the lord Charles, when exercising lordship, had a royal throne: *When I sat like a king.* Proverbs 20 (8): *The king, that sits on the throne of judgement, scatters away all evil with his look.*—Secondly, in the Kingdom (*or* Regno) he had a faithful retinue:[86] *with the army standing about* me. 1 Maccabees 6 (41): *for the army was exceedingly great and strong.*—Thirdly, in showing compassion for the pious soul: *yet I was a comforter of them that mourned.* Ps. (118: 173): *Let your hand be with me to save me.*

Thirdly, to sit belongs to a wise man or teacher. Luke 5 (3): *sitting, he taught* them. And in this way King Robert sits. One could apply to him the words of Kings 23 (8): *The wisest among the three sits.*—See, firstly, the emotions which have been calmed: John 11 (20): *sat at home.*—Secondly, the illuminated intelligence: *the wisest.* (Eccles. 12: 9–10:) *Whereas Ecclesiastes was very wise, he taught the people, and declared the things that he had done, and seeking out he set forth many parables. He sought profitable words, and wrote sermons which were most correct and full of truth.*—Thirdly, see the approved number: *among three. Among,* that is: 'above', three kings of the house of France, that is, the kings of France, Hungary, and Navarre; or among grandfather, and father— and he himself, the third, sits, being the wisest. For these are *the three who give testimony on earth: the spirit and the water and the blood. The spirit* is King Charles II; *the water,* King Robert, the most wise; and the blood, King Charles I.

Primo dico quod est triumphantis. Postquam enim princeps habuit triumphum, sedet. Unde post triumphum Christi concluditur, Mc.[87] ultimo (16: 19): *Sedet a dextris dei.* Et isto modo sedet rex Karolus primus; post multas uictorias sedet in solio Regni, ut de eo exponatur

---

[86] Perhaps a rather free translation of *consortium.*
[87] Mc.] Mt. *ms?*

illud Apoc. 3 (21): *Qui uicerit, dabo ei sedere in trono meo.* Ubi tria:—Primo gloria triumphantis: *Qui uicerit.* Secundo iura possidentis: *dabo ei.* Tertio excellentia presidentis: *se(det) in so(lio).*[88] De primo, Apoc. 6 (2):[89] *Exiuit,* scilicet de Francia, *uincens ut uinceret.* De secundo, quia scilicet sibi datum est regnum ab ecclesia, et sic habet iura possidentis. Et sic ei potest dici illud Gn. 13 (15): *Omnem terram quam conspicis dabo tibi et semini tuo usque in sempiternum.* Et sequitur (Gen. 17: 6): *Reges de te egredientur,* quia non solum super unum regnum sed duo, scilicet regnum Sicilie et Ungarie. De tertio, Hebr. 1 (8): *Tronus eius in seculum seculi.*

Secundo dico quod sedere est actus condolentis. Unde Iob dolens[90] iacebat in terra; similiter amici sui: Iob 2 (12). Et isto modo sedet rex Karolus secundus, sedens cum merentibus [*fo. 131ᵛᵃ*] et afflictis et pauperibus per animi compaxionem, quod ostendunt elemosine et beneficia pauperibus religiosis et ecclesiis largita, ut de eo exponatur illud Iob 29 (25): *Cum sederem quasi rex, circumstante*[91] me *exercitu, eram tamen merentium consolator.* Ecce quod dominus Karolus in dominando habuit regale solium *cum sederem quasi rex.* Prouer. 20 (8): *Rex qui sedet in solio iudicii dissipat omne malum intuitu suo.*—Secundo in regno habuit fidele consortium: *circumdante me*[92] *exercitu.* 1 Mach. 6 (41): *erat enim exercitus magnus ualde et fortis.*—Tertio in compatiendo pium animum: *eram tamen mere(entium) conso(lator).* Ps. (118: 173): *Fiat manus tua*[93] *ut saluet me.*

Tertio sedere est sapientis seu docentis. Luc. 5 (3): *sedens, docebat eos.* Et isto modo sedet rex Robertus, de quo posset exponi illud 2 R(eg.) 23 (8): *Sedet sapientissimus inter tres.*—Primo uidete affectum quietatum. Io. 11 (20): *domi sedebat.*—Secundo intellectum illuminatum: *sapientissimus.* (Eccles. 12: 9–10:) *Cum esset sapientissimus Ecclesiastes, docuit populum et narrauit que fecerat; et inuestigans composuit parabolas multas. Quesiuit uerba utilia, et scripsit sermones rectissimos et ueritate plenos.*—Tertio uidete numerum approbatum: *inter tres.* Inter, id est, supra, tres reges de domo Francie, scilicet Francie, Ungarie, et Nauarre. Uel inter auum, et patrem, et ipse tertius sedet sapientissimus. Isti enim sunt *tres qui testimonium dant in terra: spiritus, aqua, et sanguis.* Spiritus, rex Karolus secundus; *aqua,* rex Robertus sapientissimus; et *sanguis,* rex Karolus primus.[94]

[88] solio] *sic (i.e. not* trono *as in Rev. 3: 21)*
[89] Apoc. 6 (2)] Apoc. 3 *ms*
[90] dolens] doles *ms*
[91] *circumstante*] circumstantem *ms*
[92] *circumdante me*] *sic ms*
[93] tua] tue *ms*
[94] MS Munich, Staatsbibliothek Clm. 2981, fo. 131ʳᵇ⁻ᵛᵃ.

The representations of Charles II and of Robert will be examined shortly. What of the characterization of Charles I? It is
very brief. To anyone not familiar with his life it would say
little. The preacher seems to be working on the assumption
that he can achieve his effect by evoking latent pictures or
memories of the man's life, with which his audience would
presumably have been fairly familiar. A good rule of thumb
with this genre is that the shorter the characterization, the
more background the historian needs to supply if the audience's
reception of the sermon is to be appreciated; therefore an
excursus on the career of Charles I is required at this point.

Until 1282 his career was a crescendo of triumphs. A grandson
of King Philip Augustus of France and a younger brother of
Louis IX, he received Anjou—captured by his grandfather
from King John of England—as his share of the Capetian lands.
He married a daughter of the count of Provence; his wife's
sisters married Henry III of England, Louis IX, and Richard of
Cornwall (later a claimant to the Holy Roman Empire), but it
was Charles who, through his wife, inherited the county of
Provence. After accompanying Louis IX on the latter's first
crusade, Charles laid the firm if unspectacular foundations
of his later dramatic successes by holding down the urban
communal movement in Provence, intervening (profitably) in
Hennegau at the request of the countess of Flanders, and
establishing a power-base in Piedmont.[95] This was how to
acquire a reputation as a winner. Charles's brother-in-law Henry
III of England, of whom popes had hoped that he would oust
the Hohenstaufen on behalf of his son, had shown himself to
be something of a loser. The papacy turned to Charles. In that
sense 'the Kingdom [of Sicily, including Southern Italy] was
given him by the Church', as Federico Franconi put it.[96] Charles
had to take it first, and it is impressive that he managed it. The
emperor Frederick II's (illegitimate) son Manfred was by this
time established. It took careful preparation and a pitched
battle at Benevento (1266) to take the kingdom; then another,
two years later at Tagliacozzo, to keep it, after Frederick's

[95] P. Herde, *Karl I. von Anjou* (Stuttgart, Berlin, Cologne, and Mainz, 1979),
35–6, 38–41.
[96] MS Munich, Staatsbibliothek Clm. 2981, fo. 131[rb].

grandson Konradin had marched down from Germany, strengthened by Lombard supporters, Tuscan Ghibellines, and heavily
armoured Spanish knights.[97]

According to Villani, he died claiming that he had conquered
the Kingdom more to serve the Holy Church than his own
profit or other covetousness.[98] Whether or not he did say this,
one can well imagine him doing so. He was certainly religious.
The ubiquitous Salimbene narrates at first hand how Charles's
prayers and genuflections once kept his brother Louis waiting
(happy to wait, of course).[99] However, he seems to have been a
hard man and above all a fighter. A story told in Salimbene's
*Cronica* makes vivid for us the personality which Federico
Franconi was bringing to his audience's mind. It actually does
not matter whether the story is true, so long as it was the kind
of thing people said about Charles I in the late thirteenth
and early fourteenth century, or if it embodies an image then
current of his character. Charles had heard about the prowess
of a knight from Campania and insisted that his son arrange a
fight between this champion and a certain new knight. The
two knights duly turned up, and charged each other so hard
that their lances were shattered; but both managed to stay in
the saddle. Then Charles—for the new knight was he—wished
to continue the fight with club or mace as weapon, and chose
to bear the first blow, as a result of which he was completely
knocked out and broke two ribs. When the knight from
Campania learnt the identity of his opponent he was under-
standably alarmed (he mounted his charger, took flight, and
stayed hidden for a long time). However, when Charles came
to he asked his son if the knight was still waiting for him: he
wanted to return the blow![100] Salimbene explains that Charles
I's motive for this encounter was to preserve the honour of the
French,[101] and elsewhere he describes Charles as an *optimus*

---

[97] Herde, *Karl I.*, 59.

[98] Villani, *Nuova cronica*, 9. 95, i. 557 Porta; E. Léonard, *Les Angevins de
Naples* (Paris, 1954), 160.

[99] Salimbene, *Cronica Fratris Salimbene de Adam*, ed. O. Holder-Egger (MGH
Scriptores, 32; Hanover and Leipzig, 1905–13), 325.

[100] Salimbene, *Cronica*, p. 599 Holder-Egger.

[101] '. . . pro conseruando Gallicorum honore' (ibid., pp. 599–600 Holder-
Egger).

*preliator*, excellent warrior, who 'took away the disgrace which the French had incurred beyond the sea under St Louis'.[102]

All this gives us a better idea of how Federico's words could have worked on the minds of his listeners. The image of *the spirit and the water and the blood* is especially successful. Charles I, symbolized by blood, is effectively defined by contrast with his two successors.

His successor Charles II is symbolized as 'the spirit': a little puzzling, but most probably an allusion to Charles's compassion, which is emphasized as characteristic of him earlier in the sermon. Since Federico had included a reference to alms received by religious,[103] he may have had Charles II's favour to his own order, the Dominicans, especially in mind. Charles had been in part responsible for the creation of their great church of S. Domenico Maggiore.[104] Charles also made substantial contributions to the building of a church in honour of the Dominican Pietro da Verona (Peter Martyr).[105]

The contrast implicit in this sermon with the war-leader Charles I is born out by Charles II's career. Few men have tried so hard for peace. Perhaps the devastating naval defeat he suffered at the hands of the king of Aragon's superb admiral Ruggero di Lauria,[106] followed by the long imprisonment first of himself then of three of his sons,[107] may have developed in him this preference for peace and diplomacy. (Incidentally, we should not assume that he took this attitude because incompetence ruled out any other: Ruggero di Lauria was a persistent winner, who continued to be successful when diplomacy brought him into alliance with Charles II, later on.)

Charles II of Naples is hardly the best known of later me-

[102] '. . . abstulit opprobrium Gallicorum, quod sub sancto Lodoico incurrerant ultra mare' (ibid., p. 564 Holder-Egger).
[103] 'Quis, karissimi, non diceret regem Karolum fuisse magne clementie, cuius tot fuerunt elemosine siue circa ecclesias siue *circa personas religiosas* siue circa uiduas? Quis non diceret eum fuisse clementem qui fuit tante com*paxionis, siue pauperibus, siue infirmantibus siue merentibus?' (MS Munich, Staatsbibliothek Clm. 2981, fo. 130$^{rb}$, my emphasis).
[104] Cf. De Frede in E. Pontieri (ed.), *Storia di Napoli* (Naples, 1967– ), iii (n.d.), 142; cf. ibid. 140, 731.
[105] Ibid. 143.
[106] Herde, *Karl I.*, 109–10.
[107] Louis (= St Louis of Toulouse), Robert (later king), and Raymond Bérenger. See Léonard, *Les Angevins*, 171.

dieval monarchs, but we need to pay close attention to him because of the relatively large number of surviving memorial sermons for him. The personality behind the funeral sermons is in fact full of human interest, though one must descend into the minutiae of political history to get a real sense of it. Here a few selected details must suffice.

Charles was released from his Aragonese captivity in 1288, in large part thanks to the efforts of his cousin Edward I of England. The deal involved far-reaching political concessions by Charles to the king of Aragon. Charles had undertaken to try and persuade the pope and Philip IV of France to confirm the agreement that had been reached (though it was rather unfavourable to himself). Shortly after his release he gave evidence of his tender conscience by writing to the king of Aragon to ask if he ought to assume the title of king of Sicily, as the pope had asked him to do.[108] Unsurprisingly, he received no encouragement. Charles reached the French Court for Christmas, and there his efforts to plead the cause of peace were overridden by King Philip IV. Pope Nicholas IV pushed him in the same direction, away from his agreement with the king of Aragon, and Charles allowed himself to be solemnly crowned by the pope at Rieti in 1289. Not long afterwards Pope Nicholas reaffirmed that Charles's undertakings to the king of Aragon were illegitimate, and absolved Charles of his oath.[109]

Nevertheless, Charles seems to have been unhappy about the situation into which he had been hustled. He joined the Neapolitan forces at Gaeta, where they had managed to corner the Sicilian army and their king, James of Aragon. Revenge for years of humiliation was at hand, but instead Charles accepted a truce. The terms were not even particularly favourable.[110]

Why did he do it? Envoys from Edward I of England, who was anxious for peace in Christendom in view of a future crusade, played a part in persuading him,[111] and he was doubtless very anxious about the sons who were being kept hostage. However, according to both E. Léonard and A. Nitschke—two

---

[108] Léonard, *Les Angevins*, 171.
[109] Ibid. 171–2, 177; and A. Nitschke, 'Carlo II d'Angiò', in *Dizionario biografico degli italiani*, xx (Rome, 1977), 227–35, at 229.
[110] Nitschke, 'Carlo II d'Angiò', 229; Léonard, *Les Angevins*, 175–6.
[111] Léonard, *Les Angevins*, 176.

historians who have made a serious effort to understand Charles—conscientious scruples were also a factor.[112]

Charles II's behaviour later in the same year lends plausibility to their interpretation. He had promised to return to captivity if he could not negotiate a peace between the Church, France, and Aragon which was satisfactory to the Aragonese.[113] On 1 November 1289 Charles II actually presented himself at the Aragonese border; he had promised a lot as a condition of release from captivity and he had failed to deliver what he had promised; though no one was there to arrest him, it is remarkable that he felt himself bound to go to these lengths before notifying the king of Aragon that he would not from then on be bound by their agreement.[114]

Peace continued to be his end, and diplomacy his chosen means. He did not do badly, and with a little more luck he might have recovered Sicily through his patient negotiations. He had a card in his hand: the threat to the crown of Aragon from France. The previous king of Aragon had been deposed by the then pope (for his part in the revolt of Sicily against Charles I), and the crown conferred on Charles de Valois, brother of Philip IV. In view of the power of France, and with the analogy of the original Angevin conquest of Naples and Sicily no doubt still alive, the threat was one to take seriously. The far from subservient Cortes of Aragon took it very seriously indeed.[115] What Charles II could offer Aragon was the abandonment by Charles de Valois of his dangerous claim. The plan of a marriage between Charles II's daughter Marguerite and Charles de Valois, coupled with the cession to Charles de Valois of Maine and Anjou itself, secured the latter's co-operation.[116] By sacrificing these family lands[117] Charles II came near to achieving his ends in Italy. The king of Aragon—first Alfonso III, then, after his death, James II—decided to come to terms. The details of how the deal was put together

[112] Ibid.; Nitschke, 'Carlo II d'Angiò', 229.
[113] Nitschke, 'Carlo II d'Angiò', 229.
[114] Léonard, *Les Angevins*, 177.
[115] Ibid. 178.
[116] Ibid. 177.
[117] There was a partial compensation (even apart from the trade-off with Charles of Valois): Philip IV ceded the French part of the territory of Avignon to Naples (ibid. 178).

are too intricate to be set out here (much of the credit must go to Pope Boniface VIII), but by summer 1295 James II had given up Sicily (which he had retained when he succeeded to the crown of Aragon). James II married Charles II's daughter Blanche, and a real alliance was formed between the two families, and thus between Aragon and Naples.

Unfortunately for Charles, the Sicilian part of the plan did not come off. James II's younger brother, who had ruled Sicily for him, was to be compensated by a marriage to the heiress of Constantinople, Catherine de Courtenay. (She did not actually control the Greek Empire, but the hope was that they would reconquer it, with some military and financial help.) The lady refused.[118] Moreover, anti-Angevin feelings remained powerful in Sicily, and in defiance of James II of Aragon the Sicilians offered his younger brother the crown, which he accepted. However, the conflict between the kingdoms of Aragon and Naples, which had been started after the Sicilian Vespers of 1282 and which might have gone on indefinitely, had been resolved.

In consequence Charles II now had the help of James II and the admiral Ruggero di Lauria, who with his customary brilliance won a major victory in 1299 over the Sicilians. Even so, it was not until 1302 that Charles II obtained the peace for which he had tried so hard.

It was not a triumphant peace, for he had to give up his claim to Sicily for the lifetime of its king Frederick.[119] On the other hand, Frederick became Charles II's son-in-law. Once again, a marriage union cemented the reconciliation between the Angevins of Naples and a son of Peter III of Aragon, who had been their bane.[120]

---

[118] There was . . . to Naples, 184–6.

[119] Ibid. 195. Sicily was not in the event returned to the Angevins, and it seems that Frederick and his elder brother were contemplating 'une succession réciproque aux couronnes de Sicile et d'Aragon, qui déjouait déjà les stipulations de Caltabellota [the peace of 1302]'. (ibid.). If Frederick had died shortly after the peace, however, there might have been a serious chance of Sicily returning to Naples; and this is not an absurd scenario, since, as Léonard observes, 'ces princes aragonais mouraient jeunes' (ibid.). It is at any rate worth remembering that Frederick's son and successor was a grandson of Charles II and great-grandson of the first 'Angevin of Naples'.

[120] Ibid., and Nitschke, 'Carlo II d'Angiò', 233.

The war between Sicily and the mainland was over, at least for Charles II's lifetime, and the island was reconciled to the Church by papal legates. Even in purely pragmatic terms, peace may have been the wiser alternative. During the remainder of his reign (he died in 1309) he was able to advance the cause of the dynasty with notable success: reconstituting Angevin power in Piedmont and winning recognition for his grandson as king of Hungary.[121]

In the sermon which compares the first three Angevins of Naples Charles II's preference for peace is merely implicit in the contrasting description of his father. In another sermon by the same preacher, Federico Franconi, the characterization is more explicit. It is drawn as follows:

And it may fittingly be said that he was king of Sicily and Jerusalem. For the kingdom of Sicily is a fertile kingdom, and the kingdom of Jerusalem is pacific, because 'Jerusalem' is interpreted to mean 'Vision of Peace'. Thus he was fertile in begetting sons (*or* children), and pacific in the government of kingdoms. Therefore he may be called another King Solomon, that is, the pacific king . . .

Et merito potest dici quod fuit rex Sicilie et Ierosolem. Regnum enim Sicilie est regnum fecundum, et regnum Ierosolem pacificum, quia Ierosolem visio pacis interpretatur. Sic ipse fuit fecundus in filiorum generatione, et pacificus in regnorum gubernatione. Unde potest dici alter rex Salomon, scilicet rex pacificus . . .[122]

The interpretation of 'Jerusalem' to mean 'Vision of Peace' is in itself a perfectly banal example of the technique of *Interpretationes nominum Hebraicorum* which was commonly employed by preachers in the period,[123] but once one knows the details of Charles II's career it ceases to seem a tired and stereotyped formula and becomes a lens which focuses attention on a salient characteristic of his personality.[124]

---

[121] Nitschke, 'Carlo II d'Angiò', 233; Léonard, *Les Angevins*, 196–9, 202–4.

[122] MS Munich, Staatsbibliothek Clm. 2981, fo. 130rb, sermon on the text *Ego constitutus sum rex* (Ps. 2: 6); Schneyer, *Repertorium*, iv. 223, 'Nicolaus de Asculo', No. 216.

[123] See Amaury d'Esneval, 'Le perfectionnement d'un instrument de travail au début du xiiie siècle: Les trois glossaires bibliques d'Étienne Langton', in G. Hasenohr and J. Longère (eds.), *Culture et travail intellectuel dans l'Occident médiéval* (Paris, 1981), 163–75.

[124] The likeness is close in another respect: Charles did indeed have many children, and in one way or another they played an important part in the

In the same sermon there is another passage which effectively, if quaintly, represents the general attitude of mind or disposition of which Charles II's peace policy was a particular manifestation:

Secondly, I say that he [a king] ought to be established in the gentleness of mercy. And there is a reason, because experts say that men who guard pigs are choleric, whereas shepherds of sheep are generally gentle. A king, according to Aristotle, is called a shepherd. Therefore Aristotle says, in the *Ethics*, book 8, that a king, like a good shepherd, has the care of his subjects, to make sure they act well, in the same way that a shepherd has the care of sheep: and therefore Homer called Agamemnon the shepherd of peoples. And Seneca says, *De clementia*, book 2, that nothing befits a ruler more than mercy. An example from nature: the king of the bees, according to Ambrose, has no sting. And Aristotle says to Alexander, 'O Alexander, help in your mercy the needy, the poor and the weak in all their need.'

Secundo dico quod debet esse constitutus[125] in dulcedine clementie, et ratio est, quia experti dicunt quod custodes porcorum sunt iracundi, sed pastores ouium communiter sunt mansueti. Rex, secundum Philosophum, dicitur pastor ouium; Unde Philosophus 8 Ethicorum[126]

---

history of the reign. Table IV at the end of Léonard's *Les Angevins* (this part not paginated) gives an idea of their significance. As for the reference to Solomon, one is tempted to suggest that there was a further layer of meaning, beyond the idea that Solomon and Charles II were both pacific kings. The preacher and some of his audience may have remembered that Solomon did not remain a paragon of virtue for the whole of his reign, for 'he had seven hundred wives as queens, and three hundred concubines. And the women turned away his heart' (2 Kgs. 11: 3). Charles II was reputed to have had a weakness for women in later life: cf. Léonard, *Les Angevins*, 174, and H. Finke, *Aus den Tagen Bonifaz VIII.: Funde und Forschungen* (Vorreformationsgeschichtliche Forschungen; Münster, 1902), 245. It was allegedly said—but there may be good grounds for scepticism here—that Charles II's sexual mores became loose after he had been told by Boniface VIII that 'to sleep with any woman one liked (*cognoscere mulieres quascumque*) was not a sin but only a work of nature' (ibid.). All testimony connected with the propaganda machine around Philip IV is suspect, and in any case one should not try to be too clever in winkling allusions out of these sermons.

[125] constitutus] costitutus *ms?*
[126] '. . . benefacit enim subditis, si quidem bonus ens curam habet ipsorum ut bene operentur, quemadmodum pastor ouium. Unde et Homerus *Agameimona* pastorem populorum dixit . . .' *Aristoteles Latinus*, xxvi/1–3, fasc. 4, ed. R. A. Gauthier, *Ethica Nicomachea, Translatio . . . Grosseteste . . . Recensio Recognita* (Union Académique Internationale, Corpus Philosophorum Medii Aevi; Brussels and Leiden, 1973), 535, 1161ª12–15 Bekker.

dicit quod rex sicu*t* bonus pastor curam habet subditorum, ut bene
operentur, quemadmodum pastor ouium; unde Omerus Agemenona
pastorem populorum dixit. Et Seneca dicit, 2 libro De Clementia,[127]
quod nichil magis decorum est regenti quam clementia. Exemplum in
natura: Apum rex sine aculeo est secundum Ambr(osium).[128] Et
Ar(istoteles) ad Alexandrum dicit:[129] O Alexander, subueni [*fo. 130^{rb}*]
de tua clementia indigentibus pauperibus et debilibus in omni eorum
indigentia.[130]

The qualities of character that come through this passage may
be the same that Saba Malaspina tried to convey by putting
into Charles II's mouth the following words to Sicilian rebels:

For my works have never done you harm, but you have always heard
that my efforts have tended towards peace, not towards war, and that
they have been directed to the alleviation of your grievances; never
have I heard of anything harsh (*graue*) done to you, without it displeasing me greatly.[131]

The passage in which Federico compares Charles II to a
gentle shepherd (as opposed to a choleric pig-keeper) is actually
a fair representation of the general tendency of Charles II's
internal government, to which he brought the same tempera-
ment that we have seen at work in his foreign policy. He made
efforts to provide accommodation, care, and material support
for men blinded or mutilated.[132] One may also mention here
his part in the establishment of a hospital, providing free treatment, at Pozzuoli. It depended to a great extent (though not

---

[127] Seneca, *De clementia*, 1. 19. 1, ed. P. Faider, i (Université de Gand,
Recueil de travaux publiés par la Faculté de Philosophie et Lettres, 60; Ghent
and Paris, 1928), 89.
[128] Federico probably got this idea too from Seneca, *De clementia*, 1. 19. 3, i.
89, Faider, unless Ambrose himself somewhere quotes it (and the passage
referred to in the previous note?).
[129] Probably from the *Secretum secretorum*, 19: 'O Alexander,, indaga de
inopia et necessitate miserabilium personarum et debilium.. Subueni indigentibus in sua indigentia' (I have used the Latin text included in *Hiltgart von
Hürnheim: Mittelhochdeutsche Prosaübersetzung des 'Secretum Secretorum'*, ed. R.
Möller (Deutsche Texte des Mittelalters herausgegeben von der deutschen
Akademie der Wissenschaften zu Berlin, 56; Berlin, 1963), 44).
[130] MS Munich, Staatsbibliothek Clm. 2981, fo. 130^{ra-b}.
[131] Cited by A. Nitschke, 'Karl II. als Fürst von Salerno', *Quellen und
Forschungen aus italienischen Archiven und Bibliotheken*, 36 (1956), 188–204, at 189
n. 9.
[132] On this see De Frede in Pontieri (ed.), *Storia di Napoli*, iii. 147.

exclusively) on the generosity of the king, who appointed to it
the master physician Giovanni di Simone 'for the purpose of
visiting the sick . . . and of giving consultations (*consulendo*) and
of indicating to each of them the curative baths appropriate to
the disease of each one of them'.[133]

When Federico Franconi speaks of mercy and gentleness he
may also have had at the back of his mind Charles II's efforts to
protect his subjects from his own officials. If so, one should
take this section on mercy together with the preceding section
on justice:

Especially useful for his subjects or for a kingdom is justice, because,
according to Augustine, *City of God*, book 1,[134] 'Without justice,
what are kingdoms but brigandage?' But this brigandage, and acts of
violence, and theft are removed by royal and legal justice. . . . King
Charles of holy memory became illustrious because of . . . justice . . .

Maxime utile subditorum seu regno est iustitia, quia secundum
Agustinum 1 De ci(uitate) dei: Remota iustitia, quid sunt regna nisi
latrocinia? Que quidem latrocinia et violentie et furta remouentur
regali et legali iustitia. . . . [*fo. 130^{ra}*] . . . Hac iustitia dominus rex
Karolus sancte memorie claruit, . . .[135]

An abstract commonplace? Not once applied to the details of
Charles's government. After the revolt of 1282 (the Sicilian
Vespers), and before his defeat and capture, acting as his
father's vicar in south Italy, Charles showed his concern for
justice courageously by arresting and putting on trial some of
the highest officials of the kingdom, accusing them of injustices
towards his subjects and all kinds of extortions.[136] He believed
that crimes had gone unpunished in the past, and made clear
his intention to clean up his beautiful inheritance.[137] The future
king Charles II was almost certainly acting on his own initiative
in bringing charges against his father's advisers: when Charles
I got back (his son being by then already in captivity) he
hanged one of the jurists involved in the trial; and one of the

---

[133] *Storia di Napoli*, iii. 146.
[134] In fact the remark is from book 4, ch. 4, of the *De civitate Dei*.
[135] MS Munich Staatsbibliothek Clm. 2981, fos. 129^{vb}–130^{ra}.
[136] Nitschke, 'Karl II. als Fürst von Salerno', 193 and n. 35.
[137] 'Ad exstirpanda uitia, que iam diu in regno Sicilie preclaro hereditario
nostro propter impunitatem scelerum multipliciter inoleuerunt' (ibid. 193 n.
37).

accused, against whom legal proceedings were still pending, was acquitted instantly.[138]

Not long before this, Charles of Salerno (he was prince of Salerno before succeeding to the throne) had held a meeting of estates at San Martino—the first parliament for many years.[139] Major reforms were introduced here to meet the wishes of his subjects: notably the freedom to marry without the king's consent and the right of the nobility to judgement by their peers, issues familiar to students of medieval English history. It used to be thought that Charles was merely acting as his father's agent at San Martino, but it has been strongly argued that he, rather than Charles I, was responsible for the majority and the most important of the reforms.[140] Some years later (in 1295) he said that the reforming measures of San Martino went 'beyond the power delegated to us by our father'.[141]

After his return from captivity and to Naples, Charles II confirmed the ordinances of San Martino and sought to improve them by adding new laws designed to give the population more protection against abuses by royal officials and soldiers. Officials were forbidden to requisition animals for their own use, for instance, and judges of the *magna curia* were to make periodic visits to individual provinces to investigate and put right abuses by justices and other officials.[142]

Set against this background, the following words of Federico Franconi (from the same sermon) look like a definite allusion rather than a vague commonplace:

. . . that kingdom could say to him the words of 3 Kings 10 (9): *Blessed is the lord God, who made you king, to do judgement and justice.* And in fact not only that you might do it, but also that you might write it. For he made constitutions or statutes of the kingdom which contain both justice and judgement, so that he could be called not only an executor of the law, but also a legislator . . .

. . . regnum istud potuit sibi dicere illud 3 R(eg.) 10 (9): *Benedictus dominus deus qui constituit te regem ut faceres iudicium et iustitiam.* Et re

---

[138] Ibid. 196.
[139] Ibid. 191.
[140] Ibid. 191–6 (esp. n. 42 to p. 194).
[141] '. . . ultra paternam nobis traditam potestatem': cited by Nitschke, 'Carlo II d'Angiò', 228.
[142] Ibid. 230.

uera non solum ut faceres, se*d* etiam ut scriberes. Ipse enim fecit constitutiones seu statuta regni in quibus et iustitia et iudicium continentur, ita quod non solum potuit dici legis executor, se*d* etiam legis lator . . .[143]

It may be concluded that, within certain limits, the two sermons on Charles II which we have discussed represent him in a way that seems more realistic the more one knows about the facts of his career. The limits are that only a few characteristics are selected, that the brush-strokes are economical, and that one is given little sense of progress within the individual's life.

Between the two sermons on Charles II in this manuscript there is another, also by Federico Franconi.[144] It is an interesting source for attitudes to kingship, and we must return to it in that context, but it need not detain us here. There is another batch of sermons on Charles II, however, which have some immediate relevance, because they approach his character from a slightly different angle but give an interesting representation of at least one side of it. They are by Giovanni da Napoli, OP, and are preserved in MS Naples, Nazionale VIII AA 11.[145]

A favourite theme in these sermons is the love between Charles II and God, and the idea is elaborated with reference to Charles's generosity to churches (etc.), the intensity of religious worship in the royal chapel and household, and the revelation which enabled him to find the body of Mary Magdalen. The picture of Charles II's love of God is reproduced with some repetition from one sermon to the next. (Were they preached to different audiences? Or in different years on the anniversary of his death?) For our purposes one passage will suffice:

[143] MS Munich, Staatsbibliothek Clm. 2981, fo. 130[ra].

[144] Begins: 'In annuali eiusdem regis. *Memoriam habundantie suauitatis tue eructabant* Ps. (144: 7). Mortui reducuntur ad memoriam . . .' (fo. 130[va]); ends: '. . . in laude eius. Et hoc de primo' (fo. 131[ra]) (Schneyer, *Repertorium*, iv. 223, 'Nicolaus de Asculo', No. 217).

[145] The sermons are listed in Schneyer, *Repertorium*, iii. 607, 'Johannes de Neapel', Nos. 35, 37, 38, 39. No. 36 is part of the series, and has the rubric 'In eodem anniuersario alius sermo de eodem themate aliqualiter uariatus' (fo. 24[vb]), but in fact it is probably about his son Charles Martel (Dante's friend), or conceivably his grandson Charles of Calabria. The evidence is that near the beginning the dead man is referred to as 'principis' rather than 'regis' (fo. 24[vb]), and that the preacher speaks of him leaving this present life 'in iuuentute seu in adolescentia' (fo. 25[va]).

. . . we can prove the love of God lying hidden in the inner side of the mind of Charles through the twofold action of charity open to view on the outside. He undoubtedly continued to give many and generous alms right up to the end of his life, and to show active kindness to the poor for the sake of God is a sign and an action of the love of God. He also greatly loved and expanded the liturgical worship of God, and it was a source of delight to him, so that in his household and chapel the liturgical worship of God flourished much and continuously, and was great always, and without doubt this was by his doing and ordaining; and in his lands he founded, constructed, and endowed many churches and religious places, which could easily be set forth in detail; and to be delighted by the liturgical worship of God or the praises of God is a sign of the love of God. God also loved him in a particular special way, revealing to him a certain great secret of his, that is, a certain very precious treasure, namely the body of St Mary Magdalen, which by divine revelation or inspiration he found in his county of Provence; and from a humble place he transferred it, divided into various small parts, to various precious objects, created out of gold and silver and precious stones.

. . . amorem dei in mente Kar(oli) latentem interius probare possumus per duplex opus [*fo. 26^{rb}*] caritatiuum patens exterius. Ipse siquidem multas et amplas elemosinas usque ad finem uite sue continuauit, et bene facere propter deum pauperibus est signum et opus diuini amoris. Ipse etiam cultum dei multum dilexit et ampliauit, et in eo delectatus fuit, sic quod in domo et capella sua continue cultus dei multum uiguit et semper magnus fuit, et procul dubio ipso faciente et ordinante; et in terris suis multas ecclesias et loca religiosa fundauit, construxit, et dotauit, que de leui explicari possent; et delectari in cultu dei seu dei laudibus signum est diuini amoris. Deus etiam ipsum quodam modo speciali amauit, reuelando ei quoddam magnum secretum suum, thezaurum scilicet quemdam multum pretiosum, uidelicet corpus sancte Marie Magdalene, quod diuina reuelatione seu inspiratione inuenit in comitatu suo Prouincie, et de humili loco, in diuersas particulas diuisum, transtulit in diuersa iocalia pretiosa, fabricata ex auro et argento et lapidibus pretiosis.[146]

Charles II's generosity to good causes (including the Dominican Order) has already been noted, and the rest of the description also points up an aspect or aspects of his character. The

---

[146] MS Naples, Nazionale VIII AA 11, fo. 26^{ra–b}, from a sermon on the text *Amice ascende superius* (Luke 14: 10); Schneyer, *Repertorium*, iii. 607, 'Johannes de Neapel', No. 38.

king's piety seems to have struck contemporaries. According to a Sicilian chronicler, some knights of Charles's army (visiting the Sicilian king's lines after the truce of 1289) expressed frustration with their own camp, which they clearly felt to be religiously and ecclesiastically saturated.[147] Tholomaeus of Lucca has Charles's father Charles I say of him (after Ruggero di Lauria had captured him): 'Congratulate me and rejoice with me, for today we have lost a priest who obstructed our government and the vigour of our war-making.'[148]

As for the body of Mary Magdalen, Charles II (then still just prince of Salerno) had indeed been the promoter of the researches which lead to its discovery (as he believed) at Saint-Maximin, and he himself later said that he had acted under the inspiration of God.[149] The discovery was probably a high point in Charles's life. According to one source he flung himself into the task of digging with ardour, the sweat pouring off him.[150]

The sermon by Federico Franconi on the text *The lord our king shall sit for ever* (Ps. 28: 10), with which we began our discussion of the Angevins, portrays Charles II (it will be recalled) alongside his father Charles I and his son Robert the Wise: 'to sit belongs to a wise man or teacher . . . And in this way King Robert sits.'[151] Federico refers to the calm of Robert's emotions, and the illumination of his intelligence; he seems to imply that Robert is wiser than the kings of France, Hungary, and Navarre and also wiser than his father Charles II or his grandfather Charles I.[152] In the middle of the section on Robert's wisdom he quotes Eccles. 12: 9–10: 'Whereas Ecclesiastes was very wise, he taught the people, and declared the things that he had

---

[147] A. Barbero, *Il mito angioino nella cultura italiana e provenzale fra duecento e trecento* (Deputazione Subalpina di Storia Patria, Biblioteca Storica Subalpina, 201; Turin, 1983), 123–4.

[148] '. . . congratulamini mihi et congaudete mecum, quia hodie perdidimus [perdimus *in Nitschke*] unum sacerdotem, qui nostrum impediebat regimen ac uigorem bellandi' (cited by Nitschke, 'Karl II. als Fürst von Salerno', 188 n. 5).

[149] V. Saxer, *Le Culte de Marie Madeleine en Occident des origines à la fin du Moyen Âge* (Cahiers d'archéologie et d'histoire, 3; Auxerre and Paris, 1959), 235.

[150] Ibid.

[151] See above, text at n. 94 (final paragraph of sermon).

[152] 'Tertio uidete numerum approbatum: *inter tres*. Inter, id est, "supra" tres reges de domo Francie, scilicet Francie, Ungarie, et Nauarre; uel inter auum, et patrem, et ipse tertius sedet sapientissimus' (MS Munich, Staatsbibliothek Clm. 2981, fo. 131[va]).

done, and seeking out he set forth many parables. He sought profitable words, and wrote sermons which were most correct and full of truth.'[153] Federico uses the same passage in another sermon, on the text *Ecce rex uester* (*Behold your king*, John 19: 14), which has the rubric 'At the funeral obsequies of the lord King Robert'[154] (so he is the main character here and not just a member of the supporting cast).

The text from Ecclesiastes must have seemed remarkably apt, for Robert does seem to have made a hobby of writing and delivering sermons, which was an exceptional thing for an orthodox layman to do in this period.[155] One sensitive twentieth-century portrait of Robert has argued that the purpose of Robert's homiletic activity 'can hardly have been other than an inner need'.[156]

This sermon is full of praise for Robert's wisdom:

Who would not admire his wisdom, with respect to the natural world, or to Ethics, or to Medicine, or to Laws, or to Grammar, or to Logic? And in short, I believe that in his time the world did not have a man who was so wise in so many fields. Thorough instruction had made him competent in all the Liberal Arts, and he was a great theologian. One could therefore say of him the words of Matthew 12 (42): *Behold, a greater than Solomon here.*[157]

[153] Quoted above, text at n. 94 (final paragraph of sermon).

[154] 'In exequiis domini Regis Roberti' (MS Munich, Staatsbibliothek Clm. 2981, fo. 131ᵛᵇ; Schneyer, *Repertorium*, iv. 223, 'Nicolaus de Asculo', No. 219).

[155] For his sermons see Schneyer, *Repertorium*, v. 196–219. For a discussion of the problem of lay preaching in the Middle Ages see R. Zerfass, *Der Streit um die Laienpredigt: Eine pastoralgeschichtliche Untersuchung zum Verständnis des Predigtamtes und zu seiner Entwicklung im 12. und 13. Jahrhundert* (Freiburg i.B., Basle, and Vienna, 1974). For some important and intriguing remarks in a newly edited source from the early 13th cent. see Thomas de Chobham, *Summa de arte praedicandi*, ed. F. Morenzoni (CCCM 82; Turnhout, 1988), 57, 59, and (indirectly relevant) 62.

[156] W. Goetz, *König Robert von Neapel (1309–1343): Seine Persönlichkeit und sein Verhältnis zum Humanismus* (Universität Tübingen, Doktoren-Verzeichnis der philosophischen Fakultät, 1908; Tübingen, 1910), 32. Darleen Pryds is engaged on an important investigation of Robert of Naples as preacher, and Suzanne Cawsey has in hand a more general study of speech-making (including preaching) by kings in this period.

[157] 'Quis non admiraretur eius sapientiam, siue naturalem, siue moralem, siue medicinalem, siue legalem, siue gramaticalem, siue logicalem? Et breuiter, credo quod tempore suo mundus non habuit ita generalem sapientem. Omnibus liberalibus artibus fuit sufficienter edoctus, et theologus magnus. Unde potest dici de eo illud Mt. xi: *Ecce plus quam Salomon hic*' (MS Munich, Staatsbibliothek Clm. 2981, fo. 132ʳᵃ). For 'Mt. xi' read 'Mt. xii'.

'... He was very wise indeed in all branches of knowledge ...'[158] He was wiser than Charles I or Charles II.[159] He was 'a wise philosopher, a wiser statesman, and most wise of all as a theologian'.[160] All this sounds exaggerated and a little absurd, but Robert does indeed seem to have been exceptionally learned—for a king.

The portrayal of Robert in this sermon is confirmed by various sources.[161] Boccaccio called him 'the most learned king whom mortals have seen since Solomon'.[162] Petrarch, orchestrating the preliminaries to his own coronation as poet laureate, said that Robert was the only mortal whom he would willingly accept as judge of his talents.[163] There does indeed seem to be a foundation of truth for Federico's enthusiastic remarks both about the range of different fields over which Robert's learning extended and about the place of theology among them, to judge from Robert's library.[164]

Robert's theological tastes included civilized controversy. He wrote a treatise on the Beatific Vision,[165] and (earlier) intervened in the argument, which was to split the Franciscan Order, about the poverty of Christ, the apostles, and, by extension, the ideal religious order. Was even communal possession compatible with a perfect state? Robert argued in his treatise

---

[158] 'Fuit sapientissimus in omnibus scientiis: in responsionibus, questionibus, sermonibus' (ibid., fo. 132$^{rb}$).

[159] '... inter regem Karolum primum et secundum ipse fuit sapientissimus' (ibid., fo. 132$^{va}$).

[160] '... sapiens philosophus, sapientior politicus, sapientissimus theologus' (ibid.).

[161] Cf. Goetz, *König Robert*, 35; Léonard, *Les Angevins*, 282–3.

[162] Quoted by Léonard, *Les Angevins*, 282.

[163] Ibid. 285.

[164] See Goetz, *König Robert*, 35–6: 'Die Fürsorge für seine Bibliothek ist ihm offenbar ein wichtiges Anliegen gewesen; sie zeigt zugleich den Kreis seiner Interessen. Da stehen nun entschieden die theologischen Bücher im Vordergrund und unter diesen die Schriften Augustins und Gregors d. Gr. Es folgen an Zahl die juristischen Werke, dann geschichtliche, medizinische, naturwissenschaftliche und antike, auch Übersetzungen aller Art...' Goetz does not provide references for these interesting observations. See, however, *Robert d'Anjou, Roi de Jérusalem et de Sicile, La Vision bienheureuse: Traité envoyé au pape Jean XXII*, ed. M. Dykmans (Miscellanea Historiae Pontificiae, 30; Rome, 1970), p. 41* and n. 1, and Cornelia C. Coulter, 'The Library of the Angevin Kings at Naples', *Transactions and Proceedings of the American Philological Association*, 75 (1944), 141–55.

[165] Ed. M. Dykmans (see previous note).

that it was not compatible.[166] Like his brother St Louis of
Toulouse, he had in his youth come under the influence of
Franciscans who took a hard-line stance on poverty,[167] and the
influence of his wife Sancia seems to have pushed him in the
same direction.[168] Nevertheless, he affirmed his submission to
the doctrinal authority of the pope.[169] The tone of his treatise
on poverty is serene and uncombative. It will be remembered
that Federico, in the sermon (on Ps. 28: 10) with which we
began this discussion of the dynasty, had used the words
*affectum quietatum*, 'the emotions which have been calmed', in
connection with Robert.[170]

Paradoxically, Robert was Pope John XXII's champion against
Ludwig of Bavaria, protector of a group of Franciscans (including William of Ockham) who broke away from the pope on
the poverty issue. It was the last great conflict between the
medieval empire and the papacy. The pope was of course in
Avignon, and when Ludwig tried to establish his power and
his antipope's authority in Italy, the opposition of Robert and
his son Charles of Calabria (d. 1328) helped neutralize what
was regarded at the time, at least by Guelphs, as a grave threat
to the Church.[171] Robert was indeed on the whole a good
friend to the papacy: even his record of tribute payment, though
not perfect, was relatively respectable.[172] Therefore, it is not
pure hyperbole when the sermon praises his subjection and
obedience to the papacy:

Who would not say that our lord king was subject and obedient to the
Roman Church, which he obeyed so promptly, so faithfully in every-

[166] G. Siragusa, *L'ingegno, il sapere e gl'intendimenti di Roberto d'Angiò, con
nuovi documenti* (Palermo, 1891), 128–46, e.g. 133.
[167] Cf. M. R. Toynbee, *S. Louis of Toulouse and the Process of Canonisation in the
Fourteenth Century* (Manchester, 1929), 73.
[168] Siragusa, *L'ingegno*, 125–7; *Robert . . . La Vision*, ed. Dykmans, p. 34*.
[169] Siragusa, *L'ingegno*, 130 and n. 1.
[170] See above, p. 91.
[171] For a succinct account of the events see P. Partner, *The Lands of St. Peter:
The Papal State in the Middle Ages and the Early Renaissance* (Berkeley and Los
Angeles, 1972), 318–48; more fully, Léonard, *Les Angevins*, 248–56 (my emphases would differ from Léonard's), and also H. S. Offler, 'Empire and
Papacy: The Last Struggle', *Transactions of the Royal Historical Society*, 5th ser., 6
(1956), 21–47, and J. Miethke, 'Kaiser und Papst im Spätmittelalter: Zu den
Ausgleichsbemühungen zwischen Ludwig dem Bayern und der Kurie in
Avignon', *Zeitschrift für historische Forschung*, 10 (1983), 421–46.
[172] Léonard, *Les Angevins*, 281–2.

thing, whether by giving the financial help that was owed to it, or by defending it militarily, or by obeying its commands? Therefore one may say of him the words of John 19 (26): *Woman*: that is, the Church, which is gentle and compassionate—*behold your son*.

Quis non diceret dominum nostrum regem Robertum subiectum fuisse et obedientem ecclesie Romane, cui tam prompte, tam fideliter in omnibus obediuit, siue subueniendo in debitis,[173] siue defendendo[174] armis, siue obediendo mandatis? Dicatur ergo de eo illud Io. 19 (26): *Mulier*, id est, ecclesia, que mollis est et pia, *ecce filius tuus*.[175]

It is true that Robert found himself in opposition to papal policy in Italy when Pope John XXII decided to support the bizarre adventure of John of Bohemia in Italy. John XXII's experiment, which drastically realigned Italian politics and provoked an alliance of Guelphs and Ghibellines, could (if successful) have cost Robert a great deal politically,[176] and it is arguable that this disruption of the cordial understanding between the papacy and Naples was more Pope John's doing than his; and there is evidence that the pope did not break with him even after they had become political adversaries.[177] The sermon's version of Robert's relations with Rome is not really invalidated by this odd episode (which, one may add quite incidentally, is rather typical of John of Bohemia's adventurous career, which ended at the battle of Crécy, a last, fatal adventure from which even blindness could not keep him away).

The sermon also praises Robert as a defender of his kingdom:

He defended the kingdom with power against the emperor Henry, up to the death of the said Henry, [and] against the Bavarian. And, in short, by his strength and power he defended his subjects, put his enemies to flight, and showed that he was a man to be feared. . . . Did not Tuscany, Lombardy, etc. fear to touch his kingdom?

Defendit potenter regnum ab Herrico *im*peratore usque ad mortem predicti Herrici, contra Bauarum. Et breuiter, eius potentia et potestate

---

[173] subueniendo in debitis] *probably better than* subueniendo indebitis, 'helping with [aids] not due [from him]'. But there is room for argument about the exact sense. See below, ch. 3 n. 174.

[174] defendendo] defedendo *ms*

[175] MS Munich, Staatsbibliothek Clm. 2981, fo. 132ra.

[176] Léonard, *Les Angevins*, 263–4; for another project furthered by John XXII, in conjunction with John of Bohemia, which also posed a threat to Robert, see ibid. 267–9.

[177] *Robert . . . La Vision*, ed. Dykmans, p. 11*.

subditos[178] defendit, inimicos fugauit, et se metuendum ostendit. . . .
Nonne Tussia, Lombardia, etc. uerebantur tangere regnum eius?[179]

Though Robert was hardly a warrior in the mould of his grandfather Charles I of Anjou, it is indeed arguable that he was an effective defender of his kingdom. His position was not easy, for he had Sicily in the south as well as expeditions from the north (the emperor Henry VII, Ludwig of Bavaria, John of Bohemia) to think about.[180] His efforts to keep negotiations with Henry VII open, and his Fabian tactics against Ludwig of Bavaria, were arguably the best course of action, even in terms of *Realpolitik*, for the kingdom of Naples.[181]

It may therefore be said that Federico Franconi's sermon is not a representation of depersonalized royal virtue, but a picture which does some justice to the realities of Robert's reign and to his individual style as a ruler. There are other Angevin portraits that we might consider—sermons on the death of Charles of Calabria, of John of Durazzo, and of Philip of Taranto[182]—but these do not add much to our conclusions about individuality. In the case of Bertrand de la Tour's sermon on Charles of Calabria (Robert's son), it seems to me harder than in most of the cases we have considered to find a resemblance between the portrait painted by the preacher and what we know of the man, though this may be because we do not know so much about him. We know even less about Philip of Taranto and John of Durazzo.

A lot of space has been devoted to Edward I, Philip IV,

[178] subditos] per subditos *ms; perhaps read*: ipse subditos
[179] MS Munich, Staatsbibliothek Clm. 2981, fo. 132$^{rb}$.
[180] Compare the analysis in Goetz, *König Robert*, 14–15.
[181] Ibid. 15.
[182] The sermon on *Charles of Calabria* is by Bertrand de la Tour, OM; see Schneyer, *Repertorium*, i. 583, No. 1123. I have found it in only two manuscripts—Kremsmünster 44, fos. 121$^{vb}$–125$^{rb}$, and Seville Cathedral, Biblioteca Capitular Columbina 82-4-1 (unfoliated)—and the fact that it is about Charles of Calabria only emerges as one reads the content. The incipit gives no hint: 'Sermo lxviii$^{us}$. Qui potest fieri in exequiis alicuius magni ducis uel principis, etc. *Propter sapientiam et scientiam horum que dicuntur, ducis uita longior erit.* Prouer. xxviii° (2). Rumores flebiles . . .' *Philip of Taranto*: apart from the sermon by Juan d'Aragon, we have at least four by Giovanni da Napoli, OP: see Schneyer, *Repertorium*, iii. 606, Nos. 25–6; 609, No. 59; 615, No. 141. *John of Durazzo*: at least one by Giovanni da Napoli: Schneyer, *Repertorium*, iii. 608, No. 58; and at least three by Federico Franconi: Schneyer, *Repertorium*, iv. 223, 'Nicolaus de Asculo', Nos. 220–2.

Charles II, and Robert the Wise precisely because so much is known about their personalities: so that we can form a good idea of what the preachers' allusions would have meant to their listeners. In the course of analysing the sermons on these kings the first half of the conclusion about characterization has already been adumbrated, namely, that the portrayal of individuality does seem to have been possible and indeed rather successful within the genre.

This conclusion is corroborated when one looks at a memorial sermon on Pope Innocent IV, by Eudes of Chateauroux, which falls almost within the direct scope of this study since he exercised political power in Italy in addition to his papal office proper.[183] It is not a pure panegyric, and comes close to criticizing the pope's attitude of mind in his attempts to control the papal state:

> . . . the lord Innocent had already acquired part [*but, Eudes seems to want to stress, not all*] of the land of the Church when he died . . . perhaps he had sinned in this matter ( *facto*), by oppressing the churches for its sake; or perhaps his heart had been raised up, and the Lord did not want his efforts to do harm to himself. And the Lord reserved that victory for another, as he did with David, in respect of the building of the Temple.[184]

Eudes also makes what many may feel is a distinctly discriminating assessment of Innocent IV's gifts and strengths. We are told that God gave him a great grace for solving cases and bringing them to an end. The Life of Innocent IV by Nicolas of Calvi (Nicolaus de Carbio) also remarks on the way in which Innocent gave good justice and brought to an end in a short time, thanks to his hard work and wisdom, cases that had dragged on from long before he had become pope. Further-

---

[183] I do not address here the question of what sort or sorts of temporal power Innocent IV may have claimed as pope, though I myself (probably in the minority) do not think that he would have included temporal power *tout court* within the scope of his Petrine office. For a good study see J. A. Watt, *The Theory of Papal Monarchy in the Thirteenth Century: The Contribution of the Canonists* (London, 1965).

[184] Transcription of the Latin in P. Cole, D. L. d'Avray, and J. Riley-Smith, 'Application of Theology to Current Affairs: Memorial Sermons on the Dead of Mansurah and on Innocent IV', *Historical Research*, 63 (1990), 227–47, at 239 n. 82. (In what follows I plagiarize freely from my contribution to this article.) The point about David is that it was not granted to him to build the Temple.

more, Eudes succeeds in humanizing his picture of Innocent as judge, imparting nuances of individuality to the justice–mercy topos: 'those whom as justice dictated he cast down in one thing, he would raise up in another, prompted by mercy'.[185]

All the same, the direct portrayal of Innocent IV's personality takes up a relatively modest proportion of the sermon, a good deal if not most of which seems to be about the exercise of hierarchical authority. Close examination suggests that one of Eudes's primary concerns was to administer a stinging rebuke to the *curia* under the current pope, Alexander IV, and much of what he says is not about Innocent IV's pontificate at all.[186]

Though the sermon on Innocent IV and the sermons on kings examined in this chapter make well-directed allusions to aspects of the dead man's life, they give little narrative detail— in the case of Juan de Aragon's sermons (on his father and on Philip V of France), and of Remigio's on Louis X, virtually none. Even if the oral sermon included narrative which the written version omits, it is significant that this putative narrative detail was easily detachable from the representation. There may be a significant contrast here with, say, Italian humanist funeral oratory or with the *oraisons funèbres* of 'classical' France, which leave the reader (as well as no doubt the original listeners) with a fairly detailed knowledge of the dead person's career. A similar but partially distinct point is that vivid anecdotes characteristic of personality, such as Salimbene uses so effectively, were not as a rule integrated into the representation (apart from the mysterious reference to the lady who called Philip IV dumb in Remigio de' Girolami's sermon). Nor do descriptions of the ruler's appearance, comparable to the descriptions of Edward I in Nicholas Trevet, seem to play much of a role (the statement that Philip IV of France was fair or handsome does not amount to much of an exception).

Thus there seem to be two contrasting tendencies in the evidence set out in this chapter. On the one hand, it is clear that preachers were able to capture and represent individual personality, or aspects of it. The sermons on Charles II of Naples and Edward I of England would alone be enough to

---

[185] For the foregoing see Cole, d'Avray, and Riley-Smith, 'Application', 241.
[186] Ibid. 241–6.

demonstrate that. On the other hand, those that do so leave out a lot that one might expect in a modern memorial address, and other sermons seem to show no interest in individuality.

In reality these two tendencies may be converging rather than contrasting. The apparent tension can perhaps be traced back to one modern idea of 'the individual', which is roughly speaking the conception criticized by the biographer of Josef Knecht. Seen from that historian's imaginary future, the preceding period (our own, in fact) sought the essence of personality in differentness, departure from the norm, uniqueness: 'we are astonished to find in the biographies of that time that for instance the author recounts at length how many brothers and sisters the hero had or what psychological marks and scars were left on him by leaving childhood behind, by puberty, the struggle for recognition, the striving to win love.'[187] Contrasted with this is the idea that someone is 'worthy of special interest if placed by nature and formation in a condition to let his personality open up almost completely in its hierarchical function, yet without losing the strong, fresh, admirable driving force which makes up the aroma and worth of the individual'.[188] Something like this second conception of individuality may have informed the sermons considered above. In so far as

---

[187] 'Es ist ja allerdings das, was wir heute [= in the imaginary future] unter Persönlichkeit verstehen, nun etwas erheblich anderes, als was die Biographen und Historiker früherer Zeiten damit gemeint haben. Für sie, und zwar namentlich für die Autoren jener Epochen, welche eine ausgesprochene biographische Neigung hatten, scheint, so möchte man sagen, das Wesentliche einer Persönlichkeit das Abweichende, das Normwidrige und Einmalige, ja oft geradezu das Pathologische gewesen zu sein, während wir Heutigen von bedeutenden Persönlichkeiten überhaupt erst dann sprechen, wenn wir Menschen begegnen, denen jenseits von allen Originalitäten und Absonderlichkeiten ein möglichst vollkommenes Sich-Einordnen ins Allgemeine, ein möglichst vollkommener Dienst am Überpersönlichen gelungen ist. . . . Wir erstaunen, wenn wir in den Biographien jener Zeiten etwa weitläufig erzählt finden, wie viele Geschwister der Held gehabt oder welche seelischen Narben und Kerben ihm die Loslösung von der Kindheit, die Pubertät, der Kampf um Anerkennung, das Werben um Liebe hinterlassen haben' (*Das Glasperlenspiel: Versuch einer Lebensbeschreibung des Magister Ludi Josef Knecht samt Knechts hinterlassenen Schriften*, ed. Hermann Hesse (1943; 1975 printing), 9–10).

[188] 'Uns ist nur jener ein Held und eines besonderen Interesses würdig, der von Natur und durch Erziehung in den Stand gesetzt wurde, seine Person nahezu vollkommen in ihrer hierarchischen Funktion aufgehen zu lassen, ohne daß ihr doch der starke, frische, bewundernswerte Antrieb verlorengegangen wäre, welcher den Duft und Wert des Individuums ausmacht' (ibid. 10).

personality found expression in the prince's office, it might be vividly represented.

Whether or not the evocation of this other sort of individuality was an objective in its own right, it could certainly have helped preachers impart instruction about the ruler's role. A preacher could make a general point about the role of king or prince by emphasizing an individual trait of character. It was a matter of singling out the particular aspect of kingship which the man most strikingly embodied. Edward I's crusading and his good counsellors, Charles II's instinct for peace, Robert's wisdom— all these qualities were commonplace as abstractions, yet the application of the stereotype to the individual invests the stereotype itself with new intensity.

From this point of view, the omission of detailed narrative and physical description makes good sense. When the representation of the particular is meant to exemplify the general, selectivity is essential. It has been said that

the scarcity of specific characterization in a Boccaccio story or in Voltaire's *Candide* makes for a more rarefied literary climate, in which the characters are to be taken as mere types of human attitude . . . if a reader by means of his imagination endows all the violations of Cunégonde's womanhood with the concreteness of the pain felt by the cat that, in Flaubert's *Bouvard et Pécuchet*, escapes from a kettle of boiling water, he destroys the very substance of the author's conception.[189]

The hypothesis that fits the data best is therefore that to represent the second of the two sorts of individuality defined above was probably an end in itself and almost certainly a means of conveying the preacher's message about kingship. It is now time to define this message more precisely. The sermons are a by no means minor source for attitudes to political authority, especially if one is prepared to descend below the cerebral stratosphere of political philosophy proper. As evidence for political attitudes, furthermore, one may use model sermons for the death of a king or prince alongside the sermons for real rulers examined above. What they say about the role of a ruler is partly predictable and partly not. Something which

---

[189] R. Arnheim, 'Abstract Language and Metaphor', in his *Toward a Psychology of Art* (Berkeley and Los Angeles, 1966), 266–82, at 277.

may or may not seem predictable, furthermore, but which is certainly a prominent feature of the genre, is that the political doctrines of the sermons are by and large neither submerged in nor separated from their more other-worldly teachings. These two distinct but complementary aspects of the message are the subject of the next two chapters. The final chapter (Chapter 5) will develop the same argument about complementarity with reference to the relation between representations and political reality, thus developing also an implication of the present chapter, viz. that the image of kingship presented by memorial sermons was not detached from the realities of rulers' lives.

# 3   The Prince

AN attraction of memorial preaching as an object of research is that comparisons between periods can usefully be drawn. Since the funeral oratory of Italian humanists has recently been analysed, by John McManamon,[1] with an emphasis on ideas about social roles, it is natural to ask how far these ideas were new, and how far they were similar to the idea of the prince which is found in medieval memorial sermons.[2]

The humanists use funeral oratory to put over a positive and optimistic view of politics and of the things of this world. They praise 'external goods', notably education and ancestry.[3] 'Greed was reprehensible, but wealth was neutral', their historian tells us, and could have 'a civic reference'.[4] The first known 'fully classicizing funeral oration', by Pier Paolo Vergerio (the Elder), 'reflected the culture of subdital humanism'[5]—humanism in the service of *signori* or princes, that is—by demonstrating the benefits of monarchical rule.[6] The Florentine Leonardo Bruni, in his oration for Nanni Strozzi (1428), argued that virtue went with republican rather than monarchical rule.[7] The Milanese humanist Andrea Biglia found classical and biblical precedents for ducal ideology.[8] In the first half of the fifteenth century there is a certain emphasis on military virtue; in the second

---

[1] John M. McManamon, *Funeral Oratory and the Cultural Ideals of Italian Humanism* (Chapel Hill and London, 1989).

[2] Here the comparison will be concerned with ideas rather than rhetoric, in so far as the two can be distinguished. At the surface rhetorical level the sharp contrast between the genres is obvious after the most cursory comparison.

[3] McManamon, *Funeral Oratory*, ch. 3.

[4] Ibid. 114, 115.

[5] Ibid. 92.

[6] Ibid.

[7] Ibid. 96. This republican ideology is less relevant to our comparative purpose, as I do not know of any real equivalent—in the genre of memorial preaching—from the period before 1350. Republican ideology and civic humanism can of course be found in the 13th and early 14th cents.: see D. L. d'Avray, 'Another Friar and Antiquity', in K. Robbins (ed.), *Religion and Humanism* (Studies in Church History, 17; Oxford, 1981), 49–58 (this contains misprints for which I am not responsible, since I was not sent proofs).

[8] McManamon, *Funeral Oratory*, 98.

half, peaceful virtues are given more prominence than before.[9] Virtues and achievements include justice, clemency,[10] and the building of civic and Christian edifices.[11]

McManamon does not compare his humanist orations with medieval memorial sermons, though he seems obliquely to imply that the latter differed in not attempting to 'depict an inspirational image of the deceased',[12] which is not borne out by the findings of the previous chapter. The expectation of some Renaissance scholars might be that medieval sermons would tend to 'other-worldiness' and a comparative indifference to secular values. If there are still Renaissance scholars with such expectations, this genre should help them to think again.

The fact is that medieval memorial sermons anticipate many of the attitudes to political authority which humanist funeral orations put forward. As will shortly be demonstrated in detail, pre-humanist preachers were quite capable of praising the dead man's ancestry and even his wealth. They seem to take it for granted that political power as such is good, and, like the humanists, they expatiate on the warlike virtues of courage and energy, as well as on the dead ruler's justice, mercy, etc. Like the humanists, they make these ideals concrete by reference to the dead man's deeds.

It is true that (as observed in the previous chapter) we do not have much evidence that medieval memorial sermons included detailed chronological narratives of events in the dead man's life, as the humanist orations often did, but this is not a universal feature of humanist funeral oratory either,[13] and may in any case be regarded as more of a rhetorical than an ideo-logical difference. Again, one would obviously not expect to find, in the earlier period, the humanists' preoccupation with

[9] McManamon, *Funeral Oratory*, 101, 107, 109.
[10] Ibid. 110. Cf. p. 116: 'Marsi's speech pleads for the principal political ideals of humanist orators: for impartial justice, for generous clemency, for order within the state, for peace and concord throughout the peninsula, for *humanitas* as the informing spirit of governors and the governed.'
[11] Ibid. 97, 112 (esp. n. 75).
[12] Ibid. 33.
[13] Ibid. 21: 'By rejecting the thematic sermon and returning to classical forms of panegyric, humanists assured that the heart of their funeral orations focused upon the deeds of their subjects, often disposed in chronological order'— 'often', so not always.

their own educational programme and with the ruler's patronage of humanists. Furthermore, a study of the concept of
*humanitas* from a comparative perspective would probably point
up a real contrast, for it is very hard to find, if indeed it
appears at all, in memorial sermons on kings and princes
before 1350.[14] Conversely, it may possibly be significant (though
it is unfair to argue from silence) that McManamon's study has
no index entry under 'humility', whereas the virtue is mentioned several times in surviving medieval sermons in memory
of rulers.[15]

The fact remains that the medieval and the humanist
preachers shared an appreciation of the 'external goods' of the
dead ruler, and a tendency to dwell on his political virtues in
war and peace.

This is actually rather predictable, if old *idées fixes* about
Renaissance dawns are put aside, but we would do well not to
confuse the retrospectively predictable with the inevitable. Here
a further comparison across time—this time with the four
known surviving funeral sermons by Martin Luther—is a

---

[14] For *humanitas* as a humanist political ideal, see ibid. 101, 116.
[15] *Giovanni da San Gimignano, OP*: 'Quarta quoque questio est de ipsius
humilitate, cum subinfertur: et ubi est—supple—*Ana. Ana* enim interpretatur:
"humilis in genere fratrum". Nam siue rex siue prelatus, licet sit superior
dignitate, tamen debet se reputare fratrem et coequalem caritate, secundum
illud Ecci. 32 (1): *Rectorem te posuerunt? Noli extolli; sed esto in illis quasi unus ex
eis*. Unde rex debet esse humilis in genere fratrum, id est, ipsorum subiec-
torum, uel in genere, id est, in naturali generatione (*corrected from* genera-
tionem) quia omnes descendimus ab uno patre, scilicet, primo homine' (MS
Siena, Biblioteca Comunale, F. X. 24, fo. 103ra, from a sermon *In funere regis* on
the text *Rex hodie est et cras morietur* (Ecclus. 10: 12); Schneyer, *Repertorium*, iii.
762, No. 503); *sermon on the death of Edward I*: 'in prosperitatibus et uictoriis
istius mundi non fuit in superbiam eleuatus, sed magis humiliatus' (Transcription C:c, 4: 1); *Bertrand de la Tour, OM*: 'In scola autem dyaboli docetur omnibus
uelle (*supply* preesse?) et nulli uelle subesse; sed in scola Christi docetur
oppositum, uidelicet omnibus uelle subesse propter deum et nulli uelle preesse
contra deum. Istam lectionem studuit in principio Iehu (Iere. *ms*) rex Israel, cui
dixit deus, sicut habetur iiii° R(eg.) x (30): *studiose egisti quod rectum erat, et
placebat in oculis meis*. Reuera, nichil magis rectum est quam uita humilis' (MS
Kremsmünster 44, fo. 123rb, from a sermon beginning 'Sermo lxviiius. Qui
potest fieri in exequiis alicuius magni ducis uel principis, etc. *Propter sapientiam
et scientiam . . .*' (Prov. 28: 2); Schneyer, *Repertorium*, i. 583, No. 1123); *Giovanni
da Napoli, OP*: 'Cum omnibus inferioribus humiliter conuersabatur' (MS Naples,
Nazionale VIII AA 11, fo. 37ra, from a sermon beginning 'In translatione
domini ducis Duracii. *Placuit deo . . .* (Ecclus. 44: 16)'; Schneyer, *Repertorium*, iii.
608, No. 58).

salutary corrective. They too are on dead princes: two of them
on the elector Frederick the Wise, delivered in 1525,[16] and two
on his brother and successor John, delivered seven years later.[17]
These texts show that it was possible to write a long funeral or
memorial sermon without saying much at all about the ruler's
social role.[18] Luther gives the impression that he does not feel
it is his business to develop ideas about specifically political
virtues:

I shall not praise him now for his great virtues, but rather let him
remain a sinner like all the rest of us, who also purpose to go to the
judgement and hand over to our Lord God many a grievous sin, as we
too hold steadfast to that article which is called 'the forgiveness of
sins.' Therefore I am not going to make out that our beloved lord was
altogether pure, though he was a very devout, kindly man, free of all
guile, in whom never in my lifetime have I seen the slightest pride,
anger, or envy, who was able to bear and forgive all things readily
and was more than mild. I shall say no more of this virtue now.
    If along with this he sometimes failed in government, what can be
said against that? A prince is also a human being and has ten devils
around him where another man has only one, so that God must give
him special guidance and set his angels about him. When we see them
sometimes make a false step in government we are quick to say, Ah, I
would have done so and so, but if we were to govern we would
probably drive the cart into the mire or even turn it upside down. So
nobody can do right as far as we are concerned, and if we look
at ourselves we have never yet been right. All this we shall pass
over now and we shall stick to praising him, as St. Paul praises his
Christians, saying that God will bring with him those who are in
Christ . . .[19]

Luther goes on to talk about the elector John's 'death' (i.e.
his severe trial) at Augsburg two years before, when the elector

[16] E. Winkler, *Die Leichenpredigt im deutschen Luthertum bis Spener* (Forschungen zur Geschichte und Lehre des Protestantismus, 10th ser., 34; Munich,
1967), 25; I have used the edition in *D. Martin Luthers Werke: Kritische
Gesamtausgabe*, xvii/1 (Weimar, 1907), 196–227. Note the remarks on the context
of these sermons ibid., pp. xxxii–xxxiv.
[17] Winkler, *Die Leichenpredigt*, 25; I have used, for convenience, the translation in *Luther's Works*, gen. ed. Helmut T. Lehmann, li. *Sermons I*, ed. and
trans. John W. Doberstein (Philadelphia, 1959), 231–55. (The English *Luther's
Works* edition appears not to include the two sermons listed in the preceding
note.)
[18] See Endnote 12, below, pp. 283–4.
[19] *Luther's Works*, li. 236–7.

'openly confessed Christ's death and resurrection before the whole world and he stuck to it'.[20] These four *Leichenpredigten* by Luther make powerful and vivid reading, but the lack of attention to the role of the prince in this world is perhaps more striking than the few things actually said on that theme.[21]

The comparison with Luther shows that the approach to rulership which we find in both the humanist and the medieval phases of the genre (and for that matter in much subsequent funeral preaching) was not inevitable, but conventional—in the sense of being a choice from alternative possibilities. The convention of analysing the dead ruler's extraneous goods, his achievements, and his virtues *qua* ruler has quite probably been the dominant one in the history of memorial preaching. This is not surprising either in itself or in view of the combined weight of the medieval and humanist traditions in the genre.

Against this background of comparisons, we may now look more closely at what memorial sermons before 1350 have to say about extraneous or external goods and political virtues. The former topic deserves the closest attention, because one could not so easily have guessed at its importance in the genre's medieval phase.

Nobility was one of the 'external goods' which, as we saw above, the fifteenth-century humanists rated highly in their funeral oratory. As was briefly suggested, this preoccupation with ancestry was not a novelty which they introduced into the genre. We may begin with an anonymous sermon on the death of a prince which, so far as one can date the manuscript, probably falls just within the period before 1350 (the recent scholarly catalogue dates the manuscript to the middle of the fourteenth century, and of course the text cannot be later than the manuscript though it could be earlier).[22] The preacher

---

[20] Ibid. 237.
[21] It may be relevant that when Luther gave his first sermon on the death of Frederick the Wise, Philip Melanchthon had already preached a *Funebrem orationem* in Latin: see Winkler, *Die Leichenpredigt*, 31; Luther, *Werke* (Weimar edn.), vol. xvii/1, p. xxxiii and n. 1; and *Philippi Melanthonis opera quae supersunt omnia*, ed. Carolus Gottlieb Bretschneider (Corpus Reformatorum, 11; Halis Saxonum, 1843), 90–8.
[22] G. Achten, *Die theologischen lateinischen Handschriften in Quarto der Staatsbibliothek preußischen Kulturbesitz Berlin*, ii. *MS Theol. lat. qu. 267–378* (Wiesbaden, 1984), 69.

asserts that noble ancestry (*altitudo generis*) does much for greatness. He qualifies this by remarking that every such person ought to fear lest he leave a stain on his lineage, and become the point where nobility ends. Far better to be the beginning of fame (*claritatis*) than the end of it. For this reason man should strive for good morals. Even so, someone choosing whom to entrust with temporal authority should not only consider good morals, but also noble blood (*genus clarum*). Then the preacher quotes a quite lengthy passage from Gauthier de Châtillon's *Alexandreis*, the gist of which is that *arrivistes* are harsh and a danger to their lords (though it is reasonable to raise up men who lack noble blood if their character is outstanding).[23]

According to a model sermon by Giovanni da San Gimignano, OP, 'it is fitting that a prince should be able to be called happy more than other people can, at least in respect of political (*politica*) happiness, for which, as Aristotle tells us in *Rhetoric*, book 1, intrinsic and extrinsic goods are required'.[24]

Turning from models to sermons in memory of specific rulers, we find Federico Franconi extolling the lineage of Charles II of Naples. He is arguing that a king should have high glory, and that Charles evidently had it, for one reason, because of his origin, 'because he was born of the [royal] house and lineage of France'.[25]

The theme of family greatness is prominent in sermons on Neapolitan Angevins by Giovanni da Napoli, OP. In a sermon which, according to the rubric, was given in memory of Charles

[23] See Transcription A, **2**: 1–9, passage beginning 'Fuit maximus morum claritate' and ending 'et gloria sanguinis alti' (fo. 1ᵛ). For articulations in two recent books, by creatively *engagés* medieval historians, of the view that there was a real correlation between nobility and virtue, see M. Keen, *Chivalry* (New Haven and London, 1984), 160–1 (cautious implication), and, in a different interpretative context and more explicitly, A. Murray, *Reason and Society in the Middle Ages* (Oxford, 1978), chs. 13–15.

[24] 'Decet enim principem pre ceteris posse dici felicem saltem felicitate politica, ad quam, sicut tradit Philosophus in primo Rethoricorum, requiruntur bona intrinseca et extrinseca' (MS Siena, Biblioteca Comunale F. X. 24, fo. 106ᵛᵃ). Cf. below, text at n. 30.

[25] 'Quam celsitudinem glorie habuit dominus Karolus rex Sicilie sancte memorie, quod apparet tam ex origine, quam ex regimine. Quis non diceret eum habuisse celsitudinem glorie ex origine, quia natus est de domo et stirpe Francie?' (MS Munich, Staatsbibliothek Clm. 2981, fo. 130ʳᵇ, from a sermon on the text *Ego constitutus sum rex* (Ps. 2: 6); Schneyer, *Repertorium*, iv. 223, 'Nicolaus de Asculo', No. 216).

II, but which may in fact have been given in memory of his son and Dante's friend Charles Martel,[26] Giovanni alludes to the dead man's connection by blood (*carnali origine*) (as well as by love and devotion) with St Louis of France and Louis, bishop of Toulouse. Christ drew Louis the king and Louis the bishop to himself, so it was appropriate that he should not draw to himself the man thus attached to them, who also had the love of God.[27]

Both the spiritual and the worldly excellence of the royal family of France, of which the Angevins of Naples were a branch, are enthusiastically called to mind in a sermon in memory of Philip of Taranto, a brother of Robert the Wise. The authority of Matt. 7: 17 is invoked: *a good tree brings forth good fruit*. The royal house of France can be called a good tree with respect to both God and the world: with respect to God, as a lover and defender of the Church—and Giovanni adds a mention of the recent canonization of Louis IX and Louis of Toulouse; with respect to the world, as being outstandingly noble among all the families (*domos*) of the world. It is appropriate, Giovanni argues, that the fruits born from such a tree should not only be good with respect to God, but also great with respect to the world. He seems to mean that they should be kings, dukes (*duces*), princes, and the like. The dead man came from such a house, since his grandfather was the son of the king of France. So it is fitting that he should be a prince. (Giovanni also claims that the empire of Constantinople was Philip's *de iure*.)[28] Similar ideas recur in Giovanni's second

[26] Or, less probably, Charles II's grandson Charles of Calabria. See above, ch. 2 n. 145.

[27] My abridged paraphrase omits the skilful symbolism: 'Et quantum spectat ad presens, ferrum forte fuerunt sancti Ludouicus rex Francie et Ludouicus episcopus Tholosanus, ambo fortes in amore dei, quibus fuit iunctus carnali origine et mentis dilectione et deuotione dominus N. Et primos duos lapis Christus ad se traxit, ergo rationabile fuit quod hunc etiam tertium, habentem, up supra declaratum est, caritatem dei, ad se traheret' (MS Naples, Nazionale VIII AA 11, fo. 25ʳᵇ, from a sermon on the text *In caritate perpetua* (Jer. 31: 3); Schneyer, *Repertorium* iii. 607, No. 36).

[28] 'Quantum ad primum est sciendum quod sicut dicitur Mt. 7 (17): *bona arbor bo(nos) fructus facit*. Arbor bona potest dici domus Francie, que est bona: et quo ad deum, utpote amatrix et defensatrix ecclesie—de qua de nouo duo sancti Ludouici canonizati sunt, scilicet rex Francie et episcopus Tholosanus; et quo ad mundum, utpote inter domos omnes mundi excellenter nobilis. Ergo decet quod fructus qui nascuntur de tali arbore sint non solum boni quo ad

sermon on the death of Philip of Taranto.[29] Then, in a sermon
for the translation of Philip's body to a more honourable resting-
place, we meet the distinction between extrinsic and intrinsic
again.

Goodness is of two kinds, for present purposes. There is the extrinsic
goodness of the flesh, which people of noble blood have; for the
nobility or aristocracy of the flesh is the goodness of the family or of
ancestors, from whom the noble person draws his origin. There is also
the intrinsic goodness of mind, which virtuous people have . . . and
the aforesaid prince had both kinds of virtue. He was very noble, that
is, he was the son of a king from the most noble house of France
through the direct or masculine line. . . .

Bonitas autem est duplex quantum spectat ad presens, scilicet extrinseca carnis, quam habent persone generose, quia generositas seu
nobilitas carnis est bonitas generis seu progenitorum, a quibus generosus trahit originem;—et intrinseca mentis, quam habent persone
uirtuose . . . et utramque bonitatem habuit princeps predictus. Fuit
enim multum generosus, scilicet filius regis de domo nobilissima
Francie per rectam lineam seu masculinam ortus. . . .[30]

After balancing the foregoing remarks with a passage about
Philip's virtue,[31] Giovanni implicitly gives a religious rationale
for the attention that he (with other preachers) pays to ancestry,
arguing that goodness and evil in a person of great nobility or
rank are known and seen by many.[32] Much the same reasoning

---

deum, sed etiam magni quo ad [*fo. 18$^{vb}$*] mundum, scilicet reges, duces, principes, et huiusmodi. Dominus autem N. habuit ortum ex tali domo, quia eius
auus fuit filius regis Francie. Ergo decuit quod esset princeps. 2° R(eg.) 3° (38):
*princeps et maximus*—quia ad eum de iure spectabat *imperium* Constantino-
politanum—*cecidit*, scilicet casu mortis, *hodie'* (MS Naples, Nazionale VIII AA
11, fo. 18$^{va-b}$, from a sermon on the text *Princeps dei* (Gen. 23: 6); Schneyer,
*Repertorium*, iii. p. 606, No. 25). On the claim to the empire of Constantinople,
see Emile Léonard, *Les Angevins de Naples* (Paris, 1954), 297.

[29] MS Naples, Nazionale VIII AA 11, fo. 19$^{ra}$, passage beginning 'Quantum
ad primum est sciendum quod sicut dicitur Mt. 7'; Schneyer, *Repertorium*, iii.
606, No. 26.

[30] Ibid., fo. 37$^{va}$, from a sermon on the text *Ante translationem testimonium
habuit* (Heb. 11: 5); Schneyer, *Repertorium*, iii. 609, No. 59.

[31] Ibid., passage beginning 'Fuit etiam satis uirtuosus'.

[32] 'Bonitas enim intrinseca mentis [*fo. 37$^{vb}$*] habet annexum testimonium
intrinsecum conscientie, sicut Apostolus de se et sibi similibus dicit, secunda
ad Cor. primo (12): *gloria nostra est hec, testimonium conscientie nostre*, que in
persona generosa habet annexum testimonium extrinsecum multorum. Sicut

is set out in the same preacher's sermon for the translation of the body of Philip's brother John of Durazzo. After referring to the dead man's ancestry, Giovanni outlines the dead man's virtues;[33] then he pulls his argument together:

And of him one can truly say the words of Hebrews 11 (5): *he had testimony that he had pleased God.* Here one should note carefully the fact that it says: *he had testimony.* For just as among bodily things something which is in a high place is evident to many, whether it is beautiful to see, like a light, or unpleasant, like gallows, so in spiritual things goodness or wickedness in a person of excellent birth or rank is known and seen by many, and in consequence has the testimony of many, in accordance with the rule of Christ, who said, John 3 (11): *What we know we speak, and to what we have seen we bear witness.* But the lord N.[34] was of excellent birth, as was said above, and of excellent rank, because he was a duke, and therefore his goodness, because of which *he pleased God,* has the testimony of many, that is, of all who knew him.

Et de eo uere dici potest illud ad Hebr. xi° (5): *testimonium habuit placuisse deo.* Ubi diligenter notandum est hoc quod dicitur *testimonium habuit.* Sicut enim in corporalibus existens in eminenti loco multis apparet, siue sit pulcrum ad uidendum ut lumen, siue sit turpe ut patibulum, sic bonitas in spiritualibus et malitia existens in persona excellentis generis seu gradus a multis scitur et uidetur, et per con-

enim in corporalibus, existens in eminenti loco multis apparet, siue sit pulcrum ad uidendum, ut lumen, siue sit turpe, ut patibulum, sic, in spiritualibus, bonitas et malitia existens in persona excellentis generis seu gradus a multis scitur et uidetur, et per consequens habet testimonium multorum, secundum regulam Christi dicentis, Io. 3° (11): *quod scimus, loquimur, et quod uidimus testamur.* De quo testimonio extrinseco ait Apostolus, prima ad Thimotheum 3° (7): *Oportet testimonium habere ab hiis qui foris sunt.* Sed dominus N., ut supra declaratum est, fuit multum generosus et uirtuosus. Ergo ipse habuit duplex testimonium supradictum, ut de eo possit dici illud prime Io. 5 (9): *Si testimonium hominum accipimus, testimonium dei maius est'* (MS Naples, Nazionale VIII AA 11, fo. 37va–b, from a sermon on the text *Ante translationem testimonium habuit* (Hebr. 11: 5); Schneyer, *Repertorium,* iii. 609, No. 59). (dominus N.] N. interlined.)

[33] Ibid., fos. 36vb–37ra, passage beginning 'Bonitas autem est duplex' and ending *'per omnia placentes',* from a sermon on the text *Placuit deo et translatus est* (Ecclus. 44: 16); Schneyer, *Repertorium,* iii. 608, No. 58. He includes an allusion to the recent canonization of John of Durazzo's brother Louis of Toulouse, and of Louis IX, brother of John of Durazzo's grandfather.

[34] Reference to 'N.' is normal even when rubric and/or content make it clear that the sermon was in memory of a particular historical person.

sequens habet multorum testimonium, secundum regulam Christi dicentis, Io. 3° (11): *quod scimus loquimur, et quod uidimus testamur.* Sed dominus N. fuit excellentis generis, ut supradictum est, et fuit excellentis gradus, quia fuit dux, et idcirco[35] bonitas eius, propter quam *placuit deo,* habet testimonium multorum, omnium scilicet qui cognouerunt eum.[36]

Thus it was not uncommon to bring up the subject of the dead ruler's noble ancestry in memorial sermons before 1350, a fact which is not astonishing once known but which could not have been confidently predicted either. The way in which ancestry is made relevant differs. The anonymous sermon (in a Berlin manuscript) which was cited first implies that virtue is more likely to be found in combination with nobility, though either can exist without the other—an attitude which was no doubt widely diffused.[37] Giovanni da San Gimignano, OP, calls on the authority of Aristotle. Giovanni da Napoli, OP, makes the common-sense point that the example of a man of great family has an exceptional impact on others. In general, as with the humanists, noble ancestry is treated in positive terms.

The attitude to wealth is more ambiguous. It is not the same thing as their attitude to avarice, which we are hardly surprised to find condemned by Giovanni da San Gimignano.[38] The anonymous sermon on the death of a prince in a Berlin manuscript, however, seems to incline to a negative evaluation of wealth. The context, the previous progression of the sermon, leads one to expect comments of a positive nature, instead of which the author claims that 'today, those who are pre-eminent in riches dominate others, even if they have scarcely anything

---

[35] idcirco] *ms adds and deletes* paupertas.

[36] MS Naples, Nazionale VIII AA 11, fo. 37[ra] (same sermon).

[37] Note the interesting discussion in the immensely influential *De regimine principum* of Egidio 'Colonna' da Romano, OESA (i.e. Aegidius Romanus or Giles of Rome): 1. 4.5, pp. 204–7 of the Rome, 1607 edition. See too W. Berges, *Die Fürstenspiegel des hohen und späten Mittelalters* (Leipzig, 1938), 10–11.

[38] 'Quartum est odium uitiorum, precipue auaritie. Prouer. 28 (16): *Qui odit auaritiam longi fient dies eius.* Ad litteram, enim, multi auaritia citius moriuntur, quia uel immoderate laborant pro diuitiis adquirendis, uel quia mortalibus periculis se exponunt, uel quia propter suas diuitias nonnulli occiduntur:—que omnia effugit qui auaritiam odit; uel *longi fient dies eius,* id est, participes erit eterne claritatis, sicut glossa exponit' (MS Siena, Biblioteca Comunale F. X. 24, fo. 104[vb], from a sermon 'in funere alicuius ducis uel diuitis' (fo. 103[vb]), on the text *Dux de terra Aegypti non erit amplius* (Exod. 30: 13); Schneyer, *Repertorium,* iii. 762, No. 504).

else: which is a wicked thing, however, and more in accordance with the depravity of the world than the ordinance (*institutum*) of God'.[39] Even this preacher seems to admit the possibility of a ruler who uses wealth well (though his words are not very direct).[40]

On the other hand, Giovanni da San Gimignano, OP, his condemnation of avarice notwithstanding, is quite explicit in defending a connection between power and wealth (he was, after all, an Italian of the early fourteenth century):

Thirdly, too, in the authority which I introduced the prince is commended for the opulence of his riches, since *he was great in this city-state*.[41] For in city-states it is the commonest thing for men to be made great because of riches. And sometimes this can happen in a just and rational way: that is, because in the commonwealth of a city-state or country that man should be raised highest who is or can be most useful to the republic. But it is obvious that in many things rich men can help the commonwealth more than poor men. Therefore if rich men are more honoured or raised up higher and become great in offices of a kind in which they are or can be more useful to the community and the city-state, it is not inappropriate or a sin, since this is not to honour them because of riches, but because of the necessity and utility of the commonwealth. And where rich men obtain a higher place in the commonwealth than the poor, it is not unworthy that they should be more honoured, so far as external respect is concerned, because it is one thing to honour a man on account of his person, and another to do so because of his station. For the man who is more virtuous deserves to receive more honour because of his person: that is to say, the honour of praise or reputation and that kind of thing. However, the man who obtains the higher place in the commonwealth deserves to get more honour because of his station. Moreover, great riches are especially fitting for a prince, for it is proper for a prince to be magnificent, that is, by taking on himself, in a virtuous and rational way, great expenses, which cannot

[39] The passage in context: 'Fuit maximus morum claritate . . . armorum strenuitate . . . auctoritate officii . . . Copiositate thesauri. Unde illi qui preminent diuitiis hodie aliis dominantur, etiam si aliud uix habeant, quod tamen est iniquum, et magis secundum prauitatem mundi quam secundum institutum dei.' (See Transcription A, 2: 1, 3: 1, 4: 1, 5: 1–2.)

[40] 'Beati sunt illi serui quos . . . *que digna sunt principe cogitabit*' (Transcription A, 5: 4).

[41] This is perhaps a rather free translation of *ciuitate*. In the passage which immediately follows, 'commonwealth' translates *republica* and 'country' translates *patrie*. The phrase is from 1 Macc. 2: 17.

be managed without great riches. It is also sometimes necessary for a prince to create armies and wage wars, and these cannot happen without expenses, nor great expenses without great riches: if, in time of war, he did not have them from his own resources, but wanted simply to extort them from his subjects, it would sometimes be necessary for him to bear so heavily on them that they would hate him, and would not be so faithful; and this would be dangerous. It is also sometimes necessary for a prince to give great gifts and presents freely to knights[42] or others who have deserved well. In this too he ought to practise the virtue of magnificence, just as it is said in Esther 2 (18) of King Assuerus that *he gave gifts freely according to princely magnificence*, that is, things which were fitting for a prince.[43] And thus it is fitting for a prince to be great, that is, of great riches, as is said of Job, Job chapter 1 (3), that *this man was great among all the peoples of the East*, that is, richer in wealth, as the interlinear gloss explains it.

Tertio quoque in auctoritate inducta commendatur princeps de opulentia diuitiarum, quia *magnus in ciuitate hac* (1 Machab. 2: 17). Nam maxime efficiuntur homines magni propter diuitias in ciuitatibus. Et hoc aliquando potest iuste et rationabiliter fieri, quia scilicet ille est in republica ciuitatis uel patrie magis promouendus qui magis est uel esse potest utilis reipublice. Sed manifestum est quod in multis diuites possunt iuuare rempublicam magis quam pauperes. Unde si in talibus officiis diuites magis honorarentur uel promouerentur et magni fiant in quibus utiliores sunt uel esse possunt communitati et ciuitati, non est inconueniens neque peccatum, quia hoc non est honorare eos propter diuitias, sed propter reipublice necessitatem et utilitatem. Et ubi [*fo. 106^{va}*] diuites altiorem locum optinent in republica quam pauperes, non est indignum quod magis honorentur quantum ad reuerentiam exteriorem, quia aliud est honorare hominem propter personam, aliud propter statum. Nam propter personam, ille est magis honorandus qui est magis uirtuosus, scilicet honore laudis uel reputationis et huiusmodi.[44] Sed propter statum ille est magis honorandus qui altiorem locum in republica optinet. Competit autem specialiter principi magnitudo diuitiarum, quia decet principem esse magnificum, scilicet faciendo uirtuose et rationabiliter magnos sumptus, qui sine magnis diuitiis fieri non possunt. Oportet etiam quandoque principem facere exercitus et bella gerere,[45] que sine magnis expensis fieri non possunt, nec magne expense sine magnis diuitiis, quas si tempore

---

[42] *militibus.*
[43] If 'decebant' is emended to 'decebat', the translation would instead be: 'that is, magnificence which befits a prince'.
[44] huiusmodi] *corrected from* ha-
[45] gerere] guerre *ms*

guerre ex se non haberet, se*d* uellet eas tantum extorquere ab subditis, oporteret interdum quod in tantum grauaret eos quod odirent eum, et non essent ita fideles, et hoc esset periculosum. Oportet etiam interdum principem largiri dona magna et munera militibus uel aliis bene meritis, in quo etiam uti debet uirtute magnificentie, sicut dicitur Hester 2 (18) de Assuero rege quod *dona largitus est iuxta magnificentiam principalem*, id est, que principem decebant,[46] et ita oportet principem esse[47] magnum, id est, magnarum diuitiarum, sicut dicitur de Iob, c. 1 (3) Iob, quod *erat uir ille magnus inter omnes orientales*, id est, ditior in diuitibus, sicut exponit glossa interlinearis.[48]

Giovanni da San Gimignano's remarks probably reflect first-hand observation of political realities. Perhaps the *principes* he has in mind are the *signori* who were coming to power in Italian city-states.[49]

The attitude to wealth of the Franciscan Bertrand de la Tour, a contemporary of Giovanni, has an extra interest because of his place in the poverty controversy. In 1323 Pope John XXII condemned the doctrine that Christ and the apostles were absolutely without property, individual or common. The Franciscan Order was already a mass of tension where the poverty idea was concerned, and some broke away as a result of John's decision: not only members of the rigorous 'spiritual' party but others too (including William of Ockham). Even 'soft-liners' on poverty in practice had been able to claim that in principle the order owned no property (relying on what might seem to us a legal fiction, one which John XXII had knocked away in the previous year[50]). For many of them, too, it had

---

[46] decebant] *corrected from* debe-; *emend to* decebat?

[47] esse] n *added and deleted*

[48] MS Siena, Biblioteca Comunale F. X. 24, fo. 106[rb–va], from a sermon 'in funere alicuius principis' (fo. 105[vb]) on the text *Princeps maximus cecidit hodie* (2 Kgs. 3: 38); Schneyer, *Repertorium*, iii. 762, No. 505. On the interlinear gloss see B. Smalley, *The Study of the Bible in the Middle Ages*, 3rd edn. (Oxford, 1982), 56.

[49] It seems likely that the word *princeps* could be used loosely enough to cover *signori*. See the remarks of H. Koller quoted above, ch. 1 n. 238.

[50] In the bull *Ad conditorem canonum*: see J. Moorman, *A History of the Franciscan Order from its Origins to the Year 1517* (Oxford, 1968), 316–17. For a fascinating appraisal of a central figure in the poverty controversy in the immediately preceding period see D. Burr, *Olivi and Franciscan Poverty: The Origins of the Usus Pauper Controversy* (Philadelphia, 1989). Jean Dunbabin, *A Hound of God: Pierre de la Palud and the Fourteenth-century Church* (Oxford, 1991), 153–5, gives a sane summary. Among earlier studies note M. Lambert's lucid *Franciscan Poverty: The Doctrine of the Absolute Poverty of Christ and the Apostles in the Franciscan Order, 1210–1323* (London, 1961).

doubtless been important to feel that their order came nearest
to the way of life of Christ and the apostles. John XXII brought
in Bertrand de la Tour to help pick up the pieces: after the
order's minister-general had seceded to the pope's opponent
Ludwig of Bavaria, Bertrand was given the task of ruling the
order as caretaker.[51] Though Bertrand himself would seem to
have believed (at least before the pope closed what had been
an open question) that Christ and the apostles did not own
property,[52] he seems to have done an effective job.[53] Whatever
his views on the poverty of Franciscans, he takes an up-beat
tone when discussing wealth in the context of a sermon for a
dead king or prince.[54] He begins cautiously, sounding at first
rather negative about wealth:

Therefore that noble prince died *full of days*; he also died *full of riches*,
including temporal riches. For there was none richer than he in these
parts. It is true that these riches would not have made his death
precious, nor, strictly speaking, could he be said to be *dead full of riches*
because of them, for so far as he is concerned they have passed away
totally. And so it is said in Psalms (75: 6): *they have slept their sleep*—'of
death' is understood here—and *all the men of riches have found nothing
in their hands.*—Nothing, I say, except the alms and the good things
which they did with their riches—if indeed they did do so. Therefore
the damned will say in hell as it is said in Wisdom 5 (8): *What has pride
profited us? Or what advantage has the ostentation of riches brought us?* As if
to say: 'Nothing.' For it continues (5: 9): *All those things have passed
away like a shadow.*

---

[51] Moorman, *History*, 321.

[52] Ibid., following P. Gauchat, *Cardinal Bertrand de Turre: Ord. Min.: His
Participation in the Theoretical Controversy concerning the Poverty of Christ and the
Apostles under Pope John XXII* (Rome, 1930), 80. Gauchat argues (p. 89) that after
*Cum inter nonnullos* Bertrand must have submitted to the authority of the pope,
since 'the part that he took when Cesena broke into open conflict with the
Pope shows us that Bertrand was a man in whom the Pope placed his fullest
confidence. This fact excludes any opposition from Bertrand to the Papal
authority.' For Bertrand's views at the time when the pope was still collecting
opinions see Felice Tocco, *La quistione della povertà nel secolo XIV, secondo nuovi
documenti* (Nuova Biblioteca di Letteratura, Storia ed Arte, 4; Naples, 1910), 14,
64–74, 85–6 (I was directed to this book by an anonymous OUP reader, to
whom thanks).

[53] Moorman, *History*, 321.

[54] See Transcription B:a. I can find no hard evidence for when this sermon
was preached or written down; from its tone, one might hazard a guess that it
was after 1323.

Those riches, I say, would not have made his death precious were it not for the fact that in him, together with those riches, other riches came together, that is, the riches of salvation, of which it is said, Isaiah 33 (6): *riches of salvation are wisdom and knowledge: the fear of the Lord itself is his treasure.*[55]

Then there is a smooth and almost imperceptible transition to a defence of riches:

Those, I say, are the riches which made his death precious and made him *full of riches* in death. For he had wisdom for tasting and desiring heavenly things, knowledge for governing and dispensing earthly things, and the fear of the Lord for shunning sin.

Through these spiritual riches he justly acquired temporal riches when he was alive, kept them justly, distributed and dispensed them justly, and also justly ordered and arranged their distribution. And it is certain that in such a man temporal riches are fruitful. Therefore Ambrose says, commenting on Luke:[56] 'Let men learn that no reproach is attached to material resources, but to those who do not know how to use them. For just as riches are an impediment to virtue in wicked men, so too they are a help to it in good men.'[57]

With respect to wealth and to ancestry, therefore, there was no general tension between the ideology conveyed by the memorial sermons and the attitudes current among the lay ruling class. One would not perhaps expect an attack on these attitudes, but it would have been easy for preachers to remain silent about them, as there were plenty of other possible themes. In this sense the medieval genre, like the humanist genre which was to follow it, was in tune with secular attitudes.

The positive attitude to the things of this world extends to fame and power. One must be careful here, because sometimes worldly greatness is emphasized mainly to point up the fact that it must pass. Even the sermon on the death of Philip IV, which begins like a celebration of the French monarchy's greatness, then comes close to reversing the point of these remarks

---

[55] Transcription B:a, **12**: 1–**13**: 1.

[56] See PL 15. 1882.

[57] Transcription B:a, **13**: 2–**14**: 3. For the same idea and quotation (but attributed to Gregory the Great!) see D. L. d'Avray, 'Sermons to the Upper Bourgeoisie by a Thirteenth Century Franciscan', in D. Baker (ed.), *The Church in Town and Countryside* (Studies in Church History, 16; Oxford, 1979), 187–99, at 196 n. 40.

by turning to the theme of transience.[58] There are other cases, however, where enthusiasm for fame and power does not seem to be double-edged. Giovanni da San Gimignano says that the good prince is commended for celebrity and fame (on account of his virtues).[59] The anonymous sermon in a Berlin manuscript also praises fame, provided that the facts warrant the reputation: 'For when a man is great, in himself with respect to his life, and with respect to others through fame, then he can properly defend his people from enemies.'[60] The word 'power', *potentia*, seems to have good associations. Giovanni da San Gimignano says that the more powerful a king is, the more he is feared, and the more he is feared, the greater the reverence and veneration in which he is held.[61] Bertrand de la Tour argues that supreme power to carry things through enhances the dignity of a king: prudence would not be enough if the power to execute decisions (*exequens potentia*), overthrowing all evil, were not there at the same time.[62]

Robert the Wise of Naples is compared to a lion by reason of his power in a sermon by Federico Franconi of Naples: by his strength and power he defended his subjects, put his enemies to flight, and showed he was a man to be feared.[63] Federico ap-

---

[58] D. L. d'Avray, 'The Comparative Study of Memorial Preaching', *Transactions of the Royal Historical Society*, 5th ser., 40 (1990), 25–42, at 31–2.

[59] 'Secundo quoque in auctoritate allegata superius commendatur bonus princeps in fame celebritate, quia *clarissimus* (cf. 1 Macc. 2: 17). Dicitur 1 Cor. 15 (41) quod *alia* est *claritas solis, alia lune, et alia stellarum.* Nam clara est stella, clarior uidetur luna, sed clarissimus est sol. Habet claritatem stelle princeps qui est famosus de sapientia', and so on (MS Siena, Biblioteca Comunale F. X. 24, fo. 106$^{rb}$, from a sermon on the text *Princeps maximus cecidit hodie* (2 Kgs. 3: 38); Schneyer, *Repertorium*, iii. 762, No. 505).

[60] Transcription A, 7: 5 (and 1–7 *passim*). Cf. a passage from Bertrand de la Tour (Schneyer, *Repertorium*, i. 581, No. 1100), associating honour with office and indirectly with virtue: Transcription B:c, 4: 1–4.

[61] 'Ratio uero secundi est quia quanto rex est potentior, tanto magis timetur, et quanto magis timetur, tanto in maiori reuerentia et ueneratione habetur' (MS Siena, Biblioteca Comunale F. X. 24, fo. 102$^{vb}$, from a sermon on the text *Rex hodie est et cras morietur* (Ecclus. 10: 12); Schneyer, *Repertorium*, iii. 762, No. 503).

[62] Transcription B:d, 6: 1–2.

[63] 'Secundo assimilatur leoni ratione potentie. Defendit potenter regnum ab Herrico *imperatore* usque ad mortem predicti Herrici et (*om. ms*) contra Bauarum. Et breuiter eius potentia et potestate subditos (persubditos *ms*) defendit, inimicos fugauit, et se metuendum ostendit' (MS Munich, Staatsbibliothek Clm. 2981, fo. 132$^{rb}$, from a sermon on the text *Ecce rex vester* (John 19: 14); Schneyer, *Repertorium*, iv. 223, 'Nicolaus de Asculo', No. 219).

preciates Robert's military qualities, as he did those of Robert's conquering grandfather, Charles I of Anjou.[64] (It will be remembered, however, that he also implies approval for the peacetime virtues of Charles II.[65])

Military virtues are praised in memorial sermons by other preachers also: the anonymous preacher in a Berlin manuscript,[66] Bertrand de la Tour,[67] and Giovanni da San Gimignano[68] (not to mention the quite stirringly warlike passage in the sermon on Edward I translated at the start of Chapter 2[69]). Here too we find no sharp contrast with humanist funeral orators.[70] The medieval preachers are also in harmony with an older tradition, the chivalric ethos. It is worth remarking here that the content of the chivalric ethos had much in common with that of Renaissance Italian humanism. Both wealth and ancestors were highly desirable for medieval knights,[71] as of course were honour and fame.[72] Moreover, both Renaissance humanism and chivalry managed to combine Christianity with secularity[73]—of which more below.

[64] See ch. 2, text at n. 94 (first paragraph of passage quoted).

[65] See ch. 2, text at n. 94 (second paragraph of passage quoted) and at nn. 122 and 130.

[66] Transcription A, 3: 1–3.

[67] See his sermon in memory of Charles of Calabria: 'Et certe iste dominus Karolus fuit "manu fortis", quia probus et strenuus (strenuu$^{us}$ *ms*) contra hostes' (MS Kremsmünster 44, fo. 124$^{rb}$, from a sermon on the text *Propter sapientiam et scientiam* (Prov. 28: 2); Schneyer, *Repertorium*, i. 583, No. 1123).

[68] 'Secunda ratio est propter eius strenuitatem . . . Antiquitus enim, quando principes fecerant aliquos actus strenuos, puta quod strenue se habuerant in bello et uictoriam reportabant, tunc obuiabant eis chori mulierum et iuuenum gaudentium et canentium laudes eorum' (MS Siena, Biblioteca Comunale F. X. 24, fo. 107$^{ra}$, from a sermon on the text *Princeps maximus cecidit hodie* (2 Kgs. 3: 38); Schneyer, *Repertorium*, iv. 762, No. 505). See too the following passage, earlier in the same sermon: 'Quidam uero ita sunt indigni principatu propter defectum fortitudinis et strenuitatis. Nam quia non habent fortitudinem contra bella spiritualia, scilicet contra temptationes et contra uitia, sed corruunt in eis, ideo facit deus eos plerumque corruere (*minor error in ms*) etiam in bello corporali' (ibid., fo. 106$^{ra}$).

[69] See also below, Transcription C:a, para. 4.

[70] McManamon, *Funeral Oratory*, tends to stress the humanists' predilection for peace (ch. 5, e.g. p. 106); however, he makes it clear that they were prepared to celebrate military heroes: pp. 93, 101–2, 117.

[71] Good discussion in Keen, *Chivalry*, ch. 8, esp. pp. 154 (wealth), 160 (nobility).

[72] See e.g. ibid. 171–4.

[73] See esp. ibid., ch. 2 ('The Secular Origins of Chivalry'). Keen does not mean to imply that chivalry was hostile or indifferent to Christianity: his

One of the words associated with military virtue is *fortitudo*, bravery,[74] which was one of the four cardinal virtues. This schema of virtues is another part of the common stock of ideas which chivalry shared with the humanist ideal of princely government.[75] It is no surprise to find that the schema is also important in memorial preaching before 1350. Of course this is not the only such 'compound' or schema. The whole method of preaching encouraged schematic 'arrays' of concepts, including virtues.[76] Some at least of the other schemata have their interest, notably where the preacher groups a virtue or virtues with assets which might be categorized as success or good fortune rather than strictly ethical achievements.[77] Nevertheless, it is my tentative impression that the schema of the cardinal virtues—prudence, justice, fortitude, and temperance—is as stable as or more so than any other 'compound'.[78]

view, as developed in the next chapter, is that 'the attitude that underpinned the conception of chivalry as a Christian vocation . . . was ultimately the fruit of the ancient marriage of Teutonic heroic values with the militant tradition of the Old Testament, rather than of later developments in ecclesiastical thinking—an attitude with a royal, not a priestly genealogy' (p. 63).

[74] *Strenuitas* (vigour) and *probitas* (prowess), with their derivatives, are also important.

[75] In a section on 'The humanist ideal of princely government' Quentin Skinner says with special reference to the later humanists that 'It is . . . claimed that no one can be accounted a man of true *virtus* unless he displays all the leading Christian virtues as well as the "cardinal" virtues singled out by the moralists of antiquity. This aspect of the analysis is simply a reiteration of the arguments we have already found in the writings of Petrarch and the early *quattrocento* humanists' (*The Foundations of Modern Political Thought*, i. *The Renaissance* (Cambridge, 1978), 126). Cf. Keen, *Chivalry*, 158: 'Once settled on virtue as the prime factor, a good many chivalrous authors could not resist the opportunity offered to display their learning further by a lengthy discussion of the four cardinal virtues in their relationship to nobility.'

[76] In this connection I should acknowledge the stimulus of Judson Boyce Allen's *The Ethical Poetic of the Later Middle Ages: A Decorum of Convenient Distinction* (Toronto and London, 1982).

[77] See Endnote 13, pp. 284–5.

[78] In fact I have noted only a few occurrences, but they are spread among different preachers, and this (in view of the fact that the proportion of sermons in memory of kings that have survived from this period is probably small) is enough to suggest that it was a topos. (1) Giovanni da San Gimignano: 'uidelicet, cuius subditi prudentia dirigantur, cuius iustitia conseruentur (*corr. from* conb-), cuius fortitudine defendantur, et temperantia hedificentur' (MS Siena, Biblioteca Comunale F. X. 24, fo. 103$^{vb}$, from a sermon beginning *Dux de*

The schema had become an integral part of Christian tradition. It seems to have been St Ambrose who gave them the name 'cardinal'.[79] In the age of Charlemagne Alcuin gave impetus to a new interest in the schema.[80] In the thirteenth century they are given a prominent position by the Franciscan John of Wales in his enormously popular *Breviloquium de uirtutibus*,[81] and in the *Summa theologica* of Thomas Aquinas.[82]

Nevertheless, there are two senses in which the tradition of the four cardinal virtues may be described as secular. Firstly, the idea of the four virtues flourished (long before the Italian Renaissance) in a secular social and literary milieu: that of Italian city-states.[83] Secondly, they belong to a pre-Christian classical tradition, one that goes back to Plato rather than Aristotle—although, interestingly enough, the schema was inserted into William of Moerbeke's Latin translation of Aristotle's *Rhetoric*.[84] The pre-Christian ancestry of the schema would of

*terra Aegypti non erit amplius* (Ezek. 30: 13); Schneyer, *Repertorium*, iii. 762, No. 504); (2) Giovanni da Napoli: 'fuit pulcrior mente, quam pulcritudinem causant generaliter omnes uirtutes, scilicet tres theologice et quattuor cardinales, sed singulariter caritas' (MS Naples, Nazionale VIII AA 11, fo. 25ra, from a sermon on the text *In caritate perpetua* (Jer. 31: 3); Schneyer, *Repertorium*, iii. 607, No. 36); (3) Bertrand de la Tour: 'Multa etiam egit prudenter, fortiter, temperanter, et iuste' (MS Kremsmünster 44, fo. 122rb, from a sermon on the text *Propter sapientiam* (Prov. 28: 2); Schneyer, *Repertorium*, i. 583, No. 1123—the sermon in memory of Charles of Calabria).

[79] S. Mähl, *Quadriga Virtutum: Die Kardinaltugenden in der Geistesgeschichte der Karolingerzeit* (Beihefte zum Archiv für Kulturgeschichte, 9; Cologne and Vienna, 1969), 8.

[80] Ibid. 168.

[81] Jenny Swanson, *John of Wales: A Study of the Works and Ideas of a Thirteenth-century Friar* (Cambridge, 1989), 42 (and p. 213 for the work's popularity).

[82] 'Prologus' to the *Secunda secundae*.

[83] For Giovanni da Viterbo's *Liber de regimine ciuitatum* see Q. Skinner, 'Ambrogio Lorenzetti: The Artist as Political Philosopher', *Proceedings of the British Academy*, 72 (1986), 1–56, at 3 and 26, and also his *Foundations*, i. 33–4; for Brunetto Latini's *Li livres dou tresor* see Skinner, 'Ambrogio', 3–4, 28, and G. Holmes, *Florence, Rome, and the Origins of the Renaissance* (Oxford, 1986), 75–80; for Bono Giamboni's *Il libro de' vizî e delle virtudi* see Holmes, *Florence*, 80.

[84] On the prehistory of the four virtues see O. Kunsemüller, *Die Herkunft der platonischen Kardinaltugenden* (Erlangen, 1935). For the insertion of the words 'aut et partes ipsius prudentiam, fortitudinem, temperantiam, iustitiam' into the translation see *Aristoteles Latinus*, xxxi/1–2, ed. B. Schneider, *Rhetorica: Translatio anonyma sive vetus et translatio Guillelmi de Moerbeka* (Union Académique Internationale, Corpus Philosophorum Medii Aevi; Leiden, 1978), 175. 10–11, 1360b Bekker. In the following pages the Bekker references (column- and line-

course have been no secret: it is significant that Aquinas cites Cicero as his only authority when refuting the thesis that there are other virtues which have a better claim to pre-eminence than the cardinal four.[85]

Aquinas was extremely fond of Cicero,[86] but Aristotle was obviously a deeper influence; probably the same is true of our memorial sermons. At any rate, the Aristotelian contribution to the genre is too great to be ignored. Aristotle cannot be described as an other-worldly philosopher, and the respect paid to him by preachers in this genre tends to reinforce the positive attitude to the things of this world which has already been discerned in many if not all of their sermons.

A striking case in point is a passage from Giovanni da San Gimignano where he provides a list of virtues which includes but goes well beyond the four 'cardinal' ones, and which links them with extrinsic goods and with 'political' happiness. He acknowledges his debt to Aristotle:

For it is fitting that a prince should be able to be called happy beyond other people, at least with a political happiness, for which, as Aristotle tells us in his *Rhetoric*, book 1, intrinsic and extrinsic goods are required. I call intrinsic either those things which pertain to the soul, like honourable goods, that is, virtues such as justice, fortitude, temperance, magnificence, magnanimity, liberty, gentleness, prudence, and wisdom, for those are above all the virtues which make a prince especially worthy of honour;—or even the goods which belong to the body are called intrinsic: like health, beauty, strength, size, and athletic power or skill,[87] and a good old age.

Decet enim principem pre ceteris posse dici felicem saltem felicitate politica, ad quam, sicut tradit Philosophus in Primo Rhethoricorum,

numbers of Immanuel Bekker's standard edition of the Greek text of Aristotle, which are used as a reference system in other editions) will be accurate to the column but not necessarily to the precise line, since I have in some cases taken them from the margins of other texts (e.g. of the Latin Aristotle).

[85] 'Sed contra est quod Tullius in sua *Rhetorica*, ad has quatuor omnes alias reducit' (*Prima secundae*, q. 61, art. 3; and see *De inventione*, 2. 159). See also E. K. Rand, *Cicero in the Courtroom of St Thomas Aquinas* (The Aquinas Lecture, 1945; Milwaukee, 1946). Skinner emphasizes a way of thinking about the four virtues which rivalled the dominant Ciceronian tradition; he traces this back to Seneca and associates Giovanni da Viterbo and Brunetto Latini with it: see 'Ambrogio', 26–30.

[86] Rand, *Cicero*, *passim*.

[87] I do not know what the scribe thought the text meant here. See next note.

requiruntur bona intrinseca et extrinseca. Intrinseca autem dico uel
que pertinent ad animam, sicut sunt bona honesta, id est uirtutes sicut
iustitia, fortitudo, temperantia, magnificentia, magnanimitas, libertas,
mansuetudo, prudentia, et sapientia, quia iste sunt maxime uirtutes
que reddunt principem maxime honorabilem; uel etiam bona que insunt
corpori dicuntur intrinseca, ut sanitas, pulcritudo, robur, magnitudo,
et potentia, siue ars, agonistica,[88] et bona senectus.[89]

If Giovanni da San Gimignano is working directly from
Aristotle—which seems entirely likely though it would be rash
to rule out an intermediate source—he has synthesized and
modified passages which are at some little distance from each
other in the first book of the Philosopher's *Rhetorica*.[90]

The last two of the virtues listed, prudence and wisdom
(*prudentia, et sapientia*), appear with predictable frequency in
these sermons; indeed, it is my impression that 'intellectual
virtue' may have been as highly regarded in a prince as any
other kind of virtue, if not more so, to judge by the evidence of
these sermons. (Justice, of which more below, would probably
be the main competitor in the quantitative analysis which, in
view of the patchy survival of memorial sermons, it has not
seemed worth while to attempt.) A full catalogue of passages
where wisdom, prudence, or knowledge is praised would
rapidly become tedious, but another sermon by Giovanni

---

[88] agaristica *ms*. (I am grateful to Dr Jill Kraye for finding the place in the
*Aristoteles Latinus* and showing me that this is a corruption of *agonistica*.) Cf.
below, n. 90.

[89] MS Siena, Biblioteca Comunale F. X. 24, fo. 106^va, from a sermon for a
prince on the text *Princeps maximus cecidit hodie* (2 Kgs. 3: 38); Schneyer, *Repertorium*, iii. 762, No. 505. 'Prudentia' has an otiose abbreviation-sign.

[90] The two relevant passages seem to be as follows: 'Si itaque est felicitas
tale, necesse ipsius esse partes nobilitatem, multitudinem amicorum, bonorum
amicitiam, diuitias, bonam prolem, multitudinem prolis, bonam senectutem;
adhuc corporis uirtutes (puta sanitatem, pulcritudinem, robur, magnitudinem,
potentiam agonisticam), gloriam, honorem, bonam fortunam, uirtutem aut
et partes ipsius prudentiam, fortitudinem, temperantiam, iustitiam; sic enim
utique per se sufficientissimus erit, si existant ipsi interiora et exteriora bona;
non enim sunt alia preter hec. Sunt autem in ipso quidem que circa animam et
que in corpore, extra autem bonitas generis .et amici et pecunie et honor,
adhuc autem conuenire putamus potentiam inesse et fortunam; sic enim utique
securissima uita erit' (Aristoteles Latinus, *Rhetorica*, p. 175 Schneider). Then,
some way below: 'Iustitia, fortitudo, temperantia, magnanimitas, magnificentia,
et alii tales habitus; uirtutes enim anime'—with surrounding context (ibid.
180).

where Aristotle puts in an appearance is relevant to the argument.

Giovanni da San Gimignano says that

> . . . according to Aristotle, it belongs to the wise man to reflect on the highest cause; it is according to this cause that judgement is formed, with the greatest certainty, about other things, and that all things ought to be ordered. And since a *dux* has to order and govern not only himself, but also others, it is therefore necessary for him to be wise in such a way that he may know and reflect upon that highest cause, according to which, that is, according to whose rules, all things, and especially things and acts of human beings, ought to be ordered and governed.

> . . . secundum Philosophum, sapientis est considerare altissimam causam, secundum quam certissime de aliis iudicatur, et secundum quam omnia ordinari oportet. Et quia dux non solum se ipsum, se*d* etiam alios habet ordinare et gubernare, ideo oportet eum sic esse sapientem ut cognoscat et consideret illam altissimam causam, secundum quam, id est, secundum cuius regulas, debent ordinari et gubernari omnia et precipue res et actus humani.[91]

Here Giovanni may have taken a short cut to Aristotle through Aquinas, who cites the *Metaphysics* as his authority in a passage which could well have been before the eyes of his confrère.[92] Giovanni used Aquinas a lot,[93] which is not a surprising thing in an Italian Dominican active in the earlier fourteenth century,[94] though it goes without saying that familiarity with Aristotle was not a peculiarity of Thomas Aquinas's order. Some familiarity with Aristotle would be a natural thing in any educated

---

[91] MS Siena, Biblioteca Comunale F. X. 24, fo. 104ra, from a sermon on the text *Dux de terra Aegypti non erit amplius* (Ezek. 30: 13); Schneyer, *Repertorium*, iii. 762, No. 504.

[92] 'Obiectum autem sapientiae praecellit inter obiecta omnium uirtutum intellectualium: considerat enim causam altissimam, quae Deus est, ut dicitur in principio *Metaphys*. Et quia per causam iudicatur de effectu, et per causam superiorem de causis inferioribus; inde est quod sapientia habet iudicium de omnibus aliis uirtutibus intellectualibus; et eius est ordinare omnes; et ipsa est quasi architectonica respectu omnium' (*Summa theologica, Prima secundae*, q. 66, art. 5, *Respondeo* section).

[93] A. Dondaine, 'La vie et les œuvres de Jean de San Gimignano', *AFP* 9 (1939), 128–83, at 178.

[94] M. Grabmann, 'Die italienische Thomistenschule des XIII. und beginnenden XIV. Jahrhunderts', in id., *Mittelalterliches Geistesleben: Abhandlungen zur Geschichte der Scholastik und Mystik*, i (Munich, 1926), 332–91.

cleric by the fourteenth century, and in Bertrand de la Tour's
sermon in memory of Charles of Calabria Aristotle is grouped
quite naturally with St Paul and Augustine in a passage about
wisdom and knowledge.[95]
The unobtrusive phrase 'legal justice' is a symptom of the
Aristotelian ideas in the atmosphere. It may be remembered
that in a sermon in memory of Edward I of England it was said
that he 'loved not just any justice, but legal justice'.[96] The idea
of 'legal justice' as a semi-technical term would seem to go back
to Aristotle's *Nicomachean Ethics*, book 5,[97] but it had been given
wide currency, notably by Thomas Aquinas, in whose political
thought it is a key concept (one which perhaps deserves more
concentrated attention from historians of political thought).[98]
According to Aquinas, 'it pertains to legal justice that the acts
of all the virtues be ordered towards a higher end, that is, to
the common good of the multitude, which takes precedence
over the good of one individual person'.[99] Viewed in this light,
legislation of the right kind could be thought to carry a strong
positive moral charge (as in Aristotle's own world and more

[95] '... sciendum quod quamuis Apostolus distingwat inter sapientiam et scientiam, dicens, primo ad Cor. xii° (8), *Alii datur sermo sapientie, alii sermo scientie*, et secundum etiam Augus(tinum), ibi supra, et etiam secundum Aristotelem, sexto Ethicorum, scriptura tamen sacra sepe unum sumit pro alio. Unde et ego nunc tantum uolo loqui de sapientia, et sub eius nomine de scientia' (MS Kremsmünster 44, fo. 122ᵛᵃ, from a sermon on the text *Propter sapientiam* (Prov. 28: 2); Schneyer, *Repertorium*, i. 583, No. 1123). Bertrand probably has the following passages in mind: '*Sunt utique quibus uerum dicit anima affirmando vel negando, quinque secundum numerum; hec autem sunt ars, sciencia, prudencia, sapiencia, intellectus*' (*Aristoteles Latinus*, xxvi/1–3, fasc. 4, ed. R. A. Gauthier, *Ethica Nicomachea, Translatio... Grosseteste... Recensio Recognita* (Union Académique Internationale, Corpus Philosophorum Medii Aevi; Brussels and Leiden, 1973), 480, 1139ᵇ15 ff. Bekker; see also, in the same edition, 1139ᵇ19–35, 1141ᵃ9 ff. Bekker). As for the reference to St Augustine, it is possible that he meant Gregory: at least, he seems to have made this mistake a little earlier in the sermon. I suspect that the relevant passage is in PL 75. 592–3.
[96] See also below, Transcription C:a, 3: 5.
[97] See the illuminating discussion by F. Rosen, 'The Political Context of Aristotle's Categories of Justice', *Phronesis*, 20 (1975), 228–40, at 228–9.
[98] Note, for instance, the following fascinating attempt to explain why Aristotle neglected humility as a virtue: 'Philosophus intendebat agere de uirtutibus secundum quod ordinantur ad uitam ciuilem, in qua subiectio unius hominis ad alterum secundum legis ordinem determinatur, et ideo continetur sub iustitia legali' (*Summa theologica, Secunda secundae*, q. 161, art. 1 ad 5).
[99] Ibid., q. 58, art. 6 ad 3.

than in a modern liberal state, where it is usually seen either as promoting material, rather than moral, well-being, or as protecting citizens from each other).

Aquinas could have been the intermediary between Aristotle and the following passage from Juan de Aragon's sermon in memory of his deceased father King James II (and for his brother the successor):

Therefore let us ask justice for this son of a king, both that justice which is a general virtue, which is called legal justice by philosophers and saints, and particular justice, which is between subjects—and this is twofold: commutative, which relates to exchanges, and distributive, which has its place in the distribution of benefits and honours—so that thus we may be able finally to say of him the words of Ecclesiasticus 30 (4): *His father is dead and is not dead, for he has left* a son *like unto himself.*

Pro isto ergo filio regis postulemus iustitiam: et illam que generalis est uirtus, que a philosophis et sanctis uocatur iustitia legalis, et iustitia particularis que est inter subditos—et ista est duplex: scilicet comutatiua, que est in commutationibus, et distributiua, que consistit in beneficiis distribuendis et honoribus—ut sic possimus tandem de ipso dicere illud Ecclesiastici xxx (4): *Mortuus est pater eius et non est mort(uus), quia dimisit* filium *similem sibi.*[100]

The relevant articles from the *Summa theologica* deal with the questions of 'Whether there is such a thing as particular justice as well as general justice',[101] and 'Whether it is appropriate to posit two species of justice, distributive and commutative'[102] ('justice' hear meaning 'particular justice').[103] Juan de Aragon's remarks look closer to these articles than to the Latin Aristotle.[104] Whether or not Aquinas was the proximate source, the passage is a tribute to Aristotle's authority, the more so,

[100] MS Valencia, Cat. 182, fo. 128$^{vb}$, from a sermon on the text *Deus iudicium tuum regi da* (Ps. 71: 1); Schneyer, *Repertorium*, iii. 314, No. 256.

[101] *Secunda secundae*, q. 58, art. 7, especially: 'ita etiam praeter iustitiam legalem oportet esse particularem quandam iustitiam, quae ordinet hominem circa ea quae sunt ad alteram singularem personam.'

[102] Ibid., q. 61, art. 1.

[103] 'Utraque enim sub iustitia particulari continetur, ut dictum est (a. 1)' (ibid., q. 61, art. 2 ad 1).

[104] *Aristoteles Latinus*, xxvi/1–3, fasc. 4, ed. Gauthier, pp. 466–7, 1134$^{b}$ Bekker.

perhaps, because the remarks about distributive and commutative justice seem a little superfluous in this context.[105] A casual reference by Bertrand de la Tour to justice *ad distribuendum* of an imaginary prince or king may also be a case of this Aristotelian idea's influence.[106]

Federico Franconi introduces another Aristotelian notion, also from the *Ethics*:

> Thirdly, one should speak of him as a father, and thus of his clemency or mercy. Here it should be known that Aristotle, *Ethics* 5, says that the just is twofold, that is, political and paternal. The 'paternal' just is with the greatest mercy, and that of a king towards his subjects ought to be of this sort. . . . Thus our lord king, like a father, ruled in accordance with a father's law, that is, according to mercy, and not according to the rigour of justice.

> Tertio loquendum est de eo sicut de patre, et sic de eius clementia uel misericordia. Ubi sciendum quod Ar(istoteles), 5 Ethicorum, dicit: duplex est iustum, scilicet politicum et paternum. Iustum paternum est cum maxima misericordia, et tale debet esse regis ad subditos. . . . Sic dominus noster rex tamquam pater secundum ius paternum rexit, hoc est, secundum misericordiam et non secundum rigorem iustitie.[107]

The passage in *Ethics* 5 to which Federico is probably referring is not about precisely the same idea,[108] and one may speculate that unconscious association of ideas had allowed a passage about paternal authority from a later book of the *Ethics* to colour his memory. (In book 8 Aristotle says that 'The relationship of father to sons is regal in type, since a father's first care is for his children's welfare. This is why Homer styles Zeus

---

[105] It is possible (but not certain!) that their pertinence would be more evident if the sermon were unabridged.

[106] Transcription B:c, **11**: 1.

[107] MS Munich, Staatsbibliothek Clm. 2981, fo. 131^ra, from a sermon on the text *Memoriam habundantiae suauitatis tuae* (Ps. 144: 7); Schneyer, *Repertorium*, iv. 223, 'Nicolaus de Asculo', No. 217.

[108] The relevant passage of the Latin Aristotle is as follows: 'Dominatiuum autem iustum et paternum non idem hiis, set simile; non enim est iniusticia ad que ipsius simpliciter; possessio autem, et filius usque utique sit pelicon et separetur, quemadmodum pars ipsius, *si* ipsum autem nullus eligit *necesse*; propter quod non est iniusticia ad se ipsum. *Non* ergo iniustum, neque iustum politicum; secundum legem enim erat et in quibus natum erat esse lex' (*Aristoteles Latinus*, xxvi/1–3, fasc. 4, ed. Gauthier, p. 466, 1134^b9 ff. Bekker; note the variant *nocere* for *necesse* in Gauthier's apparatus).

"father," for the ideal of kingship is paternal government.'[109])
If so (and it is a guess), the mistake would be of a kind that
people make with a text so familiar to them that they rely too
much on memory.

It will have been noticed that the *Ethics* is relatively prominent among the Aristotelian citations in the sermons.[110] Since
the *Nicomachean Ethics* is in a sense a book about politics, or
politics and society, in their relation to virtue,[111] it was an
obvious source once the preacher had decided to discuss political authority (which, as was argued above from comparisons
with Luther, a preacher in that situation was not compelled to
do). The connection between ethics and politics—and between
Aristotle's *Ethics* and his *Politics*—is particularly strong in a
fascinating discussion by Remigio de' Girolami of the difference
between kingship and tyranny. The whole analysis takes up a
large part of the written version of his sermon in memory of
King Louix X of France. In the following passages Aristotle's
authority is woven closely into the argument. Remigio has
been listing differences between kingship and tyranny:

Again, [they differ] because a king is temperate, speaking of temperance in accordance with what Aristotle says of it in the *Ethics*, that
is, in so far as it is a virtue relating to the pleasures of taste and touch.
A tyrant, however, is intemperate, according to the words of Aristotle
in book 5 of the *Politics*: For the tyrant aims at that which is pleasurable, whereas a king aims at that which is good. . . . But with respect
to what is pleasurable to the sense of touch it is said in Proverbs 22
(11): *He who loves purity of heart, for the* word *of his lips, he will have the
king as his friend.* But, conversely, Aristotle says of tyrants in *Ethics*,
book 1, that many of those who are in power suffer the same kind

[109] Aristotle, *Nicomachean Ethics*, 1160ᵇ, ed. and trans. H. Rackham (Loeb
edn.; Cambridge, Mass., and London, rev. edn. 1926), 493; for the Latin see
Gauthier's edition, p. 534.
[110] Another case, from Giovanni da San Gimignano: 'Sed ille potest dici
clarissimus tanquam sol qui habet famam de magna iustitia. Nam sicut Philosophus dicit in 5 Ethicorum, iustitia est preclarissima uirtutum, et neque
Lucifer neque Experus est ita clarus. Et ideo ille princeps est clarissimus
sicut sol qui est famosus de iustitia' (preclarissima] *a scribal mess*) (MS Siena,
Biblioteca Comunale F. X. 24, fo. 106ʳᵇ, from a sermon on the text *Princeps
maximus cecidit hodie* (2 Kgs. 3: 38); Schneyer, *Repertorium*, iii. 762, No. 505). Cf.
*Aristoteles Latinus*, xxvi/1–3, fasc. 4, ed. Gauthier, pp. 454–5, 1129ᵇ Bekker.
[111] Cf. Alasdair MacIntyre, *A Short History of Ethics* (London and Henley,
1967), 57.

of things as Sardanapallus, the man, that is, who was king of the Assyrians and totally given over to pleasure.

Item, quia rex est te*m*peratus, loquendo de temperantia secundum quod loquitur de ea Philosophus in l(ibro) Ethicorum,[112] scilicet prout est uirtus consistens circa delectabilia gustus et tactus. Tirannus autem est inte*m*peratus, iuxta illud Philosophi in l(ibro) 5 Pol(iticorum):[113] Est autem intentio tirannica quidem quod delectabile, regalis autem quod bonum. . . . Quantum uero ad delectabile tactus dicitur Prouer. 22 (11): *Qui diligit cordis munditiam, propter* uer(bum)[114] *la(biorum) s(uorum) ha(bebit) amicum regem.* Sed, e contra, dicit de tirannis Philosophus in l(ibro) 1 Ethicorum: multi eorum qui in potestate sunt similia patiuntur Sardanapolo,[115] qui scilicet fuit rex Assiriorum et totaliter uoluptatibus deditus.[116]

Later on Aristotle reappears, as Remigio contrasts the workings of the reason, and then of the will, in kings and tyrants:

Thirdly with respect to the reason, since the king relies on reason which is true and really exists, in accordance with the words of Proverbs 20 (28): *Mercy and truth guard the king*, but the tyrant relies on reason which is false and apparent, that is, on flattery, according to the words of Aristotle in the *Politics*, book 5: With tyrants, those

---

[112] 'Circa tales utique delectaciones temperancia et intemperantia est, *quibus* reliqua animalia communicant; unde seruiles et bestiales uidentur; hee autem sunt tactus et gustus' (*Aristoteles Latinus*, xxvi/1–2, fasc. 4, ed. Gauthier, p. 427, 1118ª Bekker).

[113] This would seem to refer to the words that follow it. Since the Aristoteles Latinus series has not yet published the main text of the *Politics*, I quote from the text edited by F. Susemihl, *Aristotelis Politicorum libri octo, cum vetusta translatione Guilelmi de Moerbeka* (Leipzig, 1872): 'est autem intentio tyrannica quidem quod delectabile, regalis autem quod bonum' (1311ª4, p. 558). (I am most grateful to L.-J. Bataillon for advice about editions of the Latin *Politics*.)

[114] uerbum] gratiam *in the Clementine Vulgate*

[115] 'Multi quidem igitur omnino bestiales uidentur esse, pecudum uitam eligentes. Adipiscuntur autem racionem, quia multi eorum qui in potestate sunt *similia* Sardanapolo' (*Aristoteles Latinus*, xxvi/1–3, fasc. 4, ed. Gauthier, p. 378, 1095ᵇ19–22 Bekker). Note the variant reading: similia + paciuntur L²Rt, corr. Rp³, Rp⁴. Gauthier, ibid., fasc. 1, Praefatio (1974), p. ccix, states that 'postea . . . in Italia praesertim recensio L² pervulgata est'; he also suggests (ibid., p. ccxxv) that the Rt recension may have an Italian origin. The likelihood is that Remigio's text could be linked with the L² or Rt recension.

[116] MS Florence, Nazionale Conv. soppr. G. 4. 936, fo. 389ᵛ, left-hand margin, from a sermon on the text *Mortuus est rex Ozias* (Isa. 6: 1); Schneyer, *Repertorium*, v. 95, No. 466. This sermon is hard to track through the margins of the manuscript. I could hardly have done so without the meticulous guidance of E. Panella, 'Un sermone in morte della moglie di Guido Novello o di Beatrice d'Angiò?', *Memorie domenicane*, NS 12 (1981), 294–301, at 299.

whose conversation is humble receive honour—which, indeed, is an act of flattery. For tyrants rejoice when they receive flattery.

Fourthly with respect to the will, since the king loves the good of his subjects, but the tyrant loves profit and his own interest, according to Aristotle in book 5 of the *Ethics*. . . .

Tertio quantum ad rationem, quia rex innititur rationi uere et existenti, iuxta illud Prouer. 20 (28): *Misericordia et ueritas custodiunt regem*, tirannus autem innititur rationi false et apparenti, scilicet adulationibus, iuxta illud Philosophi in l(ibro) 5 Pol(iticorum):[117] apud tirannos honorati sunt qui humiliter collocuntur, quod quidem est opus adulationis. Tiranni enim recipientes adulationes gaudent.

Quarto quantum ad uoluntatem, quia rex diligit bonum subditorum, tirannus autem diligit lucrum et commodum proprium, secundum Philosophum in l(ibro) 5 Ethicorum.[118] . . .[119]

To conclude our extracts from Remigio's analysis of kingship and tyranny, it is worth citing the whole of his section on the use of lordship, which twice quotes from the *Politics*. (The references to Seneca, incidentally, should also be noted: they should warn us against separating the Aristotelian and the Roman Stoic traditions too sharply.[120]) Remigio deals with the use of lordship under four headings:

And first with respect to the imposition of punishments, because a king imposes them with a sorrowful heart, for the sake of the common good, but a tyrant takes delight in imposing them, in accordance with the words of Seneca in the passage to which I referred earlier: a tyrant takes pleasure in using violence, whereas a king does so because the needs of the state make it necessary. Secondly, respecting promotion

---

[117] '. . . et enim demus uult esse monarchus. propter quod et adulator apud utrosque est honoratus, apud demos quidem demagogus (est enim demagogus demi adulator), apud tyrannos aut qui humiliter collocuntur, quod quidem est opus adulationis' (1313$^b$38–1314$^a$1, p. 577 Susemihl).

[118] Cf. *Aristoteles Latinus*, xxvi/1–3, fasc. 4, ed. Gauthier, p. 533, 1160$^b$2–3 Bekker.

[119] MS Florence, Nazionale Conv. soppr. G. 4. 936, fo. 390$^r$ (right-hand margin). In one or two places the scribe may have tried to modify 'tir-' to 'tur-', but I have not noted this here or below. The abbreviation which I have tentatively extended as 'quidem' is very unusual.

[120] With his customary originality and clarity, Quentin Skinner has brought out 'the remarkable extent to which the vocabulary of Renaissance moral and political thought was derived from Roman stoic sources' (*Foundations*, vol. i, p. xiv), but I suspect that from the later 13th cent. on, if not earlier, it would often be difficult to assign a given work or writer to an Aristotelian *or* a Roman Stoic tradition, as if they were mutually exclusive.

to office, since a king promotes people who are truly good and useful to the state, in accordance with the words of the Psalm (44: 12): *the king shall desire your beauty*. But a tyrant promotes flatterers, as we said. Thirdly, with respect to the protection of his land and person, since the king looks to friends and citizens for protection, whereas the tyrant looks to aliens, as Aristotle says in the place cited above: so he says that it is a characteristic of tyranny especially to distrust friends; for since he himself loves no one, he therefore believes that he is loved by no one, and he puts his trust in no one. Therefore he sometimes even looks for protection to beasts; and so Valerius [Maximus], book 9, chapter 13:[121] Massimissa the king, putting little faith in the hearts of men, used guard-dogs to defend his safety. Fourthly, with respect to defence by arms, for as Seneca says in the passage to which I referred earlier: a king uses arms as a means of defending peace, while a tyrant uses them in order to repress great feelings of hatred with great fear. And for this reason Dionysius the tyrant had *potagōgides*, that is, men running with their feet, as Aristotle says in book [5] of the *Politics*, that is, in order to make enquiries and report back on the feelings of each individual, so that in this way he might be better able to resist plotters.

Et primo quantum ad irrogationem penarum, quia rex irrogat eas cum dolore cordis, propter bonum commune, se*d* tirannus delectatur in irrogatione earum, iuxta illud Sen(ece) ubi supra:[122] tirannus uoluptate seuit, se*d* rex necessitate publice[123] utilitatis. Secundo quantum ad promotionem honorum, quia rex promouet uere bonos et utiles rei publice, iuxta illud Ps. (44: 12): *concu(piscet) rex decorem t(uum)*. Se*d* ti(rannus) promouet adulatores, ut dictum est. Tertio quantum ad custodiam terre sue et persone, quia rex facit custodiam per amicos et ciues, tirannus autem facit eam per extraneos, ut dicit Philosophus ubi supra:[124] unde dicit: tirannicum autem maxime discredere amicis. Quia enim ipse neminem diligit, ideo ipse a nemine credit diligi, et de nemine confidit. Unde aliquando etiam per bruta facit custodiam; unde Ualerius, l(ibro) 9, c. 13:[125] Massimissa rex parum fidei in pec-

---

[121] 13] 14 *ms*

[122] See *De clementia*, 1. 11. 4, 1. 12. 1, ed. Faider (Université de Gand, Recueil de travaux publiés par la Faculté de Philosophie et Lettres, 60; Ghent and Paris, 1928), 83.

[123] publice] *my microfilm unclear here*

[124] '. . . et regnum quidem saluatur per amicos, tyrannicum autem maxime discredere amicis, tamquam uolentibus quidem omnibus, potentibus autem maxime' (p. 576 Susemihl, $1313^b29$–32 Bekker). (I do not know if there is a more precise source in the *Politics* for the words 'rex facit custodiam . . . extraneos'.)

[125] 13] 14 *ms*. See *Valerii Maximi Factorum et dictorum memorabilium libri novem*, 9. 13, ed. Carolus Kempf (Leipzig, 1888), 465.

toribus hominum reponens, salutem suam custodia canum uallauit.
Quarto quantum ad munimentum armorum, quia ut dicit Sen(eca),
ubi supra:[126] rex utitur armis in munimentum pacis, tirannus uero
ut [*fo. 390ᵛ*] magno timore magna odia compescat. Et propter hoc
Dyonysius tirannus habebat pectagogitas,[127] id est, homines pedibus
discurrentes, ut dicit Philosophus l(ibro) [quinto][128] Pol(iticorum),[129]
ut inquirerent scilicet et referrent affectus singulorum, ut sic melius
posset insidiantibus resistere.[130]

Remigio's is by far the fullest discussion of kingship and
tyranny that I have come across in memorial sermons of this
period, but it is not the only one. Bertrand de la Tour raises the
subject as well, employing also the Aristotelian concepts of
'political' and 'royal' government. Aristotle uses these words
in a semi-technical sense, contrasting them with 'despotic'
government. At one point in the *Politics* he says that 'the soul
rules the body with a despotical rule, whereas the intellect
rules the appetites with a constitutional (πολιτικήν, *politico*)
and royal rule'.[131] Further on he characterizes the authority of
husband over wife as political/constitutional, and that of father
over children as royal, making it clear that authority over
a wife or over children is different from despotic authority
because exercised over free persons (*tamquam liberis quidem
ambobus*).[132] Now compare Bertrand de la Tour:

Alas, not all other princes are like that man. Many of them govern
their subjects with a government which is not political or royal, not as
a guardian towards his wards, for they oppress them, torment them,
rob them, and indeed despoil them and kill them. To them it is said,
Micah 3 (1–2, cf. 9): *Listen, princes of the house of Jacob: Is it not your part*

---

[126] *De clementia*, 1. 12. 3, p. 84 Faider.
[127] pectagogitas] the Greek is ποταγωγίδες: see 1313ᵇ13. Remigio clearly
misunderstood the word, but there may be a copying error as well.
[128] Blank left in manuscript for book-number.
[129] '... et tentare non latere quaecunque exititerit quis dicens uel agens subditorum, sed esse attentos, uelut circa Syracusanos uocatae potagogides et
auribus audientes, quos misit Hieron, ubi fuerit aliqua congregatio et collectio
(confident enim minus timentes tales et, si confidant, latebunt minus)' (pp.
574–5 Susemihl, 1313ᵇ11 ff. Bekker).
[130] MS Florence, Nazionale Conv. soppr. G. 4. 936, fo. 390ʳ⁻ᵛ (in margins).
[131] 1254ᵇ4–5, *The Complete Works of Aristotle: The Revised Oxford Translation*,
ed. J. Barnes, ii (Princeton and Guildford, 1984), 1990; p. 18 Susemihl for the
Latin.
[132] 1259ª37–ᵇ17, pp. 49–51 Susemihl.

*to know judgement? You that hate good and love evil, who violently pluck off the skin of your subjects from them, and their flesh from their bones.* For such men are not princes, but tyrants . . .[133]

The Franciscan Bertrand de la Tour is thinking along the same lines as the Dominican Remigio de' Girolami—not that one should find that surprising.

Thus Aristotle's *Ethics* and *Politics* left a clear mark on ideas about justice, kingship, and tyranny[134] in this genre. This seems to me to be symptomatic of an underlying attitude. The *Ethics* and the *Politics* provide a specific and constructive analysis of the ways in which humans can achieve fulfilment through virtue in this life. To accept the values of these two works is to adopt a relatively positive and optimistic attitude towards life this side of the grave—a frame of mind best described by the untranslatable German adjective *weltbejahend*. (This applies even to the discussion of tyranny, because the essential goodness of its antithesis, kingship, is taken for granted.) To work from these two works of Aristotle was to accept substantial elements, at least, of a secular value-system.

One more Aristotelian virtue deserves mention: 'magnificence'. The following passage, from Federico Franconi of Naples, is an Aristotelian way of praising generosity. He is speaking of Charles II of Anjou:

Secondly, one should speak of his magnificence. According to Aristotle, *Ethics* 4, it is the part of the magnificent man to go to great expense and to make donations, and especially in connection with

---

[133] Transcription B:c, **11**: 2–4.

[134] The distinction between kingship and tyranny must have been part of the general consciousness of the intelligentsia by the early 14th cent. In the following passage from Giovanni da San Gimignano's sermon in memory of a prince it is linked to the standard question of whether a prince should want more to be loved than to be feared (on which see the interesting discussions in Skinner, *Foundations*, i. 33–4, 127–8, 135–6): 'Circa primum aduertendum est quod inter tyrapnnum (*sic*) et bonum principem est differentia, quia tyrampnus plus curat timeri quam amari, sicut dicit Seneca de Alexandro in libro De Beneficiis . . . sed bonus princeps quamuis sciat utrumque esse necessarium, scilicet et amari et [*fo. 107ra*] timeri, tamen plus appetit amari quam timeri. Et est differentia inter principis amorem et timorem, quia quando princeps solum timetur ut tyrampnus et non amatur a subditis, sed oditur, tunc subditi gaudent de eius absentia, et tristantur de eius presentia', and so on (MS Siena, Biblioteca Comunale F. X. 24, fos. 106vb–107ra, from a sermon on the text *Princeps maximus cecidit hodie* (2 Kgs. 2: 38); Schneyer, *Repertorium*, iii. 762, No. 505).

God and the building of temples. Thus our lord King Charles acted as
befits a magnificent man and went to great expense and made gifts to
knights, counts, and the like, and especially in connection with God
and the building of temples. How great were the gifts he made to
clerics and religious! Indeed, too, how many were the churches and
monasteries, how many were the convents that he built and endowed.

Secundo, loquendum est de eius magnificentia. Secundum Philosophum, 4 Ethicorum,[135] magnifici est dare magnos su*m*ptus et donaria,
et precipue circa deum [*fo. 131*ra] et preparationes te*m*plorum. Sic dominus rex Karolus ta*m*quam magnificus fecit, et dedit magnos su*m*ptus
et dona militibus, comitibus, et huiusmodi, et precipue circa deum et
preparationem te*m*plorum. Quam magna donauit clericis et religiosis! Quot etiam ecclesias, monasteria, quot conuentus hedificauit et
dotauit.[136]

It is tempting to indulge in a long analysis of this passage. The
transition from Aristotelian values to those of the medieval
nobility and courtly generosity—a king giving gifts to knights,
counts, and the like—is smoothly made. The difference is
slight, but new associations with the military retinue or household come to mind.[137] Suffice it to note again the common ground shared by Aristotelian, chivalric, and indeed
humanist[138] ideas, and the ease with which secular attitudes
are incorporated into preaching.

Generosity, which in the foregoing passage goes under the
name 'magnificence', is praised with relative frequency in our
corpus of sermons under other headings. In the following
passage it comes under the heading of charity. It will be perceived that here the atmosphere is distinctly less secular than
in passages analysed up to this point. The preacher is Giovanni
da Napoli, who says that Charles II of Anjou and Naples

showed that he had the love of God or charity in many and great
works, but especially in two, according to the two precepts of charity.

---

[135] Cf. *Aristoteles Latinus*, xxvi/1–3, fasc. 4, ed. Gauthier, pp. 436–9, esp. p.
437 (1122b20 Bekker).

[136] MS Munich, Staatsbibliothek Clm. 2981, fos. 130vb–131ra, from a sermon
on the text *Memoriam abundantiae suauitatis tuae* (Ps. 144: 7); Schneyer, *Repertorium* iv. 223, 'Nicolaus de Asculo', No. 217.

[137] For emphasis on the importance of the royal household (without specific
reference to its military aspect) see Transcription B:d, 7: 1 (if I am right to
understand *familia* as 'household' here).

[138] On magnificence in humanist funeral orations see McManamon, *Funeral
Oratory*, 97 (with n. 25 on pp. 216–17), and index s.v. 'Magnificence'.

For the worship of God flourished greatly where he stayed[139] and in his chapel, at his command and with his active intervention, and he greatly increased the worship of God in the lands of his domain, by building churches and monasteries and religious places, and endowing them; and this is with respect to the first commandment of charity. And with respect to the second, he gave alms frequently and abundantly to the poor for the sake of God, so that it would truly have been possible to say of him that text of 1 John 4 (17): *In him the charity of God is perfect.*

se habuisse dei amorem seu caritatem ostendit in multis et magnis operibus, sed precipue in duobus, secundum duo precepta caritatis. Nam cultus diuinus multum uiguit in eius hospitio et capella ipso ordinante et faciente, et cultum diuinum multum ampliauit in terris dominii sui, ecclesias et monasteria et loca religiosa construendo et dotando; et hoc quantum ad primum preceptum caritatis. Et quantum ad secundum, multas et amplas elemosinas fecit pauperibus propter deum, ut de ipso uere dici potuerit illud prime Io. quarto (17): *In hoc caritas dei perfecta est.*[140]

Strong emphasis on charity is a feature of Giovanni da Napoli's preaching on Angevins of Naples.[141] He shows in a sermon for the translation of the prince of Taranto (that is, presumably, on the transference of his remains to a new resting-place) that Aristotle can be brought into a discussion of this central Christian virtue, at least by association:

Therefore he had in himself the love of God or charity, which according to the theologians connects all the virtues . . . just as prudence does according to the philosophers, as is evident in *Ethics* 6.

Ergo ipse habuit in se dei dilectionem seu caritatem, que secundum theologos connectit omnes uirtutes . . . sicut prudentia secundum philosophos, ut patet in sexto Ethicorum.[142]

---

[139] A tentative translation of *in eius hospitio.*

[140] MS Naples, Nazionale VIII AA 11, fo. 24$^{va}$, from a sermon on the text *In caritate perpetua dilexi te* (Jer. 31: 3); Schneyer, *Repertorium*, iii. 607, No. 35.

[141] See esp. sermons 37 (MS Naples, Nazionale VIII AA 11, fos. 25$^{va}$–26$^{ra}$) and 39 (ibid., fos. 26$^{vb}$–27$^{rb}$) in Schneyer's list, *Repertorium*, iii. 607.

[142] MS Naples, Nazionale VIII AA 11, fo. 37$^{va}$, from a sermon on the text *Ante translationem testimonium habuit* (Heb. 11: 5); Schneyer, *Repertorium*, iii. 609, No. 59. If he has a precise passage of bk. 6 of the *Ethics* in mind it might be 1144$^b$30–2. Cf. Thomas Aquinas, *Summa theologica, Secunda secundae,* q. 166, art. 2 ad 1: 'Ad primum ergo dicendum quod prudentia est completiua omnium uirtutum moralium, ut dicitur in VI *Ethic.*' This might be the proximate source.

There is nevertheless a difference between this reference to
Aristotle and others discussed above. Giovanni is drawing an
analogy between the place of prudence among the natural
virtues and charity's place among the supernatural virtues, but
the analogy assumes that the two sets of virtues are not on the
same level. In one direction, charity impinges on secular life, as
we have just seen, but in another it enters a more exclusively
religious zone, as when it is related to the sacraments:

And he [the prince of Taranto] was a friend of God . . . He showed
this love in many things while he was alive, hearing mass every day
and saying the divine office, and on feast-days hearing it sung in his
chapel, and going to confession frequently . . .

Et fuit amicus dei . . . Quem amorem ostendit in multis dum uiueret,
omni die audiendo missam et dicendo officium diuinum, et in festis
audiendo cantari in capella sua, et sepe confitendo . . .[143]

This conjures up rather an other-worldly atmosphere. The first
part of this chapter stressed the positive attitude found in the
sermons towards secular things (wealth and nobility, power
and fame), and an Aristotelianism which implied acceptance of
a natural political order such as a pagan philosopher could
analyse with insight. The themes of the love of God and of the
sacraments belong to a more specifically spiritual sphere.[144]
Although the approving attitude which the preachers tend to
take towards the things of this world deserves the emphasis
it has been given above, it would be wrong to infer that
the sermons betray any indifference to things spiritual and
ecclesiastical.

Service to ecclesiastical authority, obedience of secular to
spiritual power, is praised in several sermons. Perhaps the
most interesting is Bertrand de la Tour's sermon in memory of
Charles of Calabria, the son of King Robert of Naples, who
held the *signoria* of Florence from 1326 to 1328. Charles had the

[143] MS Naples, Nazionale VIII AA 11, fo. 37ᵛᵇ, from a sermon on the text
*Ante translationem testimonium habuit* (Heb. 11: 5); Schneyer, *Repertorium*, iii. 609,
No. 59. (The sentence continues: 'et multas alias elemosinas pauperibus
faciendo, et cum religiosis personis et seruitoribus dei libenter conuersando'.)
For another passage about the reception of the sacraments (the Eucharist and
almost certainly Confession) see Transcription B:b, 1: 9–10.
[144] The theme of generosity is somewhere in between: it could be regarded
as either 'this-wordly' or 'other-worldly'.

task of leading resistance to Ludwig of Bavaria. Pope John XXII had refused to recognize Ludwig as emperor, even after the decisive defeat of his Habsburg opponent at Mühldorf in 1322.[145] When a cardinal warned John to beware of German ferocity, it is reported that he replied: 'By God! They shall discover fury and discover it again!'[146] However, by the time Charles of Calabria died in November 1328,[147] the situation had come to look dangerous for the papacy. Marsiglio of Padua's *Defensor pacis*, written under Ludwig's protection and condemned in 1327, must have seemed a significant intellectual threat to papal claims. At the beginning of 1328 Ludwig had been crowned emperor in Rome. In May he had an antipope, Peter of Corbara, elected and crowned.[148] It was also in May 1328 that the minister-general of the Franciscan Order (and, with him, William of Ockham) had fled from Avignon; at Pisa they joined Ludwig of Bavaria.[149] Bertrand de la Tour was close to these events. It was noted in another context that he was made caretaker of the leaderless Franciscan Order (on 13 June 1328).[150] The Franciscan factor was near the centre of the crisis. The argument that John XXII was a heretic on the subject of Franciscan poverty, and therefore that he automatically ceased to be head of the Church, could be used to legitimate Ludwig of Bavaria's (Franciscan) antipope,[151] as could a more diffuse sense that John XXII represented a false, wealthy Church,

---

[145] For a good account of the background to the battle see H. Thomas, *Deutsche Geschichte des Spätmittelalters 1250–1500* (Stuttgart, 1983), 153–60. (John's reasons need not concern us here.)

[146] P. Partner, *The Lands of St. Peter: The Papal State in the Middle Ages and the Early Renaissance* (Berkeley and Los Angeles, 1972), 317 n. 1.

[147] F. Schevill, *History of Florence from the Founding of the City through the Renaissance* (New York, 1961, edn.), 207.

[148] J. N. D. Kelly, *The Oxford Dictionary of Popes* (Oxford and New York, 1986), 216.

[149] H.-G. Beck, K. A. Fink, *et al.*, *From the High Middle Ages to the Eve of the Reformation* (Handbook of Church History, ed. H. Jedin and J. Dolan, 4; New York and London, 1970), 373; Gauchat, *Cardinal Bertrand de Turre*, 100.

[150] Gauchat, *Cardinal Bertrand de Turre*, 101; *Bullarium Franciscanum*, v, ed. Conradus Eubel (Rome, 1898), No. 716, pp. 349–50. See also above, at n. 51.

[151] B. Tierney, *Origins of Papal Infallibility 1150–1350: A Study on the Concepts of Infallibility, Sovereignty and Tradition in the Middle Ages* (Studies in the History of Christian Thought, 6; Leiden, 1972), 199–204, esp. 201, shows how Michael of Cesena came to deny that John was pope, since a pope who became a heretic automatically ceased to be head of the Church.

as opposed to the real, poor, 'spiritual' Church. It could be argued that Ludwig had a more formidable ideological arsenal at his disposal than Henry IV in the eleventh century, Barbarossa in the twelfth, or Frederick II in the thirteenth. All he had to do, it may have seemed, was smash the Guelphs. No wonder that Bertrand spoke emotionally—a lot of feeling comes through the sermon—about the Guelph leader's death. For him, Charles had been the champion of the Church. His sermon includes an extended statement of the idea that it is the role of the *dux* (which is perhaps better translated as 'leader' than as 'duke') to protect the papacy. It is unusual and remarkable for so full a version of a memorial sermon to be transmitted from this period, and the relevant passages are worth quoting:

And this lord Charles was certainly most faithful to God, and also to the vicar of God, to his father [King Robert of Naples], and to the people of the whole kingdom of Sicily [i.e. Naples]. For he fulfilled the word—that is, the command—of God and the pope and his father . . . the House of France, from which this leader is descended, often had the leadership of the Christian people against evil men, rebels against God and the Church and the Catholic faith—all these people being prefigured by the Canaanites and the Benjaminites. For 'Canaan' means 'changed', while 'Benjamin' means 'son of grief'. And truly, unbelieving men and heretics are changed from bad to worse, and indeed to the worst of all: that is, from original sin to actual sin and to the sin of unbelief, which is the greatest of them all. They are also 'sons of grief', eternal grief, that is, which they will endure for ever.

And indeed, there have been many leaders from the House of France against those 'changed men' and 'sons of grief': [leaders] such as Chlodoremus [Clovis?], Pippin, Charles the Magnificent [i.e. Charlemagne], St Louis, and indeed Charles [I of Anjou], the great-grandfather of that leader—and also that lord Charles [of Calabria]. For he was a leader against those 'changed men' and 'sons of grief', that is, against [Ludwig the] Bavarian and the antipope and [the] other rebels against the holy Church of God.

Et certe iste dominus Ka(rolus) fuit fidelissimus deo, dei etiam uicario, patri suo, et totius regni Scicilie populo. Dei enim et pape et patris sui impleuit uerbum, id est preceptum, . . . [*fo. 124^{ra}*] . . . domus[152] Francie, de qua dux iste descendit, habuit sepe ducatum christiani populi contra malos homines, rebelles deo et ecclesie et fidei catholice,

---

[152] domus] dominus *ms*

qui omnes figurantur[153] per Cananeos et Beniamites. Canaan enim interpretatur 'co*m*mutatus', Beniamyn autem interpretatur 'filius doloris'. Et certe, infideles homines et heretici sunt co*m*mutati a malo in peius,[154] y*m*mo et in pessimum, scilicet a peccato originali ad peccatum actuale, et ad peccatum infidelitatis quod est inter omnia maximum. Sunt etiam filii doloris, scilicet eterni, quem[155] perpetuo sustinebunt.

De domo autem Francie fuerunt multi duces contra istos co*m*mutatos et filios doloris, sicud Clodoremus, Pypinus, Karolus magnificus, sanctus Ludowicus, Karolus etiam proauus istius ducis, et iste etiam dominus Karolus. Fuit enim dux contra istos conmutatos et filios doloris, id est, contra Bauarum et antipapam, aliosque rebelles ecclesie sancte dei.[156]

Next, Charles of Calabria is compared to King David, and the subject is rapidly brought round again to the war against Ludwig of Bavaria:

David means 'strong of hand' and 'one whose countenance is desired'. And certainly that lord Charles was strong of hand, since he showed prowess and vigour against enemies. He was indeed also one whose countenance was desired, because he was just and honest. It is also read of David that he acted with especial vigour against Goliath the Philistine, whom he killed, as we find in 1 Kings 17 (50). For 'Goliath' means 'snare', and signifies the Bavarian and antipope and their followers, who are without doubt in a snare of the Devil, vilely taken in by him. They are also a trap for many others, whom they take in and bring to ruin. Truly, that lord acted with great vigour against them. For he prevented them from going any further, indeed he compelled them to depart from the City [of Rome]. Therefore it is well said of him (1 Kgs. 13: 14) that *the Lord*—that is, God, or the pope, or the king—*sought a man after his own heart, and commanded him to be a leader over his people*; and he faithfully obeyed. And because of that obedience, because he laboured much under arms [*or in armour?*] during the summer, he departed from this life.

Dauit enim interpretatur 'manu fortis' et [*fo. 124^{rb}*] 'wltu desiderabilis'. Et certe iste dominus Karolus fuit manu fortis, quia probus et strenuus

---

[153] figurantur] figuratur *ms*
[154] peius] penis *ms*
[155] quem] quam *ms*
[156] MS Kremsmünster 44, fos. 123^{vb}–124^{ra}, from a sermon on the text *Propter sapientiam* (Prov. 28: 2); Schneyer, *Repertorium*, i. 583, No. 1123. In addition to the scribal errors proper, there seems to be an otiose abbreviation-mark on 'proauus'.

contra hostes. Wltu etiam desiderabilis, quia iustus et honestus.
De Dauid etiam legitur quod specialiter fuit strenuus contra Golyath
Philisteum, quem interfecit, sicut habetur 1° R(eg.) xvii° (50). Golyath
enim interpretatur 'decipula', et significat Bauarum et antipapam et
sequaces eorum, qui proculdubio sunt in decipula dyaboli turpiter[157]
decepti per eum. Sunt etiam decipula multorum aliorum, quos ipsi
decipiunt, et interitum mergunt.[158] Certe iste dominus fuit multum
strenuus contra istos. Inpediuit enim eos ne ultra procederent, ymmo
coegit eos exire de urbe. Bene ergo dicitur de ipso: *Quesiuit Dominus—*
scilicet deus uel papa uel rex—*uirum iuxta cor suum, et precepit ei ut
esset dux super populum suum*, et ipse fideliter obediuit. Et propter istam
obedientiam, quia multum laborauit cum armis estiuo tempore, ab ista
uita migrauit.[159]

Even after all this, Bertrand is only getting into his stride.
He next compares Charles of Calabria with Ezechias, whose
measures against idolatry symbolically represent Charles's war
against 'the Bavarian' and the antipope. Ezechias (4 Kings 18:
4).

*destroyed the high places and broke the statues in pieces and cut down the
groves and broke in pieces the bronze serpent to which the children* [of Israel]
*burnt incense*. For he was very severe, especially against those things
which stood in the way of the worship of God. In the same way, I say
to you of that lord Charles that he for his part[160] *destroyed the high
places*, that is, the proud men who wished to worship in a place other
than where it had been laid down by God, that is, in a place under
interdict and, for the time being, profane, splitting the Church, and
believing that the vicar of Christ and the true emperor were in another
place, a place where they were not. For the vicar of Christ was not at
Rome then, but at Avignon, nor was the true emperor (who is now in
no place) at Rome.

There, too, he *broke the statues in pieces*. For a statue appears to be
that which it is not. For sometimes it seems to be a man, and is not a
man, sometimes a lion, and yet has nothing of a lion. In this way the
Bavarian is a statue of a kind. For he seems to be a true emperor when
he wears the emperor's insignia, and yet he is only a sham emperor.
Thus, too, that antipope seems to be pope when he bears the papal
insignia, and yet he has nothing of the truth of the papacy. What need

[157] turpiter] *correction in ms*
[158] interitum mergunt] *emend to* quibus interitum ingerunt?
[159] MS Kremsmünster 44, fo. 123[ra–b].
[160] Or perhaps 'so far as was in his power', if one emends 'est' to 'erat'.

we say, then? Truly that lord Charles *broke in pieces* those *statues*, that is, their power, for in resisting them he made it apparent that they were statues having little or nothing of virtue. . . .

Again, he *broke the bronze serpent*, that is, the Bavarian and the antipope. For the bronze serpent seemed a true serpent, yet it had nothing of the truth of a serpent. So too one of those men seemed to be emperor, when he nevertheless was not; and the other seemed to be the pope, and nevertheless he had nothing of the papacy. And as it is said that *the sons of Israel burnt incense* to that bronze serpent, so too many people who were foolish and fooled worshipped and honoured one of these men as emperor and the other as pope. Therefore that man broke the bronze serpent, that is, the Bavarian and the antipope.

*dissipauit excelsa, contriuit statuas, succidit lucos*[161] *et contriuit serpentem eneum* [ *fo. 124*$^{va}$] *cui filii [Israel]*[162] *adolebant incensum.* Ffuit enim multum seuerus, maxime contra[163] illa que impediebant diuinum cultum. Sic dico de isto domino Ka(rolo) quod ipse quantum est de se *dissipauit excelsa,* id est, homines superbos, qui uolebant alibi adorare quam ubi erat a deo institutum, scilicet in loco interdicto et ad tempus prophano, scindentes ecclesiam, et in alio loco credentes esse Christi uicarium et imperatorem uerum ubi non erant. Christi enim uicarius non erat tunc Rome, sed in Auinion., nec imperator uerus, qui modo nusquam est, ibi erat.

Ibi etiam *contriuit statuas.* Statua enim apparet esse id quod non est. Aliquando enim uidetur esse homo et homo non est, aliquando leo, et tamen nichil habet de leone. Sic est Bauarus quedam statua. Uidetur enim esse imperator uerus quando portat imperatoris insignia, et tamen imperator non est nisi fictus. Sic et ille antipapa uidetur esse papa cum portat insignia papalia, et tamen nichil habet de ueritate papatus. Quid ergo? Certe iste dominus Ka(rolus) *contriuit* istas *statuas,* id est, uirtutem eorum, resistens enim eis fecit apparere quod erant statue modicum aut nichil de uirtute habentes. . . .[164]

Iterum iste *confregit serpentem eneum,* id est, Bauarum et antipapam. Serpens enim eneus [*fo. 124*$^{vb}$] uidebatur serpens uerus,[165] et tamen nichil habebat de ueritate serpentis. Sic et unus istorum uidebatur esse imperator, cum tamen non esset, et alius uidebatur papa esse, et tamen nichil habebat de papatu. Et sicut[166] dicitur quod *filii Israel*

[161] *lucos*] lutos *ms*
[162] *Israel*] om. in *ms*
[163] contra] qua *ms*
[164] Some words, starting a new sentence, may have dropped out of the text at this point.
[165] uerus] uetus *ms*
[166] sicut] sic *ms*.

*adolebant* illi serpenti eneo *incensum*, ita multi fatui et seducti adorabant et honorabant unum istorum sicut imperatorem et alium sicut papam. Iste igitur *confregit serpentem eneum*, id est Bauarum et antipapam.[167]

So Bertrand continues, even referring to the antipope by name:

It is said of Alcimus, 1 Maccabees 7,[168] that he was the leader of the evil men, and that he wanted to be made high priest through Demetrius the king. And he stands for that Peter of Corvaria,[169] who wants to be high priest, not indeed by canonical election, but through that Bavarian, who has no power to do this.

De Achymo autem dicitur i° Machab. vii°, quod fuit dux iniquorum, et quod uoluit fieri[170] sacerdos summus per Demetrium regem; et significat istum Petrum de Corvaria, qui wlt esse summus sacerdos, non quidem per electionem canonicam, sed per illum Bauarum, qui nullam habet ad hoc potestatem.[171]

The analogy is that just as Jonathan, in Maccabees, was a leader especially against Alcimus and Bacchides (another enemy of Jewish freedom), so too Charles of Calabria was made leader against the antipope and Ludwig of Bavaria.[172]

Bertrand de la Tour's passages about the defence of the Church stand out because they are long and quite emotional. Similar ideas about the service of the Church are much more briefly expressed in a sermon on Robert the Wise himself and

[167] MS Kremsmünster 44, fo. 124^{rb–vb}.

[168] See esp. vv. 5, 9, 21.

[169] The antipope Nicholas (V) was called Pietro Rainalducci, and was born at Corvaro in the Abruzzi (Kelly, *The Oxford Dictionary of Popes*, 216). Note that contemporaries mockingly called Nicholas Ludwig of Bavaria's 'idol' (ibid.), which makes Bertrand de la Tour's imagery more appropriate.

[170] fieri] firi *ms?*

[171] MS Kremsmünster 44, fo. 124^{vb}.

[172] 'Et bene significatur ille per Alchymum, qui interpretatur "fermentum uani consilii". Et significat istum miserum qui fermentatus uano consilio fecit istam iniquitatem ut ostenderet se Christi uicarium, cum tamen [*fo. 125^{ra}*] sit eius inimicus. Contra istum ergo pessimum Alchymum qui fuit dux eorum qui comprehenderunt Iesum,—id est, comprehendere uoluerunt Iesu Christi uicarium, sicut dicitur de Iuda, Act. i° (16 seq.)—ffuit iste dominus factus dux ut faceret eum mori magno tormento, sicut fuit mortuus ille Alchymus, ut habetur i° Machabeorum ix° (56). Bachides autem interpretatur luctus fortis, et significat Bauarum, qui nunc luget fortiter quos opprimit et uexat, et tandem fortissime lugebit in inferno. Igitur contra istos duos duces pessimos et latronum principes fuit iste factus dux ad bellandum bellum nostrum—dicunt fideles christiani' (MS Kremsmünster 44, fos. 124^v–125^r). ([Iesum] *read* Iudam? (i.e. Iudas Maccabaeus); luget fortiter] *read* lugere facit?; inferno] infernum *ms*.).

on his younger brother Philip, prince of Taranto. Of the latter, Giovanni da Napoli says that 'he exposed his life to death often, twice at least, that is, in Sicily and in Tuscany, fighting for Christ, who is God, his friend, and for his Church, against the enemies of the Church'.[173] Of Robert the Wise Federico Franconi asks rhetorically: 'Who would not say that our lord king was subject and obedient to the Roman Church?', and specifies that Robert defended it militarily and obeyed its commands, and also (if I interpret an obscure phrase correctly), gave it financial help.[174]

There is an affinity between the ideas of Thomas Aquinas about the relation of State to Church and the ideas we have been examining. Thomas believed, on the one hand, in a political order that was good and in some sense autonomous; however, he also believed that secular government was subject to the authority of the Church.[175] Similarly, the preachers take an extremely positive attitude towards political power, but, in several cases at least, make a point of praising the prince's obedience to the Roman Church. (Incidentally, this attitude does not mark off medieval from humanist memorial preaching: a very humanist oration on the death of the emperor Frederick

[173] '. . . uitam suam morti exposuit sepe, saltim bis, scilicet in Sicilia et in Tuscia, pro Christo deo amico suo et eius ecclesia contra hostes ecclesie pugnando' (MS Naples, Nazionale VIII AA 11, fo. 37$^{va}$, from a sermon on the text *Ante translationem testimonium habuit* (Heb. 11: 5); Schneyer, *Repertorium*, iii. 609, No. 59).

[174] 'Secundo "ecce" notat eius subiectionem et obedientiam. Quis non diceret dominum nostrum regem Robertum subiectum fuisse et obedientem ecclesie Romane, cui tam prompte, tam fideliter in omnibus obediuit, siue subueniendo in debitis siue defendendo (desedendo *ms*) armis siue obediendo mandatis?' (MS Munich, Staatsbibliothek Clm. 2981, fo. 132$^{ra}$, from a sermon on the text *Ecce rex uester* (John 19: 14); Schneyer, *Repertorium*, iv. 223, 'Nicolaus de Asculo', No. 219). The tricky phrase is 'subueniendo in debitis' (or 'indebitis'). This presumably refers to financial help, but apart from that the sense is not clear. If *in* and *debitis* are to be taken as two words, as is most likely, one might render the phrase as 'by giving the financial help that was owed to it'. Cf. Léonard, *Les Angevins*, 282: in 1340 the kingdom 'éteignait une dette [to the papacy] remontant au grand-père du souverain régnant. . . . En dix ans, le roi Robert avait amorti sa dette extérieure après avoir lutté pendant les deux tiers de son règne pour ne pas l'accroître.' Later in the same sermon Robert is praised because he 'Defendit potenter regnum ab Herrico *imperatore* usque ad mortem predicti Herrici et (*om. ms*) contra Bauarum' (etc.) (fo. 132$^{rb}$).

[175] A. P. d'Entrèves, introduction to his *Aquinas: Selected Political Writings* (Oxford, 1965), p. xxiii; also pp. ix–xv, xx.

III lays emphasis on his defence of and reverence for the papacy.[176])

The comparison with Aquinas can in fact be carried further, for the attitudes of the sermons to the whole relation between this world and the next have the same kind of balance of emphasis that we find in the theology and philosophy of Thomas, who was by and large relatively optimistic about this world and the natural order, while subordinating it in the last analysis to the overriding objective of permanent union with God after death. The things of this world are thus linked and subordinated to the things of the next, without being denigrated or marginalized by other-worldly preoccupations.

This chapter has been mainly concerned with ideas about the things of this world. The Aristotelian (and so 'this-worldly') strain in the ideology of the sermons and their generally positive attitude to noble birth, wealth, power, and fame have been illustrated (the parallels to humanist and chivalric values being noted in passing). So far we have not taken more than a glimpse at the other, complementary aspect: the subordination of all this to religious priorities. The central theme of death and all that was thought to follow after it has been held over, as being too big for the confines of this chapter. Nevertheless, the two aspects of the message—politics and virtue on the one hand, death and afterlife on the other—should be held before the mind together. For the preachers are not primarily interested in life, or in death, in isolation, but in both together and in their relation to each other.

---

[176] Bernhard Perger, *Oratio Wienne habita in funere imperatoris* [Frederick III] (Vienna, [1493]; I have used the copy with British Library call No. IA 51513), fo. 3$^r$. (Perger alludes to Frederick's opposition to Conciliarism—the sense seems clear behind the circumlocutions—and also tells how 'rursus beatorum Apostolorum limina reuidens, sacra Romana iterum adorauit Christique uicarium deuotissimus ecclesie Romane cultor, defensor et auctor plus quam dignitas imperialis admittebat ueneratus'.)

# 4 Death and the Afterlife

THE previous chapter concentrated on passages orientated towards life this side of the grave (viewed by the preachers from a moral perspective, unsurprisingly, but not in an unfriendly light). To balance the passages about the goodness of ancestry, riches, renown, etc., and the Aristotelian outlook on political society, the sermons also present what is perhaps the nearest thing to a medieval theology of death. Death and the afterlife are of course treated in numerous places in medieval theological writings, but it is my impression[1] that the subject tends to be treated in separate segments rather than as a unity. However that may be, memorial sermons are a good place to find in a nutshell the medieval Church's idea of death.

In fact it seems likely that serious discussion of death may have been commoner in sermons as actually delivered orally than some written versions (whether models or records of sermons in memory of real people) might suggest. An analogy with preaching on saints may be pertinent here. If you were preparing a sermon on a saint, you would be likely to have two separate written sources in front of you: a collection of model sermons for the feast-days of saints (where one would not expect to find a detailed narrative of the saint's life), and a book of saints' lives such as the *Golden Legend*; thus material that was separate in its written form would be brought together in oral delivery.[2] In the same way a preacher might take his material about virtue in this life from one model memorial sermon, and material about death and the afterlife from another—perhaps from a sermon for the feast of All Souls. Similarly, the written version of a sermon in memory of a real ruler might abridge the reflections about death and the last things more drastically than the remarks about the dead man's

---

[1] Inexpert, it should be said, where the history of speculative theology is concerned.

[2] Cf. D. L. d'Avray, *The Preaching of the Friars: Sermons Diffused from Paris before 1300* (Oxford, 1985), 70 and n. 5.

office and virtues. The historian should sometimes try to reconstruct what the oral cocktail was like by mixing surviving written texts in the imagination.

Definite evidence that ideas about death could be added to an apparently self-contained sermon in memory of a king or prince is provided by Bertrand de la Tour.[3] The sermon in question has a fair amount to say about the virtues of a ruler: material that could be classified with themes discussed in the first half of this book. Bertrand does not ignore the subject of death, but never seems to grapple with it head on,[4] and the prince's achievements in this world are never far away. There is an interesting passage about mourning, but it is about the prince's virtues as well as about death: the prince should be mourned because he was so useful to the republic and the Church, but we should rejoice because he is destined directly or indirectly for heaven, since his life was good—which takes one back to his virtues.[5]

At the end of the sermon, however, we find the following cross-reference: 'You may, if you wish, say what I have noted about death or the dead in the first sermon, that is, *Beati mortui*.'[6] Though the sermon on the text *Beati mortui* seems primarily intended for All Souls' Day,[7] it is evident from the

---

[3] The sermon is on the text *Mortuus est David in senectute* (1 Chron. 29: 28); Schneyer, *Repertorium*, i. 578, No. 1063 (Transcription B:a).

[4] This is a subjective reaction, but readers may form their own impression from Transcription B:a.

[5] Transcription B:a, **7**: 1–8: 3. Compare Bertrand on the death of Charles of Calabria, in his sermon on the text *Propter sapientiam et scientiam horum, quae dicuntur uita ducis longior erit* (Prov. 28: 2); Schneyer, *Repertorium*, i. 583, No. 1123: 'Uerum, licet sua mors sit nobis lamentabilis, unum tamen est quod in hoc lamento nos consolatur, uidelicet, quod taliter se habuit in uita presenti et in puncto sue mortis quod sic firmiter debemus credere quod eius uita post mortem erit sic longa quod numquam habebit finem' (MS Kremsmünster 44, fo. 122$^{ra}$). Also Giovanni da San Gimignano, in his sermon for the death of a prince on the text *Princeps maximus cecidit hodie* (2 Reg. 3: 38); Schneyer, *Repertorium*, iii. 762, No. 505: 'Sed quando moritur princeps robustus et sanus et totus uirtuosus et reipublice utilis, tunc est materia flendi... de morte boni principis lugendum est et dolendum triplici ratione: Primo ratione amabilitatis... Secundo ratione strenuitatis... Tertio ratione dignitatis' (MS Siena, Biblioteca Comunale F. X. 24, fo. 106$^{vb}$) (before *strenuitatis, in* is written and deleted).

[6] Transcription B:a, **17**: 5.

[7] 'Precipue ergo fit hodierna commemoratio pro illis qui non habent carnales amicos per quos iuuentur spiritualiter' (MS Kremsmünster 44, fo. 5$^{rb}$). The rubric in this manuscript is 'Sermo primus de epistola preexposita in die

cross-reference to it in the other sermon that it could be used for the commemoration of a particular individual (including a prince)—which prompts the reflection that other All Souls' Day sermons could be and probably were used in the same way, in combination with remarks about the life of the dead person.

*Beati mortui* is about death. After a long preamble, Bertrand works through the themes of death as calamity, the way to die in the grace of God, and the different fates of souls after death. If we put together the two sermons under consideration, therefore, we find that themes relating to this life, to death itself, and to the afterlife are held in balance.

It is worth dwelling a little on *Beati mortui* (one of a small group of Bertrand de la Tour's *de mortuis* sermons that seem to travel together in late medieval manuscripts from German-speaking areas)[8] because it is an extended reflection on death and the afterlife. It is also a good introduction to medieval topoi about death, for it collects a good many of them together. It begins, after a preamble and a division of the subject,[9] with the catastrophic character of death, on the natural level.[10] Bertrand alludes to the fall of Adam and Eve as the cause of death.[11] Not long after, he quotes Aristotle's dictum that death

mortuorum et in missa qualibet que de mortuis celebratur etc.' (ibid., fo. 3$^{va}$; sermon on the text *Beati mortui* (Rev. 14: 13); Schneyer, *Repertorium*, i. 577, No. 1052).

[8] I have seen the sermon in the following manuscripts now held in libraries in the German *Sprachraum*: Klosterneuburg 486, fos. 129$^{vb}$–131$^{va}$; Klosterneuburg 265, fos. 52$^{ra}$–54$^{va}$; Innsbruck, Universitätsbibliothek 234, fos. 117$^{va}$–119$^{rb}$; Vienna, Schottenstift, 379 (379), fos. 169$^{va}$–171$^{va}$.

[9] '... in hoc uerbo breuiter tria innuuntur, uidelicet nature casus terribilis, gratie status laudabilis, glorie fructus optabilis. Primum autem innuitur in calamitate mortis, secundum in securitate finis, tertium autem in perhennitate mercedis' (MS Kremsmünster 44, fo. 3$^{vb}$). (status] *after scribal correction;* innuitur] *extra minim in* ms; perhennitate] perhennitatem ms?)

[10] 'Primo dico tangitur nature casus terribilis in calamitate mortis, cum dicitur: *mortui*. . . . Reuera magnus [*fo. 4$^{ra}$*] est iste casus nature humane, quo cadit a uita naturali in mortem, quo casu natura cecidit et cadit in omnibus hominibus' (ibid., fos. 3$^{vb}$–4$^{ra}$). (mortui] *supplied in margin;* cecidit] *alteration in* ms; et cadit] *supplied in margin*)

[11] 'Magnus etiam fuit nature humane casus, quo cecidit in primis hominibus ab inmortalitate status innocentie ad mortalitatem status miserie, id est ad necessitatem moriendi, que fuit et est et erit in omni homine propter primi hominis peccatum' (ibid., fo. 4$^{ra}$).

is the most terrible of all things.[12] He argues that it should
strike terror into every man, and make him careful to live
in such a way that he may die well and afterwards live in
eternity.[13] Death is a lamentable fall of our nature.[14] On the
one hand, it is inevitable: a penalty for the sin of our first
parents, who passed down to their descendants the necessity
of dying, just as they would have passed down immortality if
they had not sinned.[15] (This is not the only sermon to discuss
the origins of death in terms of original sin.[16]) Then Bertrand
goes on to what was doubtless a topos, the idea that death is
certain but nothing is less certain than the hour, place, and

[12] '. . . secundum Aristotelem, mors est ultimum terribilium' (ibid.).
(Aristotelem] Ap^lem *ms?*) Cf. *Aristoteles Latinus*, xxvi/1–3, fasc. 4, ed. Gauthier,
p. 421, 1115ª26 Bekker.
[13] 'Debent enim eum reddere sollicitum ad taliter uiuendum, ut bene possit
mori et postea uiuere in eternum' (MS Kremsmünster 44, fo. 4^ra).
[14] 'Est enim mors casus nature nostre flebilis et lamentabilis' (ibid., fo. 4^ra).
[15] 'Est, dico, mortis cursus necessarius et ineuitabilis. Dicit enim Apostolus
ad Rom. x (*recte* Heb. 9: 27) quod (*alteration in ms?*) *statutum est hominibus
semel mori*. Uere statutum in penam grauissimam propter peccatum primorum
parentum. . . . Istam enim mortalitatem, id est moriendi necessitatem, trans-
fuderunt (transfundunt *ms?*) primi parentes in omnes posteros [fo. 4^rb] quia
peccauerunt, sicut transfudissent inmortalitatem si non peccassent' (ibid., fo.
4^ra–b).
[16] Cf. below, Transcription C:b, 2, *passim*, and also the following two
passages from Giovanni da San Gimignano: (1) 'Tanquam enim scintille
fulgentes fuerunt primi parentes, ex quorum scilicet materia nostra propagata
sunt cinerea corpora, se*d* ex eorum extinctione, id est peccati transgressione,
relicta est nobis fauilla modica, id est, breuis et curta uita, quia *per unum
hominem peccatum intrauit in mundum et per peccatum mors*, ut dicit Apostolus Ro.
5 (12)' (MS Siena, Biblioteca Comunale F. X. 24, fo. 107^rb, from a sermon on the
text *Princeps maximus cecidit hodie* (2 Kgs. 3: 38); Schneyer, *Repertorium*, iii. 762,
No. 505). (2) 'Et est dicendum quod sententia mortis et resolutionis in terram
data est propter peccatum primi hominis. Nam deus creauit primos parentes
cum dono originalis iustitie, et si in hac iustitia perseuerassent, non fuissent
per mortem in terram resoluti, se*d* sine morte in celum assumpti. Se*d*, peccante
Adam, sicut dicit Apostolus Ro. 5 (12, 18): *per unum hominem*, scilicet primum,
*peccatum intrauit in mundum*, quia scilicet *per unius delictum* peccatores constituti
sunt multi. Nam in Adam omnes peccauerunt, et per peccatum mors etiam in
omnes pertransiit, et per consequens resolutio in terram. Et ideo post peccatum
dixit Dominus Ade: *reuertaris in terram de qua sumptus es, quia puluis es et in
puluerem reuerteris*, Gn. 3 (19). Unde quia ista humiliatio in terram per mortem
consecuta est ex originali peccato in quo omnes effecti sunt peccatores, ideo
peccatoribus attribuitur humiliatio talis' (ibid., fo. 102^ra, from a sermon—death
of an emperor—on the text *Is qui uidebatur fluctibus maris imperare* (2 Macc. 9: 8);
Schneyer, *Repertorium*, iii. 761, No. 502).

manner of death.[17] Accordingly, one should not wait until
death to confess and turn to the Lord.[18] Shortly afterwards
Bertrand moves into a description of the unpleasant fate of the
body after death: 'May it please God that [our] souls may have
a better inheritance after death than our bodies will have. For
they will perhaps inherit beasts of the water or the land which
will devour them; serpents too and worms which will gnaw at
them and rest in them.'[19] After this he turns to the irreversibility
of death, continuing to stress its calamitous character.[20] Then,
changing the tone, Bertrand explains how grace makes the end
of human life different by giving the man who dies in the Lord
through grace and charity the security of eternal blessedness.[21]

Shortly afterwards the idea of what 'dying in the Lord' means
is set out in a sort of miniature 'Art of Dying':

You should know . . . that those people die in the Lord who die openly
confessing [faith in the Lord] with a firm expectation of the glory of
the Lord, in the sincere love of the goodness of the Lord, in the
perfect fulfilling of the commandments of the Lord, in asking whole-

[17] 'Dico etiam quod mortis modus est (et *ms*) subitus (*ms* subidus?) et
inperceptibilis. Nichil (uel *ms*?) enim secundum Senecam (senectam *ms*?) est
morte certius, sed proculdubio nichil est incertius hora, loco, et modo mortis'
(MS Kremsmünster 44, fo. 4$^{rb}$).
[18] 'Uiuens ergo et sanus debet homo confiteri et conuerti ad dominum, et
non expectare usque ad horam mortis, quia subito uenit mors et dum (deum
*ms*?) non speratur' (ibid., fo. 4$^{rb}$). Cf. Matt. 24: 50 and Luke 12: 46 (also, as L.-J.
Bataillon pointed out to me, Ecclus. 17: 26–7, and perhaps Job 34: 20).
[19] 'Placeat deo quod anime post mortem habeant meliorem hereditatem
quam nostra (uestra *ms*) corpora sunt habitura (habitatura *ms*). Hereditabunt
enim forsan bestias aquaticas (*correction in margin*) uel terrestres que ipsa
deuorabunt; serpentes etiam et uermes que ipsa rodent et in ipsis requiescent'
(ibid., fo. 4$^{rb}$). Bertrand had just cited Ecclus. 10: 13, which speaks of serpents
and beasts and worms.
[20] 'Mortis etiam status est horridus et inpermutabilis. . . . Omnes homines
(*ms adds* uadunt) ad mortem uadunt ut subtus terram maneant, et nullus inde
reuertitur super terram. [*fo. 4$^{va}$*] Casus igitur iste (*interlined*) nostre nature
multum est terribilis. Plenus enim est calamitate et miseria. O peccati stipend-
ium! O nature debitum! O ultimum terribilium! O uniuersale iudicium! *Omnes*
enim *morimur*. Sic igitur patet primum quod in hoc uerbo innuitur (imnuitur/
innuutur *ms*?), uidelicet nature casus terribilis, qui innuitur in calamitate mortis'
(ibid., fo. 4$^{rb-va}$).
[21] 'Secundo innuitur gratie status laudabilis in securitate finis . . . Mors enim
humane uite finis est. Nunc autem finis est securus, cum homo qui moritur per
gratiam et caritatem manet in Domino. Talis enim securus est de adipiscenda
beatitudine eterna' (ibid., fo. 4$^{va}$).

heartedly for the pardon of the Lord, which is done through a fitting
penance, in devout reception of the Lord's body, in a true recognition
of their own littleness and of the greatness of the Lord, in the liberal
distribution of their goods to the poor of the Lord, and in certain other
things which are pleasing to the Lord and necessary for acquiring the
Lord's salvation. And I say 'necessary' for adults and people who
have the means of doing this kind of thing, since, when there is no
possibility, good will without the exterior deed is sufficient. In truth,
any man who in this way dies in the Lord has a secure end, and
where he is concerned there is convincing evidence that he lived in
the Lord, and so he can say the words of the Psalm (15 [16]: 8–11)
when he is dying: *Always I kept the Lord in my sight*, that is, when I
lived I always had the Lord before my eyes, *since he is at my right hand*,
i.e.,[22] now when I am dying, *lest I be shaken*, that is, from his love, by
any temptation of demons. *Because of this my heart has rejoiced*, within
me, that is, *and my tongue has been exultant*, outside me, that is; *my
flesh, too, shall rest in hope*, that is, of the glorious resurrection, *since you
will not leave my soul in hell*, that is, in purgatory, *for ever, nor will you
allow your holy one*, that is, myself—made holy by your grace—*to
see*—to experience, that is—*corruption*, that is, for eternity. *You have
made known to me*, that is, when I was living, *the ways of life*, your
commandments, that is; *you will fill me with joy with your countenance*,
which I hope to gaze at for ever. Indeed, in the sight of it there will be
perpetual delights. So he adds: *at your right hand are delights right up till
the end*—that is, without end.

Sciendum autem quod illi moriuntur in Domino qui moriuntur
in aperta confessione (*supply* Domini), in firma expectatione Domini
glorie, in sincera dilectione bonitatis Domini, in perfecta impletione
mandatorum Domini, in plena requisitione uenie Domini, que fit
per dignam penitentiam, in deuota perceptione corporis Domini, in
uera recognitione paruitatis proprie et magnitudinis Domini, in larga
distributione bonorum suorum pauperibus[23] Domini, et in quibusdam
aliis que placita sunt Domino et necessaria acquisitioni salutis Domini.
Et dico necessaria adultis hominibus et habentibus ad huiusmodi
facultatem, quoniam ubi non est possibilitas, sufficeret sine exteriori
opere bona uoluntas. Reuera, quilibet homo qui sic moritur in Domino
habet finem se|curum, [*fo. 4$^{vb}$*] et de ipso argumentum euidens est

---

[22] Bertrand weaves scriptural quotation into his argument with the help of
little glosses prefaced by 'id est' or 'supple' (indeed his use of the latter word
almost becomes a distinctive stylistic trait). I have not tried to be consistent in
translating the words that introduce these glosses.

[23] pauperibus] pamperibus *ms?*

quod uixit[24] in Domino. Unde ipse potest dicere illud Ps. (15 [16]:
8–11) cum moritur: *Prouidebam Dominum in conspectu meo semper*, id
est, cum uixi[25] semper habui Dominum pre oculis, *quoniam a dextris
est michi*, supple, nunc cum morior, *ne commouear*, supple ab eius
dilectione, per aliquam demonum temptationem. *Propter hoc letatum est
cor meum*, supple interius, *et exultauit lingwa mea*, supple, exterius;[26]
*insuper et caro mea requiescet in spe*, supple, gloriose resurrectionis,
*quoniam non derelinques*[27] *animam meam in inferno*, id est in purgatorio,
*semper, nec dabis sanctum tuum*, id est, me, gratia tua sanctificatum,
*uidere*, id est experiri, *corruptionem*, supple sempiternam. *Notas fecisti
michi*, supple, cum uiuerem, *uias uite* id est mandata tua; *adinplebis me
letitia cum wltu tuo*, quem spero perpetuo uidere. In cuius quidem
aspectu erunt perpetue delicie. Unde subdit: *delectationes in dextera tua
usque in finem*, id est, sine fine.[28]

Bertrand then suggests further Psalm texts that might be said
by a dying person. One of them is Ps. 115 [116]: 16–17: 'You
have broken my chains, O Lord; To you I will make a sacrifice
of praise'—Bertrand adding the idea that the chains had bound
the soul to the body.[29] A little later he returns to this passage
of the Psalms, quoting a commentary on it from the *Glossa
ordinaria*: 'And see in the Gloss, if you like, how much power
and efficacy that verse *Disrupisti uincula mea: tibi sacrificabo hostiam
laudis* has, when it is said at the hour of death.'[30] The *Glossa
ordinaria* does indeed say of *Disrupisti uincula mea* that 'this
verse is believed by some to be of such power, that a man has
his sins forgiven if it is spoken out three times (*trina confessione
dicatur*) when life is ending'.[31]

So much for the Art of Dying. The next topic is the afterlife.
Some go to heaven, the *patria* or home country, without any
purgatory: like baptized children, like those crowned with

[24] uixit] uexit *ms*
[25] uixi] uixit *ms*
[26] *et exultauit . . . exterius*] *supplied in margin*
[27] *derelinques*] delinques *ms, corrected from* delinquas?
[28] MS Kremsmünster 44, fo. 4[va–b].
[29] 'Iterum cum est propinqus exitus anime de corpore, potest dicere etiam
illud (*ms adds and deletes* aliud Ps.) *Disrupisti Domine uincula mea*, supple, quibus
anima mea corpori alligabatur; *tibi sacrificabo hostiam laudis*' (ibid., fo. 4[vb]).
[30] 'Et uide (?—*smudged in ms*) in glosa (gloriosa *ms*?), si placet tibi, quante
uirtutis et efficacie est uersiculus ille *Disrupisti Domine uincula mea: tibi sacrificabo
hostiam laudis*, quando dicitur in hora mortis' (ibid., fo. 5[ra]).
[31] PL 113. 1038.

martyrdom, and also like those whose repentence is perfect.[32]
The previous day's feast—All Saints—was celebrated for all
these people, Bertrand says, and they do not need our prayers,
which might even be an insult to them; however, because of
our uncertainty (about their fate, presumably) such prayers will
not be fruitless for the one who prays.[33]

There are others who go to purgatory.[34] Bertrand compares
these to Jacob and Joseph, who died in the land of Egypt but
whose bones were transported to the Promised Land, as a sign
that the souls of people in purgatory, after being purified
(*purgate*), are transferred to paradise.[35] The audience is urged
to help people in purgatory through prayer and in other ways,
e.g. almsgiving; and Bertrand makes the dead in purgatory
speak in language from the books of Job and Genesis, to convey
to his listeners a sense of their need.[36]

The reprobates, on the other hand, who have not died in
the Lord—'not in the Lord, and without the things that are
pleasing to the Lord'—cannot be helped.[37] To them will be said
on the day of judgement: 'Outside, dogs and sorcerers, the
impure and the murderers and everyone who loves falsehood
and lives in it' (Rev. 22: 15). Bertrand says that such people are

[32] 'Notandum autem quod (quot *ms*) illorum qui moriuntur in Domino quidam
statim euolant ad patriam sine alio purgatorio, sicud pueri baptizati, sicud
martires laureati, sicud etiam penitentes penitentia perfecta' (MS Kremsmünster
44, fo. 5[ra]).

[33] That is how I interpret a slightly obscure passage: 'De istis omnibus fuit
celebrata hesterna festiuitas. Unde pro illis non oportet orare, ymo forsan
iniuria fiet eis, quia sunt ualde boni; quia tamen nobis incertum est, non est
sine fructu oratio: conuertetur enim in synu (*recte* synum?) orantis' (ibid.).

[34] 'Alii (*correction in ms?*) autem sunt qui (que *ms*) non statim euolant, sed
uadunt ad purgatorium' (ibid.).

[35] 'Isti moriuntur cum Iacob et Ioseph in terra Egypti, quorum ossa fuerunt
transportata in terram promissionis, in signum quod anime istorum postquam
(p̄tquam *ms*) [*fo.* 5[rb]] purgate fuerunt, transferuntur in paradysum' (ibid., fo.
5[ra-b]).

[36] 'Pro istis ergo orandum est efficaciter, quia ut dicitur in ii Machab. (12: 46):
*Sancta et salubris est cogitatio pro defunctis exorare ut a peccatis soluantur.* Per alia
etiam suffragia, utpote per elemosinas, subueniri debet eis. Ipsi enim dicunt
illud Iob (19: 21): *Miseremini mei, miseremini mei, saltem uos amici mei* etc. Et
quilibet eorum dicit cuilibet nostrum illud Gen. xl (14): *Memento mei cum tibi
bene fuerit ut suggeras* (*ms* suggerat, *corrected?*) *Pharaoni,* id est, deo, *ut educat me
de isto carcere.* Isti ergo omnes iuuandi sunt, quia prosunt eis nostra suffragia,
quia *mortui sunt in domino*' (ibid., fo. 5[rb]).

[37] 'De reprobis autem, qui mortui sunt non in Domino, et sine illis que
placent Domino, non est curandum, quia sunt ualde mali, nec sunt in statu in
quo possunt eis proficere nostra bona' (ibid., fo. 5[rb]).

prefigured by those Jews who died in the desert on the way between Egypt and the Promised Land, and whose bodies he does not think were ever brought to it. To die in mortal sin is to die in the desert.[38]

The last part of the sermon is on heaven. Those 'who die in the Lord' are blessed straight after death, with a blessedness of the soul now, and in the end with a blessedness of the body.[39] Borrowing language from the Apocalypse of St John, Bertrand says of them that they have washed their robes in the blood of the lamb, which is to say that they have washed their bodies and souls in the Church's sacraments, whose efficacy derives from blood (he must mean from the blood of Christ).[40]

The language of the last chapter of the Bible leads him on to the image of the city of heaven. All those who have died in the Lord have entered this city through the gate of death; this applies both to those who are already blessed, have entered it *in re*—i.e. in actual fact—and also to the rest, who are in purgatory, for though they have not actually entered it, they have the certain hope of doing so, and soon.[41] 'And may Jesus Christ himself, whose radiance illuminates that city . . . make us belong to that city in the end . . .'[42]

---

[38] '*Foris* (*fores ms*) *canes et uenefici et inpudici et homicide et ydolis seruientes, et omnis qui amat et facit mendacium.* Isti omnes sunt figurati per illos qui fuerunt mortui in deserto, quorum nullus legitur fuisse translatus in terram promissionis, in signum quod illi qui moriuntur in mortali peccato, quod per desertum interdum intelligitur, [*fo. 5ᵛᵃ*] eo quod a gratia deseritur, numquam transferentur (transferetur *ms?*) in celum' (ibid., fo. 5ʳᵇ⁻ᵛᵃ).

[39] '*Sequitur tertium,* ubi innuitur fructus glorie optabilis in perhennitate mercedis, quam tangit uox celestis cum dicit de morientibus in Domino quod statim post mortem sunt beati, supple nunc beatitudine anime, et tandem erunt beatitudine corporis' (ibid., fo. 5ᵛᵃ).

[40] 'Isti enim sunt illi de quibus dicitur Apoc. xix (9): *Beati qui ad cenam agni nuptiarum uocati sunt*; et illud Apoc. ult. (22: 14): *Beati qui lauant stolas suas,* id est animas et corpora, *in sangwine agni,* id est in sacramentis ecclesie habentibus efficaciam a sangwine' (ibid.).

[41] '. . . *ut sit* (sic *ms?*) *potestas* (*peccata ms*) *eorum in ligno uite et per portam intrent ciuitatem,* supple, celestem. Quam quidem ciuitatem per mortem et portam pretiose mortis omnes qui iam mortui sunt in Domino intrauerunt, et hoc uel in re, sicut illi qui iam actualiter beati [sunt] (*not in ms*), uel in firma spe, sicut qui adhuc sunt in purgatorio, qui nondum intrauerunt actualiter, sed sunt certi de introitu et sunt in proximo ingressuri' (ibid.). (in firma spe *supplied in margin; text has* in spe *deleted*).

[42] 'Cuius quidem ciuitatis nos tandem consortes efficiat ipse Iesus Christus, cuius claritas ipsam illuminat, et qui ipsius est inextingwibilis lucerna. Amen' (ibid.).

The sermon is thus a short essay on death: original sin and the origins of death, its awfulness, how to turn it with God's grace into a triumph, by preparing for it and meeting it in the right way; and, finally, what happens on the other side of death. In this period *de mortuis* sermons were one—or perhaps even the—principal vehicle for the theology of death. Here, as with most of the *de mortuis* sermons I have read, the theology is unpretentious, and mainly interesting as an attempt to look at the topic head on, rather than splitting it up into several other theological categories. Betrand clearly thought *Beati mortui* had value, however, for he cites it not only in *Mortuus est Dauid* (which was our cue for the foregoing analysis) but also in a number of his other model sermons.[43] For our purposes too *Beati mortui* has considerable value: as a reminder that material about death from a general *de mortuis* sermon (in this case, a sermon for All Souls' Day) could be added to a sermon— whether a model or one actually delivered—in memory of a king or some other particular person.

A preacher who constructed a sermon on a dead king or prince from material in *Mortuus est Dauid* and *Beati mortui* together, or from similar sermons, would both give a religious sense to the dead man's worldly achievements and produce a commentary on death and the afterlife. As with sermons on the saints, the memorial sermons actually preached could have been made up of two blocks of material joined together. It is easy to forget this possibility, since the historian is necessarily at least one degree removed from the sermon actually preached.

Nevertheless, even in the written sermons transmitted to us the material about virtue in this life is frequently integrated within the same structure as the ideas about death and the next world. One interesting example is a sermon which has already been discussed in connection with the question of 'individualism', the sermon beginning '*Inclinauit*' on Edward I of England.[44]

---

[43] See e.g. the sermon for 'the exequies of some noble and powerful man', on the text *Iste moritur robustus diues et felix* (Job 21: 23) (Schneyer, *Repertorium*, i. 577, No. 1057), MS Kremsmünster 44, fos. 10ra–11va, at end of sermon; or again, for the exequies of a great prelate, bishop, or abbot, dying in old age, on the text *Mortuus est Abraham in senectute* (Gen. 25: 8) (Schneyer, *Repertorium*, i. 577, No. 1058), ibid., fos. 11va–13ra, at end.

[44] See above, ch. 2, at nn. 24–6, and below, Transcription C:b.

In this sermon it is the last part which deals with Edward's life: his journeys to Spain, to beyond the seas (which must mean on crusade), to Flanders, and to Scotland; the different roles he filled, how he passed with honour through many and various conditions in temporal things; and how his defence of the faith, help to the poor, etc., in these temporal things earned the reward for his soul. This concluding section is drawn out of the sermon's text: [He/it] *inclined from this to that, but the dregs of it are not emptied; all the sinners of the earth shall drink from it* (Ps. 74: 9). This text is, similarly, the basis for the preceding section, which is not about Edward at all but about mutability and death. It is a thought-provoking little synthesis, which needs to be read as a whole to be appreciated:

As we have said, in this same text it can be made clear to us what the human condition is, and we can say that the human condition is expressed in a twofold way in the text. Firstly, with respect to its mutability, when *inclined from this to that* is put first. Secondly, with respect to the inevitability of death, when it is added, *but the dregs of it are not emptied; all the sinners of the earth shall drink from it.*

Because of the first, it should be understood that it was a feature of human nature from its first creation that it should be variable and mutable, *from this to that*, i.e. from health to illness, from joy to sadness, from life to death; since just as it was produced from nothing so far as the soul is concerned, and from something mutable with respect to the body, since it was from the mud of the earth, so too human nature, in itself, tended towards nothingness and corruption. And so St John Damascene says in book 1, chapter 4, that every creature, taken in itself, is subject to mutability, and things which had their beginning in change have been made subject to change. However, this gift was given by grace to human nature, that if it wished to remain in obedience to God, by whom it had been produced, it could preserve itself from that mutability, because, while it remained in that state of obedience, it was not compelled to *incline from this to that*, that is, from good to evil, from health to sickness, or from life to death, because it had the power not to die, not to fall ill, and not to be sad, by observing the commandment given to it by God. But so soon as it showed contempt for the command, and lost the aforesaid gift which had been conferred by grace, human nature, thrown back on its own resources, so to speak, was compelled by its own condition to be changed *from this to that*, because it immediately crossed over from joy to sadness, from health to sickness, and from life to death. And straight away it subjected itself to so many changes and questions that a person can scarcely stay for one hour with some joyful feeling without something displeasing happening to his soul or body. Therefore it is said in Ecclesiastes 7 (30) that *God made man right, and he has entangled himself with an infinity of questions*. Therefore, when it is said *inclined from this to that*, the idea of human mutability is encapsulated, but when it is added: *but the dregs of it are not emptied; all the sinners of the earth shall drink from it*, the inevitability of death is encapsulated. For with the sin of Adam we are all made sinners, and since death was the due for that sin—death, which is called by the name of 'dregs', because it makes human bodies decompose into dregs and ashes—therefore *the dregs*, or death, *are not emptied*, but it is unavoidably necessary for all the sinners of the earth to pay this debt of death and to drink these dregs. And if it is said that Christ did satisfaction for that sin through his passion, we shall say that a double punishment was due for that sin, one eternal, that is, the lack of the vision of God, and the other bodily, such as death, sickness, and all the other penalties that pursue the body. Therefore Christ did indeed liberate us from the first punishment, since the vision of the divine essence, of which we had been deprived, has been restored to us through his passion; and so as soon as we have been baptized and become members of him, the blessedness of God and the vision of God are due to us immediately, unless something should stand in the way, say an actual sin[45] which we have committed. But from bodily death, and from the other bodily penalties, Christ did not liberate us. Indeed, just as he first paid that debt of death and drank those dregs due for sin, when he was nevertheless not a sinner and consequently not a debtor of death either, so too must all we sinners drink these dregs, and rightly so, because *they have not been emptied*, that is, destroyed or reduced to nothing, since, as was stated above, we have not been freed by the passion of Christ from bodily death and the penalties of the body. And so St Paul says, Philippians 2 (7–8), that Christ *emptied himself*, that is, lessened himself or reduced himself to nothing, in that *he became obedient unto death*. For before the son of God became incarnate and before he drank the dregs of the passion, he was not emptied or reduced to nothing or lessened, since he was in no respect lesser, but when he died and drank the dregs of the passion, then he was, so to speak, emptied, that is, lessened, since he not only became less than his father, but even than himself. Therefore the dregs of the Lord, that is, death, which is a debt the whole human race has to pay, are not emptied or destroyed, but all the sinners of

---

[45] Actual sin: as opposed to original sin.

the earth, i.e. all those involved in the sin of the first parents must drink it, as they must all pay the debt of death.[46]

Though brief, relatively, it is an ambitious synthesis. Big problems are solved succinctly. Mutability is a feature of man as created, but until the fall of Adam and Eve a special gift preserved human nature from it. The Fall made us mortal and mutable (the preacher's analysis of changeableness is psychologically perceptive). Christ's passion restored to us the possibility of the vision of God, but we must still undergo death, just as Christ drank the dregs of his passion.

*Inclinauit* says later on that Edward passed through many experiences, with honour, so far as his body is concerned, and that as for his soul, he was given his reward.[47] There is an antithesis here, but perhaps it is merely rhetorical. Some other sermons in memory of princes, however, are a little more forthcoming about the relation of body and soul after death. These sermons deserve attention, because they attempt to grapple with a hard intellectual problem within their system of belief—What happens to the body–soul union after death?—rather than simply drawing into a succinct synthesis various theological topoi about death, as many other sermons do.

The antithesis between soul and body is taken well beyond rhetoric in another of the sermons on Edward I (*Rex in eternum*):

For man lives for ever in himself through the separation of soul from body and the working of the intellect, for although the human body undergoes corruption, withers away, and grows putrid, because it is composed of contraries, and everything composed of contraries is necessarily corruptible, yet the soul itself lives for ever. For, as Aristotle testifies in the second book of the *De anima*,[48] the soul itself is separated from the body as something perpetual from something corruptible; and he says in the *Metaphysics*, book 12,[49] that 'life' is spoken of especially in connection with the working of the intellect, which is eternal and immortal.[50]

[46] Transcription C:b **2**: 2–14. The last clause of the passage looks otiose; perhaps there is a scribal error.
[47] Transcription C:b, **4**: 4–5.
[48] 413$^b$26–7 (in the standard 'Bekker' system of referring to Aristotle's works).
[49] Perhaps 1072$^b$26–8 Bekker.
[50] Transcription C:e, **2**: 4–5

This passage about the soul after death is a reminder that even Aristotle's psychology can be read with a mildly dualist emphasis, bringing out the Plato in him, as it were. A passage from Federico Franconi's second sermon in memory of John, duke of Durazzo, leaves a similar impression at least on the surface, though when read closely it also clearly takes for granted the tight bond between body and soul.

On the first point, it should be known that the duke of Durazzo has a firm subsistence,[51] and is able to say: *I am* (Rev. 1: 17), not in respect of the fact that his body is dead, by the law of nature, but in respect of the fact that his soul lives with the life of grace or the life of glory. Therefore Paul appeared after his death to Nero, and blessed Agnes to her relatives—note their words in their Lives. And the reason is that, according to logicians, the whole can be designated by a principal part: just as a man is called Curly (*crispus*) from his head, so, since the soul is the principal part of man, according to Aristotle, *Politics* 1—so, if the soul lives, the whole man can be said to be alive. And from that the holy doctor,[52] *Sentences* 4, establishes why—since it is only the soul of Peter, and of many saints, that is in heaven—one says: 'O St Peter', or 'O St Paul', when Peter and Paul, *qua* men, are not in heaven, because 'man' means: body and soul. To which the holy doctor replies in the way just stated.

Circa primum sciendum quod dominus dux Duratii habet firmam subsistentiam, et potest dicere: *Ego sum* (Apoc. 1: 17), non ratione qua mortuum est corpus lege nature, sed ratione qua uiuit anima uita gratie uel uita glorie. Unde Paulus post mortem apparuit Neroni, et beata Agnes suis consanguinibus. Nota uerba eorum in eorum legendis.[53] Et ratio quia secundum logycos totum potest denominari a parte principali: sicut homo dicitur crispus a capite, sic—cum anima sit principalis pars hominis secundum Philosophum, 1 Politice[54]—sic, si anima uiuit, totus homo potest dici uiuens. Et ex hoc sanctus Doctor, 4 Sententiarum,[55] uerificat quare—cum solum anima Petri et

---

[51] If used in a technical sense, subsistence may mean here: 'existing not in something else, but in itself'. Cf. Thomas Aquinas, *Summa theologica, prima pars*, q. 29, art. 2, *Respondeo* section: 'Secundum enim quod per se existit et non in alio, vocatur *subsistentia*: illa enim subsistere dicimus, quae non in alio, sed in se existunt.'

[52] He almost certainly means Thomas Aquinas.

[53] Cf. Jacopo da Varazze (Jacobus a Voragine), *Legenda aurea, vulgo Historia Lombardica dicta*, 24, 90, ed. Th. Graesse (Bratislava 1890), pp. 116, 384.

[54] Aristotle, *Politics*, 1254ª34 ff. Bekker.

[55] Probably Thomas Aquinas, *Commentum in Lib. III Sententiarum*, dist. 22, quaestio 1, articulus primus, Vivès edn., ix (Paris, 1873), 325–6. (I use the

multorum sanctorum sit in celo—dicitur 'sancte Petre' uel 'sancte Paule', cum Petrus et Paulus, ut sunt homines, non sint in celo, quia homo dicit animam et corpus. Ad quod respondet sanctus Doctor ut dictum est nunc.[56]

(Then Federico goes on to say how good a death John died, with contrition and after the sacraments of confession, the Eucharist, and extreme unction.[57])

Federico is thus a long way from the view, which Aquinas attributes to Hugh of St Victor, that the soul can be equated with the man.[58] Actually it seems to me at least possible that Aquinas has misundersood Hugh of St Victor (unlikely as that may sound).[59] Hugh's line seems to have been that 'man' in the usual sense of the term was a combination of two substances, body and soul; though the soul can be identified with the human person.[60] On this last point Hugh really does

Vivès edition for convenience, but in fact there is no satisfactory modern critical text: see J. A. Weisheipl, *Friar Thomas d'Aquino*, (Oxford, 1975), 359.) See also Aquinas's *Summa theologica*, tertia pars, q. 50, art. 4, esp. 2 and ad 2.

[56] MS Munich, Staatsbibliothek Clm. 2981, fo. 133[vb], from a sermon on the text *Ego uobiscum sum* (Matt. 28: 20); Schneyer, *Repertorium*, iv. 223, 'Nicolaus de Asculo', No. 221.

[57] 'Sic ad propositum dominus dux Duratii laudande memorie mortuus est cum deuota contrictione, confessione, et corporis Christi susceptione, et cum extrema *(supply* unctione?)' (ibid.).

[58] 'Quidam tamen confessi sunt Christum in triduo hominem fuisse, dicentes quidem uerba erronea, sed sensum erroris non habentes in fide: sicut Hugo de Sancto Victore, qui ea ratione dixit Christum in triduo mortis fuisse hominem, quia dicebat animam esse hominem. Quod tamen est falsum' (*Summa theologica*, tertia pars, q. 50, art. 4, *Respondeo* section).

[59] Cf. Hugh of St Victor, *De sacramentis*, 2. 1. 11 ed. PL 176. 401–16, esp. the following passages: 'Remanet itaque separata anima a carne, eadem persona spiritus rationalis, quae licet fortassis secundum usum loquendi homo jam dici non possit; quia id quod de terra sumptum erat, jam sibi unitum non habet, non tamen ideo minus persona est' (col. 411): 'Quapropter Christus etiam in morte carnis suae nec Deus esse desiit . . . nec homo esse desiit, quia diuinitas ejus ab humanitate sua non recessit. Sola anima a carne ad tempus diuisa est, sed diuinitas nec ab anima nec a carne separata est' (cols. 411–12). L.-J. Bataillon, whom I consulted on this point, argues in a personal communication that 'Actually, Hugh concedes that it is not usual to say that the soul is man, but that it would be truer than the usual identification of body and man. Thus it is perhaps with some lack of nuances, but not false to say that Hugh [said] that soul was the man.'

[60] E. H. Wéber, *La Personne humaine au XIIIᵉ siècle* (Bibliothèque Thomiste, 46; Paris, 1991), 48–9 (Michael Sylwanowicz drew my attention to this book), and D. L. d'Avray, 'Some Franciscan Ideas about the Body', *Archivum Franciscanum Historicum*, 84 (1991), 343–63, at 348–9.

look dualist by comparison with Aquinas, who thought that soul without body was not a person. However, that was not a distinctively Thomist view: Bonaventure's thinking was along similar lines.[61]

In view of this convergence towards an 'un-dualist' idea of the body–soul union, the content of the following passage from the Franciscan Bertrand de la Tour need not in itself cause surprise, though it is interesting to find such an analysis in a sermon. He too thinks that the soul alone, after death, is neither a man nor a person:

For the word 'death' comes from 'biting' (*mors . . . mordendo*), because it bites cruelly, because it spares no one;—and in biting it takes away everything, as it were.

For it takes away the act of subsisting, the mode of knowing, the speech by which man can confess (*uerbum confitendi*), and the state of existence in which merit can be earned. I say that it takes away the act of subsisting. For previously, he was a man and a person subsisting[62] in himself. But now he is neither a man nor a person. Even his soul or his body is not a man or a person. For *man, when he shall be dead, and stripped*—i.e. of life—*and consumed*—i.e. by worms—*I ask you, where is he?* (Job 14: 10) As if to say: 'Nowhere is he a whole in himself (*secundum se totum*)', for he is not a whole in himself, though he may be in his parts. But because he is not, he does not have a 'where' in which he might be. Therefore the bite of death is hard, because it takes away the humanity and the subsistence of the person.

It also takes away the mode of knowing. For previously, this lord had knowledge through the intellect, but also through sense-

---

[61] Wéber, *La Personne humaine*, 157–8. (The discussion of the body–soul problem and 'dualism' in the foregoing paragraphs was written before I read C. Walker Bynum's 'Material Continuity, Personal Survival and the Resurrection of the Body: A Scholastic Discussion in its Medieval and Modern Contexts', in her *Fragmentation and Redemption: Essays on Gender and the Human Body in Medieval Religion* (New York, 1991), 239–97 and 393–417. Though it is a surprise to find Giles of Rome as a Dominican (n. 57 on p. 404), and though not everyone will share her evident endorsement of the 'few perceptive Catholic philosophers' who 'argue that what Aquinas's teaching actually threatens is *body*, since, in denying the plurality of forms, Aquinas must assert that the soul (our only form) is the form of our bodiliness, too, reducing what is left over to mere primary matter or potency' (p. 255), her provocatively thoughtful approach will breathe life into the whole subject. Perhaps the most remarkable thing about this fascinatingly original paper is the use of Anglo-American analytical philosophy: something of a historiographical landmark in this area of medieval studies.)

[62] For the concept of 'subsistence' see above, n. 51.

perception. For sense-knowledge has now perished in him; but it is from this that intellectual knowledge has its origin in this life. Therefore a soul separated from the body understands, even so far as the intellect is concerned, in a different way from a soul which is joined to the body. This is why I said that death takes away the mode of knowing. For it is said in Ecclesiastes 9 (5) that *the dead know nothing*—i.e. so far as sense-perception is concerned. And so it is said, in Proverbs[63] 22 (10): *Weep for the dead, for his light has failed*—the light, indeed, of the present life, which is perceived [through] sense-perception; or they *know nothing* intellectually in that manner in which they used to understand before.

It also takes away the speech by which man can confess. For the separated soul cannot confess—i.e. vocally—either its crimes, or even the sublimity of God, because it does not have the instruments with which it might form an utterance. Therefore it is said in the Psalm (113: 17–18): *The dead shall not praise you, O Lord*—i.e. 'vocally'; or: 'they *shall not praise you* as you deserve (*ad meritum*). But *we that live bless the Lord.*[64]

Finally, Bertrand argues that death puts an end to the state of existence in which we can earn merit. The implication of this passage[65] is that eternal life can be merited only by deeds done in the body. There follows a summing up and a conclusion:

Thus it is clear that the bite of death is most hard, since it took away from that king of ours the act of subsisting, the mode of knowing, the speech by which man can confess, and the state of existence in which merit can be earned.

Therefore if his soul is undergoing punishment, let us help it with prayers, alms, and other forms of intercession, that God may snatch it swiftly from punishment and lead it to eternal life.[66]

The assumption that the dead king is quite probably in purgatory (i.e. that he has not gone directly to heaven—hell seems not to be contemplated) is quite compatible with the presentation of his life as a model of virtue. This sermon, like the others we have discussed,[67] includes plenty of praise for the dead man.[68] The preacher presumably wanted both to use

---

[63] In fact, not Proverbs but Ecclus. 22: 10.
[64] Transcription B:d, **12**: 2–**15**: 3.
[65] Transcription B:d, **16**: 1–8.
[66] Transcription B:d, **16**: 9–**17**: 1.
[67] Not excluding *Beati mortui*, if seen as an extension of *Mortuus est Dauid*.
[68] Transcription B:d, **5**: 1–8: 3.

the dead man's life as an edifying pattern and to persuade the audience to help the soul in purgatory. Any tension between these two functions is more apparent than real. To say that someone was probably in purgatory was only to say that he was probably not actually a saint. Even if a person's life had been admirable on the whole, it would still be normal to have some penance to complete after death.

In another sermon[69] Bertrand shows how naturally a train of thought could lead from assurance of the dead person's salvation to the need of the dead for help from the living:

But in this Israel, that is, in the faith and the unity and the sacraments of the Church, this great man died. Therefore he was in a state and in a place of great security when he passed away from this life. Therefore we ought to find comfort against the grief which has entered into us because of his death, because when he departed from this world he was certain of having the life of glory. Certain—I say—with the security of faith and hope. For *he is fallen in Israel* (2 Kgs. 3: 38)—that is, in the Church, which is to say as one of the faithful who are of its number and its merit. . . . we ought firmly to believe that he is already *saved in the Lord* [cf. Deut. 33: 29] so far as his soul is concerned, and this either in fact or in firm hope.

Since, therefore, we are not certain that his soul is already actually delighting in God, nor is it part of the common law (*nec est de communi lege*) that the souls of the faithful should fly immediately after death to their native country of heaven—although they have complete certainty of this, even when still enduring punishment—therefore we who survive him in this life ought to help him with alms, prayers, and the intercessions of masses, in order that he might be more quickly snatched from torments and be admitted to eternal blessedness.[70]

In this sermon too, it may be added, the reflections on death and the afterlife are combined with an (earlier) part dealing with the virtues.[71]

To persuade people to pray for the souls of the dead was doubtless at least a subsidiary function of all or many memorial sermons,[72] but we should not expect them (on the whole) to

[69] Schneyer, *Repertorium*, i. 581, No. 1100.

[70] Transcription B:c, **20**: 3–**21**: 1.

[71] Transcription B:c, **3**: 3–**11**: 1.

[72] Note the following passage from a sermon by Juan de Aragon: 'De primo: honor paternus, licet intelligatur de exibitione reuerentie, tamen principalius de subuentione in casu necessitatis; quod probatur auctoritate Christi Mt. xv

add a lot to the theological history of purgatory, or even of heaven.[73] By and large they do not even go into a wealth of imaginative detail, at least as they are transmitted to us. Only, they do connect. They bring together thoughts about political power and thoughts about last things. The death of a prince, or a ceremony to remember him, was a good moment to represent the relation between this world and the next.


# EXCURSUS

*[Some Recent Work on the History of Death]*

The foregoing chapter may appear to have failed adequately to engage with the voluminous recent literature on the 'history of death'.[74] One might argue in defence that the heterogeneity of the topics which tend to be brought under this heading leaves it without any integrated identity as a subject,[75] but that would be a little evasive since there is

---

(4–6), ubi reprehendit scribas et phariseos, qui faciebant afferri dona a filiis, patribus pauperibus relictis. Quod reprobat Dominus, et dicit facere contra preceptum hoc. Non potest esse alicubi maior necessitas et indigentia quam in loco purgatorii, ubi anime cruciantur et nichil ex se lucrantur, quia non sunt in statu merendi. Non enim pro hiis qui sunt in patria oramus, nec pro hiis qui in inferno, quia nichil eis prodest, sed pro hiis qui sunt in penis ad purgandum. Et ideo honor iste, scilicet suffragiorum, est eis necessarius, non alius, et a nobis debetur. Ecc(li.) iii (8): *Qui timet deum, honorat parentes'* (MS Valencia, Cat. 182, fo. 127[vb], from a sermon 'in anniuersario parentum suorum' on the text *Honora patrem tuum* (Exod. 20: 12); Schneyer, *Repertorium*, iii. 313, No. 254).

[73] However, the following passage from Federico Franconi has a certain interest, for its combination of philosophical and scriptural language when describing the dead Charles II's peace in heaven: 'Quarto, sedere est quiescentis; et sic sedet anima regis Karoli in pace. Can. 2 (3): *Sub umbra illus quem (quam ms) desideraui [fo. 131[vb]] sedi.* Ubi tria que sunt in illa gloria. Primo eius irascibilis est sine timore, quia est *sub umbra*; Ys. 49 (2): *Sub umbra manus sue protexit me.* Secundo eius concupiscibilis est sine dolore, quia iam habet omnem desiderium. Ps. (37: 10): *ante te omne desiderium meum.* Tertio eius intelligibilis est sine errore, quia *sedi.* Sedes anime secundum philosophos est ueritas, et ibi erit plenarie ueritas. Ps. (109: 1): *Dixit dominus domino meo: sede a dextris meis, etc.'* (MS Munich, Staatsbibliothek Clm. 2981, fo. 131[va–b], from a sermon on the text *Sedebit dominus rex noster in eternum*; Schneyer, *Repertorium*, iv. 223, 'Nicolaus de Asculo', No. 218).

[74] See Endnote 14, below, pp. 285–6.

[75] Thus in *La Mort* (Strasburg, 1977) a study of 'La famine et la mort dans les campagnes du Royaume de Navarre au XIVe siècle' (pp. 67–80) rubs shoulders with a paper on 'La danse macabre de 1485 et les fresques du charnier des Innocents' (pp. 81–6).

indeed a small set of overlapping themes which stand out in the midst of this variety. These themes have been made prominent by the work of a small number of scholars writing in France. The striking talents of these historians, their courage in addressing large problems, and the powers of synthesis displayed in their big books make it impossible to pass over their work without comment, and necessary to explain why their interpretative frameworks have not received more attention here.

The following four themes, then, would seem to call for special mention. (1) Philippe Ariès and Michel Vovelle incorporate into their own syntheses Johann Huizinga's presentation of a late Middle Ages obsessed with death (*artes moriendi*, *danse macabre*, images of decomposition).[76] (2) Thanks to the stimulus of Jacques Le Goff's already classic study, the development of ideas about, or images of, purgatory as a 'third place' between heaven and hell has become a focal point of historians' attention. (3) A less precise idea that keeps turning up is the 'rise of individuality', linked by Jacques Chiffoleau with the loss by the urban population of their solidarity with dead ancestors.[77] (4) Pierre Chaunu and Michel Vovelle believe that ancient, pre-Christian beliefs about the dead remain powerful in the Middle Ages, blending in, to some degree, with Christian attitudes. Other themes discussed by historians of death will certainly occur to readers, but this set has been especially prominent, and some explanation of how the present work stands in relation to them may reasonably be expected.

In fact none of these four themes can be connected to the subject of this book so usefully as one might expect. The popularity in the late fourteenth and fifteenth centuries of texts and images dealing with death and dying is a problem which falls outside the chronological scope of this study (otherwise I would stop to question whether people were really more preoccupied with death then than earlier,[78]

[76] It is worth emphasizing the extent to which Huizinga anticipated later interpretations of this phenomenon. Vovelle has written that 'La fin du Moyen Âge enrichit ce faisceau d'attitudes de la prolifération, connue de longue date, du thème macabre, dans lequel Philippe Ariès à la suite de Tenenti voit surtout l'expression d'un amour féroce de la vie, dans la lignée donc de l'individualisation des attitudes qui reste l'élément dominant de cette phase' ('Les attitudes devant la mort: Problèmes de méthode, approches et lectures différentes', *Annales*, 31/1 (1976), 120–32, at 126); but Huizinga had already said that 'At the bottom the macabre sentiment is self-seeking and earthly. It is hardly the absence of the departed dear ones that is deplored; it is the fear of one's own death, and this only seen as the worst of evils' (*Waning*, 145). P. Ariès, *L'Homme devant la mort* (Paris, 1977), 138, says that 'Huizinga avait bien compris la relation entre l'amour passionné de la vie et les images de la mort.'

[77] Chiffoleau, *La Comptabilité*, 429–31.

[78] It may safely be supposed that one of the reasons why so much land was given to monasteries in the early Middle Ages is that the donors were worried about the fate of their soul after death, and hoped that the prayers of the monks would continue to help them in the next world.

or whether one can trust those confident scholarly intuitions that attitudes alien to Christianity underlay the new representations).[79] The other historiographical themes mentioned above are either of limited relevance to memorial preaching, or vulnerable to criticism, or both.

Take the case of purgatory. It is true that remarkable things happened to the idea in the twelfth and thirteenth centuries,[80] the period, as it happens, from which the first medieval memorial sermons (so far as we know) have survived. It was in this period that purgatory 'acquired distinctive outlines from the scholastics, acquired a name, and received an official right to exist'.[81] Furthermore, the later thirteenth century and the first half of the fourteenth, when, as it happens, *de mortuis* sermons become much more common, were an important period for the diffusion of the élite's ideas about purgatory. (The ideas were spread through popularizing texts,[82] though not yet, apparently, through art.[83]) Nevertheless, it has been convincingly argued that

[79] See above, n. 76. As a throw-away remark, Huizinga's idea is thought-provoking and probably applicable to some texts and images, but one must feel uneasy about passages like the following: 'Peu à peu ils se dégagent de la tradition religieuse et classique, bien qu'ils en tiennent compte constamment, bien que le divorce intime dont ils témoignent échappe sans doute à la conscience des hommes qui vivent le drame. On voit apparaître dans l'iconographie macabre une contradiction avec les concepts chrétiens, l'expression chorale d'un sentiment réaliste, l'image d'une entité spirituelle jusque-là ignorée' (Tenenti, *La Vie*, 85); or again: 'Quand ils eurent pris conscience de la limite infranchissable de leur existence terrestre, celle-ci, par ce fait même, prit ouvertement une signification que la croyance religieuse empêchait jusqu'alors de lui conférer' (ibid. 88); or for an equally confident value-judgement, from an apparently different standpoint, about what was really religious: 'Es ist keine religiös gedeutete Situation, wie hier jeder Lebende vom Tod eingeheimst wird, sondern eine rein menschlich-tragische' (Haas, *Todesbilder*, 178; note also his value-loaded judgement on the *artes moriendi*, pp. 177–8).

[80] As will become clear *en passant*, Le Goff's dating of the 'birth of purgatory', as an idea and image affecting the whole society, to the 12th and 13th cents., is regarded as too late by Gurevich, who traces it back to the early Middle Ages; and too early by Vovelle, for whom the 15th cent. is the turning-point. What probably happened is that ideas and images passed successively from vision literature (early Middle Ages) to official theology and mendicant exemplum collections (12th to early 14th cent.), and finally to art. Le Goff is surely right to see the middle phase as a crucial one.

[81] Gurevich, 'The *Divine Comedy*', 148.

[82] Le Goff, *La Naissance*, ch. IX, esp. pp. 422–3, 430–3.

[83] Cf. Vovelle, *La Mort*, 66, 135. Despite the great interest of Vovelle's empirical observation, one need not assume that the absence of an idea from art implies that it was absent from popular consciousness. For purgatory and art see also Michelle Fournié, 'Deux représentations méridionales du Purgatoire: Flavin en Rouergue et Martignac en Quercy', *Annales du Midi*, 98 (1986), 363–85, esp. 385: 'Les testaments prouvent que l'essor de la dévotion au Purgatoire dans les campagnes du Sud-Ouest date de la fin du xive siècle et du

'The notion of an otherworldly place or places where souls are subjected not merely to torments but also to expiatory procedures arose
already at the beginning of the Middle Ages',[84] which weakens the
chronological correlation between the notion and the rise of memorial
and other *de mortuis* preaching. Furthermore, sermons in memory of
rulers seem not to dwell much on purgatory in this period.[85] That is
not a universal rule. Eudes de Chateauroux makes rather a point of
Innocent IV's need for help.[86] Even he is brief about it and does not
indulge in vivid description. It will be apparent to anyone who reads
the transcriptions appended to this volume that purgatory is not a
dominant or even perhaps a prominent theme.[87]

'The birth of purgatory', which has been a most fruitful field of
investigation, has been linked, not very convincingly, with the 'rise of
individualism', a concept which has arguably been something of a
liability in the historiography on death. According to Le Goff, in the
twelfth and thirteenth centuries the new idea of purgatory favoured
individualism by focusing interest on the individual death and the

début du xve, comme le montre la création des bassins des âmes, alors qu'il
faut attendre la fin du xve siècle pour voir se multiplier les images du troisième
lieu.' For discussions of how the idea of purgatory spread in particular regions
see M. Bastard-Fournié, 'Le Purgatoire dans la région toulousaine au xive et au
début du xve siècle', *Annales du Midi*, 92 (1980), 5–34, and Chiffoleau, *La
Comptabilité*, 389–424. For representations of hell in art see the forthcoming
study (originally a 'thèse de doctorat "Nouveau régime"' of the École des
Hautes Études en Sciences Sociales, 1989) by Jérôme Baschet, of which an
extensive typewritten summary by the author was kindly communicated to me
by Nicole Bériou, who also directed me to the two articles by Fournié.

[84] Gurevich, 'The *Divine Comedy*', 148–9.

[85] Contrast S. Powell and A. J. Fletcher (noting, however, that they are
writing about a later period): 'Up until the final overthrow of Catholicism after
Mary's reign, the aim of these [funeral or memorial] sermons is a narrow one.
Such a ritual had built up around the doctrine of purgatory that the placation
of souls in purgatory had become a never-ending task which many preachers
saw as sufficient end in itself' ('"In die sepulture seu trigintali": The Late
Medieval Funeral and Memorial Sermon', *Leeds Studies in English*, NS 12 (1981)
(for 1980 and 1981): *Essays in Honour of A. C. Cawley*, 195–228, at 206.

[86] P. Cole, D. L. d'Avray, and J. Riley-Smith, 'Application of Theology to
Current Affairs: Memorial Sermons on the Dead of Mansurah and on Innocent
IV', *Historical Research*, 63 (1990), 227–47, at 241.

[87] Which is not to say that it never puts in an appearance. Thus see Giovanni
da San Gimignano's sermon in memory of a *dux*, MS Siena, Biblioteca Comunale
F. X. 24, fo. 105[rb]: 'etsi (*ms adds* non *in error*) forte adhuc in purgatorio
detentus' (from a sermon on the text *Dux de terra Aegypti non erit amplius* (Ezek.
30: 13); Schneyer, *Repertorium*, iii. 762, No. 504). Nevertheless, allusions to
purgatory like this one do not exactly spring to the eye in the corpus of
sermons studied.

judgement which followed it.[88] Le Goff qualifies this claim in advance
by pointing out ways in which the idea reinforced feelings of social
solidarity,[89] but his short passage on individualism betrays a mistaken
assumption shared by a surprising number of good historians, viz.
that in the early Middle Ages the moment of death was not thought
to be the decisive moment of judgement that would determine the
individual's fate one way or another. For Philippe Ariès, the majority
of people did not much fear condemnation and judgement until the
twelfth and thirteenth centuries, when the idea of the last judgement
at the end of the world became widely assimilated; the idea of an
individual judgement at the point of death arrived even later.[90] Chaunu
seems to accept a good deal of Ariès's 'fulgurante analyse'.[91] According
to Vovelle, a change was under way around around 1300 from 'the
eschatology of the two places, and from the collective judgement
at the end of ages' to the eschatology of the three places, 'which
enhanced the importance of the individual judgement'; 'the revolution
introduced by the enhancement of the value of the individual judgement . . .'[92] corresponds to an incipient individualization of attitudes in
a society where each person was beginning to become conscious of his

---

[88] Le Goff, *La Naissance*, 315.

[89] Ibid.: 'Bien que ces nouvelles solidarités entre les vivants et les morts —
en germe dans l'œuvre de Cluny — renforcent les liens familiaux, corporatifs,
confraternels'.

[90] Ariès, *L'Homme*, 100–12. In the ancient traditional mentality dominant in
the early Middle Ages 'une vie quotidienne immobile mêlait ensemble et
confondait toutes les biographies individuelles. Au temps de l'iconographie du
Jugement, chaque biographie n'apparaît plus dissoute dans une longue durée
uniforme, mais précipitée dans l'instant qui la récapitule et la singularise: *Dies
illa.*' He associates this change with a growth in the sense of individuality: see
ibid. 108–9. His theory that the early medieval attitude to death was calm and
untroubled involves both his idea of a 'mort apprivoisée' that antedates the
Middle Ages and can still be found in Tolstoy's peasants (ibid. 13) and the idea
that a reassuring version of Christian eschatology was current (ibid. 101). For a
powerful critique of Ariès's theory of 'tame death' in the early Middle Ages see
A. Borst, *Barbaren, Ketzer und Artisten: Welten des Mittelalters* (Munich, 1988),
567–79.

[91] Chaunu, *La Mort*, 119, also 111. He has some doubts about 'la mort
apprivoisée': see ibid. Chaunu lays great stress on the idea of the *double*
(attenuated version of the person after death), and modifies Ariès's hypothesis
that (for early medieval people) 'les méchants, ceux qui n'appartenaient pas à
l'Église ne survivraient pas à leur mort, ils ne se réveilleraient pas et seraient
abandonnés au non-être' by adding 'ou *au moins-être d'un double de plus en plus
incertain*' (ibid. 111, Chaunu's emphasis; Chaunu gives no reference when
quoting Ariès).

[92] I omit the phrase 'et la possibilité d'un rachat à terme' because I am not
sure precisely what Vovelle has in mind.

or her personal destiny'.[93] (Vovelle goes on to make his view clear that this holds good only for an élite.[94])

It might be thought that this interesting convergence of views must be of some relevance to memorial sermons, but in fact it is not. To begin with, the chronology is questionable, to say the least. The idea of an individual judgement at the point of death was well established in and before the eighth century.[95] In any case, moreover, the surviving sermons on dead rulers tend to assume (if they raise the question at all) that the salvation of the deceased is assured, actually or in certain hope,[96] so judgement (at death or the world's end) is not a big issue.

Chiffoleau gives some distinctive twists to what one might call the topos of rising individualism. Wills are his main source, and he argues that individualism in the face of death, Ariès's *mort de soi*, is already detectable from this evidence in the years 1180–1220: individuals were affirming their identity in the face of solidarities based on blood, liberating themselves from the wardship of their ancestors.[97] Very slowly, the relations between individual, family, and society were redefined, above all in the towns.[98] Urbanization cut the traditional links between the living and the dead, by separating people geographically from ancestral graveyards.[99] In the period of social and economic crisis from 1340 to 1450 migrations of population accentuated this trend,[100] as did the Plague, which disrupted burial practices.[101] Cut off from the possibility of a return to their ancestors, people responded by developing flamboyant and macabre funeral ceremonies, which affirmed their own individuality.[102] Underlying all this was a profound melancholy: it was an unconscious protest against permanent isolation from their ancestors.[103]

Chiffoleau's admirable study is an important piece of original scholarship, but even this version of the thesis about individualism cannot be of much use to us. Sermons in memory of political rulers are the main concern of this book, and such men would be the last to feel isolated from their ancestors. Again, we are principally concerned

---

[93] Vovelle, *La Mort*, 81.
[94] Ibid.
[95] Gurevich, 'The *Divine Comedy*', 120–1.
[96] See e.g. Transcription B:b (Bertrand de la Tour; Schneyer, *Repertorium*, i. 579, No. 1082), **6**: 1 (not an isolated example).
[97] Chiffoleau, *La Comptabilité*, 429–30.
[98] Ibid. 430.
[99] Ibid. 200–1, 430–1.
[100] Ibid. 430.
[101] Ibid. 202–4, 431.
[102] Ibid. 205.
[103] Ibid. 205, 431–2.

here with the period before 1350; Chiffoleau, on the other hand, believes that it was in the period 1360–1450 that the process he describes had gone far enough to provoke a decisive break in attitudes and patterns of behaviour.[104] Moreover, Chiffoleau's whole theory of a loss of ancestors and melancholy urban individualism in the face of death contains a large element of hypothesis of a kind difficult to verify. The fact that urban funerals became more theatrical, without a corresponding change in rural customs, could surely be otherwise explained. One would expect more traditionalism from the country-side, and in a wealthy city competitive conspicuous expenditure (to suggest just one possible explanation) might have stimulated the desire for a funeral as flamboyant as or more so than one's neighbour's.[105] That hypothesis, like Chiffoleau's, would not be easy to verify, but in fact the substance of his book requires neither one nor the other. The pattern of development he has uncovered is interesting enough to do very well without any psychoanalytic arabesques. In any case, sermons of the period before 1350 do not seem so melancholy, macabre, or obsessive as to require a psychoanalytical explanation, however it may be with the funeral rites of the fifteenth century.

In short, our memorial sermons cannot be fitted into the sort of general theory of rising individualism that one finds in the big books on the history of death. Of course, the very fact that it was or became common to deliver memorial sermons in the period before indicates a certain interest in 'the individual', the precise nature of which interest was the subject of Chapter 2.

The last of the historiographical themes listed above is the theory that ancient, pre-Christian beliefs about the dead remained powerful in the Middle Ages, without being clearly marked off from official Christian beliefs.[106] If the theory is correct it might have some relevance

---

[104] Ibid. 431. The theory that the late medieval preoccupation with death is really a product of secular individualism, of horror at the death of self, may be passed by without discussion for the same reason (viz. that it has been applied to a period later than the one that concerns us). It is really a variant of the idea implicitly criticized above, n. 79. Cf. Vovelle, 'Les attitudes devant la mort', 126 (the passage quoted above, n. 76). Cf. also Haas, *Todesbilder*, on the Dance of Death: 'eigentlich christlich ist das alles nicht mehr. An die Stelle der Vorstellung von Hölle und Paradies ist die Vorstellung der eigenen physischen Vernichtung getreten, des tragischen, aber völlig menschlichen Untergangs der eigenen Person' (179).

[105] The competition might well be between families rather than individuals, in that the motive of the person who made the will might be to maintain or enhance his family's prestige.

[106] Vovelle, *La Mort*, 37–56, and Chaunu, *La Mort*, 109–12. Though not identical, the pictures presented by Vovelle and Chaunu have much in com-

to *de mortuis* sermons in general. They might be presented as part of an effort by the clergy, above all the mendicants, to put a purified form of the Christian system of death in the place of the ancient popular beliefs. However, I am not sure how much hard evidence has yet been produced for this 'very ancient system of death', if one discounts the folklore of more recent times and the possibly quite special case of Montaillou.[107] If this alternative model of death is just a creation of modern historians, it would still be true, no doubt, but more banal, to say that our memorial sermons were designed to communicate Christian ideas about death more clearly. Again, whereas the idea of a progressive Christianization of Europe in the later Middle Ages does indeed have some value as a framework of interpretation, it is evidently less applicable to the higher social strata, which were probably the context of most sermons in memory of rulers.

Apart from explaining why some widely known interpretations are not allowed much place in the preceding chapter or the rest of the book, the foregoing analysis may stimulate some healthy discussion of disputed questions. The history of death is still a relatively new subject, and the pioneering studies which have opened it up inevitably contain theses which still need to be tested rigorously. These courageous essays in the history of mentalities should not be treated like solid recapitulations of long-established findings. Some of the criticisms implicitly advanced above are also tributes to the daring and originality of the authors.

---

mon. Compare the following extracts: 'De tels rites funéraires portent témoignage d'une survie des morts près du tombeau. Ils sont le signe irrécusable d'une croyance générale et solidement enracinée dans le double' (Chaunu, *La Mort*, 110). 'Doubles ou revenants pérennisent au cœur du Moyen Âge l'une des lectures traditionnelles de l'au-delà, celle qui depuis l'Antiquité fait entourer les vivants et leur monde par le monde des morts, des larves, qu'il faut apaiser en assurant leur transit vers le lieu du repos' (Vovelle, *La Mort*, 50). The emphases (at the very least) of Chiffoleau seem different, but he does speak of the 'souvenir mythique d'un groupe de puissances tutélaires' (*La Comptabilité*, 431) in connection with ancestors, and lays great emphasis on the need felt for proximity to their place of burial.

[107] Furthermore, Vovelle's remarks about the feeding or feasting of the dead (*La Mort*, 47–9) should be read together with the far more precise and well-documented discussion by O. G. Oexle: 'Die Gegenwart der Toten', in Braet and Verbeke (eds.), *Death in the Middle Ages*, 19–77, at 48–52, 58–9, and esp. 61–3.

# 5   *Representations and Reality*

REPRESENTATION, as well as or perhaps more than demon-
stration, is the function of the texts from Scripture scattered
through the sermons studied here. This theme merges into the
second subject of the chapter, which is the 'reception' aspect of
representation. The next point will be that the selection of
topics circumscribed by the limits of a sermon is itself a sort of
representation, in that it signifies a balance of emphasis and a
relation between the different topics chosen. To be specific,
there is an equilibrium between the attention given to 'this-
worldly' and to 'other-worldly' topics which conveys a message
about the relation between secularity and eschatology (in
the sense of the individual's death, judgement, and afterlife).
Finally, this is not just a structural commonplace of memorial
preaching. The sermons distilled, concentrated, and presented
to their society a set of attitudes to politics and the afterlife
that were already widely diffused (though not necessarily
dominant) in political life. So in a sense they represent political
society, or an aspect of it, to itself. A spin-off for historians is
that by studying these sermons we may see that aspect more
clearly. This will take us back in a circle, or perhaps, rather, a
helix, to the consideration of individual personalities, their
busy occupations in the political world, and their concomitant
preoccupation with death; but first the reader's patience must
be tried by observations which lack the element of human
interest but which matter for an understanding of the medium.

There is a kind of 'likeness' where there is no resemblance
involving sense-perception between it and its object, but only
an analogy between the relations of the parts of each.[1] The
scriptural texts at the head of sermons are often representations
of this sort, and what they represent is the structure of the
whole sermon's contents. We may take as an example Giovanni
da Napoli's sermon on the text *Princeps et maximus cecidit hodie*

---

[1] *The Collected Papers of Charles Sanders Peirce*, ed. C. Hartshorne and
P. Weiss, ii. *Elements of Logic* (Cambridge, Mass., 1932), 158.

(2 Kgs. 3: 38: 'A king and a great man fell today'). The text is split into four parts: (1) *Princeps*; (2) *et maximus*; (3) *cecidit*; (4) *hodie*.[2] To each of these four parts of the initial text corresponds one of the four parts of the sermon as a whole. The first section of the body of the sermon (corresponding to the word *princeps*) argues that it is fitting that he should be a prince, because he comes from the royal house of France, which has been a 'good tree'[3]—good both with respect to God and with respect to the world.[4] Part two (going with *et maximus*) is about the dead man's love of God, which is the greatest (*maxima*) of the virtues.[5] The third part (matched with *cecidit*, 'fell') is about death. Through the 'fall' of death he will come to the life of blessedness in fact or certain hope.[6] The final part (*hodie*, 'today') deals with purgatory and the need to help the dead man's soul.

And therefore the recent death of Lord N. [= the deceased] ought to induce all those near to him to give swift help and assistance to the soul of Lord N., so that when he is freed from the pains of purgatory the words of Luke 19 (9) may be said of his soul: *Today salvation has been done to this house by God*. And Christ may say to him the words of Luke 23 (43): *Today you will be with me in paradise . . .*[7]

The initial text thus contains the whole sermon in miniature because the parts of the text and the parts of the body of the sermon have matching structures. It will have been noticed that in the preceding example the parallelism is set up with an elegance that must be intended, and that the scriptural text, as interpreted, balances this-worldly and other-worldly emphases

[2] 'In quo describitur quantum ad quattuor, scilicet, sublimitatem temporalis promotionis: *princeps*; inmensitatem uirtualis perfectionis: *et maximus*; labilitatem corporalis decessionis: *cecidit*; necessitatem spiritalis subuentionis: *hodie*' (MS Naples, Nazionale VIII AA 11, fo. 19[ra]; Schneyer, *Repertorium*, iii. 606, No. 26).
[3] Giovanni has been using the text Matt. 7: 17: 'arbor bona bonos fructus facit.'
[4] MS Naples, Nazionale VIII AA 11, fo. 19[ra].
[5] Ibid., fo. 19[ra–b].
[6] Ibid., fo. 19[rb].
[7] 'Et ideo mors recens domini N. debet inducere omnes ei coniunctos ad adiuuandum cito et subueniendum anime domini N., ut cum liberatur a penis purgatorii (purgarii *ms*) dicatur illud Luc. 19 (9) de anima eius: *hodie huic domui salus a deo facta est*. Et ei Christus dominus dicat illud Luc. 23 (43): *Hodie mecum eris in paradyso . . .*' (ibid., fo. 19[va]).

in a manner which is (it was argued in the last two chapters) characteristic of the genre.

Though the scriptural text which begins a sermon plays a special role in structuring it, citations from the Bible are important throughout, in the corpus of sermons analysed in this study as in medieval sermons generally. These quotations often illuminate the sermon's message with transient flashes of visual and other mental imagery. One could illustrate this at almost endless length, but another passage from Giovanni da Napoli, whose use of both scriptural texts and images generally is not ineffective, will suffice. Enough context will be quoted to show how the preacher's own imagery merges with images embodied in scriptural texts. The quotation is from one of Giovanni's sermons on Charles II of Naples:

It should be known that, just as in bodily things the heavy and impure sediment goes downwards, but what is light and pure goes upwards, as is evident with a barrel full of wine or oil, in which the sediment of wine, which is heavy, and similarly the oil-dregs, which are the sediment of oil, go down, but wine and oil, light and pure, go upwards . . . mortal guilt, however, weighs down the soul of the sinner spiritually, according to the words of Isaiah 1 (4): *Woe to the sinful nation, a people heavy with iniquity, ungracious children*; and at 24 (30) it is said of the sinful soul that: *its iniquity shall weigh it down*; and the Psalmist says in the person of the sinner (Ps. 37: 5): *my iniquities are gone over my head, and as a heavy burden have become heavy on me*; for it makes the soul impure or unclean, according to the words of Ps. (74: 9): *the dregs thereof are not emptied; all the sinners of the earth shall drink*;—therefore those who have a conscience weighed down and a soul that is impure because of some mortal guilt at death go down to hell, in accordance with the words of Job 21 (12–13): *They take the tambourine and the harp, and they rejoice at the sound of the organ; they spend their days in wealth, and in a moment go down to hell*. And conversely, one whose conscience has been made light and whose soul has been made pure by sacramental penance, goes up to heaven after death . . .

. . . est sciendum quod sicut in corporalibus graue et feculentum descendit, leue autem et purum ascendit, ut patet in dolio pleno uino uel oleo, in quo fex uini, que est grauis, et similiter emurca, que est fex olei, descendit: uinum autem et oleum leue et purum ascendit; [*fo.* 26*va*] . . . culpa autem mortalis spiritualiter grauat animam peccantis, iuxta illud Ysa. primo (4): *Ue genti peccatrici, populo graui in iniquitate, filiis sceleratis*; et 24 (20) dicitur de anima peccatrice: *grauabit eam iniquitas* *sua*; et psalmista in persona peccatoris dicit (Ps. 37: 5): *iniquitates mee supergre(sse) sunt ca(put) m(eum), et sicut o(nus) gra(ue) gra(uate) sunt super me*; facit etiam animam feculentam seu immundam, iuxta illud Psalmi (74: 9): *fex eius non est exinanita; bibent omnes peccatores terre;—* ergo habentes conscientiam grauatam et animam feculentam propter aliquam mortalem culpam in morte descendunt in infernum, iuxta illud Iob 21 (12–13): *Tenent timpanum et cytharam, et gaudent ad sonitum organi; ducunt in bonis dies suos, et in puncto ad inferna descendunt.* Et per oppositum, habens conscientiam alleuiatam et animam mundatam per sacramentalem penitentiam, post mortem ascendit ad celum . . .[8]

Different kinds of sense-imagery are stimulated here. The initial (non-scriptual) image of sediment sinking in wine or oil is mainly visual; the words *'heavy with iniquity'*, *'a heavy burden'*, *'heavy on me'*, 'a conscience weighed down' appeal more to the muscular or kinaesthetic sense; by saying *'the dregs thereof are not emptied; all the sinners of the earth shall drink'* the preacher would activate the sense of taste in the imagination of some listeners, while *'ungracious children'* and the final scriptural text would probably play mainly on the memory. This is the sort of analysis that could be routinely applied to almost any piece of poetry, and to some but not all prose. The prose of our memorial sermons (and of most sermons of the period) is the kind where the images amount to a good deal more than superficial ornamentation, and much of the imagery is carried by scriptural texts.

In the passage just examined the preacher moves rapidly from image to image. To dwell for long on any one of them would tend to distract attention from the point made. In the passage which follows, however, we see a more extended kind of image, which uses an evocation of Old Testament events to structure a large part of an (admittedly short or abbreviated) sermon on Edward I:

*In your strength, O Lord, the king will rejoice, and in your salvation he will exult exceedingly* (Ps. 20: 1). Dearest brethren, just as some men's punishment is initiated here in this present life, and in the future one it is increased and augmented—like that of Pharaoh, who was smitten with many plagues in this life as an intimation of future punishment—so too the joy and happiness of certain men are begun

---

[8] MS Naples, Nazionale VIII AA 11, fo. 26^rb–va, from a sermon on the text *Amice ascende superius* (Luke 14: 10); Schneyer, *Repertorium*, iii. 607, No. 38.

and initiated in the present life, and are completed and reach their
summit in the future one. We firmly believe that one of these was the
lord king whose exequies we are celebrating now. His happiness and
joy are expressed for us in a twofold way in the text of the sermon:
firstly, with respect to their beginning in this life and in time . . .
secondly, with respect to their summit in the future life and eternity.[9]

The preacher is then able to treat Edward as a sort of mirror
image of Pharaoh's fate. Though surrounded by many dangers
among Saracens and Christians, he was never abandoned by
the strength of God, who did not permit him to become elated
by success.

The allusion to Pharaoh in the sermon just discussed reminds
one of a sermon described in a Fontane novel set at the time of
Napoleon's retreat from Moscow: 'For the judgement of the
Lord had come home to our enemies, and, just as then the
waters had crashed against each other and "covered the chariots
and horsemen and all the power of Pharaoh, so that not one of
them was left", so it had happened again.' As the preacher
developed the comparison in tedious detail, and the attention
of the congregation drifted away, only the Prussian squire

followed with fresh enjoyment his pastor's speech. His own energy
retouched it; where the contours were inadequate he drew his sharply
defined lines over the shaky and uncertain ones. What came in
shadowy form acquired life and shape. He saw the Egyptians. Batal-
lions with golden eagles, squadrons of horsemen, with the black
horse-tail standards falling over their white cloaks—up they rode
before him, a column endlessly long, and over all their glory the
waves of the sea closed up. Only over *one* man they did *not* close; he
managed to reach the bank, an icy northerly shore, and behold, away
over glittering fields there now flew a sledge, and two dark deep-set
eyes stared into the driving snow. Pastor Seidentopf had no better
listener than the patron of his church, who knew—and not only
today—how to practise the friendly fine art of filling in the blanks [*des
Ergänzens*].[10]

This passage—a parable précis of reception theory[11] *avant le
mot*—reminds us that historians who use sermons must not

[9] Transcription C:c, **2**: 1–5.
[10] Theodor Fontane, *Vor dem Sturm* (Munich, 1959 edn.), ch. 5, pp. 36–7.
[11] Cf. e.g. the anthology collected by R. Warning, *Rezeptionsästhetik: Theorie
und Praxis*, 2nd edn. (Munich, 1979).

only see what is in them but also what some listeners could have added to the picture.

We know at least something about the sort of images listeners could have used to fill in blank spaces between the outlines of a sermon. There is reason to think that—as with the Prussian squire—they would have had no difficulty in bringing the images up to date. It will be remembered that most of the memorial sermons within the purview of this book are from the first half of the fourteenth century, when large numbers of people around courts would have seen some picture-books with illustrations from the Bible.

It would not have been hard for a fourteenth-century prince or noble to identify himself with the Jewish leaders shown in such illustrations. The pages of the so-called 'Morgan Picture Bible', to name a splendid example readily available in facsimile,[12] are alive with knights and kings in the armour which its contemporary readers would have worn. David, Saul, Solomon, and their followers are made to look at home in the world of chivalry: not the fantastic chivalry of fictional romances so much as the real world of princes and nobles in the century around 1300.

It would not be quite fair to dismiss as anachronistic this manner of representing Old Testament rulers. As with presentations of Shakespeare or Verdi in modern dress, the idea may have been that the essential message was not distant and alien, but one really applicable to their own time. Artists,

[12] *Old Testament Miniatures: A Medieval Picture Book with 283 Paintings from the Creation to the Story of David*, introduction and legends by Sydney C. Cockerell (London, n.d.). (I am grateful to Julia Walworth for guiding me to this volume.) In his intrduction Cockerell claims that the battle pictures are 'by far the finest . . . of the thirteenth century that have survived to this day. Henceforth this manuscript will be studied as affording the best existing evidence, not only of the armour, but of many other details in the ardent life of that romantic age' (p. 21). In view of the number of surviving sermons in memory of Angevins of Naples, it is also worth quoting from Cockerell's reconstruction of the manuscript's history: 'The date of the pictures may be about 1250. It is more than probable that they were the work of Parisian artists. But the Latin descriptions accompanying them are in an Italian script, with painted initials of Italian design, about fifty years later in date than the illustrations. In as many as fourteen instances the writer of the descriptions has misinterpreted the incidents depicted. [*paragraph*] It may be conjectured that the volume went from Paris to the Court of Naples and that it was there that the descriptions were added, c. 1300' (p. 6).

translators, and popularizers of the Old Testament could have felt that they were making manifest the relevance of biblical events to their day.

Just as in the early Middle Ages,[13] Old Testament kings and rulers are treated as currently relevant models. These allusions to biblical leaders are not necessarily inapposite. When Federico Franconi applies to Robert of Naples the words *Behold, a greater than Solomon is here*,[14] he could assume, like all educated men of his time, that Solomon was an author (of the books of Proverbs, Canticles, Ecclesiastes, and Wisdom), just like Robert, whom Boccaccio called the 'most learned king whom mortals have seen since Solomon'.[15]

Another obvious role model for medieval kings was Solomon's father King David. In Bertrand de la Tour's sermon in memory of Charles of Calabria, son of Robert of Naples, we are told in the course of an array of Old Testament comparisons that

Secondly, he was prefigured by David, by reason of his vigour. For, just as it is said of David, 1 Kings 13 (14), *The Lord has sought for himself a man after his own heart, and commanded him to be a leader* (dux) *over his people*. David is truly an appropriate type of that man, both with respect to the name and with respect to the thing.

Secundo fuit figuratus per Dauid ratione strennuitatis. Sicud enim dicitur de Dauid primo Reg. decimo tertio (14): *Quesiuit sibi Dominus uirum iuxta cor suum et precepit ei ut esset dux super populum suum.* Reuera, iste congrue figuratur per Dauid, et ratione nominis et ratione rei.[16] . . .[17]

---

[13] Cf. e.g. J. M. Wallace-Hadrill, *Early Germanic Kingship in England and on the Continent* (Oxford, 1971), 99.

[14] Cf. above, ch. 2, at n. 157. Cf. another passage from the same sermon: 'Tertio assimilatur homini ratione sapientie: Fuit sapientissimus in omnibus scientiis, in responsionibus, questionibus, sermonibus. Ecces. 12 (9–10): *Cumque esset sapientissimus Ecclesiastes, docuit populum, et ennarrauit que fecerat et inuestigans composuit parabolas multas. Quesiuit uerba utilia et scripsit sermones rectissimos et ueritate plenos.* Est ergo iste alter Salomon, magnificatus non solum diuitiis pecunie, sed sapientie et glorie' (MS Munich, Staatsbibliothek Clm. 2981, fo. 132^rb, from a sermon on the text *Ecce rex uester* (John 19: 14); Schneyer, *Repertorium*, iv. 223, 'Nicolaus de Asculo', No. 219).

[15] Cf. above, ch. 2, at n. 162.

[16] rei] dei *ms*

[17] MS Kremsmünster 44, fo. 124^ra, from a sermon on the text *Propter sapientiam* (Prov. 28: 2); Schneyer, *Repertorium*, i. 583, No. 1123.

(Bertrand then gives an interpretation of David's name (a familiar exegetical technique) and compares his fight with Goliath to Charles's fight against Ludwig of Bavaria.)[18]

In another of Bertrand de la Tour's memorial sermons in memory of princes[19]—this time a model, not about any historical prince that we know of—David is presented as the type or paradigm of prudence:

For someone who is not wise ought not to rejoice in the name of a prince. Isaiah 32 (5): *He who is a fool shall not be called a prince*. With this in mind, that man [i.e. the dead king or prince] was wise and prudent, not, indeed, with the prudence of the flesh, nor with the prudence of the world or of the Devil, but with the prudence of God. Accordingly, he was prefigured through that great prince David, of whom it is said, 2 Kings 23[20] (8): *David the most wise prince is seated on the throne*. And that man was prefigured well by David. For 'David' means 'strong of hand' for punishing crimes, that is, for carrying out works of piety. He also had an 'attractive countenance', because of the beauty of his body and the handsome structure of his face, and also because of his behaviour, which was a shining light. Therefore that David of ours sat on the throne through the authority which he had. He was indeed a most wise prince because of the prudence which was so highly developed in him. Therefore, because of that prudence, he managed his princely authority excellently and directed his subjects to that good which is virtue.[21]

Educated clerical members of the preacher's congregations—and such men would have been an important element in court circles—would have brought memories of Old Testament history to fill in and give colour to the outlines presented by the preacher. Since the stories about Jewish rulers in the books of Kings and in other parts of the Bible, notably Maccabees, are exceedingly vivid narratives, the reception of these discourses by such listeners would be different from and much livelier than that of a modern scholar who has not read those parts of the Bible. However, this leaves open the question of the reception of such passages by lay members of the congregations.

---

[18] See above, Ch. 3, at n. 159.
[19] Transcription B:c.
[20] Contrast the Vulgate text as commonly understood and punctuated (the 'most wise prince' is in fact a different person from David).
[21] Transcription B:c, 6: 2–11.

There is reason to think that a good many of the nobility could not only enjoy Bible stories in strip pictures (as with the Morgan Picture Bible) but even read the text in vernacular translation and/or paraphrase. The relevance of such translations to noble attitudes is emphasized in the modern classic history of chivalry, where Keen points out that 'The thirteenth century saw a complete translation of the Bible into French which appears in three interrelated versions . . . and Guiart de Moulins also translated Peter Comestor's bible-based *Historia scholastica*.'[22] These translations may not originally have been done to meet the needs of ordinary members of the secular aristocracy, but 'In the fourteenth century it becomes easier to find out about those who owned copies of vernacular bibles, and there was then a fair sprinkling of the lesser nobility among them.'[23] What proportion of the nobility in France, England (where the nobility spoke French), and Angevin Italy actually read these translations is hard to say in the present state of scholarship, but I doubt if the possibility that it was a substantial number can be excluded. Of course, in Italy a far higher proportion than elsewhere of the upper echelons of society would have been able to read the Bible in Latin.[24]

Among the books of the Bible made available in the French vernacular were the Maccabees, the appeal of which for fighting men can be readily imagined.[25] Judas Maccabaeus became a big name in the age of chivalry.[26] It is therefore no surprise to find it in the model sermon by Giovanni da San Gimignano for the

[22] M. Keen, *Chivalry* (New Haven and London, 1984), 120.
[23] Ibid. Cf. also the following passage: 'The magnificent Acre bible seems to have been commissioned by St Louis, King and Crusader. There were, moreover, a number of translations of individual books of the Bible in circulation earlier still, in the late twelfth and early thirteenth centuries, and among the earliest books translated were those, significantly, of the Judges, the Kings, and the Maccabees' (ibid.). See too C. A. Robson, 'Vernacular Scriptures in France', in G. N. H. Lampe (ed.), *The Cambridge History of the Bible*, vii (Cambridge, 1969), 436–52, at 443, 448, 451.
[24] For Tuscany see G. Holmes, *Florence, Rome, and the Origins of the Renaissance* (Oxford, 1986), esp. p. 72. I do not know how far these observations can be extended to southern Italy.
[25] Keen, *Chivalry*, 120; *Cambridge History of the Bible*, ii. 448.
[26] Cf. the important paper by Jean Dunbabin, 'The Maccabees as Exemplars in the Tenth and Eleventh Centuries', in K. Walsh and D. Wood (eds.), *The Bible in the Medieval World: Essays in Memory of Beryl Smalley* (Studies in Church History, Subsidia, 4; Oxford, 1985), 31–41, at 40–1.

death of a great prince. I quote it in context because this gives a
better idea of how the Old Testament image was made to seem
relevant, and also of how a biblical image could be combined
with a non-biblical one (the image of the towers, which were of
course a feature of San Gimignano):

*A prince, a very great one, fell today in Israel.* 2 Kgs. 3 (38). We see that,
when very great and high towers fall, they make a great sound in
their ruin, and sometimes great damage follows, that is, when many
are crushed (*opprimuntur*) by its fall. . . . when some great and excellent
prince has fallen through death, there follows a great sound of weeping
and lamenting, and rightly so, for not infrequently manifold loss for
the people follows from his end and death, and sometimes there even
follows from his removal and absence the oppression (*oppressio*) of
many, whether by enemies or by proud men who are emboldened to
revolt. There is an image (*figura*) of this in 1 Maccabees 9 (23), because
*after the death of Judas there emerged evil men in all the confines of Israel, and
all the workers of iniquity rose up.* And it is written after this (1 Macc. 9:
26–7) that *they sought out and made diligent search after the friends of Judas,
and took vengeance on them, and there was a great tribulation in Israel.* So,
therefore, now sounds and cries of people mourning and lamenting
for our most serene prince who is dead rightly can and should be
heard, since his life and presence were a cause of protection and peace
and well-being for all. And therefore there is no doubt at all that from
his death and absence much damage is due to follow in our people.

*Princeps maximus*[27] *cecidit hodie in Israel.* 2 R(eg). 3 (38). Nos uidemus
quod quando cadunt turres maxime et altissime quod faciunt in sua
ruina maximum sonitum et aliquando sequitur magnum dampnum,
quando scilicet ex casu eius multi opprimuntur. . . . quando aliquis
maximus princeps et optimus cecidit per mortem, sequitur magnus
flentium et eiulantium sonitus. Et merito, quia nonnumquam ex eius
occasu et morte sequitur multiplex dampnum in populo, et aliquando
etiam ex eius subtractione et absentia sequitur oppressio multorum
siue ab hostibus siue ab insolentibus qui cum audacia insurgunt.
Figura huius habetur 1 Macha. 9 (23), quia *post obitum Iude emerserunt*[28]
*iniqui in omnibus finibus Israel, et exorti sunt omnes qui operabantur iniqui-
tatem.* Et post sequitur (1 Macha. 9: 26–7) quod *exquirebant et per-
scrutabantur amicos Iude et uindicabant*[29] *in illos, et facta est tribulatio
magna in Israel.* Sic ergo modo de isto serenissimo principe nostro

[27] *Princeps maximus*] *sic—not* princeps et maximus *as in the Clementine Vulgate*
[28] emerserunt] *ms adds* se
[29] uindicabant] uindicabat *in Clementine Vulgate*

defuncto merito possunt et debent audiri sonitus et uoces lugentium et eiulantium, quoniam ipsius uita et presentia erat omnibus causa tutele et pacis[30] et salutis. Et ideo nequaquam est dubium quin ex eius morte et absentia sequi in gente nostra debeant multa dampna.[31]

In another passage from the same sermon he uses the example of the Maccabees to emphasize how useful the brothers of a prince can be (one wonders if he could have had in mind Philip of Taranto and John of Durazzo, the brothers of King Robert of Naples):

But it is especially to his adornment and a strength of the same prince that he should have good brothers, since *a brother who is helped by a brother is like a firm city*, as is said in Proverbs 18 (19). You have an example of this in Judas Maccabaeus, of whom it is said in 1 Macc. 3 (1–2) that after the death of Mathathias *his son Judas, called Maccabaeus, rose up in his stead, and all his brothers helped him.*

Sed precipue est ad eius ornamentum et robur ipsius principis quod habeat bonos fratres, quia *frater qui iuuatur a fratre quasi ciuitas firma*, ut dicitur Prouer. 18 (19). De hoc habes exemplum in Iuda Machabeo, de quo dicitur 1 Macha. 3 (1–2) quod post mortem Mathathie *surrexit Iudas qui uocabatur Machabeus filius eius pro eo et adiuuabant eum omnes fratres eius.*[32]

Any mention of Judas Maccabaeus in the context of high medieval chivalry and kingship is likely to bring the 'Painted Chamber of Westminster' to the mind of the medievalist. These representations of Judas Maccabaeus[33] can indeed help one form a general impression of the sort of image of an Old Testament leader which references in a thirteenth- or four-teenth-century sermon might have brought to a listener's mind. It has been argued that the pictures in question were probably executed under Edward I,[34] and it is natural to look for cor-respondences with the memorial sermons on Edward in MS, Rome, Angelica 158. Unfortunately no close parallel can be drawn. Judas Maccabaeus is not mentioned by name, so far as

[30] tutele et pacis] *in ms corr. from* et tutela pacis
[31] MS Siena, Biblioteca Comunale F. X. 24, fo. 105[vb]; Schneyer, *Repertorium*, iii. 762, 'Johannes de Sancto Geminiano', No. 505.
[32] MS Siena, Biblioteca Comunale F. X. 24, fo. 106[va].
[33] On which see P. Binski, *The Painted Chamber at Westminster* (The Society of Antiquaries of London, Occasional Papers, NS 9; London, 1986), 84.
[34] Ibid. 72.

I can see, or even unambiguously alluded to. One sermon[35] begins with a quotation from Maccabees (1 Macc. 1: 8), but it is about Alexander, not Judas, as is the reference to 1 Macc. 1: 2–3 on fo. 157[ra] of the manuscript (in the same sermon).[36] Furthermore, when quoting 1 Macc. 3: 4–5, 'In his acts he was like a lion and like a lion's whelp roaring for his prey. And he pursued the wicked . . . and them that troubled his people he burnt with fire',[37] the preacher—at least as transmitted—does not take the opportunity to spell out the parallel with Judas Maccabaeus. Nor can one build much on the quotation (without accompanying mention of any heroic rulers) of 2 Maccabees 1 (11) in the sermon *In uirtute*.[38] If the preacher or preachers of these sermons compared Edward to the Maccabee heroes, his or their words have not come down to us.[39]

There is a much closer and more satisfying parallel between one of the memorial sermons for Edward I and a fascinating illustrated 'Alexander Romance' manuscript, MS BN Fr. 24,364. Alexander (like Judas Maccabaeus) had been made into a hero of chivalric romance. It seems safe to assume that many fourteenth-century rulers and nobles were familiar with the literature and pictures—whose diffusion has been well studied[40]—representing Alexander. Whereas most people who think about Alexander at all today would visualize him in some sort of ancient classical armour and dress, the public that read and/or looked at illuminated manuscripts like BN Fr. 24,364 would have visualized him in the armour of their own day, fighting together with his knights in the manner with which they were personally familiar. When the sermon on Edward (which is translated *in extenso* at the start of Chapter 2) says he emulated Alexander in his 'power of warring down his enemies', scenes like those we find illustrated in BN Fr. 24,364 could have been at the back of many listeners' minds. The parallel between sermon and illuminated manuscript is even

[35] Transcription C:a.
[36] Transcription C:a, **4**: 3.
[37] Transcription C:a, **4**: 5–6.
[38] Transcription C:c, **3**: 2.
[39] The foregoing is a friendly corrective to what seems to be an overconfident inference by M. Prestwich on the basis of my transcripts (generously acknowledged) in his generally admirable *Edward I* (London, 1988), 558 n. 14.
[40] D. J. A. Ross, *Alexander Historiatus* (London, 1963).

more symmetrical, however. M. Pastoureau, F. Avril, and P. Stirnemann have shown that nearly all the identified coats of arms in the manuscript belong to knights summoned to Parliament around 1308–12, and that a number of them had been summoned by Edward I to take part in the Scottish war.[41] Obviously one must not postulate any direct influence of the sermon on pictures. Comparisons between Edward and Alexander may have been just 'in the air' around this time, for a similar parallel is drawn in the *Commendatio lamentabilis* on Edward's death which was edited long ago by Stubbs.[42] The most important thing about BN Fr. 24,364 (for our purpose) is that it demonstrates how images of Alexander and his following could merge together with images of Edward and his following. The manuscript both shows us the kind of visual imagery that the sermon would evoke and enables the historian to duplicate, even if only to a limited degree, the imaginative experience of the listeners.

Thus the images derived from chivalric romances (especially illustrated ones) could merge with memories of real events. The preacher could rely on many of his listeners to bring both kinds of images to the reception of the text.

We may now turn to a somewhat different case: a sermon where the preacher calls up images in his listeners' minds by appealing both to memory and to what they could see when he was preaching. Even though the sermon is a model, it provides a shell into which listeners could put what was before their eyes and in their memories. The modern reader of the passage can do neither, but even so this part of the sermon works well enough to give us some idea of its potential impact:

*And he fell this day*[43] so far as the perception of men is concerned, because it is apparent to all that he has died, now that he is to be seen lying on the bier. Therefore, *he fell.*

---

[41] '. . . toutes les armoiries identifiées, à quelques exceptions près, appartiennent à des chevaliers convoqués au Parlement vers 1308–1312 . . . plusieurs avaient été mandés par Edouard Ier pour participer à la guerre en Écosse' (F. Avril and P. Stirnemann, *Manuscrits enluminés d'origine insulaire, VIIe–XXe siècle* (Paris, 1987), notice 171, p. 137.

[42] *Chronicles of the Reigns of Edward I and Edward II*, ed. W. Stubbs (Rolls Series; London, 1882–3), ii. 14.

[43] An allusion to part of the initial text, 2 Kgs. 3: 38.

He fell, indeed, from a state of firmness and soundness. For before, he was a man, and now he is not. Before, his body was firm and solid, and now it is almost putrid, and near to complete decomposition.

He also fell from power. For before, he was strong in the power of his own body, and mighty with the help of armed men. But now he is deprived of all strength, both his own and that of others. For if he were to have a war in the other world, none of his friends would follow him, except as far as the tomb. It is an evident sign of this loss of his power and strength that his arms, that is, his sword, shield, and banner, are carried, not indeed upright, but as it were thrown down and turned upside down as a sign that he now has no strength against enemies.

He has also fallen from wealth. For he who had once been wealthy and full of great riches has suddenly been broken down, and he who abounded in unnumberable riches is now most poor, and with nothing but a shroud or with that garment which you see he will depart from us. Therefore he might say, and we also on his behalf, what Saladin the Sultan of Babylon arranged to be said when his body was being carried to the tomb. For before he died he ordered that when his body was being carried to the sepulchre, one of his servants would carry the shroud on a lance and shout to him, saying: 'Behold, the king of the Orient carries with him so much out of all his riches.' For that lord, who before his death held great banquets for many people, and gave sustenance to many poor people, could not now give to any man even a morsel of bread.

He has also fallen from elegance. For before, he was elegantly tall, handsome, and a fine figure of a man (*speciosus forma*), but now all is changed. For there is neither beauty nor grace in him, but foulness and filth, nor does he have wife, or son, or daughter, or any person who would willingly stay alone with him for one night.[44]

It cannot be too strongly emphasized that passages like this would have been far more effective when preached than they are when read today, since listeners could have supplied much of the mental imagery, though at the preacher's instigation.

It will have been noted that an exemplum or illustrative story about Saladin was woven into the passage.[45] Exempla about historical personages were one way of representing a sermon's message to the listener. The passages about Alexander and Old

---

[44] Transcription B:c, **12**: 3–**16**: 3.

[45] For the story see F. C. Tubach, *Index Exemplorum: A Handbook of Medieval Religious Tales* (FF Communications, 204; Helsinki, 1969), p. 333, No. 4355.

Testament kings come into this category, as does the following extract, which ultimately comes from Gregory of Tours.[46]

This awfulness was recognized by a certain king of the French named Lothar,[47] when he was dying at Compiègne. 'Well well,' he said to the people standing around: 'Don't you think the king of heaven is powerful and terrible, when he kills such powerful and strong kings?'—As if he were to say: 'Every man ought to think and know this.'

Istam autem terribilitatem recognoscebat quidam rex Francorum nomine Olocarnis, moriens apud Compendium. 'Va Va,' dicebat astantibus. 'Numquid putatis quam potens et quam terribilis est rex celestis, qui tam potentes et tam fortes interficit reges?' Quasi diceret: 'Putare et scire debet hoc[48] omnis homo.'[49]

It is interesting to speculate on how a story like this might have been received by a fourteenth-century listener, who might not have been aware of its origins in Gregory of Tours. Early fourteenth-century listeners, hearing that the king had died at Compiègne, might think of the dying king as something like a king of France in their own time. In his sermon in memory of Louis X of France (d. 1316), Remigio de' Girolami of Florence claimed that in comparison with the king of France all other kings were mini-kings.[50] A strong and vivid sense of the contemporary French monarchy's authority and power could have affected the reception of the historical exemplum, increasing its impact.

It is only a short step from exempla like this to comparisons or similitudes[51] like the following one, also from Bertrand de la Tour but from a different sermon. The comparison launches the sermon:

---

[46] *History of the Franks*, 6. 21.
[47] 'Olocarnis' *in ms*
[48] hoc] homo *ms?*
[49] MS Kremsmünster 44, fo. 122$^{ra}$, from a sermon in memory of Charles of Calabria on the text *Propter sapientiam* (Prov. 28: 2); Schneyer, *Repertorium*, i. 583, No. 1123.
[50] 'Omnes enim alii reges respectu regis Francie sunt reguli' (MS Florence, Nazionale Conv. Soppr. G. 4. 936, fo. 390$^v$, left-hand margin, from a sermon on the text *Mortuus est rex Ozias* (Isa. 6: 1); Schneyer, *Repertorium*, v. 95, No. 466).
[51] Cf. L.-J. Bataillon, '*Similitudines* et *Exempla* dans les sermons du XIII$^e$ siècle', in Walsh and Wood (eds.), *The Bible in the Medieval World*, 191–205 at 192.

*Today he is king, and tomorrow he will die*, Ecclesiasticus 10: (12). We see that when a king promulgates some law which he wishes to have duly carried out by all the men of his kingdom, in order that everyone, especially the simple people, may be willing to endure that law with patience, he shows that the law in question is borne with patience by the greater men and the notables of the kingdom. But so it is now, because, on account of the sin of the first man, God passed a law binding on all men, namely the law of death. *For this is the law of Adam*, as is said in 2 Kings 7 (19), that is, the law imposed on every man because of the sin of Adam. *For we all die*, said that woman in 2 Kings 14 (14). And St Paul says, Hebrews 9 (27): *It is appointed unto men once to die*. And because the simple and the poor might perhaps believe that this law was binding on them alone, and that they alone had to die, the same Lord showed that, on the contrary, the greater men and the notables of the human race have died, as being bound by this law.[52]

To appreciate the force of this comparison we would have to know whether any recent or well-known instances of impartial royal justice would have naturally come to the minds of people who heard this sermon. In this case it may be impossible to know. The historian must always at least ask how the audience might have practised 'the fine art of filling in the blanks'.

We have seen that a good deal can be ascertained about the reception of these sermons: for instance, that rulers from Old Testament history could have been made vivid to some listeners through vernacular versions of Scripture; that art made it easier to assimilate the dead prince visually to biblical and ancient forerunners; and that a preacher could play on the contrast between what his listeners could see and what they could remember. Often, however, as perhaps with this passage on the law of death, the best we can do is to guess at the kind of thing we might be missing.

It would be possible to go on from the similitude about law and death to analyse other comparisons, similes, metaphors, and in general all the devices used in this corpus of sermons to represent their messages vividly to the imagination. However, the techniques used by medieval preachers to appeal to the imagination in these ways have been studied before, and fur-

---

[52] Transcription B:d, 1: 2–8.

ther analysis of this particular set of texts would bear a strong family resemblance to other studies of other sets of sermons.

A couple of other aspects of representation cannot be passed over. Discussion of them will serve to draw together the main threads of this book, and there is no danger of duplicating earlier work on other bodies of sermons. Indeed, succinct formulae to describe these two sorts of representation are not easy to find, and it may be permitted to coin two innocent pieces of jargon: representation as circumscription and representation as distillation.

By the first formula I mean the boundary that marks off what is represented in a sermon from what is left out, and the selection this implies. For with a medieval sermon, as with a picture, selection is one aspect of representation. The content of both a sermon and a picture must be fitted into a limited compass, so choice is highly significant. The circumscription of a sermon is like the frame of a painting.[53] Just as a painter forces attention on a set of objects and the relations between them by selecting them, juxtaposing them, and leaving out other things, so too preachers chose a small number of themes from a large number of possible topics, and in doing so directed attention to the relation between the themes.

Perhaps the most significant thing about the selection of themes is that the limits of most sermons include both of the broad themes which were discussed in Chapters 3 and 4, political virtue and the afterlife respectively. The result must have been to focus attention on the relation between these two topics or sets of topics. We may focus on a sermon in memory of Edward I of England and a model sermon by Bertrand de la Tour, as they illustrate two distinct ways of connecting up the themes of political virtue and death.

The sermon *Inclinauit*,[54] on Edward, relates the two themes through the medium of an image which is in the initial text. The text is a slightly adapted version of Ps. 74: 9. In its modified form it reads: '[He/it] inclined from this to that, but the dregs

---

[53] J. Culler, *Framing the Sign* (Oxford, 1988), uses the metaphor in a different sense, as a substitute for 'context' with the connotation of a 'frame-up', but I am disinclined to regard the word as the property of the literary critics.
[54] Transcription C:b.

of it are not emptied; all the sinners of the earth shall drink from it.' The image seems never quite to come into focus in the sermon, but it is full of movement. To judge by the immediate context in the Psalms, it involves a 'cup of strong wine full of mixture'; the subject of *Inclinauit se* at the start of the text might be the person holding the cup, but might even be the cup itself, in which case a free translation might be: 'It is tipped this way and that . . .'

After applying the text to preaching itself, in a section that need not concern us, the preacher gives an explanation of the whole problem of death, in a passage which was examined at length in the preceding chapter.[55] Then the last part of the sermon applies the same images of tipping this way and that, and of drinking the dregs, to Edward himself, and we get the rather perceptive panegyric on Edward that was analysed in the chapter on individuals.[56] The panegyric and the reflections on death are brought within a common frame.

In the sermon on Edward these two topics are related by a rough parallelism, generated by the application of the same image to both. The sermon by Bertrand de la Tour[57] illustrates a different and (in this genre at least) probably more common kind of relation between topics: sequence or contiguity in time.[58] After a certain amount of interesting preamble, Bertrand gets down to his first topic, which is 'the dignity of the state of life of this king', and the four things which enhance (*magnificant*) it, which are prudence, the power to carry things through, a household prompt to serve and obey, and a worthy and holy family, where the wisdom of the father is manifested in well-brought-up (*bene ordinatis*) sons and daughters. This analysis of the life and context of a good prince in this world is followed,

---

[55] Above, pp. 168–71.
[56] See above, pp. 75–6.
[57] Transcription B:d.
[58] On the distinction between these types of relation, which it is not part of my purpose to analyse further here, see my 'Sermons on the Dead before 1350', *Studi medievali*, 3rd ser., 31/1 (1990), 207–23, at 209–11, and R. Jakobson, 'Two Aspects of Language and Two Types of Aphasic Disturbance', in R. Jakobson and M. Halle, *Fundamentals of Language* (Mouton-'S. Gravenhage, 1956), 53–82, at 76: 'The development of a discourse may take place along two different semantic lines: one topic may lead to another either through their similarity or through their contiguity.'

however, by sections on the brevity of life—kings and princes
do not live longer than other men, indeed sometimes they die
sooner[59]—and on the state of man after death. This latter
section, full of interest, was discussed at length in the previous
chapter.[60]

This life and ideas about death are thus brought within a
common frame in both our examples. By striking a balance
between attention to life and attention to death, the preachers
were in effect reminding their listeners to strike a similar
balance in their own lives.

This suggests a final point, about representation and reality.
The real lives of some thirteenth- and fourteenth-century
princes were briefly considered in an earlier chapter, where it
was suggested that the preachers were capable of representing
individuality, though their aims were not the same as with a
modern memorial address. Now the relation between political
society and its portrayal can be considered from a different
angle, and with reference to the balance between this-worldly
and other-worldly themes. For the distribution of emphasis we
have observed in memorial preaching between these two kinds
of themes mirrored a similar balance of emphasis in political
society itself.

'The pulpit does not mould the forms into which religious
thought in any age runs, it simply accommodates itself to those
that exist. For this reason, because they must follow and cannot
lead, sermons are the surest index of the prevailing religious
feeling of their age.'[61] Whether or not Mark Pattison's dictum
stands up as a generalization, it seems to hit the mark in this
instance at least. That does not mean that the sermons were
reflecting the 'spirit of the age'. There was more than one
'spirit' in this as in other 'ages'. In the ideological atmosphere
of the early fourteenth century various attitudes were inter-
mingled. The preachers distilled one of the current attitudes to

[59] Transcription B:d, 9: 9.
[60] See above, ch. 4, at nn. 64–6.
[61] M. Pattison, 'Tendencies of Religious Thought in England, 1688–1750', in
id., *Essays and Reviews*, 2nd edn. (London, 1860), 267. (I admit to quoting
this passage, to which Christopher Cheney originally directed me, at every
opportunity.)

the relation between this world and the next, and presented it in concentrated form. A spin-off, it may be added, is that they help open the historian's eyes to an aspect of the period that might not otherwise receive due emphasis.

Since 'secularization' and the 'orientation towards death' are both commonplaces of historical writing about the second half of the Middle Ages, it is a pity that the harmony between the trends has not been better appreciated. The majority of historians may even have half-tacitly postulated a conflict in which secularity was slowly gaining ground at the expense of an ecclesiastical and other-worldly orientation. Nor would such a view be wrong (though I shall try to show that it is very incomplete). In a well-known essay on 'The Laicization of French and English Society in the Thirteenth Century' (1940)[62] Joseph Strayer, the then doyen of American medieval historians, argued that in the thirteenth century 'the church lost much of its influence' and that 'the standards which it had set for secular activities were increasingly disregarded'.[63] Strayer argued that

The inner circle of royal advisers [in England and France] wanted to weaken the church courts, but they knew that a head-on collision of authorities was not the best way of securing this result. They never denied that the church courts should have a certain amount of power. But they were going to define that power; ecclesiastical courts were going to retain only the jurisdiction recognized by the royal council.[64]

He pointed out that the 'multiplication of the number of lay officials is one of the most striking phenomena of the thirteenth century' and that 'Many officials, especially those of lower rank who were in direct contact with the people, were openly anticlerical.'[65] 'The fact that such men could brutally disregard the church's rights and still keep their positions must have convinced many people that lay governments were going to be supreme.'[66]

---

[62] Reprinted in his *Medieval Statecraft and the Perspectives of History* (Princeton, 1971), 251–65.
[63] Ibid. 251. Strayer does also say (ibid.) that 'Europe remained sincerely and completely Catholic'.
[64] Ibid. 255.
[65] Ibid. 256.
[66] Ibid.

'That laymen have been very hostile to the clergy antiquity relates; and it is clearly proved by the experiences of the present time,' wrote Pope Boniface VIII (apropos of royal taxation of the clergy) in the bull *Clericis laicos*.[67] In the reign of Philip IV of France, who came out on top in his bitter conflicts with Boniface, we do see 'laicization' in an aggressive form. One of the king's principal counsellors, Guillaume de Plaisians, said that 'All those in the realm are ruled by the king's authority; even prelates and clerks, in temporal matters, are bound by the laws, edicts, and constitutions of the king.'[68] Guillaume de Plaisians had played his part in the second phase of the trial of strength between Philip IV and Boniface. For the benefit of a great assembly of barons and prelates at the Louvre in June 1303 he delivered a set of accusations which have been described as 'probably the most savage and vitriolic ever hurled at a bishop of Rome'.[69] Plaisians was a doctor of Roman Law and had taught it for a time.[70] He had probably studied under Guillaume de Nogaret,[71] another Roman Lawyer who entered royal service. Nogaret was the man who pushed the conflict with Boniface to its climax in Anagni. It is perhaps significant that Nogaret, after first apparently keeping his options open, settled on the secular career ladder as a 'king's knight', rather than the ecclesiastical one as a 'king's clerk'.[72] Training in Roman Law may well have given an intellectual stiffening to the work of these and other men on behalf of Philip the Fair, both against Boniface and generally, in that the whole discipline presupposed the existence of a supreme secular authority as the source of law;[73] once the idea that the French king was

[67] I quote from the translation by Brian Tierney, *The Crisis of Church and State, 1050–1300* (Englewood Cliffs, NJ, 1964), doc. 97, p. 175.
[68] Strayer, 'Laicization', 260.
[69] F. Pegues, *The Lawyers of the Last Capetians* (Princeton, NJ, 1962; repr. University Microfilms International, 1989), 39–40; J. Strayer, *The Reign of Philip the Fair* (Princeton, 1980), 275–6.
[70] J. Strayer, *Les Gens de justice du Languedoc sous Philippe le Bel* (Cahiers de l'Association Marc Bloch de Toulouse, Études d'histoire méridionale, 5; Toulouse, 1970), 57.
[71] Ibid.
[72] Strayer, *Reign of Philip the Fair*, 53–4 (and p. 59 for 'clerks' and 'knights' in royal service).
[73] Cf. R. Fawtier, *The Capetian Kings of France: Monarchy and Nation (987–1328)* (London etc., 1960; repr. 1983), 46–7.

emperor, or *princeps*, in his own kingdom had been formulated, the imperial ideology implicit in the Roman Law texts could be shifted behind the national monarchy.[74]

However, it would be wrong to think that Roman Law necessarily encouraged an anti-ecclesiastical form of secularity. After all, Roman (or 'Civil') lawyers and Church lawyers (Canon lawyers) were not separate categories of people: it became increasingly common in the course of the Middle Ages to attempt to combine the study of both kinds of law.[75] Moreover, one only has to look at the Court of King Robert of Naples to find counter-examples to Plaisians and Nogaret. There is Bartolomeo da Capua, a Civil lawyer of great distinction, and a major influence on the legislation, internal administration, and external politics of the kingdom, but at the same time a man who venerated Thomas Aquinas, promoted the latter's doctrine in his capacity as professor at the University of Naples, and played a significant part in the canonization process.[76] Or there is Andrea d'Isernia, another famous jurist in the service of Robert of Naples, who championed papal claims and the superiority of Church over state.[77] It is important to distinguish in principle between secularization or laicization on the one hand, and anticlericalism on the other. Secularization did not

---

[74] J.-F. Lemarignier, *La France médiévale: Institutions et société* (Paris, 1970), 265.

[75] H. Coing (ed.), *Handbuch der Quellen und Literatur der neueren europäischen Privatrechtsgeschichte*, i. *Mittelalter (1100–1500): Die gelehrten Rechte und die Gesetzgebung* (Veröffentlichung des Max-Planck-Instituts für europäische Rechtsgeschichte; Munich, 1973), 76.

[76] 'Anche se l'influenza di B. sulla politica estera napoletana durante i lunghi anni passati al servizio della corte angoina emerge con maggior evidenza, non fu tuttavia minore il peso esercitato dal grande giurista nella politica interna del Regno. [*paragraph*] A parte l'importante contributo alla legislazione angioina del tempo, strettamente legato alla sua carica di protonotaro, B. svolse un'intensa attività amministrativa . . . conobbe anche personalmente s. Tommaso, per il quale conservò sempre una grande devozione. Dell'Aquinate egli conobbe assai bene le opere e professò la dottrina anche pubblicamente in qualità di professore dell'università di Napoli. Tutto ciò risulta dalla testimonianza offerta da B. . . . nel corso del processo di canonizzazione' (*Dizionario biografico degli italiani*, vi (Rome, 1964), 697–704, at 700; this part of the notice is by I. Walter—there is also a separate section on Bartolomeo as a lawyer).

[77] F. Calasso in *Dizionario biografico degli italiani*, iii (Rome, 1961), 100–3, and W. Goetz, *König Robert von Neapel (1309–1343): Seine Persönlichkeit und sein Verhältnis zum Humanismus* (Universität Tübingen, Doktoren-Verzeichnis der philosophischen Fakultät, 1908; Tübingen, 1910), 37.

necessarily imply any conflict with the Church. Thus, it has been said that 'the French monarchy by the second half of the thirteenth century had transformed the ecclesiastical notion of peace into a more royal and secular form as embodied in the kingship of St Louis'[78]—but in view of Louis's profoundly religious conception of justice and his willingness to listen to friars, it would be absurd to describe this process of secularization as anti-ecclesiastical.[79]

Indeed, secularization could be actively promoted by the highest Church authority. A recent study of the ordeal has argued that 'It first flourished under a highly ideological Christian kingship. The involvement of the priesthood in the exercise of secular justice was part of that environment. When, over the course of the twelfth century, new views developed about that involvement, what resulted was a desacralization of secular justice.'[80] In this sense, the fourth Lateran Council of 1215, which flung its weight against the practice of ordeals, was an important agent of secularization.

Paradoxically, the papal and papally inspired reform movements of the later eleventh and the twelfth centuries can be viewed in a similar light. In demarcating an autonomous ecclesiastical domain, they also defined the secular domain more clearly. In 1122, at the Concordat of Worms, which ended

[78] R. W. Kaeuper, *War, Justice, and Public Order: England and France in the Later Middle Ages* (Oxford, 1988), 151; see also Y. Congar's important paper on 'L'Église et l'État sous le règne de Saint Louis', in *Septième centenaire de la mort de Saint Louis: Actes des Colloques de Royaumont et de Paris (21–27 mai 1970)* (Paris, 1976), 257–71, esp. 265, 271 (Nicole Bériou directed me to this).
[79] See Joinville, *The Life of St Louis*, pt. 2, ch. 17, in Joinville and Villehardouin, *Chronicles of the Crusades* (Harmondsworth, 1963), 328–9, for Louis's deferential attitude to instruction on kingship from a friar (admittedly one of great reputation). However, even if a king made a deliberate effort to emphasize his independence from ecclesiastics, as Alfonso XI of Castile apparently did, this need not imply de-Christianization. His knighting is a neat illustration. To 'de-clericalize' the ceremony while emphasizing its Christian character he would seem to have had a mechanical statue of St James built which would give him '*la paumée* which the Roman Pontifical and Durandus shortly before had described being done by the priest celebrating the mass of knighting' (P. Linehan, 'Frontier Kingship: Castile 1250–1350', in A. Boureau and C. S. Ingerflom (eds.), *La Royauté sacrée dans le monde chrétien: Colloque de Royaumont, mars 1989* (L'Histoire et ses représentations, 3; Paris, 1992), 71–9, at 76–7).
[80] R. Bartlett, *Trial by Fire and Water: The Medieval Judicial Ordeal* (Oxford, 1986), 101.

the 'investiture contest' between papacy and empire, the distinction between the religious and the secular powers of a bishop was expressed in the language of gesture: one inauguration ritual for the bishop *qua* bishop, another for the same man *qua* holder of secular authority, under the king or emperor.[81] Or again, when Becket resigned the chancellorship of England on being made Archbishop of Canterbury, the message of his action was that prelates should not be involved in secular government. The principle admitted of exceptions,[82] and was in fact frequently honoured in the breach rather than the observance: between Hubert Walter and Cardinal Wolsey there is a distinguished series of clerical civil servants whom the king rewarded by manipulating Church patronage; but no ecclesiastical idealist who reflected on Becket's gesture of renunciation could object on principle to an increased dependence by kings on lay administrators and counsellors.

It was of course less and less difficult to find laymen who possessed well-developed literate skills. As a fairly early case it is worth mentioning Pierre de Fontaines, who made his career under Louis IX of France, and who has been described as 'the first layman in France to have attempted to apply Roman to customary [law]'[83] in a sort of legal treatise written at Louis IX's request for the instruction of Prince Philip, the heir.[84] It would seem that Pierre's name is never followed by any other qualification than 'knight'.[85] He was made *bailli* of the Vermandois in 1253, but his tenure of the job was short and it may have been intended to groom him for higher things.[86] Afterwards his activities included service on the Exchequer of Normandy (1258) and as a judge in the *parlement*, the court at the summit of the system of secular justice in France.[87]

---

[81] See C. Mirbt, *Quellen zur Geschichte des Papsttums und des römischen Katholizismus*, 5th edn. (Tübingen, 1934), 161–2.

[82] For a good discussion of the principle and the exceptions that could be made see B. Smalley, *The Becket Conflict and the Schools* (Oxford, 1973), 118–19.

[83] Q. Griffiths, 'New Men among the Lay Counselors of Saint Louis' Parlement', *Medieval Studies*, 32 (1970), 234–72, at 256–7.

[84] Ibid. 254.

[85] Ibid. 251.

[86] Ibid. 252.

[87] According to Griffiths (ibid.), he was 'already a regular member of the *Parlement*' in 1257, and 'served regularly through 1261 as a judge in *Parlement*'.

Though a secular tribunal, its personnel was by no means all lay, even under the last Capetians. The laicization of the personnel was encouraged to a certain extent by an ordinance passed by Philip V in 1319, which limited the participation of prelates in the *parlement*.[88] Lehugeur, the enthusiastic historian of Philip V 'le Long', has shown that this was not meant to and did not mean the removal of the clerical element in the *parlement*: so far as ecclesiastics who were not prelates were concerned, nothing was changed; and some bishops remained too, though three cease to appear.[89] The reason that Philip gives for the ordinance—that he does not want prelates to be taken away from their spiritual duties—is nevertheless interesting. Lehugeur suggests that since the king 'had no subjects more devoted, even under Philip the Fair' than the prelates, Philip V's explanation may not have been a pretext but a genuine reason for the ordinance.[90]

The secularization of political society in France is relatively easy to describe because it has received a good deal of direct attention, probably more than parallel processes in other countries; but with rather more labour one could probably present for most parts of Europe a similar account of increasing use of educated laymen coupled with a sharpening sense of the autonomy of secular justice—a sense no doubt fostered by training in Civil Law.[91]

Alongside Roman Law and its ideological implications, it would be wrong to omit all mention of the influence of Aristotle on political attitudes in government: it is hard to prove but also to discount. Its importance has been strongly emphasized by Walter Ullmann, who connected these two sources of secular ideology by arguing that the study of Roman Law prepared the

---

[88] Quoted in P. Lehugeur, *Histoire de Philippe le Long, roi de France (1316–1322)*, ii. *Le Mécanisme du gouvernement* (Paris, 1931; repr. Geneva, 1975), 154.

[89] Ibid. 154–5.

[90] Ibid. 154 n. 3.

[91] Although England was outside the mainstream of the Roman Law tradition, growing stronger elsewhere, we should note Edward I's use of the jurist Accursius: Prestwich, *Edward I*, 81, 249, 269. But the cumulative experience of pleading in or judging common-law cases, by definition secular, in royal courts must have given the increasingly lay English legal profession a sense of the autonomy of secular justice. M. Clanchy, *From Memory to Written Record* (London, 1979), 200–1, is relevant here. (See now the revised and expanded 2nd edn. (Oxford, 1993), at 250.)

way for an assimilation of the Aristotelian idea of natural law.[92] In Aristotelian thought natural law and the State were intimately bound up with one another.[93] Knowledge of Aristotle made it easier to keep natural law and the State in a mental compartment distinct from the Bible and things supernatural.[94] Although Ullmann himself stresses the 'populist' aspect of Aristotle,[95] Aristotelian thought was not necessarily understood to be in any kind of conflict with a strong monarchical system like that of late Capetian France. The enormously popular treatise *On the Government of Princes* by Giles of Rome (Egidio Colonna da Roma)[96] 'makes Aristotle the advocate of hereditary monarchy!'[97]

It is worth briefly mentioning a couple of other respects in which political society and attitudes may be said to have worn a secular aspect. One is chivalry. Chivalric values could of course be combined more or less harmoniously with Christianity— even tournaments eventually won papal approval under the independent-minded John XXII[98]—but it is a principal thesis of the most important recent study of chivalry that the ethos was in the last analysis secular. 'Chivalry essentially was the secular code of honour of a martially orientated aristocracy.'[99] Kings

---

[92] W. Ullmann, *A History of Political Thought in the Middle Ages*, rev. edn. (Harmondsworth, 1970), 173.

[93] Ibid. 168–9.

[94] Ibid. 170, 172.

[95] '... the popular assembly was the "sovereign" ("supreme" in Aristotle's diction) which aimed at the promotion of the common good' (ibid. 169). (Ullmann goes on to draw a distinction which seems to me a dubious interpretation of Aristotle: between the citizen, operating on principles which belong to the political and legal order, and the man, operating on norms pertaining to ethics.)

[96] W. Berges, *Die Fürstenspiegel des hohen und späten Mittelalters* (Leipzig, 1938), 211: 'Es wurde der am weitesten verbreitete abendländische Fürstenspiegel und überhaupt eines der meistgelesenen Bücher des späten Mittelalters.'

[97] 'In einem Bravourstück seiner Interpretation der "Politik" macht er den Stagiriten zum Anwalt des Erbkönigtums!' (ibid. 225). See also ibid. 224: 'Aegidius will die antimonarchischen Gründe des Stagiriten schon bei diesem selbst zugunsten der Monarchie aufgelöst sehen. Er vergiß völlig, daß Aristoteles nur die Alleinherrschaft des politischen Genies als die beste Verfassung betrachtet.'

[98] Extrav. Ioann. XXII. Titulus IX De Torneamentis, in *Corpus iuris canonici*, ed. Aemilius Friedberg, ii (Leipzig, 1881; repr. Graz, 1955), 1215.

[99] Keen, *Chivalry*, 252.

and princes could not stand apart from this system of values (on the whole they showed no desire to do so), and it was one of the yardsticks by which they were judged. Thus the future Alfonso IV of Aragon (son of King James II, grandson of Charles II of Naples, and nephew of Robert the Wise) won the approval of the warrior chronicler Muntaner by his behaviour at the siege of Cagliari:

But, however ill the Lord Infante was, for no physician or other man would he leave the siege; rather, many times with the fever upon him he would put on his armour and order an attack. By his good endeavour and his expertness in chivalry (*la sua bona cavalleria*) he reduced the town to such a state that it surrendered to him.[100]

This rapid survey of secularization can be ended on a more peaceful note, with patronage of humanism. The humanism of Renaissance Italy was harmonized happily with Christian conviction, like most of the other sorts of 'secularity' analysed above. It was nevertheless an enthusiasm for and an effort to emulate a culture that antedated the coming of Christianity. Well in the vanguard of fashion among fourteenth-century rulers, Robert the Wise helped foster the new movement. 'It cannot have been by chance that Naples opened its doors to so many humanists, and the enthusiastic opinion which the humanists held of Robert could not be explained, if he had not quite consciously desired to prepare the ground for the new learning.'[101] In particular and above all one must mention the amiable and not unjustified mutual-admiration society of Robert and Petrarch.[102]

Robert was not only a patron but also an author, though not in genres associated with Renaissance humanism, and one

---

[100] *The Chronicle of Muntaner*, 274, trans. Lady Goodenough (London, 1920–1), ii. 662–3, and Ramon Muntaner, *Crònica*, viii. *Expedició dels Catalans a Orient*, ed. 'E.B.' (Collecció Popular Barcino, 145; Barcelona, 1951), 21. For a brief summary of the conquest of Sardinia and further references see J. N. Hillgarth, *The Spanish Kingdoms, 1250–1516*, i. *1250–1410: Precarious Balance* (Oxford, 1976), 265.

[101] Goetz, *König Robert*, 38.

[102] On Robert and Petrarch see the balanced remarks of Émile Léonard, *Les Angevins de Naples* (Paris, 1954), 285–6. Note Goetz's argument that 'vor Petrarcas Besuch in Neapel, im Februar 1341, die Wendung zur Antike bei Robert und bei einer Reihe von Männern seines Kreises längst vorhanden war' (*König Robert*, 41).

of his writings takes us to our final theme, that of the Last
Things.[103] Before completing the transition, it should be stressed
again that there is no paradox or necessary tension here. The
rise of secularity in political life was often strongly Christian in
its orientation (and even at times broadly pro-papal, as with
the Angevin kingdom of Naples), so a concomitant preoccupation with the afterlife was natural.

Robert of Naples was a remarkable hybrid: a king with a
penchant for preaching and amateur theology. Probably one
could write a study of the image of death in his sermons
(though I have not pursued this line).[104] A work on a larger
scale which has been edited and well studied, however, deals
with an aspect of the afterlife. The treatise is an attempt, with
the permission of Pope John XXII asked and given, to change
the direction of the latter's thinking about the Beatific Vision.[105]
(John had developed the theory that no one would enjoy the
direct vision of God after death until the end of the world.)

Robert was not the only ruler to take an interest in the
controversy. Ludwig of Bavaria and the theologians grouped
around him were naturally interested in the pope's contro-
versial theories, as the Bavarian's intellectuals were fighting a
propaganda war with the papacy at Avignon and this was a
gift to them.[106] King Philip VI of France also got involved.[107] A
plausible hypothesis to explain his active and persistent intervention is that he wanted the pope to grant him a tax on
clerical revenues (throughout Christendom!) for a crusade.[108]
However that may be, his interest led him to set up an event in
which royal and academic circles intersected interestingly. The

---

[103] For an interpretation of Robert which is formulated in quite different
terms from mine but convergent with it, as it seems to me, see Alain Boureau,
'Un Obstacle à la sacralité royale en Occident: Le principe hiérarchique', in
Boureau and Ingerflom (eds.), *La Royauté sacrée*, 29–37, at 34–6.

[104] On the sermons see Schneyer, *Repertorium*, v. 196 (with further references), and *Robert d'Anjou, Roi de Jérusalem et de Sicile, La Vision bienheureuse:
Traité envoyé au pape Jean XXII*, ed. M. Dykmans (Miscellanea Historiae Pontificiae, 30; Rome, 1970), pp. 44*–46*.

[105] Robert d'Anjou, ed. Dykmans, pp. 9*–30*, for careful analysis of the
work's setting.

[106] J. Dunbabin, *A Hound of God: Pierre de la Palud and the Fourteenth-century
Church* (Oxford, 1991), 182–3.

[107] Ibid. 183.

[108] Ibid. 183–4.

king called the French masters of the Paris Theology Faculty to meet at Vincennes to decide the question formally. 'The choice of Vincennes for the hearing scarcely disguised the king's interest in the matter; yet more pointed was the presence of large numbers of princes, prelates, and royal counsellors sitting around the chamber in which the masters were to debate.'[109] Whatever the politics behind this intellectual show, there is no reason to doubt that many of the great men of politics were interested in what would happen to their soul between death and the Last Judgement, even if they were less theologically sophisticated than Robert the Wise of Naples.[110]

Robert cited many authorities in his treatise, but he must have felt that it was a particularly bright idea to quote from John XXII's own canonization bull for St Louis of Toulouse, his own elder brother. It is a reminder that for Robert the debate about the Beatific Vision came close to home. If John XXII's pet theory was right, then a brother with whom Robert had gone as hostage to Aragon, and whose great desire for the religious life had made Robert heir to the throne, was not yet enjoying the direct vision of God. But John XXII's own earlier words, spoken in his official capacity, seemed to imply the opposite: 'He who in his life here walked in innocence . . . was released into a glorious death, and entered in his innocence to contemplate in joy his God, whose face was now revealed.'[111]

St Louis of Toulouse had said that he was not afraid to die, but very afraid to live; this was in response to his father King Charles II's admission that he himself was afraid to die.[112]

---

[109] Ibid. 184.

[110] Robert d'Anjou, ed. Dykmans, pp. 89*–90*.

[111] 'Item, in *Bulla* sancti Ludouici episcopi et confessoris: "Gloriosam resolutus in mortem, qui hic uiuens ambulauit in innocentia, in medio domus sue, ad Deum suum contemplandum in gaudio, facie revelata, in sua inocentia est ingressus"' (ibid. 3. 74, p. 56).

[112] '. . . cum pater suus rex, presente teste qui loquitur, diceret sibi quod ipse timebat mori, ipse respondit quod non mori timebat, sed bene timebat nimis uiuere. Ista dixit testis qui loquitur se uidisse et audiuisse, sicut ille qui familiaris erat et domesticus predicti domini Ludovici et qui in infirmitate sibi quasi continuo assistebat, ut dixit' (*Analecta Franciscana*, vii. *Processus canonizationis et legendae variae Sancti Ludovici O.F.M. episcopi Tolosani*, ed. Patres Collegii S. Bonaventurae etc. (Quaracchi, 1951), 42); I was led to this by M. Toynbee, *S. Louis of Toulouse and the Process of Canonisation in the Fourteenth Century* (Manchester, 1929), 129.

Nothing suprising about fear of death, in this or any other
period. However, there were practical steps to cope with the
fear which one might take in this period and which are cul-
turally more specific. The grandson of Charles II who would
become Alfonso IV of Aragon, and who was mentioned above
in connection with the conquest of Sardinia, may well have
feared that he might die on that expedition, which as a matter
of fact, according to Muntaner, he nearly did.[113] The war of
conquest lasted about a year, from June 1323 to July 1324.[114]
Among the entries in the papal registers for April 1323 we find
recorded a letter to Alfonso granting that if he was in danger
of death his confessor could give him full remission of all his
sins (but this power to be used only once).[115] The dates are
suggestive.

About a month earlier (4 April 1323) the pope had granted
another interesting request by absolving him from the vow—a
solemn one, made on a missal placed on the altar—that he
would choose to be buried in the Cistercian monastery of
Santas Creus in Tarragona.[116] What probably lay behind this
was Alfonso's devotion to the Franciscans (a devotion typical
of the interlaced Aragonese and Angevin dynasties in this per-

---

[113] Muntaner, *Crònica*, 274, viii. 21 'E.B.' (trans. Goodenough ii. 662), for a
near-fatal illness while besieging Iglesias, and the following chapter for the
heavy fighting in which, if we may believe Muntaner, Alfonso was exposed to
considerable personal danger. On the illness and on Alfonso's willingness to
risk his life in battle see also Pere III of Catalonia (Pedro IV of Aragon),
*Chronicle*, ed. and trans. J. N. and M. Hillgarth (Toronto, 1980), 1. 22, pp.
153–4, and 1. 29, p. 160.

[114] Hillgarth, *The Spanish Kingdoms*, i. 265.

[115] *Jean XXII (1316–1334): Lettres communes analysées d'après les registres
dits d'Avignon et du Vatican*, ed. G. Mollat, iv–v (Paris, 1910, 1909), iv. 257:
'17167.—*Praedicto Alphonso* indulget. ut confessor suus semel in mortis periculo
possit ei omnium peccatorum plenam remissionem concedere.' Note also
the two preceding entries (ibid.): '17165.—*Alphonso, primogenito Jacobi regis
Aragonum*, indulgetur ut ipsius confessor et alii fratres presb. religiosi, in
ejus existentes exercitu, possint ei et dicto exercitui ecclesiast. ministrare
sacramenta'; '17166.—*Univ. archiep.is et ep.is per Aragoniae et Valentiae regna
constitutis* conc. facul. absoluendi Alphonsum, primogenitum Jacobi regis
Aragonum, ab omni excom. per ipsum incursa, jurisdictionem in clericos
exercendo.'

[116] Ibid. 244: '17019.—*N. v. Alphonso, Jacobi regis Aragonum primogenito*, conc.
absolutio a uoto per ipsum super missali, posito in altari, emisso quod in
monast. ss. Crucum, Cisterc. ord., Terraconen. di., sepulturam eligeret.'

iod).[117] We know from another source that Alfonso arranged to be buried in the Franciscan house at Lerida, clothed in the Franciscan habit; but the funeral was to be celebrated 'well and with honour as the condition of our status requires'.[118] A probable hypothesis is that Alfonso thought that Franciscan prayers would help his soul the most.

Alfonso came through the conquest not only safe but with honour (it was possibly the high point of his life). Of course other people did die on the expedition, and in some cases at least their friends disembowelled the corpses, divided up the limbs, and boiled them to separate the flesh from the bones, which they sent to various lands.[119] There was a vogue for this treatment of corpses from the thirteenth century until well after the medieval period,[120] and many people seem to have desired it for themselves. It was thought desirable to have different parts of one's body buried in different places. This made it possible to have one's cake and eat it, so to speak. The dead man's physical remains could rest beside those of two or more of the people to whom he had been close in life,[121] and

---

[117] On this 'devoción franciscana' see J. Ernesto Martínez Ferrando, *Jaime II de Aragón: Su vida familiar* (2 vols.; Consejo Superior de Investigaciones Científicas, Escuela de Estudios Medievales, Estudios 9–10; Barcelona, 1948), i. 132.

[118] On these burial arrangements I follow Martínez Ferrando, ibid. 133 n. 25.

[119] John XXII, *Lettres communes*, No. 22342: '*Archiep.o Terraconen.* facul. absoluendi illos qui in exercitu Alphonsi Infantis, primogeniti Jacobi regis Aragonum, in Sardiniae insula existentes ossa amicorum suorum decocta et excussa carne ad diuersas terras transtulerunt; supplic. eodem Alphonso' (v. 376 Mollat); ibid., No. 22346: '*Alphonso Infanti, primogenito Jacobi regis Aragonum*, indult. ut corpora nonnullorum cler. et laicorum, qui ipsi in exercitu adeunte ad Sardiniae insulam assistebant, per nonnullos amicos eorumd. exenterata, membratim diuisa et inhumaniter decocta, ac tandem, ab ossibus tegumento carnis excusso, ad diuersas terras translata, in coemeterio ecclesiast. sepeliri⸱ ualeant' (v. 377 Mollat).

[120] E. A. R. Brown, 'Death and the Human Body in the Later Middle Ages: The Legislation of Boniface VIII on the Division of the Corpse', repr. in ead., *The Monarchy of Capetian France and Royal Ceremonial* (Aldershot etc., 1991), No. VI, pp. 221–70, at 267 and *passim*. (The article originally appeared in *Viator*, 12 (1981).)

[121] e.g. ibid. 259 on Charles of Valois's decision 'that his body should be buried between those of his first two wives in the church of the Dominicans in Paris, his heart in the Franciscan church of Paris, as near as possible to the place where his wife Mahaut of Saint-Pol chose burial, and his entrails in the abbey of Chaalis, if this was possible, or in the Cistercian house nearest the place of his death.'

one could have the sort of prayers associated with a grave and monument offered up in several places.[122] Pope Boniface VIII thought the practice barbarous and banned it, expressing the sort of repugnance towards it that many people might feel in the late twentieth century.[123]

Nevertheless, the dismemberment and boiling of bodies for burial retained and increased its attraction for many, and the papal ban was ignored by some, like one John of Brabanzon, who dismembered his father's body and had it interred in various places (John was absolved for this in 1317).[124] His case was comparable to that of the friends of the dead men on Alfonso's expedition.

Alfonso clearly went to some trouble to put the business right with the Church. On 15 May 1325 Pope John XXII gave the archbishop of Tarragona the power to absolve people in Alfonso's army who had transferred the bones of their dead friends to various lands after boiling them (etc.). It was noted that this was at Alfonso's request. On the same day another letter on the subject was issued, this time to Alfonso himself, granting that the bodies of not a few clerics and laymen who had helped him in the army that went to Sardinia and which had been given the treatment banned by Boniface and sent to various lands might be buried in an ecclesiastical cemetery.[125]

Alfonso clearly accepted papal authority over the treatment of dead bodies, even though in this case it had to be exercised retroactively. The later Capetian kings of France would appear to have adopted a similar attitude, manifesting it, paradoxically enough, in their efforts to get advance permission for division of their corpse.

These efforts have been admirably reconstructed in one of E. A. R. Brown's classic articles.[126] High French political society was in the vanguard of a widespread effort to secure dispensations from Boniface's ruling (which was not interpreted by

---

[122] 'Death . . . Corpse', app. II, p. 270: 'propter suffragia diuersorum locorum.'

[123] Ibid. 246–50; Extrav. Commun. Lib. III Tit. VI De Sepulturis Cap. I 'Detestandae feritatis', in *Corpus iuris canonici*, ii. 1272–3 Friedberg.

[124] Brown, 'Death and the Human Body', 252.

[125] Mollat's summaries/analyses of both papal letters are quoted above, n. 119.

[126] 'Death and the Human Body'. cit. above, at n. 120.

subsequent popes as an absolute ethical imperative). Philip V is an interesting example. Less than a year after his coronation as king of France Philip obtained from Pope John XXII permission to arrange for the division of his body as he wanted.[127] Despite the privilege, the will which Philip V drew up on 26 August 1321 'simply decreed that his body should be buried with his ancestors at Saint-Denis'.[128] One assumes that he was trying to enter into the spirit of the Church's normal law. However,

in the codicil that he prepared on 2 January 1322, the day before his death, he decreed . . . that after his death his body should be divided into three parts, with his body to be buried at Saint-Denis, his heart at the church of the Franciscans in Paris (where [his wife] Jeanne's body was to lie), and his entrails in the church of the Dominicans in Paris (where the heart of his grandfather Philip III was interred).[129]

That was what he wanted when death was close and real.

Would he have made the same arrangements without papal permission? The case of his elder brother Louis X suggests not. Louis's short reign coincided with a papal interregnum, and in Brown's view this explains why, 'when he drew up his final will and testament during the week before his death . . . he simply ordered that his body be buried at Saint-Denis, where it was interred intact'.[130] She further suggests that his widow Clementia was 'stunned, not only by her husband's early death but also by his inability to divide his body', so that only four days after a new pope had been installed she secured (among other privileges) permission to have her heart and body buried in different places.[131]

Submission to the pope as final arbiter in matters of this kind and an evident preoccupation with death seem to have been normal in early fourteenth-century political society. Even Philip the Fair seems to have been prepared to work through papal authority rather than disregarding it.[132]

---

[127] 'John decreed . . . that because of the king's devotion to numerous churches and other holy places, he could ordain division of his body as he wished' ('Death and the Human Body', 258).
[128] Ibid.
[129] Ibid. 258–9.
[130] Ibid. 257.
[131] Ibid.
[132] Ibid. 254–6.

'The secular impulses of the last direct Capetian kings—and particularly Philip the Fair—have received more attention than acts betraying spiritual and religious motivations, whose significance is often discounted.'[133] Thus E. A. R. Brown, who has done more than anyone to redress the balance. Philip the Fair, in particular, appears from her study of his wills to have been a man with a sometimes overmastering anxiety about the afterlife, filled with guilt about his economic and political behaviour (though not so far as one can see about his treatment of Pope Boniface or the Templars). Brown notes, for instance, that in his will of 1288 (when he was aged 20) he ordered that '10,000 l.t. [livres tournois] . . . should be divided among property-holders in or near different forests, listed in the will, who had been harmed by the king's beasts'.[134] In a second will of 1297 'he awarded . . . full recompense to all harmed by changes in the weight, alloy and value of his coinage'.[135] Clearly he felt that manipulation of the coinage for profit was a social injustice for which reparation must be made. Amazingly, he designated for payment of these reparations the revenues of Normandy and of the two northern *bailliages* of Vermandois and Amiens.[136] In his will of 1311 the provision about compensation for his manipulation of the coinage is left out. 'The omission is not surprising', Brown argues, 'since on 23 December 1305 Clement V, at the king's request, had forgiven him the damages caused by monetary alterations.'[137] We need not be too cynical about this: it is hard to imagine any modern government even contemplating compensation to victims of devaluation. Philip's conscience had certainly not become hardened. He now ordered that all Norman revenues should be available to pay debts and make restitution for undue exactions.[138]

Philip IV also laid it down that each session of the Norman

---

[133] 'Royal Salvation and Needs of State in Early-fourteenth-century France', repr. in ead., *Monarchy of Capetian France*, No. IV, pp. 1–56, at 1.

[134] Ibid. 9.

[135] Ibid. 12.

[136] Ibid. 12–3.

[137] Ibid. p. 13.

[138] Ibid. Later Brown shows how Philip's heir Louis X did not feel able to execute this extraordinary plan: pp. 30–2, 40–2. However, Louis X's own will shows that he was a man with a conscience (not least about his handling of his father's will): pp. 44–5.

exchequer should contribute 500 l.t. to complete Poissy, a Dominican nunnery that he had established where his grand-father St Louis had been born and baptized.[139] This same will of 1311 stated that he wanted his heart to be buried there,[140] where the nuns would presumably offer up especially intensive prayers for him. Philip's testamentary generosity was certainly not confined to reparations. He made notable gifts to religious institutions (not only Poissy)[141] and established chaplaincies or chantries and anniversary celebrations, both of which would ensure that his soul was helped by many masses.[142]

Princely preoccupation with the afterlife was not necessarily self-centred. A letter which Edward I of England wrote to the abbot of Cluny on 4 January 1291 is a moving example of feeling about the death of another. The king's wife Eleanor had died shortly before. The memorial crosses he had built to mark the stages of his journey southwards with her body (Charing Cross the last of them) were presumably a reminder to pray for her as well as an expression of his grief.[143] The letter to the abbot was certainly designed to help her in a practical way. After relating with resignation but with 'much bitterness of mind' the loss he had suffered,[144] he asks the abbot to have prayers and masses offered up for her 'whom we dearly loved when she lived', and 'do not cease to love while she is dead'.[145]

---

[139] Ibid. 13–14, 11.
[140] Ibid. 14.
[141] Ibid. 14, 15, 17.
[142] Ibid. 32.
[143] For an evocative account see F. M. Powicke, *King Henry III and the Lord Edward: The Community of the Realm in the Thirteenth Century* (2 vols.; Oxford, 1947), ii. 733–5. Powicke felt that Eleanor's death was an appropriate point at which to end his *opus magnum*.
[144] 'Deus, omnium Conditor & Creator, qui coelestis profunditate Consilii ordinat, vocat, disponit & revocat subjectas suae providentiae creaturas, serenissimam Consortem nostram Alianoram, quondam Reginam Angliae, ex Regali ortam Progenie, quarto Kalend. Decembris de praesenti seculo, quod uobis non sine multa mentis amaritudine nunciamus, sicut sibi placuit, euocauit' (*Foedera . . .* , ed. T. Rymer, i/3 (The Hague, 1745), 76).
[145] 'Cum itaque dictam Consortem nostram, quam uiuam care dileximus, mortuam non desinamus amare, ac opus sanctum & salubre, juxta diuinae scripturae sententiam, censeatur pro defunctis, ut a peccatorum soluantur nexibus, exorare, paternam caritatem uestram affectuosis precibus duximus excitandam, & instantius implorandam, quatenus, ipsius Consortis nostrae exequias, cum omni deuotione solempniter celebrantes, animam ejus, cum decantatione missarum, & aliis Ecclesiast. Sacram. Deo uiuo, qui aufert spiritum

Edward then asks the abbot to let him know how many masses and other intercessions have been arranged, so that he can measure how much gratitude he should show.[146]

It is interesting that Edward wrote to the abbot of Cluny, which is not generally considered to have been on the cutting edge of the religious life in this period. The order was traditionally associated with prayer for the dead, above all with the feast of All Souls.[147] The wording of the document suggests that Edward was asking not only for prayers at Cluny itself, but also at the many priories subject to it (the abbot of Cluny was also in theory abbot of the other houses which belonged fully to this loose order, so their heads were not abbots but priors).[148] It may also be that Edward wrote to heads of other religious orders as well, and that the letter to the abbot of Cluny was the only one of the set to be recorded on the roll.[149] In any case, the letter reminds us how seriously a king might take the afterlife even when not anxious about his own death.

With different examples one could put together a quite different pattern, but there are many patterns in each part of the past (quite apart from the ones historians just invent), and this one has been imperfectly perceived. Preachers of memorial sermons presented to listeners a true if simplified likeness of their own world, and they help us, also, to strike the right interpretative balance. The sermons are a mirror of early fourteenth-century kingship in their combination of secular

Principum specialiter commendetis, adjuvantes eandem, ac etiam facientes a Prioribus, Monachis, Clericis et aliis, breuibus, subditis in sacramentorum suffragiis, elemosinis, caeterisque operibus caritatis salubriter adjuuari: ut, siquid maculae, non purgatae in ipsa, forsan obliuionis defectu, vel alio modo, remansit, per utilia orationum uestrarum praesidia, juxta diuinae misericordiae plenitudinem, abstergatur' (ibid.).

[146] 'Quaesumus igitur ut de missarum & aliorum suffragiorum hujusmodi numero, quae pro praefata consorte nostra decreueritis facienda, per uestras litteras nos curetis reddere certiores, ut ex hoc metiri possimus, ad quales quantasque grates et gratias, ob praemissa, deuotioni uestrae teneri merito dobeamus' (ibid.).

[147] Jacques Le Goff, *La Naissance du Purgatoire* (Paris, 1981), 171, with further references (especially to the work of K. Schmid, J. Wollasch, and W. Jorden).

[148] Note the phrase 'facientes a Prioribus' in the passage quoted above, n. 145.

[149] Suggestion of Dr David Carpenter.

values with emphasis on death. It was once suggested, by Feuerbach, that there is a positive correlation 'between man's interest in the world and involvement in society, and his lack of interest in personal immortality'.[150] This is possibly invalid for many times and places, but certainly for the genre and the period studied here.

[150] See A. M. Haas, *Todesbilder im Mittelalter: Fakten und Hinweise in der deutschen Literatur* (Darmstadt, 1989), 28: '... wichtig ist die Anschauung [of Feuerbach], daß "ein Zusammenhang" gesehen ist "zwischen der Weltzugewandtheit und der gesellschaftlichen Verbundenheit der Menschen und ihrem Desinteresse an ... der persönlichen Unsterblichkeit".'

# Conclusion

FOR readers who have skipped to the end, the central path through the book can be plotted as follows. Christian memorial preaching goes back to the Roman empire, but in the early medieval West the tradition (if it continued) has left almost no known trace; evidence of memorial preaching begins to accumulate in the central medieval period, but it is only from the early fourteenth century that we have a substantial number of sermons in memory of princes. Princes and kings from the Angevin dynasty of Naples are forced on the historian's attention by the weight of surviving evidence. Sermons on Edward I of England are also an important batch. However, preaching of this kind would have been more common than the surviving evidence even from the period after 1300 might lead one to think, since memorial sermons could have been preached not only at funerals but also at subsequent commemorative services; and since the number of rulers who can be called princes (both in medieval and in modern categories) was relatively large. As for the function of memorial preaching, remarks in the sermons themselves indicate that they were intended not only to bring to mind transitoriness, the afterlife, and the needs of the suffering in purgatory, but also to give instruction about virtue in this life and to praise the person who was being remembered, if the life of the deceased warranted it.

The authors or preachers seem to have been capable of vividly depicting individual personality. However, they emphasize the sort of individuality that is realized through an existing social role, rather than individuality understood as departure from the norm. Whether or not the portrayal of personality was seen as an end in itself, it seems to have served as a means of conveying the ideology of kingship, in such a way as to stay quite close to realities of kingship.

The message conveyed about kingship has much in common with that of Renaissance humanist funeral orations, notably in its emphasis on external goods, ancestry, and virtue in the world. There are also significant borrowings from Aristotle's 'this-worldly' system of ethics and politics. Nevertheless, death and the afterlife, and also the primacy of the spiritual authority, are resoundingly, if more predictably, in evidence, and if anything predominate.

The combination of this-worldly and other-worldly ideology is represented to the recipient by the balance of emphasis in the sermons themselves. On the whole, achievements in the world are not just briefly touched on at the start of the sermon, nor is the afterlife just touched on at the end;[1] and both sorts of themes are usually represented at the top of the hierarchy of sections and subsections which give structural expression to emphasis in sermons of this period.

Furthermore, this balance of emphasis not only represents the message of the preachers, but also reflects the political society around the sermons, which give a representational (rather than purely idealized) likeness of a kingship orientated both to secular business and to the last things. This final conclusion might be half-seriously described as an application of the 'weak *Zeitgeist* principle'. The strong form of the *Zeitgeist* principle would not appeal to many historians nowadays, though it cannot have been totally without merit if it lies behind Burckhardt's *Civilization of the Renaissance in Italy* and Huizinga's *Waning of the Middle Ages*, as E. H. Gombrich argued in a powerful critique of the *Zeitgeist* theory.[2] Taken in this strong sense, the *Zeitgeist* is a sort of central principle to which the various aspects of a period's culture all lead back—an essence, as it were, in which art, religion, customs, politics, etc. all really participate. If one is not a conscious or unconscious Hegelian there seems no reason why this should be the case, and Gombrich suggested that cultural historians would do better to look for cultural 'syndromes', such as the association at a particular time of anti-realistic painting with Catholicism.[3] Since there is no intrinsic relation between the style and the religion this is quite different from the search for essential structural similarities between apparently diverse phenomena.

[1] Except in a few cases where it looks as though transmission or timing, rather than the preacher's original plan, may have been responsible.
[2] E. H. Gombrich, *In Search of Cultural History* (Oxford, 1969), 14–32.
[3] Ibid. 34.

In the middle of his civilized indictment, however, Gombrich
remarked that to criticize the *Zeitgeist* principle proper is not
'to deny that such structural likenesses between various aspects of a period may be found to be interesting';[4] and by the
'weak *Zeitgeist* principle' I mean no more than this. Of course
he is right that there is no 'iron law of such isomorphism'
(that is, of structural similarity), and of course 'ages' do not
have 'essences'. So far as periods are concerned, almost
everyone now believes in a plurality of forms. When a structural similarity emerges empirically, however, it need not be
ignored, and there is indeed a sort of 'isomorphism' between
the relation of secularity to eschatology in the sermons and in
the political world around 1300. This is to say no more than
that preachers stayed close to the ideas current in the milieu of
kings and princes, who thought about death as well as about
politics.

Yet the story which the book tries to tell ought not to be
reduced to the argument it develops. The argument about
secularity and eschatology is only a path through a landscape.
Progress along it has been an end in itself, and good intellectual
exercise for the writer at least, but also and even primarily an
excuse for observing the landscape along the way. Some non-
trivial findings are not essential components of the central
thesis. One might, for instance, mention the insights suggested
by sermons into Edward I's and Innocent IV's personalities;
the portrait gallery of the fascinating Angevin dynasty of
Naples which they present to us; evidence of the influence of a
neglected Aristotelian concept of justice, and of the kingship/
tyranny distinction; a Franciscan's explanation of why the soul
after death is neither properly human nor a person; and the
light which pictures in manuscripts cast on the reception end
of preaching. Or again, it would have been possible to say less
about the genre's history before 1300 without weakening the
main thesis.

Another underlying purpose of the study, however, has been
to rough out the first section of a history *à la longue durée*
of funeral preaching which various scholars have been inde-

4 Ibid. 32.

pendently compiling. Some reference was made to their labours at the start of the book.[5]

Accounts of the genre's history have tended to take off from the ancient world and land in the fifteenth century (after hovering briefly over Giovanni da San Gimignano). This *terra incognita* had to be explored, and to cut one clear track through it seemed a good way of opening up the whole area.

It should have become clear that the period covered by this book offers opportunities for further investigation into memorial preaching and *de mortuis* sermons generally. It would be possible, for instance, to do for offices and social categories such as cardinals, bishops, knights, women, and young children what this study has tried to do for kingship. The vast bulk even of the known evidence remains in manuscript, waiting for competent editors. No doubt there are also more texts to be discovered.

The period between 1350 (where one must part company with Schneyer's *Repertorium*) and the fifteenth century (where serious work has been done by McManamon, Fletcher, and others) remains more or less unexplored. If sermons in memory of the emperor Charles IV, which happen to have been edited,[6] are any indication, memorial preaching did not become less interesting during this period. The one by Bishop Očka of Prague, for instance, argues that Charles had the edge on Solomon, on the grounds that he knew what Solomon knew, i.e. the latter's books, whereas Solomon did not know what Charles knew. Furthermore, Solomon was a king, Charles an emperor; Solomon ruled the people of Israel, but Charles had a more comprehensive authority; Solomon waged war with wisdom, while Charles strengthened peace by wisdom without

---

[5] See above, ch. 1, at nn. 5–13.

[6] 'Post mortem imperatoris Karoli sermo factus per dominum Johannem archiepiscopum Pragensem, apostolice sedis legatum secundum', in *Fontes rerum Bohemicarum*, ed. J. Emler, iii (Prague, 1882), 423 [ends p. 432], and 'concio Adalberti Ranconis de Ericinio in Boemia, scolastici ecclesie Pragensis, . . . quam ordinauit pro die deposicionis seu sepulture . . . Karoli quarti, . . . de mandato domini nostri domini Johannis, archiepiscopi Pragensis et legati S. Romane ecclesie reuerendissimi' (ibid. 433 [ends p. 441]). See also H. Bansa, 'Heinrich von Wildenstein und seine Leichenpredigten auf Kaiser Karl IV.', *Deutsches Archiv*, 24 (1968), 187–223.

wars; if Solomon built the temple of God, Charles adorned the temple of God with gold and gems and precious stones . . .[7] Another passage seems to link monarchy with holy orders in a manner associated more with the early Middle Ages (and which I suspect may have been an extreme view even then).[8]

The sermons on Charles IV appear to belong to the same species as those studied in the preceding chapters, except that they seem more diffuse and loose-limbed (which may be due to transmission). The type of sermon studied in this book had not died out by the end of the Middle Ages. There is a sermon on King Henry VII of England by John Fisher (later to die for his beliefs under the dead man's son) which has a strong family resemblance to its counterparts in the period before 1350.[9] Nevertheless, in the fifteenth century the advent of humanist funeral preaching marked a thoroughgoing change in modes of representation and sermon structure, even if not in ideology. Another separate tradition would seem to have been started by Luther's *Leichenpredigten*. The relation between preaching in Protestant Germany and the humanist tradition of funeral orations, and, indeed, the former's relation to the earlier tradition studied here, remain to be worked out, just as many later chapters in the history of the genre remain to be written. So long as the scholars who conduct these investigations do

---

[7] 'Primo ipse habuit spiritum sapiencie: ipse enim fuit sapiencior Salomone, quod probari potest indiciis et argumentis multis. Primo illum enim, quod sciuit Salomon, hoc perfectissime sciuit serenissimus princeps noster, uidelicet libros suos. Salomon autem ignorauit, que iste sciuit: ergo probatur, quod iste plus sciuit quam Salomon. Ille fuit rex, iste imperator, ille prefuit populo Israelitico, iste prefuit uniuerso huius mundi et ecclesie Israelis, uerum istam et gentilium uniuersorum et confinia mundi distinguebat. Ille sapiencia bellabat, iste sapiencia sine bellis pacem firmabat. Ille templum dei edificabat, iste templum dei auro fulso gemmisque et lapidibus preciosis perornabat' (ibid. 427). I am unsure of the precise meaning of 'fulso' here. John Waś suggests emending to 'fuso' ('poured', i.e. 'moulded').

[8] 'Septimo et ultimo, breuiter transeundo, ipse habuit in se septem sacramenta ecclesie. Primo ordinem: ipse enim fuit ordinatus accolitus et eciam rex et imperator inunctus' (ibid. 429).

[9] For brief analyses see D. L. d'Avray, 'The Comparative Study of Memorial Preaching', *Transactions of the Royal Historical Society*, 5th ser., 40 (1990), 25–42, at 27–9, and William S. Stafford, 'Repentance on the Eve of the English Reformation: John Fisher's Sermons of 1508 and 1509', *Historical Magazine of the Protestant Episcopal Church*, 54 (1985), 297–338 (Maria Dowling drew my attention to this).

not work in isolation, from each other and from what has already been accomplished, the result will be a new and fascinating route through Western religious history.[10]

[10] It is appropriate to end by noting again how much Rudolf Lenz, the leading specialist in early modern German Protestant *Leichenpredigten*, has already done to create an awareness of the genre's history as transcending different periods, countries, and churches.

# Appendix
## The Character and Contents of Key Manuscripts

ONE can learn a lot about the function of a given copy of a text from the company it keeps in the manuscript, as also from its general appearance. Since I have worked mainly from microfilm, not always of the entire manuscript, I have not attempted a full description of the codices used. On the principle that the better is the enemy of the good, however, it seems useful to give a rough idea of the character of the manuscripts to which constant reference has been made in the body of the book, either in footnotes or through references to the transcriptions. (I do not include manuscripts to which only occasional reference is made in the book. Readers may follow them up through the Index of Manuscripts.)

When viewed as physical objects, the sermons most heavily studied in this book have a good deal in common. Apart from MS Kremsmünster 44, which would seem to belong to the half-century on either side of 1400, and MS Arch. de S. Pietro D 213, which was probably written before 1308, they all look as if they could have been written in the half-century between *c.* 1310 and *c.* 1360. In the sections I have studied from microfilm none is illuminated, and the general impression is of a businesslike and relatively unadorned product. Again, with the exception of MS Arch. de S. Pietro D 213, which is in a very personal 'academic' hand (probably that of Jacopo da Viterbo), and of MS Kremsmünster 44, which is in a form of secretary hand, they are all in quite regular Gothic book-hands, or *textualis*. Except for MS Berlin, Staatsbibliothek Theol. lat. qu. 298, they are all written in two columns.

Apart from manuscripts of Bertrand de la Tour, all the manuscripts listed below are the only witnesses known to me of those of the sermons they contain which are studied in this book. In several cases the manuscripts are in effect collections of writings, mainly if not entirely sermons, of distinguished individuals: MS Florence, Nazionale Conv. Soppr. G. 4. 936, for Remigio de' Girolami, OP; MS Arch. di S. Pietro D 213 for Jacopo da Viterbo, OESA; MS Naples, Nazionale VIII AA 11, for Giovanni da Napoli, OP; and MS Valencia, Cat. 182, for Juan de Aragón. In other cases, even though the manuscript is the only one known of the sermons in question, the preacher's fame was not so great that one can assume it to have been a reason for preserving the sermons, apart from their intrinsic interest. For the reasons stated in Chapter 1, however, there is cause for thinking that these 'one-off' manuscripts can be regarded as models, potentially usable for subsequent preaching, even when they were meant to be monuments to a great man's activity.

When one looks at the contents of the manuscript as a whole, one may get a sense of how far usefulness for future preachers was a primary consideration when the manuscript was being compiled. At least some if not all of the batch of 'prologue' sermons in the manuscripts of Remigio dé Girolami's sermons may be more like academic exercises than preaching in the usual sense, which tends to suggest that the main aim in compiling the manuscript had been to prevent the loss of Remigio's great thoughts; but there is no reason why service to future preachers should not have been an accompanying motive: it is a matter of degree. Other examples of manuscripts where one cannot assume that assistance to preachers was the primary rationale of the manuscript are two which have not been cited enough in the book to qualify for the list below. Much of MS Vienna, Schottenstift 379 (379), is taken up with the Matins of the Virgin (*matutinale beate Marie uirginis quod dicitur laus uirginum*), according to the printed catalogue.[1] MS. Klosterneuburg 265 does include sermons in addition to sermons from Bertrand's *de mortuis* set, but the catalogue also lists Innocent III's *De contemptu mundi*, the *Tractatus de hereticis* of Rainerius Sacconus, and several works honouring Saint Jerome.[2] In the light of their contents, one might hesitate to characterize these two manuscripts specifically as preachers' books.[3]

However that may be, the overall impression left by the descriptions of manuscripts listed below is that the texts which travel in the codices with the sermons studied here are such as one might find in books used by active preachers.

**Assisi, Comunale 448** includes *de mortuis* sermons of Bertrand de la Tour, including an important text of the sermon which is printed

---

[1] Dr P. A. Hübl, OSB (ed.), *Catalogus codicum manu scriptorum qui in bibliotheca monasterii B.M.V. ad Scotos Vindobonae servantur* (Vienna and Leipzig, 1899), 409.

[2] See H. Pfeifer and B. Cerník, *Catalogus codicum manu scriptorum qui in bibliotheca canonicorum regularium S. Augustini Claustroneoburgensi asservantur*, ii (Klosterneuburg, 1931), 12–15. The works about Jerome can be found together in PL 22. 239–326, according to this catalogue.

[3] Both these two manuscripts belong to a German/Austrian group containing Bertrand de la Tour's sermons. They are closely related textually to MS Klosterneuburg 486: see the introduction to Transcription B:b. In general appearance this family of three, and also MS Innsbruck Univ. 234, are not dissimilar to MS Kremsmünster 44.

below as Transcription B:a. See G. Mazzatinti and L. Alessandri, in Mazzatinti, *Inventari dei manoscritti delle biblioteche d'Italia*, iv (Forli, 1894), 94, and C. Cenci, *Bibliotheca manuscripta ad Sacrum Conventum Assisiensem* (2 vols.; Il Miracolo di Assisi, 4; Assisi, 1982), ii. 597–8. Though the manuscript (actually two codices joined together in the fourteenth century: see Cenci, ii. 597) does not consist entirely of sermons, its contents are of the sort a Franciscan preacher might like to have about him.

**Berlin, Staatsbibliothek, Theol. lat. qu. 298.** See G. Achten, *Die theologischen lateinischen Handschriften in Quarto der Staatsbibliothek preußischen Kulturbesitz Berlin*, ii. *MS. Theol. lat. qu. 267–378* (Wiesbaden, 1984), 69–75. Note (ibid. 69, 71) that the 'Sermones de defunctis', including the 'Sermo de principe', were not originally bound together with the other parts of this manuscript; there is old foliation (the modern fo. 1 also bears the number 37, and so on)—but we cannot tell what company the sermons originally kept.

**Florence, Biblioteca Nazionale Conv. soppr. G. 4. 936.** See Schneyer, *Repertorium*, v. 88–96; and E. Panella, 'Il Repertorio dello Schneyer e i sermonari di Remigio dei Girolami', *Memorie domenicane*, NS, 11 (1980), 632–50, at 634–43. The manuscript is a monument to Remigio's preaching activity, but note also the 'Prologi super totam bibliam seu sacram scripturam (seu super librum Sententiarum)' (see Panella, pp. 636–41).

**Kremsmünster 44.** Unpublished catalogue consulted on microfilm (MIC. 18, reel 2, of the Palaeography Room in the University Library of the University of London). The other substantial text which is the main fellow-traveller of Bertrand de la Tour's *de mortuis* sermons in this manuscript is a version of the *Lumen anime*, which Richard and Mary Rouse have characterized as a work, or rather three interrelated works, 'designed for use in the composition of sermons': 'The Texts called *Lumen Anime*', *AFP* 41 (1971), 5–113, at 8; cf. their *Preachers, Florilegia and Sermons: Studies on the* Manipulus florum *of Thomas of Ireland* (Studies and Texts, 47; Toronto, 1979), 200.

**Munich, Staatsbibliothek CLM 2981.** See *Catalogus codicum manu scriptorum bibliothecae regiae monacensis*, 3/1 (*Catalogus codicum Latinorum . . .* , 1/2), 2nd edn. (Munich, 1894), 56. Note that the manuscript belonged to the Franciscan library of Amberg, and that it also contains the *de mortuis* sermon collection of Nicoluccio di Ascoli (cf. Schneyer, *Repertorium*, iv. 224).

**Naples, Nazionale conv. soppr. VIII AA 11.** See T. Kaeppeli, 'Note sugli scrittori domenicani di nome Giovanni di Napoli', *AFP* 10 (1940), 48–76, at 59–68.

**Rome, Angelica 158.** The sermons in memory of Edward I travel with sermons by Augustinus Triumphus, OESA. The manuscript is described by P. B. Ministeri, 'De Augustini de Ancona, O.E.S.A. (d. 1328) Vita et Operibus, 2. De operibus', *Analecta Augustiniana*, 21 (1948), 148–262, at 225, 226–31.

**Seville. Biblioteca Capitular Columbina 82-4-1.** There is no printed catalogue known to me. *De mortuis* sermons of Bertrand de la Tour are the main text of the manuscript (which I have examined on microfilm). It is a very full set of Bertrand's sermons: for instance, it is the only manuscript I know besides MS Kremsmünster 44 which contains the sermon in memory of Charles of Calabria (Schneyer, *Repertorium*, i. 583, No. 1123).

**Siena, Biblioteca Comunale F. X. 24.** See A. Dondaine, 'La vie et les œuvres de Jean de San Gimignano', *AFP* 9 (1939), 128–83, at 155. Giovanni da S. Gimignano's collection of *de mortuis* sermons forms the main text in the manuscript.

**Valencia, Catedral 182.** See Dr D. Elías Olmos y Canalda, *Catálogo descriptivo, códices de la Catedral de Valencia*, 2nd edn. (Valencia, 1943), 135–6. Sermons occupy most of the manuscript; note also 'Fol. 270. Rúbreca: "Incipit tractatus breuis de articulis fidei, sacramentis ecclesie, preceptis ecclesie . . ."'', and cf. D. L. d'Avray, *The Preaching of the Friars; Sermons Diffused from Paris before 1300* (Oxford, 1985), 82–5, for the relevance of the Creed–sacraments–commandments framework to preaching. For a list of sermons in the manuscript see Schneyer, *Repertorium*, iii. 295–329.

**Vatican, Bibliotheca Apostolica Vaticana, Archivio di S. Pietro** (= Archiv. Capit. S. Petri) **D. 213.** See 'P.D.G.' in 'De Vita et Scriptis Beati Iacobi de Viterbio, II. De Scriptis', *Analecta Augustiniana*, 16 (1937–8), 282–305, at 297–8.

# Transcription A

MS Berlin, Staatsbibliothek Theol. lat. qu. 298, fos. 1ᵛ–2ᵛ

**1** ¹Sermo de principe. ²*An ignoratis quoniam princeps maximus cecidit hodie in Israel* (2 Reg. 3: 38)? ³Dauid rex pius, in Abner exequiis, dum ad fletum suos intenderet animare, protulisse legitur uerbum istud. ⁴Sumitur autem hoc uerbum de primo [*sic*] libro R(eg.), in quo proponitur nobis princeps, comes, uel baro mortuus quantum ad uite statum honorabilem, et quantum ad mortis occasum lamentabilem. ⁵Primum notatur cum dicitur: *princeps maximus*, secundum, cum additur: *cecidit hodie in Israel.*

**2** ¹Fuit maximus morum claritate. ²Multum facit ad magnitudinem altitudo generis. ²(1) Mach(abeorum 2: 17): *Princeps et clarissimus es in hac ciuitate, et hornatus filiis et fratribus.* ³Debet autem potissimum cauere omnis talis ne quam maculam per ignauiam sue uite genus suum coinquinat, et sit terminus ac finis nobilitatis. ⁴Longe namque prestantius est esse principium claritatis quam terminum. ⁵Et propter hoc debet homo multum satagere ad bonos mores, licet qui eligit preficiendos in temporalibus ad hec duo debeat considerationis aciem inclinare: ad bonos mores et ad genus clarum. ⁶Unde Alexander—et loquitur Alexandro poeta ex persona Aristot(elis):

> ⁷Consultor procerum: seruos contempne bilingues
> Et nequam, nec quos humiles natura iacere
> Precipit, exalta. ⁸Nam qui pluuialibus undis
> Intumuit torrens, fluit acrior ampne perhenni:
> Sic partis opibus, et honoris culmine, seruus
> In dominum surgens truculentior aspide surda
> Obturat precibus aures, mansuescere nescit.
> ⁹Non tamen id prohibet rationis calculus, ut non
> Exaltare uelis, si quos insignit honestas
> Quos morum sublimat apex, licet ampla facultas
> Et patrie desit et gloria sanguinis alti.

2: 6. Gauthier de Chatillon, *Alexandreis*, ed. PL 209. 466.

1: 1 *In margin*     1: 4 primo] *read* secundo     princeps] princes *ms*     **2: 3** ne quam] nequam *ms*     genus suum coinquinat] generi (*corr. from* genus?) suo conquirat *ms*     sit] sic *in ms?*     **2: 9** ut non] non *between lines*

**3** ¹Secundo armorum strenuitate. ²Paruus fuerat Camillus, qui, ut Agustinus dicit, et accipit a Tito Liuio, abductus fuit ab aratro, sed quia tantus fuit in strenuitate armorum ut ingratam patriam etiam a Gallis defenderit, sua uirtute ualde factus est magnus. ³De quo dicit idem Titus: Fama erat ea tempestate rebus humanis tantum uirum bello gerendo non esse. ⁴(4) R(eg.) (5: 1): *Naaman princeps exercitus regis Sirie fuit uir magnus et honoratus. Per ipsum enim dedit Dominus salutem Sirie.*

**4** ¹Tertio auctoritate officii. ²Ys. xxxii [*sic*]: *Princeps esto noster, aufer opbrobrium nostrum.* ³Ad hoc enim constituitur aliquis in principem ut auferat obprobrium a subiectis. ⁴Exemplum (1) R(egum) de Saule et Dauid, quorum uterque abstulit obprobrium ex Israel.

**5** ¹Copiositate thesauri. ²Unde illi qui preminent diuitiis hodie aliis dominantur, etiam si aliud uix habeant, quod tamen est iniquum, et magis secundum prauitatem mundi quam secundum institutum dei. ³Unde appellamus tales in Baruc (3: 16–18) principes gentium: *Ubi sunt principes gentium, et qui dominantur super bestias, que sunt super terram, qui in auibus celi ludunt et argentum thesaurizant et aurum in quo confidunt homines*, etc. ⁴Beati sunt illi serui quos *constituit dominus super familiam suam, ut det illis cibum in temppore* (Matt. 24: 45), si attendant et opere inpleant quod scribitur Ys. xxxii (8): *Princeps ea que digna sunt principe cogitabit.*

**6** ¹Quinto sapientie indagatione. ²Hoc modo fuit constitutus princeps Ioseph, de quo habes Ecc(li. 49: 17): *Ioseph princeps fratrum*, et Daniel, de quo in Daniele (?5: 11): quem *constituit pater* eius *principem*. ³Ys. xxxii (5): *Non uocabitur ultra is qui insipiens est princeps.* ⁴Uere, secundum Platonem, tunc beatus foret orbis terrarum, si aut reges saperent aut sapientes regnarent.

**7** ¹Sexto fame dilatatione. ²Talis princeps fuit Abraam, qui diuinis beneficiis cumulatus, diuitiis auctus [*fo. 2ʳ*] et uictoriis illustratus, princeps dei est a paganis appellatus: Gn. (23: 6): *princeps dei es apud nos.* ³Tunc autem huiusmodi est uere magnus quando facta fame concordant, alias et cui fama, non esset fama sed infamia. ⁴Unde

3: 2. ut Agustinus dicit] Not found.
3: 3. Cf. Livy, 5. 45. 1: 'aequis iniquisque persuasum erat tantum bello uirum neminem usquam ea tempestate esse.'
4: 2. Ys. xxxii] Not found, but cf. Isa. 3: 6 and 4: 1.

3: 2 ualde factus est] *then space/erasure in ms*      3: 4 (4) R(eg.) R *with a row of four dots above it. This method of giving the book-number is not noted henceforward*
5: 1 Copiositate] *read* Quarto copiositate?      5: 3 thesaurizant] thesaurizat *ms*
5: 4 *dominus super*] *super between lines*      6: 2 quem] quam *or* quod *ms?*
6: 4 tunc] nunc *ms*    saperent] *altered and illegible in ms*      7: 2 princeps . . . princeps] princeps . . . princes *ms*

dicitur in Laudibus: 'Iosue fuit magnus secundum nomen suum, maximus in salutem gentis sue.' [5]Quando enim homo magnus est, in se quantum ad uitam, et quantum ad alios per famam, tunc recte potest gentem suam ab hostibus defensare. [6]Hic autem uere fuit talis quantum ad omnia illa. [7]Adapta.

**8** [1]Hic autem tantus et talis hodie per mortem cecidit: [2]Primo in contemptum uilitatis. [3]Tren. (5: 16): *Cecidit corona capitis nostri; ue nobis, quia peccauimus.* [4]Nichil est enim quod hominem contemptibiliorem faciat quantum peccatum. Iere. (2: 36): *Quam uilis facta es nimis, iterans uias tuas, et ab Egypto confunderis.*

**9** [1]Secundo in defectum infirmitatis. [2]Quantumcumque enim strenuus, ad infirmitatem tantam in morte peruenit, ut nec se ualeat adiuuare nec alterum. [3](2) R(eg.) (1: 27): *Quomodo ceciderunt fortes et perierunt arma bellica?* [4]Et ut dimittamus de aliis qui mortui sunt ex infirmitate, Iulius Cesar nullo modo se poterat adiuuare. [5]Eccles. (8: 8): *non habet homo potestatem in diem mortis.*

**10** [1]Tertio in uermium dictionem. [2](2) Mach(abeorum) (9: 7–10): *contigit autem illum inpetu euntem de curru cadere*—narra ystoriam quomodo uenit in uermium dictionem. [3]Simile de Herode in Actibus (12: 23), qui *consumptus a uermibus expirauit.* [4]Erit quando dicere possis, si loqui liceat, tamen loqui non licebit: *qui me comedunt non dormiunt,* Iob. (30: 17). [5]Ecc(li. 10: 13): *Cum enim mortuus fuerit homo hereditabit serpentes et bestias et uermes.*

**11** [1]Quarto in nudationem corporis. [2]Iob (14: 10): *Homo cum mortuus fuerit nudatus atque consumptus: ubi queso est?* [3]Itaque qui se existimat stare, uideat ne cadat, quia *diues cum dormierit nichil secum affert* (Iob 27: 19). [4]Ergo *thesaurizate uobis thexauros in celo, ubi nec erugo nec tinea demolitur, ubi fures non effodiunt nec furantur* (Matt. 6: 20).

**12** [1]Quinto in caliginem mentis. [2]'Hac enim animaduersione', secundum Agustinum: 'percutitur peccator ut moriens obliuiscatur sui, qui dum uiueret oblitus est dei', in Sermone de Innocentibus. [3]Ys. (14: 12): *Quomodo cecidisti Lucifer qui mane oriebaris?*

7: 4. 'in Laudibus'] Not found. For bibliography on the *Laudes* see R. Elze, 'Die Herrscherlaudes im Mittelalter', repr. in his *Päpste—Kaiser—Könige und die mittelalterliche Herrschaftssymbolik: Ausgewählte Aufsätze*, ed. Bernhard Schimmelpfennig and Ludwig Schmugge (repr. London, 1982), No. X; unless the reference is to the daily liturgical office of Lauds.

12: 2. Cf. 'Appendix tomi quinti operum s. Augustini complectens sermones supposititios . . .', sermo CCXX, ed. PL 39. 2153.

7: 4 salutem] salūt *ms*  8: 4 enim] e *ms?*  quantum] *read* quam? 9: 2 adiuuare nec alterum] *correction/erasure in ms*  9: 5 Eccles.] ecc̣ *ms?* diem] *sic for* die  10: 2 narra] notatur (nōr) *ms*  ystoriam] ystor̄ *ms* 11: 2 mortuus] *correction in ms*

**13** [1]Sexto in obliuionem gentis, quia post mortem illud accidit quod propheta dicit (Ps. 9: 7): *Periit memoria eorum cum sonitu.* [2]*Sed* reuera, *in memoria eterna erit iustus* (Ps. 111: 7). [3]Huius exemplum patet in romanis principibus, et apostolis nostris pauperibus. [4]Ubi est memoria Octauiani, Neronis, et aliorum? [5]Memoria certe Petri preminet eorum memorie. [6]Adapta. [7]Faciat deus nos ita iustos ut memoria sit nostra cum laudibus, Amen.

**13:** 1  dicit] *between lines*     **13:** 7  deus] *between lines*

*Note:* In several places the scribe has put an abbreviation mark apparently in error through the descender of the first *p* of *princeps*.

# Transcription B:a

Bertrand de la Tour, Schneyer, *Repertorium*, i. 578, No. 1063;
MS Seville, Biblioteca Capitular Colombina 82-4-1 (unfoliated)

*Introduction*

I have seen four manuscripts of this sermon: Kremsmünster 44 (= K),
fos. 17$^{rb}$–19$^{rb}$; Assisi 448 (= A), fos. 39$^{va}$–42$^{rb}$ (note that I ignore the
deleted foliation); Innsbruck, Universitätsbibliothek 234, fos. 129$^{ra}$–
130$^{va}$ (= I); and Seville Cathedral, Biblioteca Capitular Columbina (=
Colomb. Cab. in Schneyer) 82-4-1 (= S). This last manuscript is unfoliated, but I selected it for the transcription because it seems rather
good textually, certainly much better than K or A. As explained in the
'Note on Transcriptions' in the Introduction, readings from other
manuscripts replace the reading in S when they are superior to S,
whose reading is relegated to the apparatus, but when the reading
from S seems preferable the other readings are not recorded unless for
some special reason.[1] In the case of A there is such a reason for
recording some variants in the apparatus or even, when the diver-
gence extends to a whole passage, in a parallel text: in these cases the
differences look like a separate version rather than errors, so that even
if they do not go back to Bertrand (which cannot categorically be ruled
out) they would deserve to be recorded as evidence for the reception
and use of the text.

Analysis of errors in the text has not revealed any really serviceable
stemmatic relationships to me. To summarize: there is at least a
possibility that each of A, K, and S agrees in error with each of the
other two in this trio against the third, which could imply contamination. I have not noticed any common errors linking I to A. In principle,
therefore, these two manuscripts might be regarded as independent of
each other, so that agreement between them would be grounds for
accepting their reading when there is no intrinsic difference in merit
between it and other variants. But cases where they agree against the
base manuscript S are few, and I have not found an instance where
their stemmatic independence helps.

The one error linking S with I that I have noticed might have been

---

[1] Where more than one manuscript other than S has what seems to be the
right reading I do not list them all, but privilege K. Agreement of more than
one witness does not logically strengthen the case for a reading if there is a
likelihood of contamination.

made independently by the two scribes, but other agreements between the two manuscripts would still not affect textual choices, since the reading of S has been adopted in any case, except when there is reason to think that it is wrong.

The following agreements in error lie behind the foregoing observations and may be useful to some future editor of Bertrand. There is room for debate about some of my judgements of what is erroneous, but for brevity's sake I have not hedged them with qualifications.

AGREEMENT IN ERROR BETWEEN A AND K

1: 4 ... ut uideantur mori male qui bene moriuntur, *et, e conuerso, bene mori qui tamen male moriuntur] male ... bene ... male ... bene *AK*

3: 1 ... cursum sue uite qui precessit ... terminum qui successit] c. s. u. que p. ... t. q. s. *AK*

AGREEMENT IN ERROR BETWEEN A, I, AND K

7: 3 habemus exempla in scriptura sacra] h. exemplum i. s. s. *AIK* (More than one exemplum follows, and previous endings in -*um* explain the error.)

AGREEMENT IN ERROR BETWEEN A AND S

1: 5 que tamen] qui tamen *AS*         (The relative must refer to *mors* rather than *conspectu*.)

6: 4 progressio uirtuosa, quia fuit per figuram Dauid] p. u., que f. p. f. D. *SA*        (In the context, it would seem that David stands for the dead man, rather than for virtuous progression.)

AGREEMENT IN ERROR BETWEEN K AND S

6: 2 ... legem carnis, que est lasciuia, ... legem mundi, que est auaritia] i. c., q. e. lasciua, ... l. m., q. e. a. *KS* (*S could read* lascuia)

AGREEMENT IN ERROR BETWEEN I AND S

4: 2 *Dauit*, inquit;—interpretatur enim Dauit] D. inquit interpretatur *IS*

**1** ¹Sermo duodecimus qui potest fieri in exequiis alicuius regis seu *magni principis.

²*Mortuus est Dauit in senectute bona plenus dierum, diuitiis et gloria,* prima Paral. xxix (28). ³Secundum quod haberi potest ex uerbis beati Augus(tini) in sermone quodam de Innocentibus, et primo libro de Ciui(tate) Dei, xi capitulo, sicut ex mala uita hominis sequitur eiusdem mala mors, quia hac animaduersione percuttitur peccator, ut moriens obliuiscatur sui qui dum uiueret oblitus est dei;—malam autem mortem temporalem sequitur mors eterna, que mortem temporalem simpliciter efficit malam; unde dicit Augustinus de Ciui(tate Dei) loco preallegato quod nichil facit malam mortem simpliciter, supple, nisi quod sequitur mortem, quod, supple, est *mors eterna; propter quod, addit, non itaque multum curandum est eis qui necessario morituri sunt quid accidat si moriantur, se*d* moriendo quo ire cogantur;—sic ex bona uita hominis sequitur bona mors temporalis eiusdem, quam sequitur uita eterna, que mortem temporalem simpliciter efficit bonam. ⁴Dicit enim idem Augustinus parum supra: neque enim putanda est mala mors se*d* potius bona in conspectu Domini, quam uita bona precessit; et signanter dico in conspectu Domini, quia in conspectu hominum sepe apparet oppositum horum, ut uideantur mori male qui bene moriuntur, *et, e conuerso, bene mori qui tamen male moriuntur. ⁵Propter quod propheta in Ps. (33: 22), considerans quod ineffabile est [*second col.*] diuinum iudicium, dicit quod *mors peccatorum pessima*— supple, in conspectu dei—que tamen interdum in conspectu hominum optima uidetur. ⁶Et alibi dicit idem in Ps. quod *pretiosa in conspectu Domini mors sanctorum eius* (Ps. 115: 15). ⁷Et tamen in conspectu hominum interdum uilissima uidetur, utpote quando moriuntur subito uel interficiuntur per malos homines, uel quando carent sepultura.

**2** ¹Quia igitur iste rex illustrissimus, dominus scilicet talis uel talis, uel iste princeps nobilissimus, scilicet dominus talis uel talis, diu bene uixit et iuste gubernauit principatum suum quantum apparere poterat hominibus, idcirco putandum est quod mors ipsius fuit pretiosa, propter quod de ipso nunc exponi possunt allegorice uerba proposita,

---

**1**: 3. 'Augustine', 'Appendix tomi quinti operum s. Augustini complectens sermones suppositicios . . .', sermo CCXX, ed. PL 39. 2153; and Augustine, *De ciuitate Dei*, I. 11.
**1**: 4. Augustine, *De ciuitate Dei*, loc. cit.

**1**: 1 Sermo . . . principis] Pro rege uel magno principe Sermo xii *A*    duodecimus] *K*: undecimus *S*    alicuius regis seu *magni principis] *K*: cuius boni episcopi *S*    **1**: 4 qui tamen male] *I*: tamen *om. S*    **1**: 5 que] *K*: qui *S*

que ad litteram fuerunt de rege Dauid scripta, scilicet: *mortuus est Dauit*, etc. ²Cursus enim uite istius uiri permaximi fuit multum laudabilis, et idcirco nunc habuit pro fine et *termino mortem trist-abilem secundum quid, simpliciter tamen gaudiosam, quia firmiter tenendum est quod eius mors fuit in conspectu Domini pretiosa.

**3** ¹Igitur in hiis uerbis breuiter tanguntur tria quorum primum respicit cursum sue uite qui precessit, alia duo respiciunt sue uite terminum qui successit. ²Primo, dico, tangitur uite huius domini pro-gressio uirtuosa; secundo autem tangitur uite sue deffunctio luctuosa; et tertio tangitur eiusdem uite conclusio gaudiosa.

**4** ¹Primum, scilicet sue uite progressio uirtuosa, tangitur in nomine 'Dauit'. ²*Dauit*, inquit;—interpretatur enim Dauit 'manu fortis' et 'uultu desiderabilis', et significabat istum illustrem regem seu nobilem principem, cuius corpus exequiatur inter nos. ³Ipse enim fuit fortis manu ad impletionem mandatorum dei, ad *sustentationem [*third col.*] et deffensionem miserorum, ad punitionem peccatorum, et ad pro-motionem bonorum. ⁴Fuit etiam uultu desiderabilis, quia fuit in uerbis cautus, in factis strenuus, in gestibus maturus, et in signis honestus. ⁵Propter ista enim desiderabant homines respicere in faciem siue suum uultum, id est exemplarem suam conuersationem. ⁶Unde de persona ipsius possumus dicere illud quod scribitur Prouer. ult. (31: 25): *for-titudo et decor indumentum eius, et ridebit in die nouissimo*—*fortitudo*, quidem, ad bene operandum, et *decor* ad exemplariter conuersandum, *et ridebit in die nouissimo*, supple, propter suppliciorum euasionem et premiorum adeptionem.

**5** ¹*Iste igitur fuit per figuram Dauid, de quo possumus con-uenienter exponere illud quod scribitur ii Reg. xxiii (8): *Dauid sedens in cathedra sapientissimus princeps inter tres*. ²Iste magnus dominus fre-quenter sedit in cathedra dum uiueret, causas audiens, proposita dis-cusciens, *sententias proferens et iudicia descernens. ³Cuius quidem cathedra stabat super quatuor pedes, quorum primus erat prudentia que principatum ordinat, secundus erat iustitia que principatum per-petuat, tertius erat constantia que principatum conseruat, quartus erat clementia, que principatum roborat.

**6** ¹Et iste Dauit noster fuit princeps *sapientissimus inter tres*. ²Cum aliquis principetur secundum legem carnis, que est lasciuia, aliquis secundum legem mundi, que est auaritia, et aliquis secundum legem

---

4: 1–2 'Dauit'. *Dauit*, inquit;—interpretatur enim Dauit 'manu fortis'] *K (but:* Dauid *and* inquid*):* 'D.'. *D* inquit interpretatur 'm. f.' *S:* 'D.'. D. enim interpretatur 'm. f.' *A*     4: 2 principem] *A adds* uel militem     4: 5 faciem siue suum uultum] *emend to* faciem suam siue uultum?     5: 2 frequ-enter] *A:* sequenter *S*     5: 3 quartus erat] erat *om. S, supplied from A*     6: 2 lasciuia] *A:* lasciua *SK* principabatur] *A:* principaliter *S*

dyaboli, que est superbia et malitia, iste principabatur secundum legem Christi, que est uera sapientia. ³Et idcirco inter alios tres qui erant et sunt principes stultissimi [*fourth col.*] iste fuit sapientissimus. ⁴Bene ergo debemus credere quod ipsius mors fuit bona quam precessit uite progressio uirtuosa, quia fuit per figuram Dauid: *Dauid,* inquid.

**7** ¹Secundo tangitur sue uite deffunctio luctuosa, cum additur: *mortuus est.* ²Certe, in morte tanti domini tantique principis lugere debent omnes sui subditi, precipue propinqui ac familiares sui. ³Et certe, de lugendo in morte magnorum uirorum reipublice utilium habemus exempla in scriptura sacra: filii namque Israel fleuerunt et plancxerunt multum in morte Iacob patris sui, sicut habetur Gen. ult(imo). ⁴Omnis etiam multitudo populi fleuit in morte Aaron, sicut habetur Numerorum uigesimo. ⁵Dauit etiam in morte illius magni principis, scilicet Abner, fleuit et dixit omni populo: *Scindite uestimenta uestra, et accingimini saccis ac plangite ante exequias Abner;* sequitur: *et rex Dauit leuauit uocem suam et fleuit super tumulum Abner, fleuitque et omnis populus,* sicut hec dicuntur ii R(eg.) tertio (31–2). ⁶Et quod maius omnibus *hiis est, saluator noster Dominus Iesus Christus fleuit super monumento Lazari. ⁷Unde dicitur Io. xi (33) quod uidens Iesus flentes sorores Lazari, *infremuit,* etc. ⁸Sequitur (11: 35): *et lacrimatus est Ihesus.* ⁹Reuera, cum princeps iste nobilissimus esset reipublice et toti *ecclesie multum utilis, reuera, sua mors et sue uite deffunctio est et debet esse quantum in se est omnibus luctuosa, quia maximum dampnum est quando unus bonus princeps qui bene gubernat rempublicam subtrahitur per mortem,

|                          *S*                          |                          *A*                          |
|-------------------------------------------------------|-------------------------------------------------------|
| tamen et si mors sua sit propter ista que dicta sunt lugubris et *flebilis, tamen propter aliqua alia debet esse gaudiosa. ¹⁰Quare? Quia conuenienter dicitur quod est mortuus *in senec\|tute* [*fifth col.*] *bona, plenus dierum, diuitiis et gloria.* | unde et si mors sua sit propter ista que dicta sunt lugubris et flebilis, tamen propter aliqua alia debet esse gratiosa, sicut in alio sermone dixi, quia securius est alibi quam hic, quia est in firma spe, si est in purgatorio, de beatitudine habenda. |
| **8** ¹Unde in hiis uerbis tertio tangitur sue uite conclusio pretiosa, ac per hoc et gaudiosa. | Tertio dico quod tangitur in hiis uerbis sue uite conclusio pretiosa, ac per hoc et gaudiosa, ubi dicitur: *in senectute bona plenus diuitiis et gloria.* |

---

**6**: 4 quia] *K*: que *SA*    **7**: 2 precipue] *A adds* consanguinei    sui] *A adds* quia natura dolet et inducit ad luctum de aliquo tibi dilecto uel sanguine uel amore    **7**: 6 maius] *A*: maior *S*    **7**: 10 conuenienter] connter *I*: communiter *K*: consequenter *S*

²Illius enim mors multum lugenda et plangenda est, de quo potest dici probabiliter quod *mortuus est diues et sepultus est in infernum* (Luke 16: 22). ³Se*d* mors illius de quo presumitur quod mortuus est sicut ille Lazarus cuius anima portata fuit per angelos in sinum Habrahe—hoc, est, in celum uel in purgatorium—plangi non debet simpliciter: sicut ista innuuntur de diuite epulone et Lazaro paupere, Luc. xvi.

**9** ¹Reuera, iste magnus dominus fuit mortuus in senectute bona, non solum annorum, se*d* etiam morum, alias non fuisset eius senectus bona. ²In ipso enim concurrit utraque senectus, uidelicet naturalis et moralis. ³Nec dicitur eius senectus bona solum propter senectutem naturalem, se*d* potius propter moralem. ⁴Illa enim est *senectus uenerabilis* que *non est*—solum, supple—*diuturna neque numero annorum conputata;* se*d* illa que est morigerata et cum *uita immaculata,* sicut dicitur Sapientie iiii (8–9).

**10** ¹De isto possumus dicere per figuram illud quod scribitur ad litteram de Gedeon, Iudicum octauo (32): *Mortuus est Gedeon in senectute bona.* ²'Gedeon' enim interpretatur 'experimentum iniquitatis', et significat istum nobilem principem qui fuit expertus iniquitates multorum hominum qui mala faciebant in terra sua; que non sustinuit, se*d* eos iuste puniuit.

S

³Interpretatur etiam experimentum *te*mptationis, propter *quod significat eundem, qui fuit expertus te*mptationes multorum malorum hominum, et etiam demonum, qui te*mptauerunt eum sepe de co*mmittendo diuersa crimina. ⁴Ipse tamen non acquieuit eis, se*d* uirtuose repulit ipsorum te*mptamenta. ⁵Mortuus ergo fuit iste noster Gedeon in senectute bona.

A

Interpretatur etiam *experimentum te*mptationis, id est, temptationes suas et aliorum suo experimento expellendo.—Si uis plus de senectute, require retro in sermone 7, qui incipit: *Abraham mortuus est in senectute bona.*

**11** [*sixth col.*] ¹Mortuus est etiam plenus dierum, non solum dierum usualium, se*d* etiam spiritualium, uirtutum scilicet et meritorum, alias non fuisset mortuus plenus dierum. ²Multitudo enim annorum na-

**8:** 2 *infernum] sic* S: inferno *in Clementine Vulgate*   **10:** 1 *bona]* A *adds* et hoc erit figura ad propositum nostrum de isto domino   **10:** 2 multorum hominum qui mala faciebant in terra sua] multorum malorum hominum A sed eos] I: ea S   **10:** 3 Interpretatur etiam] IK: etiam *om.* S   **10:** 3 ff. (*parallel text from* A) sermone 7] sermone 8 A

turalium et dierum usualium loquendo proprie non faciunt hominem plenum dierum, quia dies tales non manent, sed *transeunt. ³Dies enim hominis tales *sicut umbra pretereunt,* dicitur in Ps. (143: 4). ⁴Unde de talibus diebus potest quilibet dicere illud Iob. vii (6): *Dies mei uelocius transierunt quam a texente tela succiditur.* ⁵Sic autem in morte hominis isti dies transierunt quod penitus nichil sunt—propter quod dicit ille in persona cuiuslibet hominis, Iob. vii (16): *Parce michi, Domine, nichil enim sunt dies mei*—quod autem nichil est, nullam potest facere plenitudinem. ⁶Dies autem spirituales illi manere possunt et semper manebunt post mortem hominis. ⁷*Merita enim bona semper manebunt. ⁸Unde isti dies faciunt plenitudinem, propter quos etiam dies usuales faciunt aliquo modo plenitudinem, quia quodammodo manent in diebus spiritualibus, quia facti sunt in eis. ⁹Unde sicut dies naturales et anni dicuntur uacui *quando nichil boni factum est in eis—tales enim dies dicuntur perditi, de quibus diebus et annis dicitur Iob. vii (3): *Ego,* inquit, *habui menses uacuos,* etc.—sic etiam dies naturales quodammodo dicuntur pleni propter bona opera que facta sunt in eis. ¹⁰De talibus enim diebus dicitur in Ps. (72: 10): *Dies pleni inuenientur in eis.* ¹¹Dies autem naturales in quibus nichil boni fit, quantumcumque sint multi, dies sunt uacui, dies sunt mali. ¹²*Dies mali sunt,* dicitur de talibus ad Ephe. v (16). ¹³Et talis homo qui solum habet tales dies multos est ille cui [*seventh col.*] dicetur in morte illud Dan. xiii (52): *Inueterate dierum malorum, nunc peccata tua* apprehenderunt te, etc. ¹⁴Et quamuis isti dies possint dici semper manere, propter penam perpetuam que debetur peccatis, non tamen manent in diebus, quia in inferno non erit dies penitus, sed nox eterna.

**12** ¹Iste igitur princeps nobilis mortuus est plenus dierum; mortuus etiam plenus diuitiis etiam temporalibus. ²Nullus enim fuit eo ditior in partibus istis. ³Uerum iste diuitie non fecissent mortem suam pretiosam, nec propter eas, loquendo proprie, posset dici mortuus plenus diuitiis, quia quantum ad ipsum iam transiuerunt totaliter. ⁴Unde in Ps. (75: 6) dicitur: *Dormierunt *sompnum suum,* supple mortis, *et nichil inuenerunt omnes uiri diuitiarum in manibus suis:*—nichil, dico, nisi helemosinas et bona que de suis diuitiis fecerunt, si tamen fecerunt. ⁵Unde dampnati dicent in inferno, sicut dicitur Sapientie quinto (8): *Quid profuit nobis superbia, aut diuitiarum iactantia quid contulit nobis—* quasi dicerent: 'Nichil', quia sequitur (5: 9): *Transiuerunt illa omnia tanquam umbra.*

**11:** 4 *succiditur*] *A: succinditur S*   **11:** 8 dies usuales] *KA: om. S*   **11:** 11 quantumcumque] *KA:* quantum *S*   **11:** 14 possint] *K:* possunt *S:* posset *A*   **12:** 1 etiam²] *omit with K?*   **12:** 2 Nullus . . . istis] Quantum enim diues uos scitis *A*   **12:** 5 in inferno] in *om. S*   profuit nobis] *p. uobis S?* dicerent] dicent *S:* dicat *A:* diceret *K?*

**13** ¹Iste dico diuitie non fecissent mortem eius pretiosam nisi cum istis diuitiis in ipso alie diuitie concurrissent, scilicet diuitie salutares, de quibus dicitur Ys. xxxiii (6): *diuitie salutis sapientia et scientia: timor Domini ipse thesaurus eius.* ²Iste, dico, diuitie fecerunt mortem eius pretiosam, et ipsum fecerunt in morte plenum diuitiis. ³Habuit enim sapientiam ad degustandum et desiderandum celestia, scientiam ad gubernandum et dispensandum terrena, et timorem Domini ad declinandum peccata.

**14** ¹Per istas spiritu|ales [*eighth col.*] diuitias ipse temporales diuitias iuste acquisiuit dum uiueret, iuste retinuit, iuste distribuit et dispensauit, iuste etiam distribui mandauit et ordinauit. ²Et certe, in tali homine diuitie temporales sunt fructuose. ³Unde Ambrosius super Lucham: Discant homines non in facultatibus crimen esse, sed in hiis qui nesciunt facultatibus uti; nam sicut diuitie sunt inpedimenta in inprobis, ita sunt in bonis adiumenta uirtutis.

**15** ¹Fuit ettiam mortuus plenus gloria, id est, gloria seculi. ²Ipse enim fuit unus de gloriosis terre. ³Uerum ista gloria non fecit mortem eius pretiosam, nec propter eam posset dici proprie plenus gloria, quia ista gloria non est nisi quidam fumus et quedam umbra que cito euanescunt. ⁴Ys. xl (6; + 1 Pet. 1: 24): *Omnis caro fenum, et omnis gloria eius quasi flos feni,* qui ualde arescit cito. ⁵Sic transit cito gloria mundana, nec manet in homine post mortem. ⁶Unde dicitur in Ps. (48: 17): *Ne timueris cum diues factus fuerit homo, et cum multi(plicata),* etc.; sequitur (48: 18): *quoniam, cum interierit, non \*sumet omnia, neque descendet cum eo gloria eius.*

**16** ¹Sed iste dominus non solum habuit istam gloriam transitoriam, sed etiam habuit quandam aliam gloriam mansiuam, scilicet de uirtutibus ac meritis et testimonio bone conscientie. ²De qua gloria dicit Apostolus, secunda ad Cor. primo capitulo (12): *gloria nostra hec est, testimonium conscientie nostre.*

**17** ¹Iterum fuit mortuus plenus gloria, id est spe firmissima de habendo illam gloriam de qua dicitur in Ps. (149: 9): *Gloria hec est omnibus sanctis eius.* ²Hec est gloria celestis que manebit \*perpetuo. ³Ad quam credo firmissime quod iste dominus, propter bona que fecit [*ninth col.*] in uita sua et propter illa etiam que fecit in puncto mortis sue, quia pure confessus fuit, deuotissime comunicauit, prudenter de

14: 3. Ambrose: PL 15. 1882.

13: 1 fecissent] *K*: fecerunt *S*    14: 3 adiumenta] adiuuenta *S*: adiuuamenta *KI* uirtutis] uirtutes *S*    15: 1 Fuit] Prefuit *S?*    id est] *I*: etiam (et') *S*    15: 3 nec] *KA*: ne *S*    fumus . . . euanescunt] *A*: fumus et quedam que cito euanescunt uelut umbra *S*

bonis suis ordinauit, et de omnibus da*m*pnis *per ipsum aliis datis plene satisfieri mandauit, et ad causas pias legata pinguia fecit:—quod iam uel actu istam gloriam possidet uel saltim securus est de possidendo. [4]Quod sibi et nobis concedat, etc. [5]Dicas, si uis, de morte uel de mortuis que notaui superius in primo sermone, scilicet *Beati mortui.*

**17:** 3 possidendo] habendo *A, which adds:* et precipue purgatione facta, gloriam eternam habebit.

# Transcription B:b

Bertrand de la Tour, Schneyer, Repertorium, i. 579, No. 1082; MS Kremsmünster 44, fos. 49$^{va}$–50$^{rb}$

## Introduction

This sermon survives in more of the manuscripts of Bertrand that I have seen than any of the other sermons transcribed in this section. Before deciding which to use for the transcription I collated the following: Innsbruck, Universitätsbibliothek 234 (= I), fo. 153$^{rb-va}$; Klosterneuburg 265 (= Ka), fos. 66$^{rb}$–67$^{ra}$; Klosterneuburg 486 (= Kb), fos. 140$^{vb}$–141$^{va}$; Kremsmünster 44 (= Km), fos. 49$^{va}$–50$^{rb}$; Seville Cathedral, Biblioteca Capitular Columbina 82-4-1 (= S), unfoliated; Vienna, Schottenstift 379 (379) (= V), fos. 181$^{rb}$–182$^{ra}$.

The scribe of S, selected for Transcriptions B:a and B:d, may have been off form when copying this sermon, since there seem to be a lot of mistakes, many or most of them not shared with other manuscripts. Though I originally selected it as the base manuscript for the collation, it did not in the event come up to expectations and has not been used for the transcription.

Ka, Kb, and V form a clear group, linked by common errors which are set out below. Both severally and individually the proportion of errors they contain seems high.

I is a good manuscript. However, towards the end passages are smudged and totally illegible, at least on film. On this account it has not been chosen for transcription, though close attention has been paid to its readings.

Km is a reasonably good manuscript. Furthermore, it seems textually aloof from the others. Though there is at least one possible common error linking it to I, this could be coincidence, and I have not noticed any evidently erroneous agreements with either S or the KaKbV trio. That is in itself a reason for selecting it for transcription. Supposing that Km is stemmatically separate from S or KaKbV, then any readings which it shares either with S or with KaKbV have the authority of a coincidence of independent witnesses. By choosing Km for transcription one automatically reserves a place in the text for such readings except when manifestly doubtful.

When Km's reading seems wrong it is relegated to the apparatus, and if it has been corrected from other manuscripts (rather than by conjecture) at least one of these is listed (except when the correction imposes itself without the need for back-up). Though in principle only one of the manuscripts with the reading thought to be correct is noted in the apparatus to justify the reading's inclusion in the text, I have sometimes given more than one to show an agreement between S and the distinctive KaKbV group. Such an agreement is an extra argument, though hardly a decisive one *per se*, for the choice of the reading in question.

The following agreements in error are worth recording to underpin the foregoing and to help anyone who might undertake a 'Lach-mannian' edition of Bertrand in the future.

AGREEMENT IN ERROR BETWEEN KA, KB, AND V

**1:** 10 Sacrificium etiam eukaristie] *for* etiam *KaKbV read* autem
**3:** 1 defunctio et tumulatio] defunctis et tumulatis *Kb*: defunct(is) et tumulat(is) *V*: defunct(is) et tumulatus *Ka*      (I use '(is)'to show a truncation-mark which I would normally extend in that way.)
**3:** 5 Si enim] Si est *KaKbV*      (But see apparatus: Km has a rather similar error and S makes its own mistake. Perhaps the archetype was hard to read.)
**4:** 5 longe] longis *KaKb*: long(is) *V*

Note also the following error linking Kb, V, and possibly Ka and S in error against I and Km:

**1:** 8 iustarum] instar *KbV, ?S, ?Ka*

AGREEMENT IN ERROR BETWEEN S AND I

**3:** 4 debent] debet *IS*      (This could be coincidence.)

AGREEMENT IN ERROR BETWEEN I AND KM

**3:** 2 et sepelitione] *om. IKm*      (See also apparatus for **3:** 6.)

**1** [1]Sermo *uicesimus nonus de mort(uis), qui potest fieri quandocum-que *celebretur missa sollempnis pro anima alicuius regis in sepulcro [*fo. 49$^{vb}$*] patris sui tumulati et cetera.

[2]*Iosyas defunctus est et sepultus in sepulchro paterno*, ii Esdre primo capitulo (= 3 Ezra 1: 31). [3]Ad aliqualem recommendationem anime istius domini regis quondam illustris, et mitigationem dolorum

familiariorum suorum, ymo et omnium hominum regni sui, pro subtractione persone sue nobilissime, satis conuenienter exponuntur
uerba ista. ⁴Ipse enim congrue figuratus fuit per Yosiam regem
Iuda. ⁵Interpretatur enim Yosias 'ubi est incensum Domini et inest
sacrificium'. ⁶Et certe, in isto illustrissimo rege, dum uiueret, fuit
incensum Domini. ⁷Incensum, dico, deuotarum orationum, que di-
rigebantur in conspectu Domini, sicut incensum iuxta prophetam in
Psalmo (140: 2). ⁸Incensum *etiam iustarum operationum et piarum
erogationum que offerebantur Domino in odorem maioris suauitatis
quam possit esse incensum. ⁹In ipso etiam dum uiueret, etiam cum
esset propinquus morti, fuit sacrificium, uidelicet uere penitentie, de
quo in Psalmo (50: 19): *Sacrificium deo spiritus contribulatus.* ¹⁰Sacrificium
etiam eukaristie, quod deuotissime recepit, de quo dicit Apostolus, ad
Hebr. x (10): *sanctificati sumus per oblationem corporis Christi.*

2 ¹Bene ergo potest dici per figuram Iosias. ²Et potest dici nunc,
proch dolor, quod *defunctus est*, etc. ³In quibus quidem uerbis duo
tanguntur, que nos prouocant ad fletum et lacrimationem; et alia duo
tanguntur que nobis ingerunt risum et consolationem.

3 ¹Prima duo sunt defunctio et tumulatio, que tanguntur cum dicitur
*defunctus est et sepultus.* ²Dictum autem fuit superius in illo sermone
*Dauid patriarcha*, etc., quod inter corporalia et temporalia [*fo. 50ʳᵃ*]
nichil est miserius, nichilque tristius defunctione et sepelitione. ³Uide
in illo sermone et dic que ibi sunt notata. ⁴Et certe, ista duo que
audiuntur de morte istius illustrissimi regis debent *prouocare suos
homines ad gemitum et lacrimationem. ⁵Si enim pro morte cuiuslibet
hominis quilibet alius homo debet producere lacrimas et non despicere
sepulturam illius, iuxta illud Ecc(li.) xxxviii (16): *ffili, in mortuum produc
lacrimas, et quasi dira passus incipe plorare, et ne despicias sepulturam illius,*
multo fortius pro morte istius regis nobilissimi debemus lacrimas
producere, et plorare ad sepulchrum eius. ⁶Legimus enim ii Machab.
iiii (37) quod ille Anthyochus propter mortem summi sacerdotis,
Onye scilicet, *flexus ad misericordiam fudit lacrimas, recordatus defuncti
sobrietatem et modestiam.* ⁷Si igitur hoc fecit ille qui erat impius et
perfidus pro morte summi sacerdotis, multo fortius et nos debemus

---

**1:** 3 familiariorum] fam(i)lai̯orum *Km*: familiarium *IKbSV*: familiarum *Ka*
**1:** 7 orationum, que] *I etc.*: orationum, qua *Km*          **1:** 9 esset] *I etc.*: ē *Km*: ē
*Ka*          **2:** 1–2 potest dici per figuram Iosias. Et] *I etc.*: *om. Km (homoeoteleuton)*
**3:** 2 et sepelitione] *Ka* (sepulitione) *and SV*: *om. IKm*          **3:** 4 audiuntur] *I etc.*:
addiciuntur *Km?*     istius] *I etc.*: *om. Km*          **3:** 5 Si enim] *I*: Sic est *Km*: Si est
*KaKbV*: Sine *S*     dira] *I etc*: dura *Km*          **3:** 6 Machab.] *V etc.*: Mᵗ *I*: Math.
*Km.*? *(if so, possibly a significant error linking I with Km)*

lacrimari pro subtractione istius illustrissimi regis, recordati ipsius strennuitatem et bonitatem morum.

**4** [1]Alia uero duo, que nobis ingerunt spirituale gaudium, sunt sue uite sanctitas et sui tumuli nobilitas. [2]Sanctitas autem sue uite notatur cum ipse per figuram dicitur fuisse Iosyas, sicut patuit supra. [3]Uide illa que dicta sunt superius sub nomine Iosye. [4]Tumuli autem sui nobilitas notatur cum dicitur quod *sepultus est in sepulchro paterno*, id est, in sepulchro regali. [5]Pater enim suus rex fuit certe longe melior quam Amon pater Iosye. [6]Certe sepeliri in sepulchro patrum suorum, precipue si fuerunt reges, reputabatur antiquitus [ *fo. 50^{rb}* ] pro maxima nobilitate. [7]Unde ad confusionem illius Yoram regis Iuda, qui fuit rex malus et impius, dicitur ii Paral. *xxi (20) quod sepultus fuit in ciuitate Dauid, *uerumtamen non in sepulchris regum*. [8]Sed de illo sancto uiro Mathathya dicitur primi Machab. ii (70) quod *defunctus est et sepultus in sepulchris patrum suorum*.

**5** [1]Multum igitur est triste et flebile omnibus hominibus regni huius cum audiunt quod illustrissimus rex eorum defunctus est et sepultus. [2]Unde sicut in tota Iudea lugebant Iosyam defunctum et sepultum, sicud dicitur ii Esdr. ubi supra, ita in toto isto regno *debent omnes lugere regem suum nobilissimum iam *defunctum et sepultum. [3]Uerumtamen gaudiosum *est et omnibus multum consolabile cum audiunt quod ipse se taliter habuit dum uiueret, et etiam morti propinqus, quod potuit dici per figuram 'Iosyas', id est, 'ubi erat incensum Domini' et 'in quo fuit sacrificium', sicut expositum est supra, cum audiunt etiam quod sepultus est in sepulchro regis quondam illustrissimi patris sui.

**6** [1]Et reuera, sicut habuit uitam sanctam, ita credo firmiter quod habuit mortem bonam, et sicut corpus eius habuit nobilem sepulturam in terra, ita credo quod propter ipsius merita et uiuorum suffragia habet nunc realiter et actualiter, uel saltem in firma et certa spe, mansionem in domo patris celestis, ad quam nos perducat etc. [2]Dicas si uis illa vii uel octo que notaui superius de illis defunctis qui mortui fuerunt in Domino superius, in illo sermone *'Sancta et salubris est cogatatio'* etc.

---

3: 7 regis] *sic Km, but om. IKaKbSV*     4: 2 patuit *IV etc.: om. Km*     4: 4 Tumuli autem sui] *KaKbS:* Tumuli aut sui *I?:* Tumuli sui *V:* Tumuli sui autem *Km*     4: 8 Mathathya] *I:* Machacio/Mathatio *Km*     5: 3 consolabile cum audiunt quod] *SV:* c. quod a. q. *Km*     taliter] *d'Avray:* totaliter *Km*     id est] *KbIS:* et *Km*     6: 2 octo] viii° *Km* notaui] *I etc.:* noui *Km*

# Transcription B:c

Bertrand de la Tour, Schneyer, *Repertorium*, i. 581,
No. 1100; MS Kremsmünster 44, fos. 82$^{vb}$–85$^{ra1}$

## Introduction

Kremsmünster 44 (= K) is the only one of the manuscripts of Bertrand's *de mortuis* sermons which I have examined to include this text, something which is hard to understand since this is one of the occasions when he rises to real eloquence, such as a modern reader can appreciate—by no means always the case with Bertrand. Accordingly, my transcription is diplomatic, in the qualified sense explained in the 'Note on Transcriptions' in the introduction.

**1** [1]Sermo quadragesimus quintus. [2]Et potest fieri in exequiis alicuius regis uel magni principis, etc.

[3]*Princeps et maximus cecidit hodie in Israel*, ii R(eg.) iii (38). [4]In hoc uerbo, quondam per Dauid regem de illo magno principe Abner scilicet ad litteram, dicto, et per Ioab interfecto, de isto nostro magno principe, qui per mortem iam cecidit, allegorice tanguntur tria. [5]Quorum primum a cunctis fuit multum honorabile. [6]Secundum est a cunctis multum lamentabile. [6]Tertium est uniuersis multum consolabile.

**2** [1]Multum enim fuit honorabilis gradus auctoritatis quem habuit, qui notatur cum dicitur *Princeps et maximus*. [2]Multum autem est cunctis lamentabilis casus mortalitatis quem subiit, qui notatur cum additur: *cecidit*. [3]Sed multum est uniuersis consolabilis locus securitatis in quo obiit, qui notatur cum subditur: *in Israel*.

**3** [1]Et bene per Abner iste designatur noster princeps qui iam obiit. [2]Interpretatur enim Abner 'lapis lucidus'. [3]Et reuera, iste dominus erat lapis per constantiam. [4]Erat enim per figuram ille cui dicitur,

**1: 1** quadragesimus quintus] xlv° K    **1: 4** *The sentence is possibly corrupt, but might make sense thus: 'In these words, which were once said by King Dauid of that great prince Abner, in the literal sense that is—and he had been killed by Ioab—three things are touched on in the allegorical sense with respect to that great prince of ours who has now fallen through death.'*    **2: 1** cum dicitur *Princeps et maximus*] cum additur *cecidit* K (*error of transposition: see* 2: 2 *below*)    **2: 2** cum additur: *cecidit*] cum dicitur *Princeps et maximus* K    **3: 1** bene per] bene quod K    **3: 4** cui] qui K

[1] Foliation at centre, *not* right hand, of top margin.

Gn. penultimo (49: 24), *pastor, lapis Israel.* ⁵Sed erat lapis lucidus per morum refulgentiam. ⁶Erat enim de numero illorum de quibus dicitur, Prouerbiorum quarto (18): *Iustorum semita quasi lux splendens procedit.* ⁷Et bene per Ioab, qui interfecit Abner, designatur mors, que hunc uirum illustrissimum interfecit. ⁷Ioab enim interpretatur inimicus. ⁸Quod autem mors, que nulli homini parcit, uere sit inimica, probatur per Apostolum, qui dicit de morte, i Cor. xv (26): *Nouissime autem omnium inimica destruetur mors.* ⁹Quid igitur? ¹⁰Sicud per Ioab inimicum cecidit ad litteram ille princeps magnus Abner, ita per mortem, omnibus [*fo. 83ʳᵃ*] inimicam, iam cecidit, sicut apparet hodie per facti euidentiam, ille noster illustratissimus princeps.

**4** ¹Primo, igitur, in hoc uerbo tangitur de ipso illud quod fuit cunctis honorabile, scilicet gradus auctoritatis quem habuit, cum dicitur: *Princeps et maximus.* ²Et non solum dicitur *princeps,* sed additur: *et maximus,* ut innuatur euidenter quod non solum habuit auctoritatem, quia princeps, uerum etiam et uirtutum pluralitatem; ac per hoc fuit maximus. ³Secundum enim Aristotelem i Polit., magis decet principem habere uirtutem ad bene regendum quam subditos ad bene seruiendum. ⁴Et secundum Augustinum, v De Ciuitate Dei, apud antiquos, [edes] uirtutum et principatuum siue honoris erant coniuncte, nec aliquis poterat intrare ad edem principatus seu honoris nisi per edem uirtutis.

**5** ¹Iste autem dominus non solum fuit princeps propter auctoritatem, sed etiam maximus, ut dictum est, propter uirtutum uarietatem. ²Habuit enim uirtutem prudentie. ³Sciebat enim quod prudentia principatum ordinat. ⁴Habuit etiam uirtutem clementie. ⁵Sciebat enim quod clementia principatum roborat. ⁶Habuit etiam uirtutem constantie. ⁷Sciebat enim quod constantia principatum conseruat. ⁸Habuit nichilominus uirtutem iustitie. ⁹Sciebat enim quod iustitia principatum perpetuat.

---

**4**: 3. Aristotle: probably a reference to *Politics* I. 13. Note especially the following passage in William of Moerbeke's medieval Latin translation: 'propter quod principem quidem perfectam habere oportet moralem uirtutem (opus enim est simpliciter architectonis, ratio autem architecton), aliorum autem unumquodque, quantum immittit ipsis' (1260ᵃ17–20, ed. F. Susemihl, *Aristotelis Politicorum libri octo, cum vetusta translatione Guilelmi de Moerbeka* (Leipzig, 1872), 54).
**4**: 4 Augustine: *De ciuitate Dei,* 5. 12: 'Hoc insitum habuisse Romanos etiam deorum apud illos aedes indicant, quas coniunctissimas constituerunt, Uirtutis et Honoris, pro diis habentes quae dantur a Deo.'

---

**3**: 7 hunc] huc *K?*     **3**: 8 *Nouissime autem omnium] contrast Vulgate text*
**3**: 10 illustrissimus] illustratissimus *K*     **4**: 4 Augustinum] Augᵘˢ *K*
edes] *om. K*     et] sed *K*     principatuum] principatum *K*     **5**: 4 etiam] enim
*K*

**6** ¹Dico primo quod iste habuit uirtutem prudentie, sciens quod prudentia principatum ordinat. ²Non enim debet gaudere nomine principis qui non est sapiens. ³Ys. trigesimo secundo (5): *Non uocatur princeps is qui est insipiens.* ⁴Quod iste considerans, fuit sapiens et prudens, non quidem prudentia carnis, nec prudentia mundi, seu dyaboli, sed prudentia dei. ⁵Unde fuit figuratus per illum magnum principem Dauid, de quo dicitur ii R(eg.) uigesimo | [*col. b*] tertio *Dauid sedet in kathedra sapientissimus princeps.* ⁶Et bene per Dauid iste figuratus fuit. ⁷Dauid enim interpretatur 'manu fortis' ad puniendum scelera, id est, ad exercendum pietatis opera. ⁸Ffuit etiam 'wltu desiderabilis' propter sui corporis pulchritudinem et wltus elegantiam, et propter etiam morum refulgentiam. ⁹Iste igitur noster Dauid sedebat in kathedra propter auctoritatem quam habebat. ¹⁰Princeps utique sapientissimus propter prudentiam que in ipso uigebat. ¹¹Unde propter istam prudentiam ipse optime principatum suum ordinabat et subditos suos ad bonum uirtutis dirigebat.

**7** ¹Dico secundo quod ipse habuit uirtutem clementie, quia clementia principatum roborat. ²Dicitur enim Prouerbiorum xx (28) quod *Misericordia et ueritas custodiunt regem, et clementia roborabitur tronus eius.* ³Et secundum quod ait Seneca, libro secundo De Clementia Principis, nullum hominem sic decet clementia sicut principem. ⁴Crudelitas enim principis, sicut ibidem dicit, idem bellum est. ⁵Infra eodem: Magni animi quem princeps debet habere proprium est esse placidum et tranquillum. ⁶Ut enim dicit idem, eodem libro, Apes sunt iracundissime et aculeo in wlnera relinquunt; solus tamen rex apum sine aculeo est; uoluit enim natura regem non seuum esse ultorem. ⁷Et quidam uersificator dixit:

---

**7:** 3 Seneca: *De clementia,* 1. 3. 3. Note that the wrong book-number is given here, but that below at **8:** 7 the book-number is given correctly.
**7:** 4 Ibid. 1. 5. 2.
**7:** 5 Ibid. 1. 5. 5.
**7:** 6 Ibid. 1. 19. 3.
**7:** 7 Not found in D. Schaller and E. Könsgen, with J. Tagliabue, *Initia carminum Latinorum saeculo undecimo antiquiorum* (Göttingen, 1977).

---

**6:** 5 uigesimo tertio] xxiiii° K    **6:** 7 manu . . . scelera] *my punctuation excludes* ad puniendum scelera *from the direct interpretation of the Hebrew word* 'David', *on which see M.* Thiel, Grundlagen und Gestalt der Hebräischkenntnisse des frühen Mittelalters *(Biblioteca degli 'Studi Medievali', 4; Spoleto, 1973), 286. The sense of the sentence seems odd; perhaps it is corrupt*    pietatis] parietatis K?
**6:** 10 uigebat] K *adds* Unde propter istam prudentiam que in ipso uigebat
**7:** 2 clementia] clementiam K    **7:** 4 principis] principem K    **7:** 5 quem] *corr. from* quod?    **7:** 6 non] ne K. *The source reads* Noluit illum natura nec saeuum esse nec (*etc.*) (*see footnote*). *My emendation of Bertrand's version is not the only possible one*    **7:** 7 quidam] quidem K

Est piger ad penas princeps, ad premia uelox
Quique dolet quotiens cogitur esse ferox.

**8** ¹Reuera, iste noster princeps, ista considerans, fuit piissimus et clementissimus, parcendo reis, beneficia erogando egenis et miserabilibus personis, nullumque puniendo nisi cum dolore et compassione. [*fo. 83ᵛᵃ*] ²Unde fuit figuratus per illum principem Ionatham, cui dixerunt Iudei, sicut habetur i Machabeorum ix (30): *Ionatha te elegimus in ducem et principem ad bellandum bellum nostrum.* ³Reuera, iste potuit dici Ionathas. ⁴Ionathas propter clementiam interpretatur 'columba'. ⁵Et certe, iste fuit totus columbinus, sine felle malitie et inuidie. ⁶Fuit enim clementissimus in subleuando miserias, in remittendo iniurias, in condonando offensas, et in temperando penas malefactoribus debitas. ⁷Audiuerat enim illud quod dicit Seneca libro primo De Clementia Principis: Principes tales se debent exhibere ciuibus quales sibi uolunt esse deos. ⁸Ergo bene fuit figuratus per Ionatham. ⁹Unde sicut iste fuit electus in principem Iudeorum, ita et iste fuit electus in principem christianorum ad bellandum contra malos homines christianitatis bellum.

**9** ¹Tertio dico quod habuit uirtutem constantie, sciens quod constantia conseruat regnum. ²Ffuit enim uir constantissimus pro bono uirtutis et rei publice augmento, pro defensione fidei, et sancte ecclesie dilatatione et malorum hominum exterminatione. ³Nec quantum ad ista potuit frangi nec minis, nec blanditiis, nec muneribus aut promissis. ⁴Unde fuit figuratus per illum principem Egipti Yoseph de quo dicitur Ecc(li.) xlix (17): *Ioseph qui natus est homo princeps fratrum, firmamentum.* ⁵Reuera, ipse fuit firmamentum et stabilimentum totius populi principatus sui propter constantiam quam habuit. ⁶Semper enim considerauit suam fragilitatem, et quod natus erat homo, supple, fragilis et mortalis, sicut dicitur de Yoseph quod *natus est homo.*

**10** ¹Quarto dico quod habuit uirtutem iustitie, sciens quod iustitia principatum perpetuat. ²Iustitia enim est [*col. b*] perpetua et inmortalis,

---

8: 7 *De clementia*, 1. 7. 1.

8: 2 *bellum*] *om. K*    8: 3–4 dici . . . columba] dici Ionathas propter clementiam interpretatur columba *K*    8: 6 debitas] dibitas *K*    8: 7 ciuibus] *altered and unclear in K*    8: 9 et] etiam *K? (my photo unclear)*    9: 2 dilatatione] dilatione *K*    9: 4 de quo dicitur] *corr. from* de dicitur quo    9: 5 constantiam] instantiam *K*    10: 2 enim est] est *is unclear in K* et ideo inpossibile est quod principatus sit stabilis et durabilis ubi iustitia non uiget. ³Remota enim iustitia, quid sunt regna nisi quedam latrocinia, dicit Augustinus, quarto De Ciuitate Dei, quasi dicat: Nichil aliud sunt nisi latrocinia. ⁴Et bene dico quod iustitia regnum perpetuat, quia sicut dicitur Ecc(li.) decimo (8): *Regnum transfertur de gente in gentem propter iniustitias et iniurias et diuersos dolos.* ⁵Propter quod iste princeps fuit iustissimus, reddendo unicuique quod sibi debebat, scilicet deo obedientiam, sibi ipsi penitentiam, egenis beneficientiam, et peccatoribus penam. ⁶Unde fuit figuratus per illum magnum principem Mathathiam, cui dictum fuit, sicut habetur i Machab. ii (17): *Princeps clarissimus es et magnus in hac ciuitate.* ⁷Et bene per Mathathiam fuit iste figuratus, quoniam sicut ille habuit magnum zelum ad defensionem diuine legis et sue gentis et ad effugationem malorum hominum, ita et iste.

**11** ¹Sane ergo dictum est de isto: *Princeps et magnus,* quoniam habuit prudentiam ad dirigendum, clementiam ad miserendum, constantiam ad defendendum, et iustitiam ad distribuendum. ²Proch dolor, non sunt isti similes omnes alii principes, quorum multi principantur subditis non principatu pollitico uel regali, et sicut tutor ad pupillos, nam eos opprimunt, lacerant, spoliant, ymmo excoriant et iugulant. ³Quibus dicitur Michee tertio (1–2, cf. 9): *Audite, principes domus Iacob, nunquid non uestrum est scire iudicium? Qui odio habetis bonum, et diligitis malum; qui uiolenter tollitis pellem* subditorum *desuper eis, et carnem eorum* [*fo. 84ʳᵃ*] *desuper ossibus eorum?* ⁴Tales enim non sunt principes sed tyranni, non pastores, sed lupi, ymo leones et ursi, de quorum quolibet dicitur (Prov. 28: 15): *Leo rugiens et ursus esuriens princeps impius super populum pauperem.* ⁵Non sic de isto.

**12** ¹Secundo dico quod in isto uerbo tangitur illud quod in isto domino est multum lamentabile, scilicet, casus mortalitatis quem subiit, qui notatur cum dicitur *cecidit hodie.* ²Cecidit quidem per mortem, quia mortalis erat, et mors est casus ultimus mortalium. ³Et hodie cecidit quantum ad hominum innotescentiam, quia cunctis apparet quod mortuus est cum uidetur in feretra iacens. ⁴Ergo, *cecidit.*

---

**10:** 3 *De ciuitate Dei, 4. 4.*


**10:** 3 Remota] Oblata *K*  regna] *corr. from* regnat  quedam latrocinia] *K adds and deletes* aliud sunt nisi latrocinia. Et bene dico  dicat] d. *K*  **10:** 4 *de gente in gentem*] degentem *K*  **10:** 6 Mathathiam] Mathiam *K*  **10:** 7 Mathathiam] Mathiam *K*  **11:** 2 pollitico] pollicito *K*  **11:** 3 Michee tertio] Michee iiii° *K*  habetis] habebis *K*  desuper eis] desuper eos *K*  **11:** 4 enim non] non *om. K*

**13** ¹Cecidit quidem a consistentia. ²Ante enim homo, et modo non est. ³Ante erat corpus eius firmum et solidum, et nunc est quasi putridum, et omni dissolutioni proximum.

**14** ¹Cecidit etiam a potentia. ²Ante enim erat fortis uiribus corporis et potens armatorum auxilio. ³Sed nunc priuatus est omni uirtute, tam propria quam aliena. ⁴Si enim haberet bellum in alio seculo, nullus de amicis suis sequeretur eum nisi usque ad sepulchrum. ⁵Huius autem priuationis potentie et fortitudinis signum est euidens quod eius arma, scilicet ensis, scutum, et uexillum portantur non quidem erecta, sed quasi euersa et subuersa, in signum quot iam habet nullam fortitudinem contra hostes.

**15** ¹Cecidit etiam ab opulentia. ²Ipse enim quondam opulentus et plenus magnis diuitiis repente contritus est, et qui innumeris habundabat diuitiis, nunc pauperrimus, et cum solo sudario, uel cum illo amictu quem uidetis, recedet [*col. b*] a nobis. ³Unde posset dicere, et nos etiam uice ipsius, illud quod fecit dici Saladinis Soldanos Babylonie, quando corpus suum portabatur ad sepulchrum. ⁴Ordinauit enim antequam moreretur quod quando corpus eius portaretur ad tumulum unus de seruitoribus suis ferret sudarium in lancea ac clamaret sibi dicens: 'Ecce, rex orientis tantum portat secum de omnibus diuitiis suis.' ⁵Iste enim dominus qui ante mortem multis faciebat magna conuiuia multosque reficiebat pauperes, modo non posset dare alicui hominum etiam buccellam panis.

**16** ¹Cecidit etiam ab elegantia. ²Ante enim erat elegantis stature, pulcher facie, et speciosus forma, sed nunc totum inmutatum. ³Non enim est in eo species, neque decor, sed feditas et turpitudo, nec habet uxorem, nec filium, nec filiam, nec personam aliquam que libenter staret cum eo sola per unam noctem.

**17** ¹Ergo cecidit. ²Nec mirum, quia in Ps. (21: 30) dicitur quod *cadent omnes qui descendunt in terram*. ³*Cadent*, supple, per mortem. ⁴Unde omnes homines qui fuerunt, uel sunt, uel erunt, poterunt dicere coram Christo in die iudicii illud quod scribitur Ys. sexagesimo quarto (6): *quasi folium cecidimus uniuersi*, quasi dicat de isto casu mortis quomodo est generalis, quomodo est terribilis. ⁵Et specialiter casus istius uiri eminentissimi est omnibus nobis multum lamentabilis.

---

**13:** 2 enim homo] *read* enim erat homo?      **14:** 5 Huius] *or* Huiusmodi?
**15:** 1 opulentia] epulentia *K*      **15:** 2 opulentus] epulentus *K*      innumeris]
-ur *sign used for* -er *sign? (also elsewhere)* uidetis] uideris *K?*      **15:** 3 posset
dicere] *K adds* illud      Saladinis Soldanos] *sic K*      **15:** 4 antequam] antiquam
*K*      **16:** 2 speciosus] speciosos *K?*      **17:** 4 poterunt] poterant *K*      sexagesimo quarto] lxiii° *K*      quasi dicat de . . . generalis] *K has* Q (*or* O?) de isto
casu mortis quomodo est generalis      **17:** 5 specialiter] spiritualiter *K*

**18** ¹Unde possumus omnes dicere propter mortem istius domini illud quod dicit Ieremias propter mortem Iosie, et scribitur Tren. v (16): *Cecidit corona capitis nostri; ue nobis, quia peccauimus.* ²Reuera, peccatis nostris inputari potest quod sic ceciderit per mortem *corona capitis* [*fo. 84^{va}*] *nostri,* id est, istius domini nostri, qui erat capud nostrum. ³Et reuera, quod in ipso nunc uidemus, et debemus dicere cunctis regibus et reginis, ut humilientur et a male agendo quiescant. ⁴Dicitur enim sic cuilibet nostrum, Iere. decimo tertio (18): *Dic regi et dominatrici: Humiliamini, et sedete,* id est, a malis operibus quiescite, *quoniam de capite uestro descendet corona glorie uestre* sicut iam descendet de capite nostro.

**19** ¹Omnes etiam nobiles huius regni uel huius principatus debent et debebunt ullulare cum audiunt et audient casum istius domini nostri. ²Cuilibet enim eorum dicitur per figuram Zacharie xi (2): *Ullula, abies, quoniam cecidit cedrus.* ³Omnes enim alii nobiles se habebunt ad istum dominum sicut se habent abietes ad cedrum. ⁴Magis enim excedebat eos in altitudine quam abietes excedunt cedrum. ⁵Et non solum potest dici quot *cedrus cecidit* propter casum istius domini, uerum etiam quot *stella magna cecidit* cuius *nomen* nunc est *absinthyium,* quia casus eius est nobis amarius quam absinthium, sicud hec dicuntur per figuram Apoc. viii (10–11).

**20** ¹Uerum unum est pro uobis consolabile, quod tertio in hiis uerbis innuitur, cum subditur quod *cecidit in Israel,* ubi notabatur superius locus securitatis in quo obiit. ²Per Israel enim, quod interpretatur 'uidens deum', designatur ipsa sancta ecclesia, que quamdiu est in hoc mundo peregrinans uidet deum per fidem, et tum, facta triumphans, uidebit per speciem (cf. 2 Cor. 5: 7). ³In isto autem Israel, id est in fide et unitate ac sacramentis ecclesie, iste magnus uir obiit. ⁴Ergo in statu et in loco magne securitatis existens mi|grauit [*col. b*] ab hac uita. ⁵Consolari ergo debemus contra dolorem quem de morte sua concepimus, quia securus de habendo uitam glorie recessit ab hoc mundo. ⁶Securus dico securitate fidei et spei. ⁷*Cecidit enim in Israel,* id est, in ecclesia, hoc est *tanquam* unus de fidelibus qui sunt de numero et merito eius. ⁸Quibus dicitur, Deut. trigesimo tertio (29): *Beatus es tu, Israel: quis similis tui, popule, qui saluaris in Domino?* ⁹—Quasi dicat: Non est alius populus similis tibi qui saluetur in Domino sicut tu saluaris. ¹⁰Propter quod, quia iste dominus *cecidit in Israel,* firmiter tenere debemus quod iam sit *saluatus in Domino* secundum animam, et hoc uel in re, uel in firma spe.

**21** ¹Quia igitur non est nobis certum quod eius anima iam deo fruatur realiter, nec est de communi lege quod anime fidelium statim post mortem euolent ad patriam, quamuis etiam in penis existentes habeant de hoc securitatem plenam, idcirco nos in uita superstites debemus ipsum iuuare elemosinis, orationibus, et missarum suffragiis, ut citius eruatur a supliciis et ad eternam beatitudinem admittatur. [2]Nos, dico, debemus ipsum iuuare, quoniam sicut ipse cecidit, et nos cademus. [3]Nobis enim dicitur in Ps. (81: 7): *Uos sicut homines moriemini, et sicut unus de principibus cadetis.* [4]Sicud unus, dico, id est, sicut iste magnus princcps cecidit. [5]Et fidenter ipsum iuuare possumus, quoniam *cecidit* per mortem *in Israel.* [6]Propter quod debemus credere quod iam Dominus suscepit eum: suscepit, dico, uel ad rem beatitudinis uel ad securitatem spei. [7]Unde ipse potest dicere illud Ps. (117: 13): *Inpulsus, euersus sum, ut caderem, et Dominus suscepit me.* [*fo. 85$^{ra}$*] [8]Quod sibi et nobis concedat, qui cum patre et spiritu sancto uiuit et regnat deus, Amen.

21: 5 iuuare] iuuate *K?*     21: 7 *suscepit me*] *repeated at start of new page in* K

# Transcription B:d

Bertrand de la Tour, Schneyer, *Repertorium*, i. 582, No. 1120;
MS Seville, Biblioteca Capitular Columbina 82-4-1 (unfoliated)

*Introduction*

Two manuscripts have been collated: Kremsmünster 44 (= K), fos.
115$^{vb}$–117$^{va}$ (foliation at centre, *not* right hand, of top margin), and
Seville Cathedral, Biblioteca Capitular Columbina 82-4-1 (= S), unfoliated. (I failed to find the sermon in the manuscripts used for
Transcriptions B:a and B:b.) S emerged from the comparison as distinctly superior, so it has been used for the transcription, but as
before, its readings are relegated to the apparatus when I judge a
reading from K (or conjecture) to be better.

**1** [1]Sermo *lxv de mortuis, qui potest fieri in exequiis cuiuslibet
christiani regis.

[2]*Rex est hodie, et cras morietur*, Ecci. x (12). [3]Uidemus quod quando
aliquis rex promulgat legem aliquam, quam wlt per omnes homines
regni sui exequtioni debite demandare, ut omnes, maxime simplices,
uelint illam legem cum pascientia sustinere, ostendit ipse quod per
maiores personas et notabiliores regni illa lex est cum pascientia
tolerata. [4]Modo autem sic est quod propter peccatum primi hominis
deus legem tulit omnem hominem obligantem, uidelicet legem mortis.
[5]*Ista enim lex Adam*, sicut dicitur ii R(eg.) vii (19), id est lex inposita
omni homini propter peccatum Adam. [6]*Omnes* enim *morimur*, dixit illa
ii R(eg.) decimo quarto (14). [7]Et Ap|postolus [*second col.*] dicit ad
Hebreos ix (27) quod *statutum est hominibus semel mori*. [8]Et quia forte
simplices et pauperes possent credere quod ipsos solos lex ista
obligaret, et ipsi soli deberent mori, ostendit ipse Dominus quod ymo
maiores et notabiliores humani generis sunt mortui ta*m*quam ad istam
legem obligati.

**2** [1]De Habraham enim et aliis patriarchis scriptum est quod quamuis
diu uixerint, tamen tandem fuerunt mortui. [2]Et idem dico de omnibus
prophetis. [3]Nam et prophete mortui sunt, Io. octauo (52). [4]Idem etiam
dicendum de omnibus regibus Iuda et Israel. [5]Et, quod *in euidenti

---

1: 3 regni illa] K: regni quod illa S    1: 5 vii] xiiii S, *which adds by anticipation (and deletes?):* Et Apostolus dicit, ad Hebreos nono, quod statutum est
hominibus semel mori    1: 6 dixit illa] KS: *read* illud?

est, iste rex, quondam nobilissimus dominus talis uel talis talis uel talis regni heri uel ante heri uiuebat et agebat in humanis, set nunc mortuus est sicut patet. ⁶Unde tunc poterat dici: *Rex est hodie*, id est, dominus talis uiuit et regnat et omnes homines istius regni sunt suo dominio subditi, unde hodie rex est, set, pro dolor, cras morietur. ⁷Quod iam uerificatum est, quia iam mortuus est rex iste.

**3** ¹Et notandum quod in *hoc uerbo breuiter sapiens tangit tria, uidelicet:

> primo sui status dignitatem
> secundo sui et nostri cursus breuitatem
> tertio sui casus grauitatem.

²Primum *notatur cum dicitur *Rex*. ³Secundum *cum additur *hodie est*—et innuitur quod usque cras. ⁴Tertium cum *subditur *morietur*.— ⁵Certe huius regis statu nichil est altius, quia *Rex*; huius uite cursu nichil breuius, quia *hodie*; et dire mortis ictu nichil est grauius, quia *morietur*, id est, deficiet ictu mortis.

**4** ¹Tangitur ergo primo huius regis status dignitas. ²Certe in mundanis *nichil sublimius dignitate regis, quam dignitatem quatuor [*third col.*] magnificant que fuerunt in isto eminenter, uidelicet.

**5** ¹clara prudentia ad recte discernendum. ²Certe de isto *uidetur fuisse dictum illud Ieremie uigesimo tertio (5), *regnabit rex et sapiens erit*, etc. ³Et bene regnabit rex sapiens, faciendo iudicium et iustitiam in terra sua ac per hoc stabiliendo populum suum, quia ut dicitur Sap. vi (26), *rex sapiens stabilimentum populi est*. ⁴Et per oppositum dicitur, Ecci. x (3): *rex insipiens perdet populum suum*. ⁵Et uere, *melior est pauper et sapiens rege sene et stulto*, Ecces. quarto (13).

**6** ¹Secundo magnificat dignitatem regis firma potentia ad exequendum. ²Non enim sufficeret prudentia nisi etiam concurreret exequens potentia discipans omne malum. ³Dicitur enim Prouer. xx (8) quod *rex qui sedet in solio iudicii uultu suo uel intuitu suo discipat omne malum*. ⁴Et infra, eodem (20: 26) dicitur: *rex sapiens discipat impios*. ⁵Et uere iste rex noster fuit potens, scilicet ad discipandum omne malum in terra sua, semper tamen cum clementia. ⁶Sciebat illud Prouer. xx (28): *Misericordia et ueritas custodiunt regem, et clementia roboratur tronus eius*. ⁷Uerumptamen propter clementiam non dimittebat iustitiam, sciens illud quod scriptum est, Prouerbiorum xxv (5): *Aufer impietatem de uultu regis, et iustitia firmabitur tronus eius.*

---

**3:** 1 breuiter sapiens tangit tria] *K*: tanguntur a sapiente breuiter tria *S* **5:** 1 recte discernendum] *K*: directe cernendum *S* **6:** 2 malum] *a passage is added by an error of anticipation, and apparently deleted, in S* **6:** 7 xxv] xxx *KS*

**7** ¹Tertio magnificat dignitatem regis familia prompta ad seruiendum et hobediendum, unde dicitur Prouer. xiiii (28) [*fourth col.*] quod *in multitudine populi dignitas regis et in paucitate plebis ignominia principis.* ²Iste rex noster habuit magnam multitudinem populi, et multitudinem sibi hobedientissimam, quia uidebant in eo esse sapientiam dei ad faciendum iudicium, sicut dictum fuit de Salomone, iii R(eg.) iii (28).

**8** ¹Quarto magnificat regis dignitatem prosapia digna et sancta. ²In filiis enim et filiabus bene ordinatis apparet sapientia patris. ³Et certe iste rex noster habuit et habet multos filios, qui non sunt degeneres a sua probitate. ⁴Unde potest dici de filiis istius domini illud quod fuit dictum de filiis Dauit regis, sicut habetur ii R(eg.) octauo (18), quod omnes *filii Dauid erant sacerdotes.* ⁵Non quidem sacerdotes a sacrando, sed sacerdotes dicebantur quia uiuebant et se regebant sicut sacerdotes. ⁶Reuera, sic est de filiis istius domini, et idem de filiabus. ⁷Unde de ipsis potest dici illud Ps. (44: 9–10): *Delectauerunt te*, Iesu Christe, *filie regum*, id est, filie huius regis, que tam ex parte patris quam ex parte matris ex multis regibus descenderunt.

**9** ¹Secundo tangitur cursus uite nostre breuitas, cum additur *hodie*, et innuitur quod usque *cras.* ²*Reuera, breuior est uita nostra etiam posito quod uiueret quilibet nostrum per centum annos, respectu futuri temporis, quam sit spatium unius diei usque ad diem sequentem, respectu eiusdem, scilicet futuri temporis, *quod numquam cessabit. ³Satis ergo congrue innuit breuitatem uite hominis per hoc aduerbium, scilicet 'hodie'. ⁴Rex, inquid, *est hodie.* ⁵Unde uita et regimen huius regis nostri multum uidentur fuisse breuia, cum non uidentur durasse *ultra unam diem et noctem usque ad mane *diei sequentis. ⁶Unde quando uiuebat et [*fifth col.*] regebat poterat dici: *Rex est hodie*, et post istud hodie non erit, quia morietur. ⁷*Homo enim uanitati similis factus est; dies eius sicut umbra pretereunt*, dicitur in Ps. (143: 4). ⁸Et, Iob decimo quarto, dicit ille quod *homo breui uiuens tempore repletur multis miseriis et fugit uelud umbra.* ⁹Et certe, non diutius uiuunt reges et principes quam homines ceteri, ymo *aliquando citius moriuntur. ¹⁰*Omnis enim potentatus breuis uita*, dicit sapiens, Ecci. decimo (11). ¹¹*Ergo Rex est hodie* poterat dici dum uiuebat, sed nunc, cum mortuus est, potest dicere omni uiuenti illud Ecci. tricesimo octauo (23): *Memento iudicii mei*, id est, iudicii mortis, quod iam subii, *sic enim erit et tuum*, id est, ita morieris sicut *ego* mortuus sum; *michi* enim *est *heri*, supple, erat 'hodie' quod iam transiuit, *et tibi* est,

---

**7:** 1 dicitur] *K:* dicit *S?*      **8:** 7 huius] *K:* hominis *S (influenced by 'Son of Man'?)*      **9:** 2 etiam] *K:* quem *S?*   usque] *K: om. S*   *quod numquam] translate* quod *as 'because'? Or is the sentence corrupt?*

supple nunc, *hodie*. ¹²Ergo, cum habes tuum 'hodie', memor esto mortis, quia post tuum 'hodie' morieris, et dices *'michi heri*, sicut iam transiuit meum "hodie", propter quod dico *"michi heri".'* ¹³Mortui ergo possunt dicere 'heri', supple, fuit uita mea, 'et tunc erat meum "hodie", se*d* nunc est meum heri'. ¹⁴Sed uiuentes possunt dicere 'hodie', quod, supple, cito transibit, quia cras; et tunc poterunt dicere 'heri', supple, uita nostra erat.

**10** ¹Sic est, dico, de hominibus puris. ²Se*d* de Christo Domino, qui simul est deus et homo, dicit Appostolus ad Hebre. decimo tertio (8): *Iesus Christus heri et hodie: ipse et in secula*, id est, sua duratio, que est eternitas secundum deitatem, omnem differentiam te*m*poris ambit. ³Se*d* de aliis hominibus dicitur, Ys. xl (6), quod *omnis caro fenum, et omnis gloria eius quasi flos feni*. ⁴De feno autem dicitur Mt. vi (30); *fenum quod est hodie et cras in clibanum mittitur*. ⁵Uere sic est de homine sicu*t* [*sixth col.*] de feno. ⁶'Sicut fenum' propter breuitatem sue durationis dicitur, quod hodie uiuens est et quasi per unum diem extenditur uita eius, et cras mittitur in clibanum, id est, in sepulcrum, quod proprie dicitur clibanus—sicut enim in clibano ligna incinerantur, sic et ossa hominum in sepulcro incinerantur.

**11** ¹Breuis igitur fuit uita regis nostri. ²Durauit enim quasi per unam diem, sic uidetur nobis, ita breuis fuit; que iam terminata est. ³Iam enim transiuit suum 'hodie'. ⁴Placeat Christo, cuius 'hodie' se*m*per est, quod dicat anime istius nostri regis illud quod dixit latroni iuxta ipsum pendenti: *Amen, dico tibi, hodie mecum eris in paradizo*, Luc. xxiii (43).

**12** ¹Tertio tangitur casus istius regis crudelitas, cum dicitur *morietur*. ²Mors enim dicitur a mordendo, quia crudeliter mordet, quia nulli parcit. ³Et mordendo, quasi omnia aufert.

**13** ¹Aufert enim actum subsistendi, modum cognoscendi, uerbum confitendi, et statum promerendi. ²Aufert, dico, actum subsistendi. ³Ante, enim, *erat homo et persona in se subsistens. ⁴Modo autem nec est homo nec est persona. ⁵Etiam anima sua uel corpus suum non est homo uel persona. ⁶*Homo enim *mortuus nudatus*, supple uita, *et consumptus*, supple uermibus, *ubi queso est?* (Job 14: 10) ⁷Quasi dicat, nusquam est secundum se totum, quia non est secundum se totum quamuis sit secundum partes. ⁸Quod autem non est, non habet 'ubi' in quo sit. ⁹Durus est ergo morsus mortis, quia aufert humanitatem et subsistentiam personalem.

---

9: 14 poterunt] *K*: potuerunt *S?*     10: 4 Mt.] *K*: Mr. *S*     13: 1 promerendi] *S adds in error (anticipation)*: Modo autem nec est homo nec est persona. Etiam anima sua uel corpus non est homo uel persona     13: 6 uermibus] uiribus *S*     13: 7 nusquam] *K*: nu*m*quid *S*     13: 8 Quod] *corr. from* Quamuis *in S?*

**14** ¹Aufert etiam modum cognoscendi. ²Ante enim cognoscebat iste dominus per [*seventh col.*] intellectum, se*d* etiam per sensum. ³Periit enim nunc in ipso cognitio sensitiua, a qua tamen in uita ista habet ortum intellectiua. ⁴Propterea etiam secundum intellectum alio modo intelligit anima separata a corpore quam intelligat ei coniuncta. ⁵Propter quod dixi quod mors aufert modum cognoscendi. ⁶Dicitur enim Ecces. nono (5) quod *mortui nichil nouerunt*, supple, secundum sensum. ⁷Propter quod dicitur Prouer. [*recte* Eccli.] uicesimo secundo (10): *Supra mortuum plora, defecit enim lux eius*—lux, quidem, uite presentis, que percipitur per sensum. ⁸Uel *nichil nouerunt* intellectualiter secundum illum modum secundum quem intelligebant ante.

**15** ¹Aufert etiam uerbum confitendi. ²Anima enim separata confiteri non potest, supple uocaliter, nec sua crimina, nec etiam diuinam sublimitatem, quia non habet instrumenta quibus possit formare uocem. ³Idcirco dicitur in Ps. (113: 17–18): *Non mortui laudabunt te, Domine*—supple, uocaliter; uel *non laudabunt te* ad meritum;—*Sed nos qui uiuimus benedicimus Domino*.

**16** ¹Aufert etiam statum merendi. ²Ante enim erat anima sua in statu merendi. ³Per bona enim que faciebat in corpore poterat mereri uitam eternam. ⁴Nunc autem exiuit totaliter statum meriti, unde ac si nichil esset non potest aliquid ad meritum operari. ⁵Unde dicitur cuilibet nostrum, Ecci. xvii (26): *ante mortem confitere; a mortuo enim quasi nichil perit confessio*—id est, confessio est sibi omnino infructuosa ex quo mortuus est, quasi ipse nichil esset; uel: confessio ab eo perit quasi nichil, id est nullius ualoris. ⁶Et quod dicit de confessione, idem intelligendum est de omnibus aliis, que scilicet anima potest facere extra corpus, quod, supple, per ea mereri non potest. ⁷Transiuit enim tempus merendi [*eighth col.*] et uenit tempus mercedem accipiendi; transiuit tempus laborandi, et uenit tempus quiescendi. ⁸Unde Appoci. decimo quarto (13) *Amodo iam dicit spiritus ut requiescant a laboribus suis.* ⁹Sic igitur patet quod grauissimus est morsus *mortis, qui abstulit ab isto nostro ⸱ rege actum subsistendi, modum cognoscendi, uerbum confitendi, et statum promerendi.

**17** ¹Igitur si anima ipsius sit in penis, iuuemus eam orationibus et helemosinis et aliis suffragiis, ut deus cito eruat eam a suppliciis et introducat eam in uitam eternam. ²Oremus etiam pro successore istius regis ipsius filio, ut deus det sibi ipsius regnum regere bene, et det sibi multos annos et longam uitam. ³Unde faciamus nos sicut dicebatur

14: 2 dominus] S *adds* uobiscum *or* nobiscum *(K omits this and context)*
14: 3 Periit enim] Periit etiam S: Periit autem K     14: 4 Propterea] K:
preterea S?     14: 6 Ecces.] Ecci. S     14: 7 Prouer.] *sic* KS     per *om.*
KS     15: 2 formare] *corr. from* informare     16: 3 Per bona] K *(or* Pro
bona?)*: Persona S     17: 1 eam . . . eam . . . eam] K: eam . . . eum . . . eam S
in uitam] K: ad uitam S

illis primi Esdre sexto (10): *offerant oblationes deo celi et orent pro uita regis*, supple huius qui mortuus est, pro uita dico eterna, et pro uita *filiorum eius*, supple, temporali. [4]Nobis enim dicitur illud Baruch i (11): *orate pro uita regis*, supple, eterna, *et pro uita filii eius*, supple, temporali. [5]Sic igitur iuuemus animam istius regis nostri suffragiis, ut cito eripiatur a suppliciis, et assequatur uitam eternam. [6]Quam sibi et nobis concedat, etc., Amen.

---

**17:** 3 Esdre sexto] Esdre primo *KS*     **17:** 5 nostri] *K*: nostris *S (either reading is acceptable, but corruption from -ri to -ris is easier to explain—by influence of contiguous words)*     **17:** 6 concedat] *K*: consedat *S*

# Transcription C:a

MS Rome, Angelica 158, fos. 156$^{vb}$–157$^{rb}$

**1** ¹Collatio ad clerum in morte regis.

²*Regnauit Alexander annis xii et mortuus est.* ³Propositum uerbum, quod scribitur primo Machabeorum capitulo primo (8) quamuis dictum fuerit in persona magni Alexandri regis Grecorum possumus tamen conuenienter ipsum assumere ad propositum nostrum ut sit dictum in persona illustrissimi domini Odouardi regis Anglorum, quia uere si facta et opera istius redigerentur in scriptis sicut facta et opera illius in libris registrata fuerunt non minus i*m*mo forte magis laudabilia apparent et magnifica opera eius quam opera et facta illius.

**2** ¹Et possumus dicere quod conditio istius illustrissimi regis in uerbo assumpto dupliciter nobis notificatur et manifestatur. ²Primo quantum ad eius regiminis singularem excellentiam, cum dicitur in persona eius: *Regnauit Alexander annis xii.* ³Secundo quantum ad eius finis terminatiuam sententiam, cum additur: *et mortuus est.*

**3** ¹Primo igitur nobis notificatur et manifestatur conditio istius illustrissimi regis quantum ad eius regiminis singularem excellentiam, cum dicitur in persona eius: *regnauit Alexander annis xii.* ²Nam si Alexander magnus rex Grecorum regnauit in iustitie equitate, in debellandi aduersarios potestate, et in animi industria et sagacitate, sicut libri scripti de ipso manifestant, merito possumus dicere quod iste illustrissimus et sanctissimus rex regnauit ut Alexander quantum ad ista tria. ³Nam primo ipse regnauit non in tirannica prauitate, sed in mera iustitie equitate, omnibus subiectis suis magnis et paruis iustitiam faciendo, et uolentes tirannizare et iniuste agere grauiter feriendo et puniendo. ⁴Unde merito in persona eius possumus exponere illud uerbum Psalmi (44: 8): *Dilexisti iustitiam et odisti iniquitatem, propterea unxit te deus, deus* [*fo. 157*$^{ra}$] *tuus oleo letitie pre consortibus tuis.* ⁵Nam quia ipse dilexit iustitiam non qualemcu*m*que sed iustitiam legalem, que est omnis uirtus et omnis iustitia, et odiuit iniquitatem non qualemcu*m*que, sed talem iniquitatem odiuit que est omne uitium et omnis iniustitia, quia *omne peccatum est iniquitas,* ut dicit Iohannes in

---

**2:** 3 Secundo] *a correction*   cum] *supplied in margin*   **3:** 5 quia *omne*] omne *supplied in margin* omne peccatum est iniquitas] *Clementine Vulgate reads:* omnis qui facit peccatum, et iniquitatem facit, et peccatum est iniquitas

sua canonica (1 Io. 3: 4; cf. 5: 17), ideo deus unxit eum in regem istius populi oleo letitie, id est gratia spiritus sancti, *pre* omnibus *consortibus* suis, id est pre omnibus aliis regibus. [6]Quia uere temporibus nostris nullius regis regnum fuit firmatum et roboratum tanta iustitia et tanta clementia sicut regnum istud per bonum regimen istius sanctissimi regis. [7]Unde signanter in persona eius potest esse dictum illud uerbum Prouerbiorum xx (28): *Misericordia et iustitia custodiunt regem, et roborabitur clementia thronus eius.*

**4** [1]Secundo ipse regnauit in debellandi aduersarios potestate. [2]Nam ipse inimicos Christi et sancte matris ecclesie debellauit et expugnauit, mortis etiam periculo se et gentem suam pro expugnatione eorum exponendo. [3]Unde si de Alexandro scriptum est, Machabeorum primo (1: 2–3), quod ipse *interfecit reges* gentium *et pertransiuit usque ad fines terre et accepit spolia multitudinis gentium et siluit terra in conspectu eius,* multo fortius dici potest de isto illustrissimo rege, quod ipse pertransiuit fines terre, quia partes ultramarinas et partes orientales perlustrauit ad debellandum inimicos Christi et sancte matris ecclesie. [4]Omnes etiam uolentes perturbare populum suum atque rem publicam ipse conatus est debellare et expugnare. [5]Unde uere de eo exponi potest quod scribitur primo Machab. capitulo iii (4–5): *Similis factus est leoni in operibus suis, et sicut catulus leonis rugiens in uenatione sua.* [6]*Persecutus est iniquos et qui conturbabant populum suum succendit flammis.*

**5** [1]Tertio ipse regnauit in animi industria et sagacitate. [2]Nam ipse regnauit non in leuitate animi nec in persuasione adulatorum et malorum consiliariorum sicut multi reges faciunt hodie, sed in sui animi industria et sapientia et bonorum et sapientum uirorum consilio et prudentia. [3]Unde uere sibi potest intelligi fuisse dictum illud quod dictum fuit Salomoni iii Regum iii° (12): *Ecce, dedi tibi cor sapiens et intelligens* ad regendum populum tuum, *in tantum ut nullus ante te similis tui fuerit, nec post te secutus sit.* Regnauit ergo iste illustrissimus et sanctissimus rex ut Alexander in iustitie equitate, et in debellandi aduersarios potestate, et in animi industria et sagacitate. Propter quod signanter nobis manifestata est conditio eius quantum ad eius regiminis singularem excellentiam, cum dicitur in persona eius primo: *regnauit Alexander annis xii.*

**6** [1]Secundo notificatur nobis conditio eius quantum ad eius finis terminatiuam sententiam, cum additur: *et mortuus est.* [2]Et possumus dicere quod iste sanctissimus et illustrissimus rex mortuus est et non est mortuus. [3]Nam mortuus est humane nature conditione. [4]Nam cum ipse contraxerit originem ex propagine primorum parentum,

---

3: 6 nostris] *or* meis      3: 7 *iustitia*] ueritas *in Clementine Vulgate, but cf.*
Prov. 25: 5

quibus dictum est, Gen. tertio (3) *Quacumque* hora *comederitis de ligno boni et mali, morte moriemini,* oportet quod ipse et quilibet alius homo sententiam datam de illis incurrat, ut sicut quilibet est particeps culpe et preuaricationis illorum, sic quilibet sit particeps pene. ⁵Unde Ecclesiastici viii (8) [*col. b*] scribitur quod: *omnes morimur et in gaudium eternum uolumus peruenire.*

**7** ¹Sed possumus dicere quod ipse non est mortuus, bone hereditatis dimissione, quia nobis dimisit bonos heredes de semine suo et bonum primogenitum qui loco eius super istud regnum regnare debet, quem dominus Iesus Christus oleo sue gratie ungere dignetur ut sui patris uestigia sequi ualeat in iustitie equitate, in debellandi aduersarios potestate, et in animi industria et sagacitate; ut de ipso possimus dicere illud quod scribitur Ecclesiastici xxx (4): *mortuus est et quasi non est mortuus pater eius; similem enim sibi reliquit nobis in terra.*

**8** ¹Similiter dicere possumus quod non est mortuus uite eterne participatione, quia licet mortuus sit uita ista animali et corporali, firmiter tamen credere debemus quod uiuat cum Christo uita spirituali et eternali. Quam sibi et nobis concedat Christus, qui cum patre etc.

6: 4. Cf. Gen. 2: 17.

6: 5 *omnes . . . peruenire*] *Clementine Vulgate has* omnes morimur, et in gaudium nolumus venire

# Transcription C:b

**1** ¹Collatio in morte cuiuscunque clerici uel laici.

²*Inclinauit* se *ex hoc in hoc, verumtamen fex eius non est exinanita; bibent ex ea omnes peccatores terre* (Ps. 74: 9). ³In uerbo isto proposito, karissimi, de Psalmo assumpto, notificatur nobis breuiter qualis esse debet diuini verbi predicatoris operatio; secundo, qualis sit humane nature conditio. ⁴Propter primum est sciendum quod predicator debet esse humilis in conuersando, et debet esse seuerus in corrigendo. ⁵Predicatoris humilitas habetur cum dicitur: *Inclinauit* se *ex hoc in hoc.* ⁶Nam non debet predicator semper stare tensus per sue scientie inflationem, sed debet se inclinare, et condescendere debet infirmitati auditorum per mentis humiliationem. ⁷Unde in persona predicatoris sic se inclinantis per humilitatem scribitur in Ps. (17: 10): *Inclinavit* se *et descendit; et caligo sub pedibus eius.* ⁸Sed predicatoris seueritas notatur cum additur: *uerumtamen fex eius non est exinanita; bibent ex ea omnes peccatores terre.* ⁹Nam debet predicator arguere et obsecrare et increpare, seueritatem diuini iudicii annuntiando peccatoribus, quia fecem dei, id est, penam eterni iudicii, debet predicare numquam exinaniri et numquam terminari, sed perpetualiter bibiturum esse a peccatoribus. ¹⁰In principio igitur nostre collationis rogemus deum etc.

**2** ¹*Inclinauit* se *ex hoc in hoc, uerumtamen fex eius non est exinanita; bibent ex ea omnes peccatores terre.* ²Sicut dicebatur, in isto eodem uerbo potest nobis manifestari qualis sit humane nature conditio, et possumus dicere quod conditio humane nature dupliciter nobis exprimitur in uerbo proposito: primo quantum ad eius mutabilitatem cum premittitur primo: *Inclinauit* se *ex hoc in hoc*; secundo quantum ad mortis ineuitabilitatem, cum additur: *uerumtamen fex eius non est exinanita; bibent ex ea omnes peccatores terre.* ³Propter primum est intelligendum quod humana natura a primordio sue creationis habuit quod esset uariabilis et mutabilis, *ex hoc in hoc,* id est ex sanitate in infirmitatem, ex gaudio in tristitiam, ex uita in mortem, quia sicut ipsa ex nichilo producta fuit secundum animam, et ex re muta|bili [*fo. 157ᵛᵃ*] secundum corpus, quia ex limo terre, ita quantum est de se natura

---

humana in nichilum et corruptionem tendebat. ⁴Unde Damascenus
primo libro capitulo iiii dicit quod omnis creatura quantum est de se,
mutabilitati subiecta est, et que a uersione inceperunt hec uersioni
subiecta sunt. ⁵Fuit tamen hoc donum per gratiam tributum humane
nature, quod si uolebat stare in obedientia dei a quo producta erat,
poterat se ab ista mutabilitate preseruare, quia ipsa existente in ista
obedientia non cogebatur inclinari ex hoc in hoc, id est, ex bono in
malum, ex sanitate in infirmitatem, uel ex uita in mortem, eo quod
poterat non mori, non infirmari, et non tristari, obseruando mandatum
sibi a deo factum. ⁶Sed statim cum preceptum contempsit, et pre-
dictum donum gratuitum perdidit, humana natura quasi sibi ipsi
relicta ex sua conditione coacta fuit mutari ex hoc in hoc, quia statim
de letitia transiuit in tristitiam, de sanitate in infirmitatem, et de uita in
mortem, et *immediate* tot mutationibus et questionibus se supposuit
ut fere quis stare non possit per unam horam in aliqua letitia quin
superueniat sibi aliquid secundum animam uel secundum corpus quod
sibi displicet. ⁷Unde dicitur Ecclesiastes vii (30) quod *deus fecit hominem
rectum et ipse se infinitis immiscuit questionibus.* ⁸Per hoc ergo quod
dicitur: *Inclinauit se ex hoc in hoc,* habetur humane nature mutabilitas,
sed per hoc quod subditur: *uerumtamen fex eius non est exinanita; bibent
ex ea omnes peccatores terre,* habetur mortis ineuitabilitas. ⁹Nam
peccante Adam omnes facti sumus peccatores, et quia illi peccato
debebatur mors, que fecis nomine nuncupatur, eo quod in fecem
et cinerem facit humana corpora resolui, ideo *fex* uel mors *non est
exinanita,* sed ineuitabiliter oportet omnes peccatores terre hanc mortem persoluere et hanc fecem bibere. ¹⁰Et si dicatur quod Christus
satisfecit pro illo peccato per suam passionem, dicemus quod illi
peccato debebatur duplex pena, una eternalis, scilicet carentia uisionis
diuine, et alia corporalis, sicut mors, infirmitas et alie penalitates que
sequntur corpus. ¹¹Christus ergo bene liberauit nos a prima pena,
quia uisio diuine essentie per eius passionem nobis est restituta qua
prius eramus priuati—unde statim cum sumus baptizati et *membra*
eius facti, *immediate* nobis debentur diuina beatitudo et diuina uisio,
nisi aliud obstet, puta peccatum actuale per nos perpetratum—sed a
morte corporali et ab aliis penalitatibus corporalibus Christus non

2: 4. Just conceivably the following passage: '"quod ex elementis est compositum, et in ipsa rursus resoluitur? Compositio enim principium est pugnae,
pugna distantiae, distantia uero solutionis; solutio uero aliena est a Deo
omnino"' (Saint John Damascene, *De fide orthodoxa*, versions of Burgundio and
Cerbanus, 'Burgundionis Versio', 4. 1, ed. E. M. Buytaert (Franciscan Institute
Publications, Text Series 8; St Bonaventure, NY, etc., 1955), 19).

2: 6 non] *deleted in ms?*

liberauit nos, *im*mo sicut ipse prius ipsam mortem persoluit et ipsam fecem debitam pro peccato bibit, cum tamen ipse non esset peccator et per consequens nec debitor mortis, sic oportet omnes nos peccatores hanc fecem bibere, et merito, quia *non est exinanita*, id est, non est destructa uel adnichilata, eo quod per passionem Christi, ut predictum est, a morte corporali et penalitatibus corporis liberati non sumus. [12]Unde Apostolus ad Phil. ii (7–8) dicit quod Christus *exinaniuit semetipsum*, id est mino|rauit [*col. b*] seipsum uel seipsum adnichilauit ex eo quod factus fuit *obediens usque ad mortem*. [13]Nam antequam dei filius incarnaretur et antequam fecem passionis biberet non erat exinanitus uel annichilatus aut minoratus, quia nequaquam erat minor, sed cum mortuus fuit et fecem passionis bibit, tunc est quasi exinanitus, id est minoratus, quia non solum patre sed etiam seipso minor factus est. [14]Fex ergo Domini, id est mors, quam debet persoluere totum humanum genus, non est exinanita uel destructa, sed omnes peccatores terre, id est omnes inuolutos peccato primorum parentum, oportet ipsam bibere, sicut mortem ipsam oportet omnes persoluere.

**3** [1]Exponendo igitur uerbum propositum in presenti ad nostrum propositum, dicere possumus quod iste illustrissimus rex dominus Odouardus hanc duplicem humane nature conditionem in se habuit. [2]Nam primo ipse habuit humane nature mutabilitatem et uariabilitatem, quia *inclinauit* se *ex hoc in hoc*. [3]Inter omnes enim reges et principes qui fuerunt temporibus nostris qui plura uoluerint scire de mutationibus et uariationibus mundi, ipse fuit unus, eo quod ipse nu*m*quam sciuit quiescere, obseruans illud quod scribitur Ecclesiastes ix (10): *Quodcum*que *potest manus tua facere instanter operare*. [4]Nam *inclinauit* se *ex hoc in hoc* ex Anglia transeundo in Yspaniam, militiam ibi honorifice recipiendo, quandoque uero partes ultramarinas perlustrando, inimicos Christi ibi potenter debellando, quandoque etiam in Walliam, quandoque in Flandriam, quandoque in Scotiam, quandoque in Uasconiam, ipse cum gente sua proficiscendo, regnum suum amplificando et augmentando. [5]*Inclinauit* se similiter *ex hoc in hoc*, id est ex magnifico statu in paruum, quia nunc rex, nunc miles, nunc domicellus; nunc diues, nunc pauper; nunc iudex potentes deponens, nunc aduocatus pauperes liberans in suis operibus uideri uoluit. [6]Unde uere ipse dicere potuit illud quod dixit Salomon, Ecclesiastes primo (12–13, 17): *Ego Ecclesiastes fui rex in Israel, et proposui in corde meo querere et inuestigare sapienter de omnibus que fiunt sub sole, et congnoui quod in hiis esset labor et afflictio spiritus*. [7]Habuit ergo iste illustrissimus rex humane nature mutabilitatem, quia *inclinauit* se *ex hoc in hoc*.

**4** [1]Secundo, completo termino uite sue habuit mortis ineuitabili-

tatem, quia fecem illam quam nos omnes peccatores oportet bibere
ipse iam bibit. [2]Unde de ipso dici potest quod scribitur Sapientie iiii
(13–14): *Consummatus in breui expleuit tempora multa.* [3]*Placita enim erat
deo anima illius.* [4]Nam licet ipse in breui compleuerit uitam suam,
quia (Iob 14: 5): *Breues dies hominis sunt, et numerus mensium eius apud
deum est,* tamen multa tempora transiuit, id est, multas et uarias
conditiones in temporalibus uidit, et omnes dei gratia cum honore
transiuit, quantum ad corpus, et cum mercede, quantum ad animam,
quia suus transitus per ista temporalia semper fuit cum fidei defensione, cum pauperum subleuatione, cum superborum depressione et
humilium promotione. [5]Et quia per ista placita erat deo anima eius,
ideo deus altissimus properauit illam educere de medio iniquitatum et
remunerare ipsam eterno premio, quod sibi et nobis concedat Christus,
qui est benedictus in secula, Amen.

**4:** 4 *deum*] *corrected in margin from* te

# Transcription C:c

**1** ¹Collatio ad clerum de morte regis.

²*In uirtute tua, Domine, letabitur rex, et super salutare tuum exultabit uehementer* (Ps. 20: 2). ³Karissimi, diuini uerbi predicatio siue pro uiuis siue pro mortuis debet esse: primo, audientium letificatiua, unde in persona auditorum dicebat Psalmista (118: 162): *Letabor ego super eloquia tua sicut qui inuenit spolia multa.* ⁴Et debet esse salutis eterne ostensiua et demonstratiua, unde ille sanctus Symeon dixit, Luce secundo (30): *Uiderunt oculi mei salutare tuum quod parasti ante faciem omnium populorum.* ⁵Quantum igitur ad primum dicit propheta in uerbo proposito: *in uirtute tua Domine letabitur rex*; set quantum ad secundum ait: *et super salutare tuum exultabit vehementer.* ⁶In principio igitur nostre collationis rogemus deum ut nostra predicatio hunc duplicem effectum habere possit etc.

**2** ¹*In uirtute tua, Domine, letabitur rex, et super salutare tuum exultabit uehementer.* ²Sicut quorundam hominum, karissimi, pena hic in presenti uita initiatur, et in futura cumulatur et augmentatur, ut Pharaonis, qui in hac uita multis plagis fuit percussus ad insinuationem pene future, ita quorundam hominum gaudium et letitia in presenti uita incipit et initiatur, et in futura completur et terminatur. ³De quorum numero firmiter credimus quod fuit dominus rex cuius exequias nunc celebramus, cuius letitia et gaudium dupliciter nobis in uerbo proposito exprimitur: ⁴Primo quantum ad eius inceptionem in hac uita temporali, cum dicitur: *In uirtute tua, Domine, letabitur rex.* ⁵Secundo, quantum ad eius terminationem in futura uita eternali, cum additur: *et super salutare tuum exultabit uehementer.*

**3** ¹Primo igitur, karissimi, regis nostri domini Odouardi letitia in presenti uita est incepta et initiata quia ipse in uirtute dei letatus est in hac uita eum nunquam in aduersis relinquente, quia cum ipse fuerit in multis periculis, in mari et in terra et inter Sarracenos et Christianos, nunquam tamen dei uirtute est derelictus, sed de omnibus liberatus. ²Unde merito ipse dicere potuit illud quod scribitur secundo Machab.

2: 3 letitia] *erasure follows in ms*

primo capitulo (11): *de magnis periculis a deo liberati magnifice gratias ipsi agimus.*

**4** ¹Letatus est secundo in uirtute dei eum in prosperis eleuari non permittente, quia in prosperitatibus et uictoriis istius mundi non fuit in superbiam eleuatus, sed magis humiliatus. ²Unde ipse uere poterat dicere illud uerbum Ps. (130: 1): *Domine, non est exaltatum cor meum, neque elati sunt oculi mei.*

**5** ¹Letatus est tertio in uirtute dei eum finaliter in conscientia purgante et sanante. ²Unde ipse potuit dicere merito in fine illud Apostoli secunda ad Cor. i° (12): *Gloria et letitia nostra est testimonium conscientie nostre*: quam ipse per contritionem et sacramentorum receptionem purgauerat. ³Dicat igitur, karissimi, sanctus propheta: Domine, rex Odouardus letabitur in uita presenti in uirtute tua eum in aduersis non relinquente, in prosperis eleuari non permittente, et finaliter eum in conscientia purgante.

**6** ¹Et sic eius letitia et exultatio hic erat incepta et initiata, sed in futura uita eius letitia erit completa et terminata, quia: *super salutare tuum exultabit uehementer,* id est exultabit in vehementi gaudio et in vehementi salute quam [*col. b*] habebit in uisione tua. ²Et signanter illud salutare et illud gaudium dicitur uehemens, quia (1 Cor. 2: 9) *nec oculus uidit nec auris audiuit nec in cor hominis ascendit que preparauit deus diligentibus se.* ³Que gaudia sibi et nobis dignetur preparare Christus, qui est etc.

# Transcription C:d

**1** ¹Item collatio de morte regis.

²*Quoniam rex sperauit in Domino et in misericordia altissimi non com-mouebitur* (Ps. 20: 8). ³Karissimi, uerbi dei annuntiator caute et sagaciter debet populo predicare, quia per eum non debet annuntiari populo desperatio de seueritate diuine iustitie, immo debet dicere (Ps. 61: 9): *Sperate in Domino omnis congregatio populi, effundite coram illo corda uestra.* ⁴Nec debet per eum annuntiari nimia presumptio de diuina miseri-cordia, quia presumptio est peccatum in spiritum sanctum, et facit hominem peccare ex certa malitia. ⁵Ad remouendum igitur despe-rationem dicit propheta: *quoniam rex sperauit in Domino.* ⁶Sed ad removendum presumptionem dicit: *et in misericordia altissimi non commouebitur.* ⁷In principio igitur nostre collationis rogemus deum ut ab utroque defectu nostra predicatio sit immunis, et ut id quod petimus et cetera.

**2** ¹*Quoniam rex sperauit in Domino et in misericordia altissimi non com-mouebitur.* ²In uerbo proposito karissimi, laus et commendatio regis nostri cuius exequias facimus dupliciter nobis manifestatur. ³Primo quantum ad eius spei firmitatem, cum dicitur: *quoniam rex sperauit in Domino.* ⁴Secundo quantum ad eius remunerationis securitatem, cum additur: *et in misericordia altissimi non commouebitur.*

**3** ¹Primo igitur laus et commendatio eius exprimitur, quia ipse fir-miter sperauit in Domino. ²Et possumus dicere quod tria sunt signa que demonstrant hominem firmiter sperare in Domino. ³Primum est diuinorum uerborum delectabilis intellectio, quia: *omnis qui est ex deo uerba dei audit,* ut Saluator dicit in Johanne (8: 47). ⁴Secundum est peccatorum et uitiorum detestatio, quia homo *quasi a facie colubri fugit peccata* qui sperat in Domino, ut dicitur Ecclesiastici uigesimo primo (2). ⁵Tertium est bonorum operum operatio, quia, secundum beatum Gregorium, probatio dilectionis exhibitio est operis. ⁶Ex istis tribus,

---

3: 5. Gregory: not found.

---

**1**: 6 presumptionem] *follows* desperationem *deleted*          **3**: 4 uigesimo
primo] xx⁰ *ms*

karissimi, possumus dicere quod rex noster dominus Odouardus firmiter sperauit in Domino: ⁷Primo propter uerborum eius delectabilem intellectionem, quia uere uerba dei sibi fuerunt *delectabilia super aurum et lapidem pretiosum multum, et dulciora super mel et fauum* (Ps. 18: 11). ⁸Secundo propter peccatorum et uitiorum detestationem, quia sicut possibile fuit fragilitati humane, ipse iniquitatem odio habuit, et legem dei dilexit. ⁹Tertio propter bonorum operum executionem in mandatorum dei obseruatione et proximorum defectuum releuatione. ¹⁰Unde ipse merito poterat dicere quia *Spera*ui *in Domino et* feci *bonitatem,* ideo deus dedit michi *petitione*m *cordis* mei (Cf. Ps. 36: 3–4).

4 ¹Commendatur igitur primo quantum ad spei firmitatem, cum dicitur: *quoniam rex sperauit in Domino.* ²Secundo commendatur quantum ad remunerationis securitatem, cum additur: *et in misericordia altissimi non commouebitur.* ³Nam quia nullum bonum apud deum irremuneratum [*fo. 158ᵛᵃ*] ideo misericordia altissimi hanc remunerationem sibi faciet, ut illud quod sperauit et credidit nunc teneat et possideat, quod sibi concedat Christus qui est benedictus etc.

# Transcription C:e

## MS Rome, Angelica 158, fo. 158<sup>va–b</sup>

**1** ¹Item collatio de morte regis ad clerum.

²*Rex in eternum uiue.* ³Predicator diuini uerbi merito dicitur rex et dicitur uiuere in eternum, que duo ponuntur in uerbo proposito quod scribitur Daniel tertio (9). ⁴Nam dicitur rex propter auditorum regiam dominationem. ⁵Unde prima Petri ii (9) scribitur in persona predicatorum: *Uos estis genus electum, regale sacerdotium, gens sancta, populus acquisitionis, ut uirtutes annuntietis eius qui de tenebris uos uocauit.* ⁶Et dicitur uiuere in eternum propter eterni premii firmam expectationem, quia ipsi predicatores uerbi diuini firmius et certius aliis eternum premium expectare possunt. ⁷Unde in persona eorum dicitur, Ecclesiastici xxiiii (30–1): *Qui audiunt me, non confundentur, qui operantur in me, non peccabunt, et qui elucidant me, uitam eternam habebunt.* ⁸In principio igitur nostre collationis rogemus deum ut de numero predicatorum hanc duplicem perfectionem habentium esse possimus et ut id quod petimus, etc.

**2** ¹*Rex in eternum uiue.* ²Karissimi, istud uerbum dictum fuit Nabuchodonosor magnifico et potentissimo regi Caldeorum, nos tamen merito possumus dicere domino Odouardo magnifico et potentissimo regi anglorum, quia licet ipse amplius non uiuat nobiscum ista uita animali corruptibili et terminabili, uiuit tamen cum deo uita celestiali, spirituali et eternali, ut uere possimus dicere sibi: *Rex in eternum uiue.* ³Et possumus dicere quod *homo potest eternaliter uiuere* in se, cum proximo et cum deo. ⁴Nam in se homo in eternum uiuit per anime a corpore separationem et intellectualem operationem, quia licet corpus hominis corru*m*patur, marcescat et putrescat, quia ex contrariis est compositum, et omne compositum ex contrariis necessario est corruptibile, anima tamen ipsa in eternum uiuit, quia, ut testatur Philosophus secundo de Anima, separatur ipsa anima a corpore uelut perpetuum a corruptibili. ⁵Et xii Methaphisice dicit quod uita maxime dicitur de intellectuali operatione, que eterna est et i*m*mortalis. Saluator etiam

---

2: 4. Aristotle: *De anima*, 413ᵇ26–7: for the Latin text see Aquinas, *Opera omnia*, xlv/1. *Sentencia libri de Anima cura et studio Fratrum Praedicatorum* (Rome and Paris, 1984), 82.

noster Luce xii (4–5) ait: *Dico uobis amicis meis: Nolite timere eos qui occidunt corpus, animam autem non possunt occidere, se*d *potius eum timete qui potest animam et corpus perdere in Iehennam.*

**3** ¹Cum proximo uero homo uiuit in eternum per iustitie obseruationem et misericordie compassionem, quia sicut *iustitia perpetua est et immortalis,* iniustitia uero mortis est acquisitio, ut dicitur Sapientie primo (15), ita *iustorum anime in manu dei sunt et non tanget illos tormentum mortis;* et quamuis *oculis insipientium uisi sunt mori, spes tamen et uita illorum immortalitate plena est,* ut scribitur eodem libro capitulo tertio (1–2, 4). ²De misericordia similiter et compassione proximorum dixit angelus, Thobie xii (9): *Elemosina a morte liberat et peccata purgat et ipsa facit inuenire uitam eternam.*

**4** ¹Sed [*col. b*] cum deo homo in eternum uiuit per fidei professionem et eius intrepidam defensionem. ²Unde, Iohannis xi (26), dixit Salvator Marthe: *Omnis qui credit in me non morietur in eternum.* ³Non tamen sufficit credere nisi ipsa fides defendatur, quia (Mt. 10: 33) *qui negauerit me coram hominibus, ego negabo eum coram patre meo.* ⁴Unde post baptismum in quo quis facit fidei professionem, statim postmodum datur confirmatio, in quo sacramento quis promittit fidei defensionem, quia quilibet ex tunc efficitur pugil et bellator pro fide. ⁵Igitur quilibet homo uiuit in eternum in se per anime a corpore separationem, et intellectualem operationem, cum proximo per iustitie obseruationem et misericordie compassionem, et cum deo per fidei professionem et eius defensionem.

**5** ¹Reuera igitur karissimi, possumus dicere quod illustrissimus et sanctissimus rex dominus Odouardus, quamdiu eius anima fuit in corpore, uixit in se per intellectualem operationem, quia postquam factus est rex istius populi non uixit secundum concupiscentias sensuales et carnales et animales, sed secundum operationes intellectuales. ²Nam quamuis sit detestabile in quolibet homine quod sit insecutor passionum et temptationum carnalium et sensualium, eo quod homo magis est intellectus quam sensus, et sic magis debet homo uiuere secundum operationem anime quam carnis, potissime tamen est detestabile in rege, quia cum nomen regis dicatur a regendo, ille qui regitur passionibus et temptationibus magis regitur quam

---

**2:** 5 Aristotle: Probably *Metaphysics,* 1072ᵇ26–8. Cf. *Aristoteles Latinus,* xxv/2. *Metaphysica Lib. I–X, XII–XIV, translatio anonyma sive 'media',* ed. Gudrun Vuillemin-Diem (Leiden, 1976), 214.

Luce ii] Cf. Matt. 10: 28 (closer verbally).

**3:** 1 Sapientie primo (15)] and vv. 12–14 more loosely.

**4:** 4 pro fide] pro *supplied in margin*

regat, et ideo maxime regi et principi dicitur Ecclesiastici xviii (30–1): *Post concupiscentias tuas non eas, quia si prestaueris anime tue omnes concupiscentias et uoluptates eius, facient te in gaudium inimicis tuis.*

**6** ¹Secundo ipse uixit cum subditis suis per iustitie obseruationem et misericordie compassionem; unde ipse merito dicere poterat quod scribitur Iob xxix (14): *Iustitia indutus sum et uestiuit me sicut uestimento et diademate iudicio meo.* ²Pauperes etiam semper eum in patrocinium et subleuamen habuerunt. ³Unde sibi conueniebat dicere uere quod scribitur [Iob 31: 18] *Ab infantia mea creuit mecum miseratio, et de utero matris mee egressa est mecum.*

**7** ¹Sed cum deo ipse uixit per eius fidei defensionem, quia non solum in gente sua et in regno suo fidem Christi protexit et defensauit, sed tamquam pugil et bellator eius ad expugnandum Sarracenos et rebelles ecclesie et incredulos partes ultramarinas perlustrauit, mortis periculo corpus suum et corpora suorum subditorum exponendo.

**8** ¹Unde significanter possumus sibi dicere istud uerbum: *Rex in eternum uiue.* ²Nam possumus dicere: O domine Odouarde, rex Anglorum, uiue modo in eternum! ³Et merito uiuere debes eternaliter, quia, temporaliter existens in corpore, tu semper uixisti in teipso per intellectualem operationem, cum tuis subditis per iustitie obseruationem, et cum deo per eius fidei defensionem. ⁴Quam uitam sibi et nobis concedat deus, qui est benedictus in secula Amen.

---

**6**: 1 *uestimento*] *uestimentum ms*     **6**: 3 [Iob 31: 18]] *blank space left in ms*
**7**: 1 *defensauit*] *correction in ms?*     **8**: 1 significanter] *or* signanter     **8**: 4
nobis concedat] nobis concedat nobis *ms*

# Transcription D

## Bertrand de la Tour?
## MS Troyes 2001, fos. 46$^{va}$–47$^{vb}$

### Introduction

The following extracts illustrate principal themes of a sermon in memory of a prince whose author might or might not be Bertrand de la Tour: see above, ch. 1, at nn. 216–17. I have seen MS Barcelona, Archivo de la Corona de Aragón Ripoll 187 (= B), fos. 95$^{va}$–96$^{ra}$, MS Bibliotheca Apostolica Vaticana, Archiv. Capit. di San Pietro G 48 (= V), fos. 35$^{vb}$–36$^{ra}$, and MS Troyes 2001 (= T), fos. 46$^{va}$–47$^{vb}$ (new foliation). B is terrible. V is a little better but omits a long passage. T has been selected for transcription. If both B and V give a reading which deserves to be incorporated in the text I give only V as authority, since B's testimony is not worth much.

. . . ¹Quia mors est quoddam tributum quod omnes debemus soluere, ait Seneca, a quo tributo nullius principis excusat potentia, nullius presulis excusat scientia, nullius militis excusat prosapia, nullius denique hominis excusat prudentia seu cautela. ²Quod patet hodie. ³Quia princeps rapitur pro tributo, planum est nullus mortalium se poterit excusare. ⁴Demum si de hoc dubitas, uide quid sancta ueritas dicat: *Princeps,* etc. (2 Reg. 3:38); ubi ostenditur quod mors non ueretur: cuiusquam statum inuadere; cuiusquam gradum deprimere; cuiusquam malum infligere; cuiusquam casum ostendere.

⁵Inuadit ergo magnum in genere, ut timeas. ⁶Ideo ait: *Princeps*—non quicunque, sed: generosior germine; uirtuosior opere; uigorosior corpore; satis iunior tempore. . . . ⁷Uide ergo quem inuasit mors ut et tu paueas, quoniam si talem et tantum percussit, tibi non parcet: *non enim* [col. b] *est discipulus super magistrum, nec seruus super dominum suum,* Mt. x (24). ⁸Ideo ad te uenturam mortem cito expecta . . . ⁹Deprimit altum a culmine, ut caueas. . . . ¹⁰Uide ergo quem mors depressit, quia quem multi hostes superare non potuerunt, ictus unius doloris depressit, ut tibi caueas—certe non ad euasionem, cum non

---

1. Seneca: cf. *Naturales quaestiones,* 6. 32. 12 (source found by Alan Griffiths).

---

3 mortalium] militum *V*    5 magnum] *V*: magna *T*    8 mortem] *V*: *om. T*    9 altum] *V*: alta *T*

possis, se*d* caue ne te inueniat i*m*paratum. ... [11]Infligit da*m*pnum in
opere, ut doleas. [12]Ideo ait: *cecidit*—non anima, anima enim non
moritur, se*d* corpus, [*fo. 47^{ra}*] ad te*m*pus. ... [13]Cecidit ergo ille
dominus, cuius mors est: lancea militibus, plaga parentibus, meror
pauperibus, dolor propriis ciuibus. ... [14]Ostendit factum in te*m*pore,
ut credas. [15]Ideo ait: *hodie.* [16]Aduerbium est demonstrandi, et ostendit: extinctum dominum, afflictum populum, apertum tumulum,
amarum diem et pessimum. [17]Si de hiis dubitas, uoca dominum, si
tibi *respondeat? [18]Interroga populum, quare fleat? ... [19]Unde
legitur in uita Iohannis elemosinarii quod antiquitus, postquam
i*m*perator erat [*col. b*] coronatus, astantibus sibi exercitibus, mox
ueniebant ad ipsum monumentorum edificatores cum marmoribus
diuersicoloribus, et inquirebant ab eo: De quali metallo uel marmore
iubet tuum i*m*perium tuum fieri monumentum;—insinuantes ei quod
ta*m*quam corruptibilis et transitorius deberet habere curam anime sue
et mortis memoriam ante oculos cordis.

[20]Debet etiam thesaurizare in celo. [21]Unde narrat Barlaam de ciuitate
cuius mos fuit omni anno unum accipere principem, et in fine anni
nudare et exulare. [22]Ueniens autem quidam sapiens pro principe,
legem audiens, transmisit bona quecu*m*que potuit anno sui principatus
ad locum exilii, ad quem ueniens in fine anni, inuenit sufficientiam.
[23]Ciuitas ista mundus est qui spoliat et nudat in fine ...

19. Johannes: see Jacopo da Varazze, *Legenda aurea, vulgo Historia Lombardica
dicta,* 27, ed. Th. Graesse (Bratislava, 1890), 130 (probable source).
21–3. Barlaam: see ibid. 180, p. 817 Graesse.

11 da*m*pnum] *V*: da*m*pna *T*        12 ad te*m*pus] *T*: quod ad te*m*pus moritur
*V*        13 lancea] amara *T*      propriis ciuibus] populis *V: in T* omnibus *could be
read for* ciuibus        21 nudare et exulare] nudari et exulare *T*: nudari et exulari
*B: whole exemplum omitted in V*

# Endnotes

These notes are cued in the text at points where they cannot
conveniently be included on the page.

## Chapter 1

1. Several such sermons have been printed. The following cases are all assigned by Linsenmayer, *Geschichte*, 163 n. 2, to the 12th cent., but his
dating may be insecure. The sermon from the 'St. Pauler Sammlung', with
the heading *Pro defunctis, quando mortuus est praesens*, which Linsenmayer
appears to translate in full into modern German (*Geschichte*, 163–5), is
firmly assigned to the 13th cent. by Haas, *Todesbilder*, 47. Then there is a
German *Sermo de mortuis* among the so-called 'Weingartner Predigten': A.
Schönbach, 'Weingartner Predigten', *Zeitschrift für deutsches Alterthum*, 28 (NS
16) (1884), 1–20, at 12–13. Though the rubric *de mortuis* does not necessarily
imply a memorial sermon in our sense (it can be used for an All Souls' Day
sermon, and also, so far as one can tell, for sermons on death whose
occasion is not specified), in this one ambiguity is ruled out by the sentence
'Dar umbe sunt ir bitten got zem ersten umbe iuch selber, dar nach ubir
disen lichnamin der hie vor iuwer stat: swa der lip habe missetan, daz des
got vergezze ginædichliche hin ze der selê' (ibid. 13), and also the phrase
'dirre sælige lichname' (ibid.). K. Morvay and D. Gruber, *Bibliographie der
deutschen Predigt des Mittelalters: Veröffentlichte Predigten* (Münchener Texte
und Untersuchungen zur deutschen Literatur des Mittelalters, 47; Munich,
1974), 26, include it in their section on 'Vorfranziskanische Predigt im 12.
und in der ersten Hälfte des 13. Jahrhunderts'; I do not know whether it
can be more precisely dated. Linsenmayer, *Geschichte*, 163 n. 2, also lists, as
12th-cent. *Leichenreden*, Nos. 147–51 of the vernacular sermons printed in
A. Schönbach, *Altdeutsche Predigten*, i (Graz, 1886), 239–42. Once again I do
not know how securely one may ascribe these to the period before 1200
(Morvay and Gruber, *Bibliographie*, 13—T17, the 'Leipziger Sammlung'—
place this collection too in their 12th-/first half of 13th-cent. section).
Sermon 150 in Schoñbach's *Altdeutsche Predigten*, i. 241, seems definitely to
be a *Leichenrede*, since it contains the words 'nu bitten den almechtigen
got . . . daz er des gûten menschin sele von dem ewigen tode irlose.
alle die sine vrûnt hie sin, die gedenken sin, so sie beste mûgen, .
dise drizich tage mit irme opphere, mit irn almusen, mit irme gebete und
mit andern gûten werkin.' I confess that I do not see any firm evidence
that the other numbers Linsenmayer refers to are *Leichenreden*.
2. ' . . . uir iste iustus et timoratus ac uerus dei cultor ante oculos nostros
tamquam speculum hodie proponitur, qui cautus fuit et circumspectus in
uita, et diem istum semper ante mentis oculos habuit, et ideo se ita
preparauit ut mortis horam secure posset expectare et iudici suo uenienti
occurrere. Et quoniam in Ecclesiaste (4: 2) scriptum est: *Laudaui magis
mortuos quam uiuos*, in uita non est multum laudandus homo, sed post
mortem securius potest laudari. Unde testimonium illi possumus [*fo. 146^{ra}*]
perhibere quod corde contrito et humili de omnibus peccatis suis non
semel sed pluries confessionem fecit, et ad mandatum ecclesie satisfacere

se promisit, et sacramentorum medicamenta deuotissime suscepit. Non solum autem largis elemosinis peccata sua redemit, sed omnibus cum quibus querelam uel causam habuit sincero corde dimisit, et secundum ecclesie consilium omnibus qui circa ipsum aliquid habebant, satisfecit. Et quoniam scriptum audierat (Is. 38: 1) *Dispone domui tue, quoniam morieris et non uiues,* non solum familiam et domum exteriorem ex testamento suo prudenter ordinauit, sed et domum interiorem, id est animam propriam, ita disposuit quod de hiis que ad eius salutem pertinebant nichil omisit: pauperibus, uiduis, orphanis, et locis religiosis de bonis suis copiose reliquit, attendens illud quod ait beatus Ambrosius: "Sola misericordia comes est defunctorum". Corpus etiam et sanguinem redemptoris ut uiaticum haberet, et ducem uie deuotissime cum lacrimis recepit. Et secundum beati Iacobi consilium (Iac. 5: 14–15) et ecclesie dei constitutionem, uocauit *presbiteros ecclesie ut orarent pro ipso et ungerent oleo sancto,* ut uirtute sacramenti dimitterentur ei peccata (*corr. from* peccata ei) minora, uel penitentia pro maioribus alleuiaretur, ut facilius per purgatorium transiret et diabolus uirtute sacramenti refrenatus animam eius in exitu non adeo molestare ualeret. Et quoniam in uita sua super fidei fundamentum edificauit aurum, argentum et lapides pretiosos, si forte lignum, fenum, et stipulam superaddidit, minus patietur detrimentum propter extreme unctionis sacramentum. Sic autem saluus erit quasi per ignem' (MS Troyes 228, fos. 145$^{vb}$–146$^{ra}$).

3. The medieval table of contents at the beginning of the manuscript lists five sermons 'de s. Ludouico Rege Franc(orum)', with column-numbers:

> *Dauit in sua misericordia consecutus est sedem regni in secula* (1 Macc. 2: 57): 17.
> *Rex in eternum uiue* (2 Esdra 2: 3): 114.
> *Fecit Ezechias quod placuit deo* (Eccli. 48: 25): 247.
> *Magnificans salutes regis eius* (Ps. 17: 51): 377.
> *Tronus eius sicut sol in conspectu meo* (Ps. 88: 38): 487.

I have checked that there are sermons with these incipits in the columns listed, but have not studied the sermons themselves. Preaching in honour of royal saints and of St Louis in particular deserves a full study, which I have not undertaken myself but whose eventual results it will be useful to compare with the findings of this book. Royal saints more generally (especially of the earlier medieval period) have been the object of much research. See notably: F. Graus, *Volk, Herrscher und Heiliger im Reich der Merowinger: Studien zur Hagiographie der Merowingerzeit* (Prague, 1965); E. Hoffmann, *Die heiligen Könige bei den Angelsachsen und den skandinavischen Völkern: Königsheiliger und Königshaus* (Quellen und Forschungen zur Geschichte Schleswig-Holsteins, 69; Neumünster, 1975); R. Folz, *Les Saints Rois du Moyen Âge en Occident (VI<sup>e</sup>–XIII<sup>e</sup> siècles)* (Subsidia Hagiographica, 68; Brussels, 1984); P. Corbet, *Les Saints Ottoniens: Sainteté dynastique, sainteté royale, et sainteté féminine autour de l'an Mil* (Beihefte der Francia, 15; Sigmaringen, 1986); D. Rollason, 'The Cults of Murdered Royal Saints in Anglo-Saxon England', *Anglo-Saxon England*, 11 (1983), 1–22; Susan J. Ridyard, *The Royal Saints of Anglo-Saxon England: A Study of West Saxon and East Anglian Cults* (Cambridge Studies in Medieval Life and Thought, 4th ser., 9; Cambridge, 1988); J. Nelson, 'Royal Saints and Early Medieval Kingship', in ead., *Politics and Ritual in Early Medieval Europe* (London, 1986), No. 3; G. Klaniczay, 'L'image chevaleresque du saint roi au XII<sup>e</sup> siècle', in A. Boureau and C. S. Ingerflom (eds.), *La Royauté sacrée dans le* *monde chrétien* (Colloque de Royaumont, mars 1989; L'histoire et ses représentations, 3; Paris, 1992), 53–61. See also A. Vauchez's classic *La Sainteté en Occident aux derniers siècles du Moyen Âge d'après les procès de canonisation et les documents hagiographiques* (Bibliothèque des Écoles Françaises d'Athènes et de Rome, 241; Rome, 1981), index, s.v. 'Roi, Reine, Royauté'. An important study of Louis IX by Jacques Le Goff is imminent.

4. MS Barcelona, Biblioteca de Catalunya 661, fos. 132$^r$–133$^r$. Schneyer, *Repertorium*, i. 583, includes among his list of manuscripts of one set of Bertrand's sermons 'Barcelona, Centralb. 661 f. 105–41'. However, the sermon in question is not among the incipits listed for that set (it is not the same as No. 1100, p. 581, although they are on the same text, *Princeps et maximus cecidit hodie* (2 Kgs. 3: 38); incidentally, the Barcelona manuscript has *magnus* for *maximus* and the wrong chapter-number). Thus it would be rash definitively to assign the sermon to Bertrand.

5. 'Dixi secundo quod in uerbis propositis denotatur fragilitatis (fragilitas *ms*) istius domini euidentia, cum sequitur: *cecidit*, quia nec magnitudo, nec generis altitudo, potuerunt eum euadere (*sic*) quin ceciderit, nec fortitudo nec diuitiarum plenitudo, nec etiam populi multitudo potuerunt eum euadere debitum mortis. Quamuis tamen sic per mortem ceciderit, quia ecclesiastica sacramenta, scilicet penitentiam, eucharestiam, extremam unctionem cum maxima deuotione suscepit, ad gloriam sempiternam esurget' (MS Barcelona, Biblioteca de Catalunya, 661, fo. 132$^r$). The nearness of death had already been emphasized at the start of the sermon: '*Princeps magnus* . . . Beatus (?) Bernardus in quodam sermone nos morti preparatos esse desiderans dicit sic: Miser homo, quare omni hora te non disponis. Cogita te iam mortuum, quem scis de necessitate moriturum. Que quidem necessitas patet. Nam secundum Philosophum omne ponderosum apetit esse terra (trum *ms*?) et cadere deorsum. Nam natura humana ex terra est, sicut dicitur Gen. quarto (*error for 3: 19?*): terra es et *in terram reuerteris*, ideo ponderosa, quare oportet ipsam de necessitate cadere. Ergo cum iste dominus esset homo ex terra et ceteris elementis compositus, oportuit ipsum cadere, uitam presentem finiendo, et hoc est quod dicitur in uerbis prepositis: *Princeps magnus*, etc.' (ibid.).

6. 'Primo ergo notatur in uerbis prepositis istius domini nobilitas (*corr. from* nobilitat- ?) cum premititur *Princeps magnus*. Et uere magna fuit nobilitas huius domini, cum procesit ab initio ex progenie regali, quo ad corpus, et non solum quo ad corpus, set etiam animam habuit uirtutibus decoratam, quod quidem est euidentissimum nobilitatis indicium' (ibid.).

7. 'Dicit ergo *Princeps magnus*, ubi est notandum quod decet principem habere tria que iste dominus habuit, scilicet:—in gubernando discretionis magnitudinem;—in expugnando directionis fortitudinem;—in pacificando subiectionis rectitudinem. Dico primo quod decet regem seu principem habere [*fo. 132$^v$*] in gubernando discretionis magnitudinem, ut (*correction in ms?*) scilicet regat sapienter et discrete populum sibi comissum in iustitia et equitate. Nam iustitia respicit bonum comune, quod (qd *ms*) quidem ordinatur ad conseruationem populi, cum reddat unicuique quod suum est, scilicet deo gloriam et honorem, proximo misericordiam et amorem. Talis fuit iste presens dominus: habendo discretionis magnitudinem in gubernando reddidit deo gloriam et honorem, suum seruitium aumentando, pro ipso quidquid habere poterat exponendo, non solum hoc, uerum etiam populum sibi subditum discrete regendo . . . Set sunt multi qui talem non seruant iustitiam erga deum nec erga subditos suos, ymo potius crudelitatem, eos per uarias questias (*read* questas?) et extorssiones excoriando,

similes leoni rapienti, . . . Secundo dico quod decet principem seu regem
habere in expugnando hostes directionis fortitudinem, ut uidelicet terram
et populum sibi subditum ab aduersariorum insultatione fortiter defendat.
Talis enim fuit iste dominus rex noster. Ffuit enim fortis in expugnatione
sui regni ac populi, ipsum ab aduersariis uiriliter deffendendo et semper de
omnibus uictoriam obtinendo, et suo inperio diuersas gentes et regna
submitendo . . . Et non solum hostes sua fortitudine superauit corporales,
uerum etiam sp*i*rituales, scilicet diabolum per humilitatem, mundum per
largitatem, carnem per castitatem . . . [*fo. 133*ʳ] . . . Tertio dico quod decet
regem siue principem habere rectitudinem subiectionis seu humilitatis in
pacificando' (ibid., fos. 132ʳ–133ʳ). The passage which follows is not wholly
clear, perhaps because of textual corruption, but the problem need not
concern us here.

8. MS Troyes, Bibliothèque Municipale 817, fo. 17ʳ⁻ᵛ; Schneyer, *Repertorium*,
   ix. 634, No. 96.

9. It is very short: 'In morte alicuius principis. Ierem. (19: 1): *Hec dicit Dominus:
   Uade et accipe lagunculam figuli testeam de senioribus populi et de senioribus
   sacerdotum, et egredere ad uallem filii Ennon, que est iuxta introitum porte fictilis.
   Ire* est in bonis proficere. *Acci(pere) la(gunculam) fi(guli) teste(am)* est considerare fragilitatem humane conditionis, que bene apparet [*fo. 17*ᵛ] in
   mortibus *seniorum po(puli)*, id est, principum terrenorum et *sen(iorum)
   sacerdo(tum)*, id est, ecclesiasticarum personarum, ut episcoporum, archiepi-
   scoporum, etc. *Ennon* interpretatur fons tristitie; *filius Ennon* est homo,
   quam multa cui cum ueniunt incomoda. *Uallis filii Ennon* est mundus. Ad
   hanc uallem egredimur cum a tumultu malarum cogitationum semoti mala
   mundi contemplamur. Hic est uallis *siluestris*, in qua sunt *multi putei
   bituminis*, ut dicit Gen. (14: 10). *Introitus porte fic(tilis)* est ingressus humane
   natiuitatis, et iuxta hunc est Ennon, quia cum homine nascente nascitur
   eius miseria. Unde dicit auctoritas super epistola Pauli: Puer cum nascitur
   propheta est sue miserie. Item idem Iere. alibi (22: 29–30) monet accipere
   lagunculam figuli, ubi dicit: *Terra, terra, terra, audi sermonem domini. Scribe
   uirum sterilem qui in diebus suis non prosperabitur*. Rex dicitur *terra* quia
   terrena nos subuertunt per luxuriam, auaritiam, et superbiam. Terra scribit
   uirum sterilem quando mortem alicuius mali hominis terrenis impressi
   nobis quasi legibilem ostendit ad terrorem. Unde idem alibi: (Ierem. 17:
   13): *Recedentes a te, Domine, in terra scribentur'* (MS Troyes, Bibliothèque
   Municipale 817, fo. 17ʳ⁻ᵛ).

10. For liturgical *memoria* as the setting of our sermons, see above, Introduction,
    ad init. and n. 1. Contrast Theodor Nolte, *Lauda post mortem: Die deutschen
    und niederländischen Ehrenreden des Mittelalters* (Europäische Hochschul-
    schriften, 1st ser., Deutsche Sprache und Literatur, 562; Frankfurt am Main
    and Berne, 1983), 47: 'Die Ehrenreden sind daher wohl nicht in der Kirche
    im Rahmen der Exequien, sondern beim anschließenden gemeinsamen Mahl
    vorgetragen worden; sie gehören also nicht in den kirchlichen Bereich.'
    Nolte also states that 'Die Ehrenrede fungiert nicht als "cura pro mortuis".
    Außer der Fürbitte tauchen keine christlichen Motive auf. . . . Die Mahnung,
    sich auf den Tod vorzubereiten, läuft der Gesamtintention der Texte
    zuwider, die im Kern, wie die antike Leichenrede auch, als laudatio sich
    darstellt' (ibid. 46). Nolte cannot have known most of the sermons studied
    in the present book, and his picture of medieval funeral preaching (ibid.),
    as opposed to *Ehrenreden* (his book's main subject), is distinctly one-sided:
    he has little or no awareness of the 'this-worldly' aspect discussed below,
    Chapter 3. His theory (ibid. 46–7) of a sort of rule of complementarity, by
    which funeral sermons were widely diffused where *Ehrenreden* were not,

and vice versa, is highly speculative (though appealingly symmetrical). A related genre, the Old Provençal lament or *planh*, is assumed by D. Rieger to be a 'Vortrag vor der "maisnada" des Verstorbenen', as opposed to the Latin *planctus*, a 'Vortrag während der Bestattungsfeierlichkeiten in der Kirche' (section on 'Das Klagelied' in E. Köhler (ed.), *Les Genres lyriques* (Grundriß der romanischen Literaturen des Mittelalters, 2/1, fasc. 4B ii; Heidelberg, 1980), 83. This seems plausible so far as the *planh* is concerned; as for the *planctus*, one would like to have evidence. For some discussion of the complex of genres written in medieval Latin which are concerned with a person's death, including both memorial sermons and *planctus*, see von Moos, *Consolatio*, i. *Darstellungsband*, 'Gattungsprobleme', esp. pp. 36–44, paras. 45–69 (and the corresponding bibliographical notes in the *Anmerkungsband*). For a general survey of the lament see Claude Thiry, *La Plainte funèbre* (Typologie des sources du Moyen Âge Occidental, 30; Brepols, Turnhout, 1978). For examples of vernacular poetic laments (on Count Eudes de Nevers, on Thibaut V, count of Champagne (and king of Navarre), on Alphonse of Poitiers, and on 'monseigneur Anseau de L'Isle') see *Œuvres complètes de Rutebeuf*, ed. E. Faral and Julia Bastin (2 vols. Paris, 1959–60), i. 451–60, 479–85, 486–91, 510–16 (Patricia Stirneman drew my attention to these). It does not seem at all likely that poems like these were in any way integrated into the liturgy.

11. 'Nomen quidem exequiarum secundum primam *im*positionem significat ipsum funus. . . . Sed assumitur ulterius nomen exequiarum ad significandum cultum honoris qui exibetur mortuis. Unde dicit Hugucio quod exequie sunt officia mortuorum et obsequia que fiunt circa sepulturam, et dicuntur ab exequendo. Est enim 'exequi' perficere et ad effectum ducere, et executio dicitur effectus. Quia ergo exequimur in huiusmodi officiis quod debemus, ideo exequie dicuntur; uel sic dicuntur quia in huiusmodi officiis defunctum sequimur. Hic autem exequialis honor uel cultus exibetur mortuis triplici ratione. Primo quidem propter solatium. Sunt enim huiusmodi officia solatia quedam uiuorum, et consolantur et leuiunt tristitiam que est de morte. Secundo propter testimonium uel signum. Hic enim est testimonium uite preterite et future. Honor enim non debetur mortuo nisi in ordine ad uitam preteritam uel futuram. Non autem cuilibet uite debetur honor, sed uel uite uirtuose uel uite gloriose. Uite enim brutali non debetur honoris cultus. Honorantur ergo mortui ratione uite uirtuose que precessit, et ratione uite gloriose que successit. Honor ergo iste est testimonium uirtuose conuersationis preterite et gloriose remunerationis et resurrectionis future. Tertio propter subsidium, quia huiusmodi honor et cultus ad subsidium spirituale defuncti redundat, dum in huiusmodi cultu inducimur ad orandum pro ipso, et aliis modis, etc. Et ideo in scriptura talis cultus laudatur et exemplo patrum approbatur. . . . Propter tria uero predicta *im*pendendus est exequialis honor huic domino magnus (*sic ms!*): et propter solatium nostrum, quibus pro morte ipsius est magna causa meroris, et propter testimonium sue bone uite preterite nec non propter spem future, et propter subsidium, ut ei si indiget uelociter succurramus' (propter spem] (*suppl. in marg.*) MS Bibliotheca Apostolica Vaticana, Archiv. Capit. S. Petri D 213, col. 263).

*Chapter 3*

12. This is especially true of the two sermons on the elector John and the second sermon on Frederick the Wise. The first sermon on Frederick does

lay some emphasis on the good peace he had given to the land: e.g. *Werke*
(Weimar edn.), xvii/1. 198 (lower text): 'Ists nu lobs werd, wenn man sich
bekümert und leid tregt uber verstorbene nidrigs stands, als wenn ein
Nachbar, freunde etc. umb den andern trawret, Viel mehr ist loblich, das
man solches thu, wenn grosse Herrn oder Fürsten mit tod abgehen,
durch welche Gott fried gibt und erhelt und allerley [*p. 199*] gutes den
unterthanen erzeigt. Weil denn nu unser Heubt und lieber Landesfürst
inn Gott verstorben hie liget, sollen wir uns billich von hertzen bekümern
und leid tragen, Nicht allein seins abschieds halben von diesem Jamertal,
sonder viel mehr, das in Gott eben inn dieser ferlichen grewlichen zeit, da
schier gantz Deudschland erreget ist durch der Bawren auffrhur, so plötzlich
hinweg nimpt, dazu besorgen ist, Gott möchte uns sampt im den schönen
frieden, den er dem gantzen Land durch in, so lang er im regiment gewest,
gnediglich geben hat, auch wegnemen, Des haben wir uns am meisten zu
beklagen.' A few other passages also have some political content. P. 199
(top): 'ein solch heupt gehabt durch wilchs uns Gott fride geben hat, zu
wilches zeitten nie keyn blutvergiessen gewesen.' Pp. 200–1: Luther's idea
here seems to be that the ruler had been taken away just when most
needed. This good ruler had been deserved, because the Gospel-teaching
had never been so pure in Germany, but people had been ungrateful for
this, so God took him away. P. 210 (top): 'dieweyl uns das unglücke
itzt fur der thür ist, und hie ligt das heupt, das fride hat gehalten, Itzt
so gehet der teuffel hereyn und hats ym synn, das er land und leutte ym
bluet verschwemme.' P. 211 (top): 'Darumb so will ich euch gebetten
haben, das wyr Gott drumb dancken und unsern undanck bekennen und
bitten fur die uberkeyt, das er uns nicht all ynn eynen hauffen stosse,
Denn wo die uberkeit also nidder geleget würde, so würden wyr
kynen fride haben, Gott der wil nicht, das der gemeyne pofel regire, wie er
saget Roma. 13.: alle gewalt ist von Gotte, dazu gibt er auch seyne gnade
und gabe, wie man denn sicht, das eyn oberman odder heubt man, eyn
furst mehr gnade und tugende hat denn eyn gemeyner man, wie wol es
ettlich misbrauchen, ydoch bleyben die gabe, Wo aber die uberkeyt
auffgehaben wird, so werden die ergisten buben regiren, die nicht werd
sind, das sie die schussel solten waschen, der teuffel wolte die ordenunge
gerne auffheben, auff das er raum hette seyne büberey zuvolfuren,
gelinget es yhm, so sind wyr schon verloren.'
     Derhalben so ist nu hie stercker zu streiten mit dem gebet denn mit dem
schwert, Aber das sollen sie wissen, das wer widder uberkeit strebt, der
nympt eyn gericht uber sich. Rom 13. Das ist, eyne stauppe, neyn stauchen
odder plage werden sie haben, wie denn das wortlin auch zu den Corinth.
gebraucht wird .l. Cor. 11. wenn wyr gerichtet werden, so werden wyr
von dem Herrn gestrafft, Und disser spruch wird mehr thun denn alle
büchssen und spisse, und die bauren werden dissem spruche nicht
entgehen.' This sermon is therefore a partial exception to the generalization
that Luther has little to say about politics in his memorial sermons, though
even with this sermon the political content is slight in relation to the
whole.
13. Justice, power, wisdom, and humility (Giovanni da San Gimignano): 'excellentia regalis dignitatis tanto redditur uenerabilior quanto rex est iustior,
potentior, sapientior, et humilior. . . . Ratio uero secundi . . .' (then see
above, n. 61, for the remainder of the passage) (MS Siena, Biblioteca
Comunale F. X. 24, fo. 102^{vb}, from a sermon on the text *Rex hodie est et cras
morietur* (Ecclus. 10: 12); Schneyer, *Repertorium*, iii. 762, No. 503); justice,

mercy, and glory (Federico Franconi da Napoli): 'Circa primum sciendum quod rex debet esse constitutus tripliciter: primo in rectitudine iustitie; secundo in dulcedine clementie; tertio in celsitudine glorie' (MS Munich, Staatsbibliothek Clm. 2981, fo. 129$^{vb}$, from a sermon on the text *Ego consti-tutus sum rex* (Ps. 2: 6); Schneyer, *Repertorium*, iv. 223, 'Nicolaus de Asculo', No. 216). The section on glory turns out to be a celebration of power and ancestry: 'Tertio dico quod debet esse constitutus in celsitudine glorie uel habere celsitudinem glorie. Quam celsitudinem glorie habuit dominus Karolus rex Sicilie sancte memorie, quod apparet tam ex origine, quam ex regimine. Quis non diceret eum habuisse celsitudinem glorie ex origine, quia natus est de domo et stirpe Francie;—et ex regimine, quia rex Ierusalem et Sicilie? Est enim celsitudo glorie sue a mari usque ad mare: a mari Regni usque ad mare Prouincie, ymo a mari usque ultra mare, quia rex, ut dictum est, Ierusalem et Sicilie' (fo. 130$^{rb}$). As examples of schemata of virtues (other than the four cardinal virtues) which do not include elements from outside what we might regard as the strictly moral order, note the following passages from Bertrand de la Tour's sermon in memory of Charles of Calabria (Schneyer, *Repertorium*, i. 583, No. 1123): (1) 'Est autem sciendum quod iste nobilissimus uir fuit figuratus in scriptura per quattuor nobilis-simos duces, scilicet per Iosue ratione fidelitatis, per Dauid ratione strenuitatis (strennuitatis/strenuuitatis *ms*), per Ezechiam ratione seueritatis (serenitatis *ms*), per Ionatham ratione benignitatis' (MS Kremsmünster 44, fo. 123$^{vb}$); (2) 'Secundo fuit figuratus per Dauid ratione strennuitatis.... "Dauit" (*sic*) enim interpretatur "manu fortis" et [*fo. 124$^{rb}$*] "wltu desider-abilis". Et certe iste dominus Karolus fuit 'manu fortis', quia probus et strennuus contra hostes. Wltu etiam desiderabilis, quia iustus et honestus' (ibid., fo. 124$^{ra–b}$).

*Chapter 4*

14. The subject has been so popular that the following list is inevitably incom-plete and indeed somewhat arbitrary: J. Huizinga, *The Waning of the Middle Ages* (first published in English in 1924), ch. 11; A. Tenenti, *La Vie et la mort à travers l'art du XV$^e$ siècle* (Cahiers des Annales, 8; Paris, 1952); id., *Il senso della morte e l'amore della vita nel Rinascimento (Francia e Italia)* ([Turin,] 1957); Ph. Ariès, *Western Attitudes towards Death from the Middle Ages to the Present* (Baltimore and London, 1974); W. Goez, 'Die Einstellung zum Tode im Mittelalter', in *Der Grenzbereich zwischen Leben und Tod* (Göttingen, 1976), 111–53; articles by various authors, notably J.-C. Schmitt, R. Chartier, and M. Vovelle, in *Annales: Économies, sociétés, civilisations*, 31/1, (1976)—an issue on the theme 'Autour de la mort'; Ariès, *L'Homme devant la mort* (Paris, 1977); *La Mort au Moyen Âge: Colloque de l'Association des historiens médiévistes français réunis à Strasbourg en juin 1975 au Palais universitaire* (Publications de la société savante d'Alsace et des régions de l'est, collection 'Recherches et documents', 25; Strasburg, 1977); P. Chaunu, *La Mort à Paris: XVI$^e$, XVII$^e$ et XVIII$^e$ siècles* (Paris, 1978) (includes extensive comment on death in the Middle Ages); J. Delumeau, *La Peur en Occident (XIV$^e$–XVIII$^e$ siècles): Une cité assiégée* (Paris, 1978) (index thématique s.v. 'Mort'); *Le Sentiment de la mort au Moyen Âge: Études présentées au cinquième colloque de l'Institut d'Études Médiévales de l'Université de Montréal*, ed. C. Sutto (Montreal, 1979); J. Chiffoleau, *La Comptabilité de l'au-delà: Les Hommes, la mort et la religion dans la région d'Avignon à la fin du Moyen Âge (vers 1320–vers 1480)* (Collection de l'École Française de Rome, 47; Rome, 1980);

J. le Goff, *La Naissance du Purgatoire* (Paris, 1981); J. Whaley (ed.), *Mirrors of Mortality: Studies in the Social History of Death* (London, 1981); H. Braet and W. Verbeke (eds.), *Death in the Middle Ages* (Mediaevalia Lovaniensia, 1st ser., Studia, 9; Leuven, 1983); M. Vovelle, *La Mort et l'Occident de 1300 à nos jours* (Paris, 1983); E. Mitre Fernández, *La muerte vencida: Imágenes e historia en el Occidente medieval (1200–1348)* (Madrid, 1988) (good); A. Haas, *Todesbilder im Mittelalter: Fakten und Hinweise in der deutschen Literatur* (Darmstadt, 1989). Haas includes a good bibliography. There is an interesting discussion of the historiography of the subject by John McManners, 'Death and the French Historians', in Whaley (ed.), *Mirrors of Mortality*, 106–30. I am also much indebted to A. Patschovsky for sending me his unpublished 'Forschungsüberblick zum Thema "Tod im Mittelalter"', which prepared the way for the conference on that theme held at Konstanz in Oct. 1990. Perhaps the most original critical survey of work on death and the afterlife, in my view, is A. Gurevich, 'The *Divine Comedy* before Dante', in id., *Medieval Popular Culture: Problems of Belief and Perception* (Cambridge, 1988), 104–52. The outstanding work on liturgical *Memoria* by the group of German historians discussed at the beginning of this volume (see Introduction, n. 1 and also ch. 2 n. 4) should also be regarded as a fundamental contribution to the 'History of Death' (as well as to other themes), though it is my impression that its relevance and importance have not yet received due attention outside Germany. It gets its due, however, in Michel Lauwers, 'La mémoire des ancêtres, le souci des morts: Fonction et usages du culte des morts dans l'Occident médiéval (diocèse de Liège, XIᵉ–XIIIᵉ siècles)' (École des Hautes Études en Sciences Sociales, Groupe d'anthropologie historique de l'Occident médiéval, thèse de doctorat 'Nouveau régime' dirigé par Jacques le Goff; Paris, 1992), which I believe is to be published by Beauchesne. A study of the relations between living and dead, with special reference to ghosts, by a remarkable historian, appeared after the present work had gone to press: J. Cl. Schmitt, *Les Revenants Les vivants et les morts dans la société médiévale* (Paris, 1994).

# Bibliography

ACHTEN, G., *Die theologischen lateinischen Handschriften in Quarto der Staatsbibliothek preußischen Kulturbesitz Berlin*, pt. ii. *MS. Theol. lat. qu. 267–378* (Wiesbaden, 1984).

AEGIDIUS ROMANUS: *see* Egidio da Romano.

ALLEN, JUDSON BOYCE, *The Ethical Poetic of the Later Middle Ages: A Decorum of Convenient Distinction* (Toronto and London, 1982).

ALTHOFF, G., 'Beobachtungen zum liudolfingisch-ottonischen Gedenkwesen', in Schmid and Wollasch (eds.), *Memoria*, 649–65.

—— *Adels- und Königsfamilien im Spiegel ihrer Memorialüberlieferung: Studien zum Totengedenken der Billunger und Ottonen* (Münstersche Mittelalter-Schriften, 47; Munich, 1984).

AMBROSE, SAINT, *Sancti Ambrosii Opera, pars septima*, ed. O. Faller (Corpus Scriptorum Ecclesiasticorum Latinorum, 73; Vienna, 1955).

—— *Sancti Ambrosii Liber de Consolatione Valentiniani: A Text with a Translation, Introduction and Commentary* (The Catholic University of America, Patristic Studies, 58; Washington, DC, 1940).

*Analecta Franciscana*, vii. *Processus canonizationis et legendae variae Sancti Ludovici O.F.M. episcopi Tolosani*, ed. Patres Collegii S. Bonaventurae etc. (Quaracchi, 1951).

AQUINAS: *see* Thomas de Aquino.

ARIÈS, P., *L'Homme devant la mort* (Paris, 1977).

—— *Western Attitudes towards Death from the Middle Ages to the Present* (Baltimore and London, 1974).

ARISTOTLE, *The Complete Works of Aristotle: The Revised Oxford Translation*, ed. J. Barnes (Princeton and Guildford, 1984).

—— *Ethica Nicomachea, Translatio . . . Grosseteste . . . Recensio Recognita*, ed. R. A. Gauthier, in *Aristoteles Latinus*, xxvi/1–3 (4 fascs.; Union Académique Internationale, Corpus Philosophorum Medii Aevi; Brussels and Leiden, 1973–4).

—— *Nicomachean Ethics*, ed. and trans. H. Rackham (Cambridge, Mass., and London, 1926).

—— *Politica*, in *Aristotelis Politicorum libri octo, cum vetusta translatione Guilelmi de Moerbeka*, ed. F. Susemihl (Leipzig, 1872).

—— *Rhetorica*, ed. B. Schneider, in *Aristoteles Latinus*, xxxi/1–2. *Rhetorica: Translatio anonyma sive vetus et translatio Guillelmi de Moerbeka* (Union Académique Internationale, Corpus Philosophorum Medii Aevi; Leiden, 1978).

ARNHEIM, R., 'Abstract Language and Metaphor', in his *Toward a Psychology of Art* (Berkeley and Los Angeles, 1966).

AVRIL, F., and STIRNEMANN, P., *Manuscrits enluminés d'origine insulaire, VIIᵉ–XXᵉ siècle* (Paris, 1987).

BANSA, H., 'Heinrich von Wildenstein und seine Leichenpredigten auf Kaiser Karl IV.', *Deutsches Archiv*, 24 (1968), 187–223.

BARBER, M., *The Trial of the Templars* (Cambridge, 1978).

BARBERO, A., *Il mito angioino nella cultura italiana e provenzale fra duecento e trecento* (Deputazione Subalpina di Storia Patria, Biblioteca Storica Subalpina, 201; Turin, 1983).

BARTLETT, R., *Trial by Fire and Water: The Medieval Judicial Ordeal* (Oxford, 1986).

BATAILLON, L.-J., 'Prédication des séculiers aux laïcs au XIIIᵉ siècle de Thomas de Chobham à Ranulphe de la Houblonnière', *Revue des sciences philosophiques et théologiques*, 74 (1990), 457–65.

—— 'Similitudines et Exempla dans les sermons du XIIIᵉ siècle', in Walsh and Wood (eds.), *The Bible in the Medieval World*, 191–205.

BAUTIER, R.-H., 'Diplomatique et histoire politique: Ce que la critique diplomatique nous apprend sur la personnalité de Philippe le Bel', *Revue historique*, 259 (1978), 3–27.

BECK, H.-G., FINK, K. A., et al., *From the High Middle Ages to the Eve of the Reformation* (Handbook of Church History, eds. H. Jedin and J. Dolan, 4; New York and London, 1970).

BERGES, W., *Die Fürstenspiegel des hohen und späten Mittelalters* (Leipzig, 1938).

BÉRIOU, NICOLE, and TOUATI, FRANÇOIS-OLIVIER, *'Voluntate dei leprosus': Les Lépreux entre conversion et exclusion au XIIᵉᵐᵉ et XIIIᵉᵐᵉ siècles* (Centro Italiano di Studi sull'Alto Medievo; Spoleto, 1991).

BEUMANN, H., 'Die Historiographie des Mittelalters als Quelle für die Ideengeschichte des Königtums' (1955), repr. in id., *Ideengeschichtliche Studien zu Einhard und anderen Geschichtsschreibern des früheren Mittelalters* (Darmstadt, 1962).

*Biblia Sacra iuxta vulgatam versionem*, ed. R. Weber (2 vols.; Stuttgart, 1962).

BINSKI, P., *The Painted Chamber at Westminster* (The Society of Antiquaries of London, Occasional Papers, NS 9; London, 1986).

BOETHIUS, *Philosophiae consolatio*, ed. L. Bieler (CCSL 94; Turnhout, 1957).

BORST, A., *Barbaren, Ketzer und Artisten: Welten des Mittelalters* (Munich, 1988).

BOUREAU, ALAIN, 'Un obstacle a la sacralité royale en Occident: Le principe hiérarchique', in Boureau and Ingerflom (eds.), *La Royauté sacrée*, 28–37.

—— and INGERFLOM, C. S. (eds.), *La Royauté sacrée dans le monde chrétien: Colloque de Royaumont, mars 1989* (L'Histoire et ses représentations, 3; Paris, 1992).

BRAET, H., and VERBEKE, W. (eds.), *Death in the Middle Ages* (Mediaevalia Lovaniensia, 1st ser., Studia, 9; Leuven, 1983).

BROWN, E. A. R., 'Death and the Human Body in the Later Middle Ages: The Legislation of Boniface VIII on the Division of the Corpse' (1981), repr. in ead., *The Monarchy of Capetian France*, No. VI, pp. 221–70.

—— *The Monarchy of Capetian France and Royal Ceremonial* (Aldershot etc., 1991).

—— 'Persona et Gesta: The Image and Deeds of the Thirteenth-century Capetians, 3. The Case of Philip the Fair', *Viator*, 19 (1988), 219–38.

—— 'Royal Salvation and Needs of State in Early-fourteenth-century France', repr. in ead., *The Monarchy of Capetian France*, No. IV, pp. 1–56.

*Bullarium Franciscanum*, v, ed. Conradus Eubel (Rome, 1898).

BURCKHARDT, J., *The Civilization of the Renaissance in Italy* (New York, 1960 edn.).

BURR, D., *Olivi and Franciscan Poverty: The Origins of the* Usus Pauper *Controversy* (Philadelphia, 1989).

BYNUM, C. WALKER, 'Material Continuity, Personal Survival and the Resurrection of the Body: A Scholastic Discussion in its Medieval and Modern Contexts', in ead., *Fragmentation and Redemption: Essays on Gender and the Human Body in Medieval Religion* (New York, 1991).

CALASSO, F., 'Andrea d'Isernia', in *Dizionario biografico degi italiani*, iii (Rome, 1961), 100–3.

CARY, C., *The Medieval Alexander* (Cambridge, 1956).

CASAGRANDE, C., *Prediche alle donne del secolo XIII: Testi di Umberto da Romans, Gilberto da Tournai, Stefano di Borbone* (Milan, 1978).

*Catalogus codicum manu scriptorum Bibliothecae regiae monacensis*, iii/1 (Catalogus codicum Latinorum . . . , 1/2), 2nd edn. (Munich, 1894).

CENCI, C., *Bibliotheca manuscripta ad Sacrum Conventum Assisiensem* (2 vols.; Il Miracolo di Assisi, 4; Assisi, 1982).

CHAUNU, P., *La Mort à Paris: XVIᵉ, XVIIᵉ et XVIIIᵉ siècles* (Paris, 1978).

CHIFFOLEAU, J., *La Comptabilité de l'au-delà: Les Hommes, la mort et la religion dans la région d'Avignon à la fin du Moyen Âge (vers 1320–vers 1480)* (Collection de l'École Française de Rome, 47; Rome, 1980).

*Chronicles of the Reigns of Edward I and Edward II*, ed. W. Stubbs (2 vols.; Rolls Series; London, 1882–3).

*Chronicon Hugonis monachi Virdunensis et Divionensis Abbatis Flaviniacensis* (MGH Scriptores, 8; Hanover, 1848).

CLANCHY, M., *From Memory to Written Record: England 1066–1307* (London, 1979; 2nd, rev. edn, Oxford, 1993).

COING, H. (ed.), *Handbuch der Quellen und Literatur der neueren europäischen Privatrechtsgeschichte*, i. *Mittelalter (1100–1500): Die gelehrten Rechte und die Gesetzgebung* (Veröffentlichung des Max-Planck-Instituts für europäische Rechtsgeschichte; Munich 1973).

COLE, P., D'AVRAY, D. L., and RILEY-SMITH, J., 'Application of Theology to Current Affairs: Memorial Sermons on the Dead of Mansurah and on Innocent IV', *Historical Research*, 63 (1990), 227–47.

CONGAR, Y., 'L'Église et l'État sous le règne de Saint Louis', in *Septième centenaire de la mort de Saint Louis: Actes des Colloques de Royaumont et de Paris (21–27 mai 1970)* (Paris, 1976), 257–71.

CORBET, P., *Les Saints Ottoniens: Sainteté dynastique, sainteté royale, et sainteté féminine autour de l'an Mil* (Beihefte der Francia, 15; Sigmaringen, 1986).

*Corpus iuris canonici*, ed. Aemilius Friedberg (2 vols.; Leipzig, 1879–81; repr. Graz, 1955).

COULTER, CORNELIA C., 'The Library of the Angevin Kings at Naples', *Transactions and Proceedings of the American Philological Association*, 75 (1944), 141–55.

CRUEL, R., *Geschichte der deutschen Predigt im Mittelalter* (Detmold, 1879; repr. Hildesheim, 1966).

CULLER, J., *Framing the Sign* (Oxford, 1988).

D'AVRAY, D. L., 'Another Friar and Antiquity', in K. Robbins (ed.), *Religion and Humanism* (Studies in Church History, 17; Oxford, 1981), 49–58.

—— 'The Comparative Study of Memorial Preaching', *Transactions of the Royal Historical Society*, 5th ser., 40 (1990), 25–42.

—— *The Preaching of the Friars: Sermons Diffused from Paris before 1300* (Oxford, 1985).

—— 'Sermons on the Dead before 1350', *Studi medievali*, 3rd ser., 31/1 (1990), 207–23.

—— 'Sermons to the Upper Bourgeoisie by a Thirteenth Century Franciscan', in D. Baker (ed.), *The Church in Town and Countryside* (Studies in Church History, 16; Oxford, 1979), 187–99.

—— 'Some Franciscan Ideas about the Body', *Archivum Franciscanum Historicum*, 84 (1991), 343–63.

—— and TAUSCHE, M., 'Marriage Sermons in *Ad status* Collections of the Central Middle Ages', *Archives d'histoire doctrinale et littéraire du Moyen Âge*, 47 (an 1980), 71–119.

DELUMEAU, J., *La Peur en Occident (XIVᵉ–XVIIIᵉ siècles): Une cité assiégée* (Paris, 1978).

D'ESNEVAL, AMAURY, 'Le perfectionnement d'un instrument de travail au début du XIIIᵉ siècle: Les trois glossaires bibliques d'Étienne Langton', in G. Hasenohr and J. Longère (eds.), *Culture et travail intellectuel dans l'Occident médiéval* (Paris, 1981), 163–75.

*Dictionnaire de biographie française* (Paris, 1933– ).

DONDAINE, A., 'La vie et les œuvres de Jean de San Gimignano', *AFP* 9 (1939), 128–83.

DUBY, G., *Guillaume le Maréchal ou le meilleur chevalier du monde* (Paris, 1984).

—— 'Über einige Grundtendenzen der modernen französischen Geschichtswissenschaft', *Historische Zeitschrift*, 241 (1985), 543–54.

DUDDEN, F. HOMES, *The Life and Times of St. Ambrose* (2 vols.; Oxford, 1935).

DUNBABIN, J., *A Hound of God: Pierre de la Palud and the Fourteenth-century Church* (Oxford, 1991).

—— 'The Maccabees as Exemplars in the Tenth and Eleventh Centuries', in Walsh and Wood (eds.), *The Bible in the Medieval World*, 31–41.

EBBO: *Ebbonis Vita Ottonis Episcopi Babenbergensis* (MGH Scriptores, 12; Hanover, 1856).

EGIDIO DA ROMANO, *De regimine principum* (Rome, 1607 edn.).

ELM, K. (ed.), *Stellung und Wirksamkeit der Bettelorden in der städtischen Gesellschaft* (Berliner historische Studien, 3, Ordensstudien, 2; Berlin, 1981).

ERLANDE-BRANDENBURG, A., *'Le Roi est mort': Étude sur les funérailles, les sépultures et les tombeaux des rois de France jusqu'à la fin du XIIIᵉ siècle* (Bibliothèque de la société française d'archéologie, 7; Geneva, 1975).

FAVIER, J., *Philippe le Bel* (Paris, 1978).

FAWTIER, R., *The Capetian Kings of France: Monarchy and Nation (987–1328)* (London etc., 1960; repr. 1983).

FINKE, H., *Aus den Tagen Bonifaz VIII.: Funde und Forschungen* (Vorreformationsgeschichtliche Forschungen; Münster, 1902).

—— *Papsttum und Untergang des Templerordens* (2 vols.; Vorreformationsgeschichtliche Forschungen, 4; Münster, 1907).

FLINT, VALERIE, 'The Chronology of the Works of Honorius Augustodunensis', *Revue bénédictine*, 82 (1972), 215–42.

*Foedera . . .* , ed., T. Rymer, i/3 (The Hague, 1744).

FOLZ, R., *Les Saints Rois du Moyen Âge en Occident (VIᵉ–XIIIᵉ siècles)* (Subsidia Hagiographica, 68; Brussels, 1984).

*Fontes rerum Bohemicarum*, ed. J. Emler, iii (Prague, 1882).

FOURNIÉ, MICHELLE, 'Deux représentations méridionales du Purgatoire: Flavin en Rouergue et Martignac en Quercy', *Annales du Midi*, 98 (1986), 361–85.

FOURNIÉ, MICHELLE, 'Le Purgatoire dans la région toulousaine au XIV<sup>e</sup> siècle et au début du XV<sup>e</sup> siècle', *Annales du Midi*, 92 (1980), 5–34.

GARRIGUES, M.-O., 'L'Anonymat d'Honorius Augustodunensis', *Studia Monastica*, 25 (1983), 31–71.

GAUCHAT, P., *Cardinal Bertrand de Turre Ord. Min.: His Participation in the Theoretical Controversy concerning the Poverty of Christ and the Apostles under Pope John XXII* (Rome, 1930).

GAUTHIER, R. A.: *see* Aristotle, *Ethica Nicomachea*.

*Gerhardi Vita Sancti Oudalrici Episcopi* (MGH Scriptores, 4; Hanover, 1841).

GILES OF ROME: *see* EGIDIO DA ROMANO.

GOETZ, W., *König Robert von Neapel (1309–1343): Seine Persönlichkeit und sein Verhältnis zum Humanismus* (Universität Tübingen, Doktoren-Verzeichnis der philosophischen Fakultät, 1908; Tübingen, 1910).

—— 'Die Quellen zur Geschichte des hl. Franz von Assisi', *Zeitschrift für Kirchengeschichte*, 24 (1903), 165–97.

—— 'Zur Geschichte des literarischen Porträts', *Historische Zeitschrift*, 92 (1904), 61–72.

GOEZ, W., 'Die Einstellung zum Tode im Mittelalter', in *Der Grenzbereich zwischen Leben und Tod* (Göttingen, 1976), 111–53.

GOMBRICH, E. H., *In Search of Cultural History* (Oxford, 1969).

GRABMANN, M., 'Die italienische Thomistenschule des XIII. und beginnenden XIV. Jahrhunderts', in id., *Mittelalterliches Geistesleben: Abhandlungen zur Geschichte der Scholastik und Mystik*, i (Munich, 1926), 332–91.

—— 'Die Lehre des Jakob von Viterbo (†1308) von der Wirklichkeit des göttlichen Seins: Beitrag zum Streit über das Sein Gottes zur Zeit Meister Eckharts', in id., *Mittelalterliches Geistesleben: Abhandlungen zur Geschichte der Scholastik und Mystik*, ii (Munich, 1936), 490–511.

GRAUS, F., *Volk, Herrscher und Heiliger im Reich der Merowinger: Studien zur Hagiographie der Merowingerzeit* (Prague, 1965).

GRIFFITHS, Q., 'New Men among the Lay Counselors of Saint Louis' Parlement', *Medieval Studies*, 32 (1970), 234–72.

GUREVICH, A., *Categories of Medieval Culture* (London etc., 1985).

—— 'The *Divine Comedy* before Dante', in id., *Medieval Popular Culture: Problems of Belief and Perception* (Cambridge, 1988), 104–52.

HAAS, A. M., *Todesbilder im Mittelalter: Fakten und Hinweise in der deutschen Literatur* (Darmstadt, 1989).

HALLAM, ELIZABETH, M., *Capetian France 987–1328* (London and New York, 1980).

HASENOHR, G., and LONGÈRE, J. (eds.), *Culture et travail intellectuel dans l'Occident médiéval* (Paris, 1981).

HENNEQUIN, J., *Henri IV dans ses oraisons funèbres, ou la naissance d'une légende* (Bibliothèque française et romane, ser. C, Études Littéraires, 62; Paris, 1977).

*Herbordi Dialogus de Vita Ottonis Episcopi Babenbergensis* (MGH Scriptores, 20; Hanover, 1868).

HERDE, P., *Karl I. von Anjou* (Stuttgart, Berlin, Cologne, and Mainz, 1979).

HILLGARTH, J. N., *The Spanish Kingdoms, 1250–1516*, i. *1250–1410: Precarious Balance* (Oxford, 1976).

HILTGART VON HÜRNHEIM, *Mittelhochdeutsche Prosaübersetzung des 'Secretum Secretorum'*, ed. R. Möller (Deutsche Texte des Mittelalters herausgegeben von der deutschen Akademie der Wissenschaft zu Berlin, 56; Berlin, 1963).

*Histoire de Guillaume le Maréchal, L'*, ed. P. Meyer (3 vols.; Paris, 1891–1901).

HÖDL, L., and HETZLER, R., 'Zum Stand der Erforschung der lateinischen Sermones des Mittelalters (für die Zeit von 1350–1500)', *Scriptorium*, 46 (1992), 121–30.

HOFFMANN, E., *Die heiligen Könige bei den Angelsachsen und den skandinavischen Völkern: Königsheiliger und Königshaus* (Quellen und Forschungen zur Geschichte Schleswig-Holsteins, 69; Neumünster, 1975).

HOLMES, G., *Florence, Rome, and the Origins of the Renaissance* (Oxford, 1986).

HONORIUS AUGUSTODUNENSIS, *Speculum Ecclesiae*, ed. PL 172 (Paris, 1895), 807–1108.

HORNER, P. J., 'John Paunteley's Sermon at the Funeral of Walter Froucester, Abbot of Gloucester (1412)', *American Benedictine Review*, 28 (1977), 147–66.

HÜBL, Dr P. A., OSB (ed.), *Catalogus codicum manu scriptorum qui in bibliotheca monasterii B.M.V. ad Scotos Vindobonae servantur* (Vienna and Leipzig, 1899).

HUGH OF ST VICTOR, *De sacramentis*, bk. 2 (PL 176; Paris, 1880).

HUIZINGA, J., *The Waning of the Middle Ages* (London, 1924).

JACOBUS DE VORAGINE: *see* JACOPO DA VARAZZE.

JACOPO DA VARAZZE, *Legenda aurea, vulgo Historia Lombardica dicta*, ed. Th. Graesse (Bratislava, 1890).

JAKOBSON, R., 'Two Aspects of Language and Two Types of Aphasic Disturbance', in R. Jakobson and M. Halle, *Fundamentals of Language* (Mouton-'S. Gravenhage, 1956), 53–82.

JANER, IGNACIO DE, *El patriarca Don Juan de Aragón, su vida y sus obras (1301–1334)* (Tarragona, 1904) [not seen].

JEAN XXII: *see* JOHN XXII.

JOHN XXII, Pope, *JEAN XXII (1316–1334): Lettres communes analysées d'après les registres dits d'Avignon et du Vatican*, ed. G. Mollat, iv–v (Paris, 1910, 1909).

JOINVILLE, *The Life of St. Louis*, in Joinville and Villehardouin, *Chronicles of the Crusades* (Harmondsworth, 1963).

JÜRGENSMEIER, F., 'Die Leichenpredigt in der katholischen Begräbnisfeier', in Lenz (ed.), *Leichenpredigten als Quelle historischer Wissenschaften*, i. 122–41.

KAEPPELI, T., 'B. Jordani de Saxonia Litterae Encyclicae (1233)', *AFP* 22 (1952), 177–85.

—— 'Dalle pergamene di S. Domenico di Napoli: Rilievo dei domenicani ivi menzionati con due appendici sui priori conventuali e provinciali fino al 1500', *AFP* 32 (1962), 285–326.

—— 'Note sugli scrittori domenicani di nome Giovanni di Napoli', *AFP* 10 (1940), 48–76.

—— 'Opere latine attribuite a Jacopo Passavanti, con un appendice sulle opere di Nicoluccio di Ascoli O. P.', *AFP* 32 (1962), 145–79.

KAEUPER, R. W., *War, Justice, and Public Order: England and France in the Later Middle Ages* (Oxford, 1988).

KAMP, N., *Kirche und Monarchie im staufischen Königreich Sizilien*, i. *Prosopografische Grundlegung: Bistümer und Bischöfe des Königreichs 1194–1266* (Münstersche Mittelalter-Schriften, 10/I. 1–4; Munich, 1973–82).

KANTOROWICZ, H., 'Über die dem Petrus de Vineis zugeschriebenen "Arenga"', *Mitteilungen des Instituts für österreichische Geschichtsforschung*, 30 (1909; repr. 1969), 651–4.

KEEN, M., *Chivalry* (New Haven and London, 1984).

KELLY, J. N. D., *The Oxford Dictionary of Popes* (Oxford and New York, 1986).

KIERDORF, W., *Laudatio funebris: Interpretationen und Untersuchungen zur Entwicklung der römischen Leichenrede* (Beiträge zur klassischen Philologie, 106; Meisenheim am Glan, 1980).

KINGSFORD, C. L., 'Jorz . . . Thomas', in *Dictionary of National Biography*, x. 1091–2.

KLANICZAY, G., 'L'image chevaleresque du saint roi au XIIe siècle', in Boureau, and Ingerflom (eds.), *La Royauté sacrée*, 53–61.

KOLLER, H., 'Die Bedeutung d. Titels "princeps" in der Reichskanzlei unter den Saliern u. Staufern', *Mitteilungen des Instituts für österreichische Geschichtsforschung*, 68 (1960), 63–80.

KUNSEMÜLLER, O., *Die Herkunft der platonischen Kardinaltugenden* (Erlangen, 1935).

LA LUMIA, I., *Storia della Sicilia sotto Guglielmo il Buono* (Florence, 1867).

LAMBERT, M., *Franciscan Poverty: The Doctrine of the Absolute Poverty of*

*Christ and the Apostles in the Franciscan Order, 1210–1323* (London, 1961).

LAMPE, G. W. H. (ed.), *The Cambridge History of the Bible*, ii (Cambridge, 1969).

LANGLOIS, CH.-V., *Saint Louis. — Philippe le Bel: Les Derniers Capétiens directs* (Histoire de la France depuis les origines jusqu'à la Révolution, ed. E. Lavisse, 3/2; Paris, 1901).

LAUWERS, M., 'La mémoire des ancêtres, le souci des morts: Fonction et usages du culte des morts dans l'Occident médiéval (diocèse de Liège, XI$^e$–XIII$^e$ siècles)' (École des Hautes Études en Sciences Sociales, Groupe d'anthropologie historique de l'Occident médiéval, thèse de doctorat 'Nouveau régime' dirigé par Jacques le Goff; Paris, 1992).

LE GOFF, JACQUES, *La Naissance du Purgatoire* (Paris, 1981).

LEHUGEUR, P., *Histoire de Philippe le Long, roi de France (1316–1322)*, ii. *Le Mécanisme du gouvernement* (Paris, 1931; repr. Geneva, 1975).

LEMARIGNIER, J.-F., *La France médiévale: Institutions et société* (Paris, 1970).

LENZ, R., *Leichenpredigten: Eine Bestandsaufnahme. Bibliographie und Ergebnisse einer Umfrage* (Marburger Personalschriften-Forschungen, 3; Marburg, 1980).

—— (ed.), *Leichenpredigten als Quelle historischer Wissenschaften* (3 vols.; Vienna (vol. i) and Marburg (vols. ii–iii), 1975–84).

LÉONARD, É. G., *Les Angevins de Naples* (Paris, 1954).

LE ROY LADURIE, E., 'Chaunu, Lebrun, Vovelle: La nouvelle histoire de la mort', in id., *Le Territoire de l'historien* (Paris, 1973), 393–403.

LEYSER, K. J., *Rule and Conflict in an Early Medieval Society: Ottonian Saxony* (Oxford, 1979).

LINEHAN, P., 'Frontier Kingship: Castile 1250–1350', in Boureau and Ingerflom (eds.), *La Royauté sacrée*, 71–9.

LINSENMAYER, A., *Geschichte der Predigt in Deutschland von Karl dem Großen bis zum Ausgange des 14. Jahrhunderts* (Munich, 1886).

LUTHER, MARTIN, *D. Martin Luthers Werke: Kritische Gesamtausgabe*, xvii/1 (Weimar, 1907).

—— *Luther's Works*, gen. ed. Helmut T. Lehmann, li. *Sermons I*, ed. and trans. John W. Doberstein (Philadelphia, 1959).

McFARLANE, K.B., 'Had Edward I a Policy towards the Earls?', *History*, 50 (1965), 145–59.

MacINTYRE, ALASDAIR, *A Short History of Ethics* (London and Henley, 1967).

McMANAMON, JOHN M., *Funeral Oratory and the Cultural Ideals of Italian Humanism* (Chapel Hill and London, 1989).

McMANAMON, JOHN M., 'The Ideal Renaissance Pope: Funeral Oratory from the Papal Court', *Archivum Historiae Pontificiae*, 14 (1976), 9–70.

——— 'Innovation in Early Humanist Rhetoric: The Oratory of Pier Paolo Vergerio the Elder', *Rinascimento*, 2nd ser., 22 (1982), 3–32.

McMANNERS, J., 'Death and the French Historians', in Whaley (ed.), *Mirrors of Mortality*, 106–30.

MÄHL, S., *Quadriga Virtutum: Die Kardinaltugenden in der Geistesgeschichte der Karolingerzeit* (Beihefte zum Archiv für Kulturgeschichte, 9; Cologne and Vienna, 1969).

MARTÍNEZ FERRANDO, J. ERNESTO, *Jaime II de Aragón: Su vida familiar* (2 vols.; Consejo Superior de Investigaciones Científicas, Escuela de Estudios Medievales, Estudios 9–10; Barcelona, 1948).

MAZZATINTI, G., and ALESSANDRI, in Mazzatinti, *Inventari dei manoscritti delle biblioteche d'Italia*, iv (Forli, 1894).

MELANCHTHON, PHILIP, *Philipi Melanthonis opera quae supersunt omnia*, ed. Corolus Gottlieb Bretschneider (Corpus Reformatorum, 11; Halle, 1843).

MIETHKE, J., 'Kaiser und Papst im Spätmittelalter: Zu den Ausgleichsbemühungen zwischen Ludwig dem Bayern und der Kyrie in Avignon', *Zeitschrift für historische Forschung*, 10 (1983), 421–46.

MINISTERI, P. B., 'De Augustini de Ancona, O.E.S.A. (d. 1328) Vita et Operibus, 2. De operibus'; *Analecta Augustiniana*, 21 (1948), 148–262.

MIRBT, C., *Quellen zur Geschichte des Papsttums und des römischen Katholizismus*, 5th edn. (Tübingen, 1934).

MITRE FERNÁNDEZ, E., *La muerte vencida: Imágenes e historia en el Occidente medieval (1200–1348)* (Madrid, 1988).

MOLLAT, M., *Les Papes d'Avignon, 1305–1378* (Paris, 1930).

MONTI, G. M., *La dominazione angioina in Piemonte* (Biblioteca della Società Storica Subalpina, 116; Turin, 1930).

MOORMAN, J., *A History of the Franciscan Order from its Origins to the Year 1517* (Oxford, 1968).

MORRALL, J. B., *Political Thought in Medieval Times* (1962 edn.; repr. Toronto etc., 1980).

*Mort au Moyen Âge, La: Colloque de l'Association des Historiens médiévistes français réunis à Strasbourg en juin 1975 au Palais universitaire* (Publications de la société savante d'Alsace et des régions de l'est, collection 'Recherches et documents', 25; Strasburg, 1977).

MORVAY, K., and GRUBER, D., *Bibliographie der deutschen Predigt des Mittelalters: Veröffentlichte Predigten* (Münchener Texte und Untersuchungen zur deutschen Literatur des Mittelalters, 47; Munich, 1974).

MUNTANER, RAMON, *Crònica*, viii. *Expedició dels Catalans a Orient*, ed.

'E.B.' (Collecció Popular Barcino, 145; Barcelona, 1951); trans. Lady Goodenough (2 vols.; London, 1920–1).

MURRAY, A., 'Archbishop and Mendicants in Thirteenth-century Pisa', in Elm (ed.), *Stellung und Wirksamkeit der Bettelorden*, 19–75.

—— *Reason and Society in the Middle Ages* (Oxford, 1978).

NELSON, J., 'Royal Saints and Early Medieval Kingship', in ead., *Politics and Ritual in Early Medieval Europe* (London, 1986), No. 3.

NITSCHKE, A., 'Carlo II d'Angiò', in *Dizionario biografico degli italiani*, xx (Rome, 1977), 227–35.

—— 'Karl II. als Fürst von Salerno', *Quellen und Forschungen aus italienischen Archiven und Bibliotheken*, 36 (1956), 188–204.

NOLTE, TH., *Lauda post mortem: Die deutschen und niederländischen Ehrenreden des Mittelalters* (Europäische Hochschulschriften, 1st ser., Deutsche Sprache und Literatur, 562; Frankfurt am Main and Berne, 1983).

*Oculus pastoralis: Speeches from the* Oculus pastoralis, *Edited from Cleveland, Public Library, MS. Wq7890921M-C37*, ed. Terence O. Tunberg (Toronto Medieval Latin Texts, 19; Toronto, 1990).

OEXLE, O. G., 'Die Gegenwart der Toten', in Braet and Verbeke (eds.), *Death in the Middle Ages*, 19–77.

—— 'Memoria und Memorialbild', in Schmid and Wollasch (eds.), *Memoria*, 384–440.

—— 'Memoria und Memorialüberlieferung im früheren Mittelalter', *Frühmittelalterliche Studien*, 10 (1976), 70–95.

OFFLER, H. S., 'Empire and Papacy: The Last Struggle', *Transactions of the Royal Historical Society*, 5th ser., 6 (1956), 21–47.

*Old Testament Miniatures: A Medieval Picture Book with 283 Paintings from the Creation to the Story of David*, introduction and legends by Sydney C. Cockerell (London, n.d.).

OLMOS Y CANALDA, D., *Catálogo descriptivo, códices de la Catedral de Valencia*, 2nd edn. (Valencia, 1943).

ORDERICUS VITALIS, *The Ecclesiastical History of Ordericus Vitalis*, ed. M. Chibnall (6 vols.; Oxford, 1969–80), iv (1973).

PAINTER, S., *William Marshall, Knight-errant, Baron and Regent of England* (Baltimore, 1933).

PANELLA, E., 'Il Repertorio dello Schneyer e i sermonari di Remigio dei Girolami', *Memorie domenicane*, NS 11 (1980), 632–50.

—— 'Note di biografia domenicana tra xiii e xiv secolo', *AFP* 54 (1984), 231–80.

—— 'Per lo studio di Fra Remigio dei Girolami (†1319): *Contra falsos ecclesie professores* cc. 5–37', *Memorie domenicane*, NS 10 (1979).

—— 'Un sermone in morte della moglie di Guido Novello o Beatrice d'Angiò?', *Memorie domenicane*, NS 12 (1981), 294–301.

PARTNER, P., *The Lands of St. Peter: The Papal State in the Middle Ages and the Early Renaissance* (Berkeley and Los Angeles, 1972).

'P.D.G.', 'De Vita et Scriptis Beati Jacobi de Viterbio, II. De Scriptis', *Analecta Augustiniana*, 16 (1937–8), 282–305.

PEGUES, F., *The Lawyers of the Last Capetians* (Princeton, NJ, 1962; repr. University Microfilms International, 1989).

PEIRCE, C. S., *The Collected Papers of Charles Sanders Peirce*, ii. *Elements of Logic*, ed. C. Hartshorne and P. Weiss (Cambridge, Mass., 1932).

PERE III of CATALONIA (Pedro IV of Aragon), *Chronicle*, ed. and trans. J. N. and M. Hillgarth (Toronto, 1980).

PERGER, BERNHARD, *Oratio Wienne habita in funere imperatoris* [Frederick III] (Vienna, [1493]).

PETERSOHN, J., 'Überlieferung und ursprüngliche Gestalt der Kurzfassung von Herbords Otto-Vita', *Deutsches Archiv*, 23 (1967), 93–115.

PFEIFFER, H., and CERNÍK, B., *Catalogus codicum manu scriptorum qui in bibliotheca canonicorum regularium S. Augustini Claustroneoburgensi Servantur*, ii (Klosterneuburg, 1931).

PONTIERI E. (ed.), *Storia di Napoli* (Naples, 1967– ), iii (Naples ?, 1969).

POWELL, S., and FLETCHER, A. J., '"In die sepulture seu trigintali": The Late Medieval Funeral and Memorial Sermon', *Leeds Studies in English*, NS 12 (1981) (for 1980 and 1981): *Essays in Honour of A. C. Cawley*, 195–228.

POWICKE, F. M., *King Henry III and the Lord Edward: The Community of the Realm in the Thirteenth Century* (2 vols.; Oxford, 1947).

—— *The Thirteenth Century, 1216–1307* (London, 1964).

—— and CHENEY, C. R., *Councils and Synods with Other Documents Relating to the English Church*, ii *A.D. 1205–1313*, pt. II. *1265–1313* (Oxford, 1964).

PRESTWICH, M., *Edward I* (London, 1988).

—— *The Three Edwards: War and State in England 1272–1377* (London, 1980).

PREVITÉ-ORTON, C. W., *The Shorter Cambridge Medieval History* (2 vols.; Cambridge, 1966).

RAND, E. K., *Cicero in the Courtroom of St. Thomas Aquinas* (The Aquinas Lecture, 1945; Milwaukee, 1946).

*Recueil des historiens des Gaules et de la France*, ed. M. Bouquet *et al.*, xxi pub. by Guigniaut and de Wailly (Paris, 1855).

REMIGIO DE' GIROLAMI, *Contra falsos ecclesie professores*, ed. F. Tamburini ('Utrumque Ius', Collectio Pontificiae Universitatis Lateranensis, 6; Rome, 1981).

—— *see also* Salvadori and Federici.

RIDYARD, SUSAN J., *The Royal Saints of Anglo-Saxon England: A Study of*

*West Saxon and East Anglian Cults* (Cambridge Studies in Medieval Life and Thought, 4th ser., 9; Cambridge, 1988).

RIEGER, D., 'Klagelied', in E. Köhler (ed.), *Les Genres Lyriques* (Grundriß der romanischen Literaturen des Mittelalters, 2/1, fasc. 4Bii; Heidelberg, 1980).

ROBERT D'ANJOU, *Robert d'Anjou, Roi de Jérusalem et de Sicile, La Vision bienheureuse: Traité envoyé au pape Jean XXII*, ed. M. Dykmans (Miscellanea Historiae Pontificiae, 30; Rome, 1970).

ROBSON, C. A., 'Vernacular Scriptures in France', in G. W. H. Lampe (ed.), *The Cambridge History of the Bible*, ii (Cambridge, 1969), 436–52.

ROLLASON, D., 'The Cults of Murdered Royal Saints in Anglo-Saxon England', *Anglo-Saxon England*, 11 (1983), 1–22.

ROSEN, F., 'The Political Context of Aristotle's Categories of Justice', *Phronesis*, 20 (1975), 228–40.

ROSS, D. J. A., *Alexander Historiatus: A Guide to Medieval Illustrated Alexander Literature* (London, 1963).

ROUSE, R. H. and M. A., 'Biblical Distinctions in the Thirteenth Century', *Archives d'histoire doctrinale et littéraire du Mogen Âge*, 41 (1974), 27–37.

—— —— *Preachers, Florilegia and Sermons: Studies on the* Manipulus florum *of Thomas of Ireland* (Studies and Texts, 47; Toronto, 1979).

—— —— 'The Texts Called *Lumen Anime*', *AFP* 41 (1971), 5–113.

ROZYNSKI, FRANZ, *Die Leichenreden des hl. Ambrosius, insbesondere auf ihr Verhältnis zur antiken Rhetorik und der antiken Trostschrift untersucht* (Wrocław, 1910) [not seen].

RUBIN, M., *Corpus Christi: The Eucharist in Late Medieval Culture* (Cambridge, 1991).

RULAND, LUDWIG, *Die Geschichte der kirchlichen Leichenfeier* (Regensburg, 1901).

RUSTERHOLZ, S., *Rostra, Sarg, und Predigtstuhl: Studien zu Form und Funktion der Totenrede bei Andreas Gryphius* (Studien zur Germanistik, Anglistik und Komparatistik, 16; Bonn, 1974).

RUTEBEUF, *Œuvres complètes de Rutebeuf*, ed. E. Faral and J. Bastin (2 vols.; Paris, 1959–60).

SALIMBENE, *Cronica fratris Salimbene de Adam*, ed. O. Holder-Egger (MGH Scriptores, 32; Hanover and Leipzig, 1905–13).

SALVADORI, G., and FEDERICI, V., 'I sermoni d'occasione, le sequenze e i ritmi di Remigio Girolami fiorentino', in *Scritti vari di filologia: A Ernesto Monaci gli scolari (1876–1901)* (Rome, 1901), 455–508.

SAULNIER, VERDUN L., 'L'oraison funèbre au XVIᵉ siècle', *Bibliothèque d'humanisme et renaissance*, 10 (1948), 124–57.

SAXER, V., *Le Culte de Marie Madeleine en Occident des origines à la fin du Moyen Âge* (Cahiers d'archéologie et d'histoire, 3; Auxerre and Paris, 1959).

SCHEVILL, F., *History of Florence from the Founding of the City through the Renaissance* (New York, 1961 edn.).

SCHMID, K., and WOLLASCH, J. (eds), *Memoria: Der geschichtliche Zeugniswert des liturgischen Gedenkens im Mittelalter* (Münstersche Mittelalter-Schriften, 48; Munich, 1984).

————— 'Die Gemeinschaft der Lebenden und Verstorbenen in Zeugnissen des Mittelalters', *Frühmittelalterliche Studien*, 1 (1967), 365–405.

SCHNEIDER, B.: *See* Aristotle, *Rhetorica*.

SCHNEYER, J. B., 'Der Beitrag des Johannes Regina von Neapel zur Entwicklung eigener Predigtreihen', *(Tübinger) theologische Quartalschrift*, 144 (1964), 216–27.

————— *Repertorium der lateinischen Sermones des Mittelalters für die Zeit von 1150–1350* (11 vols. to date; Münster, 1969– ).

SCHÖNBACH, A. (ed.), *Altdeutsche Predigten*, 3 vols. (Graz, 1886–91).

————— 'Studien zur Geschichte der altdeutschen Predigt, 1. Über Kelle's "Speculum Ecclesiae"', *Sitzungsberichte der philosophisch-historischen Classe der kaiserlichen Akademie der Wissenschaften*, 135, III. Abhandlung (Vienna, 1896).

————— 'Weingartner Predigten', *Zeitschrift für deutsches Alterthum*, 28 (NS 16) (1884), 1–20.

SCHWENNICKE, D. (ed.), *Europäische Stammtafeln: Stammtafeln zur Geschichte der europäischen Staaten*, NS 2. *Die außerdeutschen Staaten: Die regierenden Häuser der übrigen Staaten Europas* (Marburg, 1984).

*Scriptores Ordinis Praedicatorum mediiaevi*, ed. T. Kaeppeli (Rome, 1970– ).

SENECA, *De clementia*, ed. P. Faider, vol. i (Université de Gand, Recueil de travaux publiés par la Faculté de Philosophie et Lettres, 60; Ghent and Paris, 1928).

*Sentiment de la mort au Moyen Âge, Le: Études présentées au cinquième colloque de l'Institut d'Études Médiévales de l'Université de Montréal*, ed. Claude Sutto (Montreal, 1979).

SIDERAS, A., 'Byzantinische Leichenreden: Bestand, Prosopographie, zeitliche und räumliche Distribution, literarische Form und Quellenwert', in Lenz (ed.), *Leichenpredigten als Quelle historischer Wissenschaften*, iii. 17–49.

————— 'Die byzantinischen Grabreden: Prosopographie, Datierung, Überlieferung, mit 24 Erstausgaben' (unpublished Habilitationsschrift; Göttingen, 1982) [not seen].

SIRAGUSA, G., *L'Ingegno, il sapere e gl'intendimenti di Roberto d'Angiò, con nuovi documenti* (Palermo, 1891).

SKINNER, Q., 'Ambrogio Lorenzetti: The Artist as Political Philosopher', *Proceedings of the British Academy*, 72 (1986), 1–56.

—— *The Foundations of Modern Political Thought*, i. *The Renaissance* (Cambridge, 1978).

SMALLEY, B., *The Becket Conflict and the Schools* (Oxford, 1973).

—— *The Study of the Bible in the Middle Ages*, 3rd edn. (Oxford, 1982).

*Speculum Ecclesiae: Eine frühmittelhochdeutsche Predigtsammlung (Cgm. 39)*, ed. G. Mellbourn (Lund and Copenhagen, 1944).

STAFFORD, WILLIAM S., 'Repentance on the Eve of the English Reformation: John Fisher's Sermons of 1508 and 1509', *Historical Magazine of the Protestant Episcopal Church*, 54 (1985), 297–338.

STENGEL, E. E., 'Land- u. lehnrechtliche Grundlagen d. Reichsfürstenstandes', *Zeitschrift d. Savigny-Stiftung für Rechtsgeschichte, germanistische Abteilung*, 66 (1948), 294–343.

STRAYER, J., *Les Gens de justice du Languedoc sous Philippe le Bel* (Cahiers de l'Association Marc Bloch de Toulouse, Études d'histoire méridionale, 5; Toulouse, 1970).

—— 'The Laicization of French and English Society in the Thirteenth Century' (1940), repr. in id., *Medieval Statecraft and the Perspectives of History* (Princeton, 1971), 251–65.

—— *The Reign of Philip the Fair* (Princeton, 1980).

SUSEMIHL, F.: *see* Aristotle, *Politica*.

SWANSON, JENNY, *John of Wales: A Study of the Works and Ideas of a Thirteenth-century Friar* (Cambridge, 1989).

TENENTI, A., *Il senso della morte e l'amore della vita nel Rinascimento (Francia e Italia)* ([Turin,] 1957).

—— *La Vie et la mort à travers l'art du XV^e siècle* (Cahiers des Annales, 8; Paris, 1952).

THIEL, M., *Grundlagen und Gestalt der hebräischkenntnisse des frühen Mittelalters* (Biblioteca degli 'Studi Medievali', 4; Spoleto, 1973).

THIRY, C., *La Plainte funèbre* (Typologie des sources du Moyen Âge Occidental, 30; Turnhout, 1978).

THOMAS, H., *Deutsche Geschichte des Spätmittelalters 1250–1500* (Stuttgart, 1983).

THOMAS DE CHOBHAM, *Summa de arte praedicandi*, ed. F. Morenzoni (CCCM 82; Turnhout, 1988).

THOMAS DE AQUINO, *Opera omnia* (Vivès edition, 1871–82), ix (Paris, 1873).

—— *Selected Political Writings*, ed. A. P. d'Entrèves (Oxford, 1965).

—— *Summa theologica*, 5 vols. (Madrid, 1961–5).

TIERNEY, B., *The Crisis of Church and State, 1050–1300* (Englewood Cliffs, NJ, 1964).

—— *Origins of Papal Infallibility 1150–1350: A Study on the Concepts of Infallibility, Sovereignty and Tradition in the Middle Ages* (Studies in the History of Christian Thought, 6; Leiden, 1972).

TOCCO, F., *La quistione della povertà nel secolo XIV, secondo nuovi documenti* (Nuova Biblioteca di Letteratura, Storia e Arte, 4; Naples, 1910).

TOYNBEE, M. R., *S. Louis of Toulouse and the Process of Canonisation in the Fourteenth Century* (Manchester, 1929).

TREVET, NICHOLAS, *Annales*, ed. T. Hog (London, 1845).

TUBACH, F. C., *Index Exemplorum: A Handbook of Medieval Religious Tales* (FF Communications, 204; Helsinki, 1969).

ULLMANN, W., 'The Curial Exequies for Edward I and Edward III', *Journal of Ecclesiastical History*, 6 (1955), 26–36.

—— *A History of Political Thought in the Middle Ages*, rev. edn. (Harmondsworth, 1970).

VALERIUS MAXIMUS, *Valerii Maximi Factorum et dictorum memorabilium libri novem*, ed. C. Kempf (Leipzig, 1888).

VAUCHEZ, A., *La Sainteté en occident aux derniers siècles du Moyen Âge d'après les procès de canonisation et les documents hagiographiques* (Bibliothèque des Écoles Françaises d'Athènes et de Rome, 241; Rome, 1981).

VILLANI, GIOVANNI, *Nuova cronica*, ed. G. Porta (3 vols.; Parma, 1990–1).

*Vita Annonis Archiepiscopi Coloniensis* (MGH Scriptores, 11; Hanover, 1954).

VON MOOS, PETER, *Consolatio: Studien zur mittellateinschen Trostliteratur über den Tod und zum Problem der christlichen Trauer* (4 vols.; Münster Mittelalter-Schriften, 3 (1–4); Munich, 1971–2).

VON SCHULTE, J. F., *Die Geschichte der Quellen und Literatur des canonischen Rechts*, ii. *Von Papst Gregor IX. bis zum Concil von Trient* (1877; repr. Graz, 1956).

VOVELLE, M., 'Les attitudes devant la mort: Problèmes de méthode, approches et lectures différentes', *Annales: Économies, sociétés, civilisations*, 31/1 (1976), 120–32.

—— *La Mort et l'Occident de 1300 à nos jours* (Paris, 1983).

WALLACE-HADRILL, J. M., *Early Germanic Kingship in England and on the Continent* (Oxford, 1971).

WALSH, K., and WOOD, D. (eds.), *The Bible in the Medieval World: Essays in Memory of Beryl Smalley* (Studies in Church History, Subsidia, 4; Oxford, 1985).

WALTER, I., 'Bartolomeo da Capua', in *Dizionario biografico degli italiani*, vi (Rome, 1964), 697–700.

WARNING, R. (ed.), *Rezeptionsästhetik: Theorie und Praxis*, 2nd edn. (Munich, 1979).

WATT, J. A., *The Theory of Papal Monarchy in the Thirteenth Century: The Contribution of the Canonists* (London, 1965).

WÉBER, E. H., *La Personne humaine au XIII^e siècle* (Bibliothèque Thomiste, 46; Paris, 1991).

WEISHEIPL, J. A., *Friar Thomas d'Aquino* (Oxford, 1975 edn.).

WENZEL, S., *Preachers, Poets and the Early English Lyric* (Princeton, 1986).

WEST, M. L., *Textual Criticism and Editorial Technique Applicable to Greek and Latin Texts* (Stuttgart, 1973).

WHALEY, JOACHIM (ed.), *Mirrors of Mortality: Studies in the Social History of Death* (London, 1981).

WILLIS, J., *Latin Textual Criticism* (Illinois Studies in Language and Literature, 61; Urbana etc., 1972).

WINKLER, E., *Die Leichenpredigt im deutschen Luthertum bis Spener* (Forschungen zur Geschichte und Lehre des Protestantismus, 10th ser., 34; Munich, 1967).

—— 'Scholastische Leichenpredigten: Die Sermones funebres des Johannes von S. Geminiano', in *Kirche—Theologie—Frömmigkeit: Festgabe für Gottfried Holtz zum 65. Geburtstag* (Berlin, 1965), 177–86.

WOLTERSDORFER IN GREIFSWALD, TH., 'Zur Geschichte der Leichenreden im Mittelalter', *Zeitschrift für praktische Theologie*, 6 (1984), 359–65.

ZERFASS, R., *Der Streit um die Laienpredigt: Eine pastoralgeschichtliche Untersuchung zum Verständnis des Predigtamtes und zu seiner Entwicklung im 12. und 13. Jahrhundert* (Freiburg i.B., Basle, and Vienna, 1974).

# Index of Manuscripts

This index lists pages where precise references are given to places in manuscripts, usually where some portion of the manuscript is transcribed. The page numbers are those on which folio numbers or equivalent are given, rather than of the full page extent of a transcribed passage, even if the transcription is in a note which has been continued from the previous page. Allusions to a manuscript without mention of folio numbers or equivalent are not listed. Cues in the main text to transcriptions in the 'Endnotes' or 'Transcriptions' sections in the end are included. Note therefore the following sigla used in notes in the main text, when reference is made to passages in the 'Transcriptions' at the end:

A = MS Berlin, Staatsbibliothek Theol. lat. qu. 298
B:a *and* B:d = MS Seville, Biblioteca Capitular Columbina 82-4-1
B:b *and* B:c = MS Kremsmünster 44
C:a,b,c,d,e = MS Rome, Angelica 158
D = MS Troyes 2001

Arras, Bibliothèque Municipale 137
(876): pp. 38, 39
Assisi, Comunale 448: p. 236

Barcelona, Archivo de la Corona de
Aragón Ripoll 187: pp. 54, 277
Barcelona, Biblioteca de Catalunya
661: pp. 55, 281–2
Berlin, Staatsbibliothek, Theol. lat. qu.
298: pp. 56, 122, 127, 133, 232

Florence, Bibliotheca Laurentiana
Plut. 33 Sin. l: p. 62
Florence, Biblioteca Nazionale Conv.
soppr. G. 4. 936: pp. 64, 84, 143,
144, 146, 199

Innsbruck, Universitätsbibliothek 234:
pp. 161, 236, 245

Klosterneuburg 265: pp. 161, 245
Klosterneuburg 486: pp. 161, 245
Kremsmunster 44: pp. 57, 58, 63, 111,
119, 132, 133, 135, 139, 147, 150,
153–6, 160–8, 176, 182, 191, 192,
198, 199, 236, 245, 257, 285

London, British Library, Arundel 395:
p. 43

Munich, Staatsbibliothek Clm. 2981:
pp. 52, 67, 90, 92–3, 95, 101, 102,
104, 106–8, 110–11, 122, 132, 141,
148, 157, 173, 177, 191, 285
Munich, Staatsbibliothek, Clm. 3555:
p. 47

Naples, Nazionale Conv. soppr. VIII
AA ll: pp. 104, 105, 119, 123–6, 135,
149–50, 157, 186, 188

Paris, Bibliothèque Nationale 15943:
pp. 34–7
Pistoia, Archi Capitolare C 112: p. 41

Rome, Angelica 158: pp. 59, 70, 73,
75–6, 78–9, 139, 168, 171, 189, 196,
201, 263, 266, 270, 272, 274

Seville, Biblioteca Capitular
Columbina 82-4-1: pp. 111, 130, 131,
132, 148, 160, 175, 200, 202, 203, 236,
245, 257
Siena, Biblioteca Comunale F. X. 24:
pp. 65–7, 119, 122, 126, 129, 132,
133, 134, 137, 138, 142, 147, 160, 162,
180, 195, 284

Troyes, Bibliothèque Municipale 228:
pp. 30–3, 280; 817: pp. 55, 282; 1729:
p. 42; 2001: pp. 54, 277

Valencia, Catedral 182: pp. 53, 63, 64, 85–9, 140, 177

Vatican, Bibliotheca Apostolica Vaticana, Archivio di S. Pietro (=Archiv, Capit. S. Petri) D. 213: pp. 48–52, 283; Archivio di S. Pietro G. 48: p. 277; Ottobuono latino 557: p. 43

Vienna, Schottenstift 379 (379): 161, 245

# General Index

Abner 58
abridgement 54, 89, 160
abstinence 80
abstract and concrete thought 46, 77, 87, 115
Accursius 209 n.
Adelbertinus O.P. 43 n.
*ad status*, see *status*
Aegidius Romanus, see Egidio da Romano
afterlife 18–19, 158–77
Agnes, S. 172
Albertano da Brescia 61 n.
Albertinus Dertonensis 43 n.
Alcuin 135
Aldobrandino da Toscanella 43
Alexander IV, pope 113
Alexander the Great 71–2, 75, 100, 196–7
*Alexandreis* 122
Alfonso III, king of Aragon 97
Alfonso IV, king of Aragon 211, 214–16
aliens 145
All Souls day 42 n., 43 n., 160, 220
alms see generosity; donations, pious; dead, help for
Ambrose, S. 15–20
analytical philosophy, Anglo-American, use of by Bynum 174 n.
ancestry, see nobility
Andrea Biglia 117
Andrea d'Isernia 206
anger 16, 77
Angevins of Naples 41, 47–54, 89–112, 123, 149
  see also Beatrice; Blanche; Carlo d'Acaia; Charles I of Anjou/ Naples; Charles II of Anjou/ Naples; Charles Martel; Isabella; John of Durazzo; Philip of Taranto; Raymond Berengar; Robert I 'the Wise'
anniversary 12, 35 n., 57, 62, 87
Anno II of Cologne, archbishop 21–2

anointing 73
antipope 151–6
appearance, physical 76
'Apulia' 41, 84, 89
Aquinas, see Thomas Aquinas
Aragon 53, 96–8
Aristotle 44–5, 46, 100, 122, 126, 135–50, 171–2, 209–10
  *Ethics*, political doctrine in 142
  and hereditary monarchy 209–10
arrays of concepts 134
*arrivistes* 122
art, see illustrated manuscripts; Westminster, painted chamber
art of dying 163–5
'artistic' method of preaching 34, 38
Arts, Liberal 107
Assisi, manuscripts at 42
audience 59–62
Augustine of Hippo 47, 102
avarice 126
Avignon 154
Azzone d'Este 47 n.

Bertrand de la Tour 47, 54–5, 57, 133, 191–2
  on the cardinal virtues 135 (note 78 from 134)
  on Church-state relations 150–6
  on death and afterlife 160–8, 174–6
  on tyranny 146–7
  on wealth 129–31
'Barons' Wars', in England 38–9
Beatrice of Anjou 47 n.
Becket, Thomas 208
bees, king of 100
Benevento, battle of 93
Berlinghieri, see Graziado Berlinghieri
Bernard of Clairvaux 24
Bible, see Scripture
Biglia, Andrea 117
Blanche, daughter of Charles II of Anjou/Naples 98
blind, provision for 101
blood relationship 123
Boccaccio 108, 191

body:
    dead man's, and transitoriness 22,
        27, 28–30, 163, 198
    division of after death 215–19
    goods pertaining to 136
    translation of 124
body–soul relation 18, 35, 45, 51, 146,
        163, 171–5
    soul's fate between death and last
        judgement 213
Boethius 86
*bona externa* 20, 117, 119, 121, 122, 136
Boniface VIII 98, 100 (n. 124 from 99),
        205, 216
Brunetto Latini 135 n.
Bruni, Leonardo 117
Burnell, Robert 74

Caligari, siege of 211
canon law 206
canonization of Louis of Toulouse
        125 n., 213
Capetians, later 216–19
    *see also* Louis IX; Philip IV; Louis X;
        Philip V; Philip VI
cardinal virtues, *see* virtues
Carlo d'Acaia 47 n.
Castille, queen of 89
Catherine de Courtenay 98
charity 148–9
    *see also* love of God
Charlemagne 58, 135
Charles I of Anjou/Naples 90–5, 133,
        152
Charles II of Anjou/Naples 67, 90, 94,
        95–106, 112, 113
    fear of death 213–14
    and Giovanni da Napoli 52–3, 57
    less wise than his successor 106
    his 'magnificence'/generosity 95,
        101–2, 105, 147–9
    and sons 49, 86, 89
Charles IV, emperor 225–6
Charles of Calabria 54, 57, 58, 63, 109,
        111
    compared to David 191–2
    praised for military qualities 133 n.
    in war against Ludwig of Bavaria
        150–6
Charles of Salerno, *see* Charles II of
        Anjou/Naples
Charles Martel, son of Charles II of
        Anjou/Naples 104 n., 123

Charles de Valois 97
chivalry 133, 148, 193, 195–7, 210–11
    *see also* knight; knights; hobility
Christ 36, 73, 164, 167, 170–1
    enemies of 72, 76
Church:
    Church–State relations 90–1, 93,
        109–10, 150–8, 206–9
    enemies of 72, 78
    holy mother, and commemoration
        of the dead 64
    'spiritual' 152
churches, building of 95, 148
Cicero 136
'circumscription' as representation
        201–3
city (*ciuitas*), heaven as 167
civil law, *see* roman law
civil servants, clerical 208
classical forms 27–8, 118
classical tradition and cardinal virtues
        135
Clement V, pope 70
Clementine constitutions 56 n.
Clovis 152
Cluny 219–20
commemoration, liturgical, see
        *memoria*
*Commendatio lamentabilis* 77–8
common good 139, 144
comparisons in sermons 199–200
    *see also* history, comparative
confession 44, 88, 150, 163, 164, 173,
        187
    'confession' impossible after death
        175
    contrition 79
Conradin, *see* Konradin
conscience 88, 97
consolation 30 n., 45, 51, 60, 61, 65,
        283
contempt of world 45, 63, 66
Cortes of Aragon 97
counsellors of ruler:
    Edward I 73–4, 115
    Philip IV 81, 82
courts as context 60, 192
crusade 72, 74–5, 76, 78, 115
*cultus* of dead 60, 283 (endnote 11)
curia, papal 113

Dante 47 n., 104 n., 123
David 190, 192

interpretation of Hebrew Name 251
(apparatus)
dead
help for the 21, 23, 25, 27, 31, 37,
166, 180, 186; and function of
memorial preaching 60–1, 64, 65,
67, 175–6
honour due to 51–2, 60, 283
(endnote 11)
see also *memoria*
death 15–68, 86, 159–84, 212–21
agony before 36 n.
body and burial 214–17, 219
certainty/uncertainty topos 26,
162–3
distinction on the word 30, 41
division of body after 215–17, 219
and original sin 35, 72–3, 161–2,
168, 170–1, 200
preparation for 30, 44, 173
'tame death' 181
theology of 159–77, esp. 159, 168
in youth 104 n.; in old age 168 n.
decomposition 163, 170, 171, 178, 198
devil 153
Dionysius the Tyrant 145
diplomacy 95–8
dispensations 81
'distillation' and representation 6,
201, 203–21, 223–4
*distinctiones, see* death, distinction on
the word
donations, pious 80, 81, 91, 95, 101,
105, 147–9
*dux* 57–9, 123, 152, 191
dying, art of 163–5
dynasty 89

education, humanist programme of
119
Edward I of England 55, 59, 111, 113,
219–20
and representation of individuality
70–9
and selection of themes in sermon
201–2
and theology of death in sermons
168–71
Edward II of England 73
Egidio da Romano 126 n., 210
*Ehrenrede* 1, 60, 282–3 (endnote 10)
Eleanor of Castile, wife of Edward
I 219–20

empire, eastern 98, 123
empire, holy roman 109–11, 151,
154–5
estates parliamentary, of San Martino
103
Ethics 107
Eucharist 44, 46, 150 n., 173
Eudes de Chateauroux 38–40, 42, 65,
180
*exempla* 30, 36, 44, 45, 47, 198, 199
external goods, see *bona externa*
extreme unction 44, 46, 173

Fall, the, *see* Death: and original sin
fame 133, 150, 159
families, multinational, as political
units 89
fear 145
feast after funeral 60
Federico Franconi da Napoli 47, 52,
67, 90–104, 111, 122, 132–3, 191
Federico Visconti 42, 62
female religious 44
Feuerbach 221
*figurae*, biblical 46–7
flattery 143–5
Florence 43, 58, 79, 150
fortune, good, 134
'frame' and representation 201–3
France, kingdom of 49, 83–4, 199
royal house of 122–3
Franciscans 109, 129–30, 151, 214–15
Frederick Barbarossa, emperor 152
Frederick II, emperor 28, 152
Frederick, king of Sicily (brother of
James II of Aragon) 98
*Fredericus Franconus, see* Federico
Franconi da Napoli
French, honour of the 94–5
frequency of memorial preaching
56–9
friars and funerals 56
function of memorial preaching 63–7
funeral 1, 12, 56, 60–1, 182–3
funeral preaching in S. Italy 41

gallows, as image 125
Gauthier de Châtillon 122
generosity 80, 91, 95, 101–2, 105, 128,
148
German *Sprachraum*, mss. of Bertrand
de la Tour in 161, 229 n.

German vernacular, sermons
transmitted in 25–6, 279
(endnote 1)
Gervais, *see* John Gervais
ghosts, see *revenants*
Gilbert, bishop of Evreux 23
Giles of Rome, see Egidio da Romano
Gregory of Tours 199
Giovanni da Napoli 47, 111 n., 126,
135 (n. 78 from 134), 148–50,
185–7
Angevins, special relationship with
52–3
on Charles II's love of God 104–6
multiple sermons in memory of
same individual 57
Giovanni Regina, *see* Giovanni da
Napoli
Giovanni da San Gimignano 45–6,
61, 122, 132, 136–8, 147 n., 193–5
on cardinal virtues 134 n.
on frequency of funeral preaching
56 n.
on military virtues 133
on tyranny 142 n.
on wealth and power 126–9
Giovanni da Simone 102
Giovanni da Viterbo 135 n.
gothic book hands 228
grace 161, 163, 168, 169
fall from 87
Grammar 107
Graziado Berlinghieri 41
Gregory the Great 47
Grief, *see* loss, sense of; lament
Guelfs and Ghibellines 109–10, 151,
152
Guibert de Tournai 34–8, 42
guile, holy 25
Guillaume de Plaisians 205, 206
Guillaume de Nogaret 205, 206
guilt 87

happiness 122
heaven 21, 37, 55, 160
S. Ambrose on 18–19
Beatific Vision controversy 212–13
Bertrand de la Tour on 163–4,
165–6, 167, 175–6
Federico Franconi on 177 n.
Hebrew names 192, 251 (apparatus)
Hegel 223
Henry VII, king of England 226

hope 167
hell 19, 37, 166–7, 175
Herimannus, prior 21–2, 24
*Historia scholastica* 193
historiography 1–6, 177–84, 282–3
(endnote 10),
285–6 (endnote 14)
Bynum's place in 174 n.
history, comparative 19–20, 13–14,
115–21, 224–7
Homer 100
Honorius Augustodunensis 26–7
honour 133
hospital, free, at Pozzuoli 101–2
household, royal 148
Hubert Walter 208
Hugh of Flavigny 23
Hugh of St. Victor 173–4
humanism 65, 113, 117–19, 133, 148,
157–8
'civic humanism' 117
and papal-imperial relations 157–8
*humanitas* 119
humility 17, 31, 79, 119, 164
and 'legal justice' in Aquinas 139 n.
Hungary 48, 91, 106

illustrated manuscripts 190, 196–7
images 19, 30, 44, 46, 125, 177,
187–200
Imbrico of Würzburg 24–5
individual, sense of the 4, 16–17, 20,
44, 69–116
individualism 178, 180–3
Innocent IV 39–40, 42, 65, 112–13
inspiration of God 106
intercession, *see* dead, help for the
'investiture contest' 208
Isabella of Anjou 48
Italy, lay culture in 193
tradition of funeral preaching in the
south 41, 47, 89

Jacopo da Viterbo 47–52, 228
Jacopo Passavanti 46
Jacques de Vitry 29–34
James II, king of Aragon 85, 96, 97, 98
Jean de Saumois 24 (n. 69 from 23)
Jerusalem 99
Jews 38, 80
Johannes de Opreno 42
John XXII, pope 109, 110, 129–30, 151,
210, 214 nn., 216–17

and Beatific Vision 212–13
election of 85
uses Giovanni da Napoli as
    consultant 53
John of Bohemia 110
John of Brabanzon 216
John of Durazzo 53, 125, 195
John Fisher, bishop 226
John Gervais, bishop of Winchester
    38–9
John of London 77–8
John of Wales 135
Thomas Jorz 70 n.
Joshua 58
joy and sadness 169–70
Juan de Aragon 47, 53–4, 63–4, 66,
    85–9, 113
Judas Maccabaeus 193–6
    *see also* Maccabee; Maccabees, books
    of
judgement 66, 88, 181–2
justice 71, 78, 102–4, 136, 137, 153
    commutative and distributive 140
    of God 87
    humanist orations on 118
    of pope Innocent IV 40, 113
    'paternal' 141
    'political' 141

kinaesthetic sense 188
knight, knights 51, 94, 133, 148, 190,
    196–7
    Edward I as 76
    French knights, valour of 83
    'king's knights' 205, 208
    knightly v. 'priestly' values 106
    model sermon in memory of 31–4
knowing, mode of, in afterlife 174–5
Konradin 94

Ladislas IV, king of Hungary 48
laicisation, *see* secularization
laity, culture of 61–2, 107–8, 192–7,
    208
laity, preaching by 107, 212
lament 28, 50–1
    poetic lament 60, 283 (endnote 10)
    *see also* loss, sense of
Langton, Stephen 28–9
language of preaching 61–2
Lateran IV, general council 207
law 139–40
    *see also* canon law; 'legal justice';

legislation; roman law
'legal justice' 71, 139–40
legislation, written 73, 103
    *see also* 'legal justice'
Leonardo Bruni 117
lèse majesté 35
library of Robert 'the Wise' 108
light, as image 19, 125
literacy 29 n., 61, 193, 208
literary theory 5–6, 115, 189
liturgical worship, enthusiasm for:
    Charles II of Anjou/Naples 105
    Philip of Taranto 150
liturgy, and context of memorial
    preaching 1–2, 60, 69–70, 282
    (endnote 10)
Logic 107
Lombardy 110
loss, sense of 22–3, 25, 28, 30, 50–1,
    160
    grief/mourning to be restrained 30,
    35, 37, 45, 51, 60, 160
Lothar 199
Louis IX, king of France 24 (n. 69 from
    23), 48, 123, 152, 280–1 (endnote
    3)
    Bertrand de la Tour on 58
    and Charles I of Anjou/Naples 93
    and Eudes de Chateauroux 38
    Jacopo da Viterbo's sermons on 48
    Salimbene, on military failure of
    95
Louis X, king of France 57, 113, 142,
    199, 218 n.
Louis of Toulouse, S. 48, 123, 213
love of God 104–6, 123, 148–9, 163
Luca da Bitonto 41
Ludwig of Bavaria 63, 109, 111,
    151–6, 192, 212
Luther, Martin 119–21, 226, 283–4
    (endnote 12)

Maccabee:
    Jonathan the 58
    Judas the 193–6
Maccabees, books of 192–6
'magnificence' 128, 136, 147
Manfred, son of emperor Frederick II
    93
Marguerite, daughter of Charles II of
    Anjou/Naples 97
Maria de Molina, queen of Castille
    89 n.

marriage
  control of by ruler 103
  and Edward I 78 n., 219–20
  ends political feud 98–9
  husband's authority over wife 146
Marshall, the, *see* William the Marshall
Marsiglio of Padua 151
Mary Magdalen 104, 106
medicine 107
melancholy 182–3
*memoria* 60, 67, 282 (endnote 10)
  German historians on 1–2, 69–70,
    282 (endnote 10), 286 (endnote 14)
  and individuality 69–70
memory 188
mentalities 2–5
mercy 71, 100, 113
  of God 87
  humanist orations on 118
merit and reward 46, 51, 169, 175
model sermons 42, 56, 58, 59, 62–3,
    159
  by Bertrand de la Tour 54
  by Giovanni da San Gimignano 45
  by Honorius Augustodunensis 26
  by Jacques de Vitry 31
  by Remigio de' Girolami 44
  as source for political attitudes 115
Mongol business 38
Montaillou 184
'month's mind', *see* Thirty Days
morality:
  and law 139–40
  sexual 78, 100 (n. 124 from 99)
'Morgan Picture Bibie' 190
mourning, *see* lament; loss, sense of
Mühldorf, battle of 151
Muntaner 211, 214
muscular sense 188
mutability 169–71
  *see also* transitoriness

names, hebrew, interpretation of 192,
    251 (app. crit.)
name symbolism 44
narrative detail 113, 118
natural law 210
Nero 172
new historicism, the 5–6
Nicholas IV, pope 96
Nicholas of Calvi 112
Nicolaus de Carbio, *see* Nicholas of
  Calvi

Nicholas Trivet 76–7
Nicolaus de Asculo, *see* Nicoluccio di
  Ascoli
Nicoluccio di Ascoli 46–7
nobility 27, 31, 55, 122, 133, 148, 150,
    159
  ancestry of Philip of Taranto 86
  attitude to, in humanist and
    pre-humanist memorial sermons
    117–18, 121–2
  knowledge of Bible 193
Nogaret, Guillaume de 205, 206

Očka, bishop of Prague 225–6
Old Testament rulers/princes 58,
    190–6
oral and written sermons 89, 159–60,
    168
ordeal, the 207
Ordericus Vitalis 23
original sin 152
  *see also* death
Otto of Bamburg 24–5
*Outremer* 72, 75

pagan beliefs, survival of 178, 183–4
palaeographical dating 42 n., 43 n.,
    55, 228
papacy 96, 109–10, 112–13, 151
  and burial 214–17
  antipope 151–7
  and preaching at funerals by friars
    56
paranoia of tyrants 145
*Parlement*, French 208–9
parts and wholes 185–7
peace 28, 95, 97–101, 115, 145
person, the human 173–5
Peter Comestor 193
Peter Rainalducci, antipope 151, 156
Petrarch 211
Philip IV, 'the Fair', of France 44, 57,
    96, 97, 111, 113
  attitude to afterlife 217–19
  counsellors of 205–6 (and cf. 49)
  personality depicted 79–84
Philip V 'le Long' of France 85, 209
Philip VI of France 212–13
Philip of Taranto 53–4, 58, 123, 149,
    157
  personality of, not represented in
    sermons 86, 111
  relations of 89

and usefulness of king's brother 195
philosophical language, combined with scriptural language 117 n.
philosophy 43
*see also* Aristotle
Piedmont 49, 93, 99
Pier Paolo Vergerio, *see* Vergerio
Pierre de Fontaines 208
pigs 100
Pippin 152
Pistoia, sermons by bishop of, *see* Graziado Berlinghieri
pity 90
plagiarism 38
Plaisians, Guillaume de 205–6
*planctus* 50, 283 (endnote 10)
*see also* lament
*planh*, provencal 283 (endnote 10)
Plato 135
pleasure, as aim 142–3
plurality of forms 174 n.
as metaphor 224
poems, vernacular memorial 60
see also *Ehrenrede*
Poissy, Dominican nunnery 219
'political' v. despotic government 146
'political' happiness 122, 136
*politicus, see* statesman
poverty, religious 109, 129–30, 151
power, political 118, 285 (endnote 13)
positive connotation of 132
and wealth 127–8
praise 16–17, 25, 31, 37–8, 65–7, 175
prayers 94
*see also* dead, help for the
preaching by laity 107, 212
pre-christian beliefs, *see* pagan beliefs
predestination 46
'prince', definition of 57–9, 129 and n. 49
French king as *princeps* in own kingdom 205–6
*princeps, see* prince
prudence, *see* virtues, intellectual
psalm texts, to be said when dying 164–5
Ptolemy of Lucca, *see* Tholomaeus
punishment for sin, 170
punishments, imposed by kings and by tyrants 144
purgatory 164, 166, 167, 176–7, 186
'birth of' 178–80

Eudes de Chateauroux on 65
Guibert de Tournai on 37
Nicoluccio di Ascoli on 46
Remigio de' Girolami on 44

Raymond Berengar, son of Charles II of Anjou/Naples 49–51
reception, by audience 6, 93, 189–99
Remigio de' Girolami 61, 64–5, 113, 199, 229
as memorial preacher 43–4
representation of individuality by 79–85
on tyranny 142–7
renaissance, *see* humanism
representation, 185–221, 226
of individual personality 69–116
retinue 148
revelation, personal, to Charles II 105, 106
*revenants* 172, 286
rhetoric 117 n., 118, 226
Robert I 'the Wise' of Anjou/Naples 58, 89, 106–12, 123, 132–3, 152
on Beatific Vision 211–13
compared with Solomon 191
Robert Burnell 74
roman Law 205–6, 208–9
Rome, city of 153–4
royal ancestry 55
Ruggero di Lauria 95, 98
Rutebeuf 283 (endnote 10)

Saba Malaspina 101
sacraments 31, 51, 55, 88, 150, 164, 167, 173
Edward I and 79
Remigio de' Girolami on 44
Nicoluccio di Ascoli on 46
saints:
preaching on 13, 24 (n. 69 from 23), 159, 168
*see also* Agnes, S.; Louis of Toulouse, S.; sanctity, royal
Saisset, bishop Bernard 82
Salimbene 40–1, 47, 69
Saladin 198
sanctity, royal 280–1 (endnote 3)
San Domenico Maggiore, Dominican Church of at Naples 86, 95
San Gimignano, towers of 194
San Martino, ordinances of 103
Sardinia 214–16

Satyras, brother of S. Ambrose 16
'scholastic' preaching, *see* 'artistic method of preaching'
science 43
Scripture:
  use of texts and images from 84 n., 90, 164 n., 177 n., 185–9
  in vernacular 193
*Secretum secretorum* 81, 101 n.
secularization 204–12
  *see also* world, positive attitude to
selection and representation 201–3
Seneca 47, 100
sense-knowledge 175
setting in life 1–2, 57, 60–2
sheep 100
shepherd, king as 100
Sicilian Vespers 98, 102
Sicily 97–9
*signori* 117, 129
Simon de Montford 38–9
Solomon 72, 99 and n. 124, 108, 190–1, 225–6
soul, *see* body–soul relation
*Speculum Ecclesiae* 26
state, value of deceased to 50
statesman (*politicus*), Robert 'the Wise' as 108
*status* preaching 13, 29–38, 45
stoic tradition 144
Strozzi, Nanni 117
structures, of scriptural text and sermon 185–7
subsisting, and afterlife 174
success 134

Tagliacozzo, battle of 93
taste, sense of 188
taxation 128
temperance 136, 142–3
Templars 80, 82, 83 n., 218
temporal power, and the Church, *see* Church–State relations
*textualis* (script) 228
Theodosius, emperor 16–20
theologian, Robert 'the Wise' as 107–9
thirty days, commemoration after 2, 12
Tholomaeus of Lucca 106
Thomas, archbishop of Reggio 27–8
Thomas Aquinas 45, 46, 136, 140, 157–8, 172–4

on 'legal justice' 139, 140
on humility and 'legal justice' 139 n. 98
Thomas Becket 208
Thomas Jorz 70 n.
Thomism, medieval 138
tournaments 210
transitoriness 28–30, 55, 56, 64, 84, 86, 132, 169, 203
  *see also* body
translation of body 124
Trevet, Nicholas 76–7
Tuscany 110
tyranny 84, 142–7

Ulrich of Augsburg 21
urbanization and attitudes to death 178, 182–3

Valentinian II, emperor 16–19
Valerius Maximus 145
Vergerio 117
Villani, Giovanni 75
virtues 17, 20, 25, 64–5, 71–5, 134–57, 160
  cardinal 134–5, esp. nn. 79, 84
  intellectual 91, 106–8, 112, 115, 132, 136–9, 143, 192
  of a knight 31–2
  in Luther's *Leichenpredigten* 120–1
  martial 23, 32, 72, 74–5 (Edward I), 90, 93–5 (Charles I of Anjou), 110–11 (Robert 'the Wise'), 153, 117–18 (humanist oratory), 132–4
  natural and supernatural 150
  sets of 284–5 (endnote 13)
Visconti, *see* Federico
vision of God, by humans, 170, 212–13

war:
  cost of 128
  *see also* virtues, martial
wars, just 80, 81
wealth 76, 118, 126–31, 133, 150, 159
  false, wealthy Church 151
  of France 83
  and transitoriness 198
Westminster, painted chamber 195
will, last 36
William the Conqueror 23
William II of Sicily 27–8
William Marshall 28–9

William of Moerbeke 135
William of Ockham 129, 151
wisdom, *see* virtues, intellectual
works, good 88
world, contempt of 45, 63, 66
world, positive attitude to 6, 64–8,

116, 117–19, 121–49, 160, 204–12
otherworldly orientation 159–77,
212–21

*Zeitgeist* 6, 203–4
'weak *Zeitgeist* principle' 223–4